奥林匹克文化概论（双语教材）

THE OLYMPIC CULTURE:
AN INTRODUCTION(Bilingual Textbook)

董进霞　〔英〕J.A.曼根　著
Dong Jinxia　J.A.Mangan

北京大学出版社
PEKING UNIVERSITY PRESS

图书在版编目(CIP)数据

奥林匹克文化概论(双语教材)[The Olympic Culture: An Introduction (Bilingual Textbook)]/董进霞,(英)J. A. 曼根(J. A. Mangan)著. —北京:北京大学出版社,2008.7

ISBN 978-7-301-12339-3

Ⅰ. 奥… Ⅱ. ①董… ②曼… Ⅲ. 奥运会-文化-研究-汉、英 Ⅳ. G811.21

中国版本图书馆 CIP 数据核字(2008)第 080624 号

书　　　名:	奥林匹克文化概论(双语教材)[The Olympic Culture: An Introduction (Bilingual Textbook)]
著作责任者:	董进霞　〔英〕J. A. 曼根(J. A. Mangan)　著
责 任 编 辑:	田　炜
封 面 设 计:	奇文云海
标 准 书 号:	ISBN 978-7-301-12339-3/G·2110
出 版 发 行:	北京大学出版社
地　　　址:	北京市海淀区成府路 205 号　100871
网　　　址:	http://www.pup.cn　电子邮箱:pkuwsz@yahoo.com.cn
电　　　话:	邮购部 62752015　发行部 62750672　出版部 62754962 编辑部 62752025
印 刷 者:	北京汇林印务有限公司
经 销 者:	新华书店
	650mm×980mm　16 开本　31 印张　450 千字 2008 年 7 月第 1 版　2008 年 7 月第 1 次印刷
定　　　价:	50.00 元

未经许可,不得以任何方式复制或抄袭本书之部分或全部内容。
版权所有,侵权必究
举报电话:010-62752024　电子邮箱:fd@pup.pku.edu.cn

作者简介

董进霞,北京大学教授,"北大妇女体育研究中心"主任,"北京大学人文体育研究基地"副主任,国际体操裁判员。20世纪80年代在北京体育大学获得学士和硕士学位,2001年在英国斯特拉斯克莱德大学获得哲学博士。1985年至2001年在北京体育大学任教。2001年9月起在北京大学任教,讲授奥林匹克文化、形体、体育社会学等课程,从事以奥林匹克文化和妇女体育为主的体育文化研究。用中英文在国内外刊物发表了近百篇论文和著作,其中《新中国的妇女、体育和社会:顶起大半边天》(*Women, Sport and Society in New China: Holding Up More Than Half the Sky*)在国际和国内获得了很好的反响。近年来,多次应邀赴美国、加拿大、德国、希腊、丹麦、日本、韩国、中国香港等国家和地区的大学和国际会议讲课和报告论文。

J. A. 曼根,英国斯特拉斯克莱德大学退休教授,英国皇家历史学会会员,是享有很高国际声望的体育史和文化研究的专家。他是《国际体育史杂志》、《社会、体育》、《足球和社会》等学术杂志的首任主编。他还是《全球社会中的体育》这一国际上广为称赞的系列书籍的首任主编,该系列已出版了100本书籍。由他专著和编著的学术书籍近40本,包括国际上影响巨大的《维多利亚和爱德华时代公立学校的体育运动:一种教育意识形态的出现和巩固》、《运动伦理和帝国主义》、《男性特征和道德:1800—1940年英美中产阶级男性》、《快乐、利润和信仰改变:1700—1914年间海内外英国文化和体育》、《文化捆绑:体育、帝国和社会》、《从公平性别到女权主义:工业和后工业时代的体育和女性社会化》、《还女性身体以自由:令人鼓舞的偶像》、《开创一个新时代:足球、女性和性解放》、《为地位而奋斗:体育和少数民族》等。

目录

致谢/1

风中舞动的稻草(代序)　　J. A. 曼根/1

前言　董进霞/1

第一部分　社会视角

第一章　奥林匹克文化概述/3

1. 概念和分类/3

(1) 文化/3

(2) 奥林匹克文化/4

2. 内容/5

3. 特征/6

(1) 共性文化特征/6

(2) 独特性/6

4. 奥林匹克运动的哲学基础/7

(1) 人生哲学/7

(2) 普世性的社学哲学/9

第二章　奥林匹克文化：制度/11

1. 奥运大家庭的构成/11

(1) 国际奥委会/11

(2) 国际单项体育联合会——奥林匹克运动的专家/18

(3) 国家奥委会/19

(4) 奥运会组织委员会(奥组委)/20

(5) 奥林匹克运动员/21

2. 奥林匹克家庭成员之间的相互关系/22

第三章　举办奥运会/26

1. 申办奥运会/26
2. 举办奥运会：程序/29
（1）组委会结构/29
（2）组委会的职责/29
3. 举办奥运会的模式/30
4. 举办奥运会：有利和不利影响/31
（1）社会影响/31
（2）城市重建/32
（3）奥运会的经济影响/33
（4）奥运会的环境影响/35

第四章　奥林匹克物质文化/38

1. 建筑/38
（1）希腊体育场/38
（2）罗马圆形剧场/39
（3）现代奥运建筑/40
（4）与体育建筑相关的问题/48
2. 技术/49
（1）设备/49
（2）更准确的成绩测量/50
（3）监督裁判/50
（4）技术和成绩/51
（5）技术和观众的更多选择/51

第五章　奥运会与大众传媒/54

1. 媒体的力量/54
2. 大众传媒的主要形式/55
（1）文字媒体/56

(2) 广播/56

(3) 电影/56

(4) 电视/60

(5) 因特网/61

3. 转播权 /63

第六章 奥运会仪式/69

1. 点火 /69

2. 圣火传递仪式/70

3. 开幕式/75

4. 发奖仪式/76

5. 闭幕式/79

6. 国际奥委会仪式礼节:开幕式的详细情况/80

第七章 艺术和奥运会/85

1. 简要的历史回顾/85

2. 现代奥林匹克文化活动方案 /92

3. 现代奥林匹克音乐/95

第二部分 历史视角

第八章 古代奥运会/101

1. 古希腊文明/101

(1) 宗教/102

(2) 战争和奥林匹克文化/103

2. 古代奥运会的发展变化 /104

(1) 节日、运动会和奥林匹亚/104

(2) 规定/107

(3) 比赛安排/108

（4）竞争和欺骗/110

3．古代奥运文化的衰亡/111

第九章　现代奥运会：苏醒与复活/115

1．现代奥运会的创建/115

（1）意识形态背景/115

（2）工业革命/116

（3）资产阶级教育改革/117

（4）体育的国际化/117

（5）考古发掘/118

（6）复兴奥运会的尝试/118

2．国际奥委会的诞生/119

3．现代奥运会的发展/121

（1）组织模式的逐渐建立/124

（2）世界大战对奥运会的影响/125

（3）奥运会规模的不断扩展/126

（4）举办城市的地理位置和它对奥运会的影响/126

（5）现代的改革变化/127

4．奥林匹克运动的未来/129

第十章　奥林匹克运动：理想主义与现实主义的冲撞/135

1．业余主义与职业主义/135

2．慈善与商业化/137

3．远离政治与亲近政治/138

4．公平竞争与暗箱操作/142

（1）兴奋剂/142

（2）其他违规操作/147

5．男性统治与男女平等/148

第十一章 奥林匹克营销：作为商业的奥林匹克运动/154

1. 从历史的视角看奥运营销/155
2. 独特性/157
3. 奥林匹克营销收入的主要来源/158
   (1) 赞助/158
   (2) 奥运票务/161
   (3) 奥林匹克纪念币/162
   (4) 奥林匹克邮票/163
4. 奥林匹克营销的管理/163
   (1) 管理结构/163
   (2) 营销收入的分配/164
   (3) 知识产权保护/165
   (4) 过分商业化的挑战/165

第三部分 中国与奥运会

第十二章 奥运会和中国：历史进程/171

1. 建立关系/171
2. 中断关系（1949—1979）/173
3. 关系正常化（1979—1992）/173
4. 举办奥运会：雄心（1993—2001）/177

第十三章 走向2008奥运会/185

1. 基础设施建设/185
   (1) 交通/185
   (2) 体育场馆和公园/187
   (3) 通讯网络/188
   (4) 环境保护/188

2. 组织建设/189

　（1）比赛管理/189

　（2）奥运营销/190

　（3）组织竞赛/190

　（4）人才培训和教育/191

　（5）准备残疾人奥运会/191

3. 人文发展/192

4. 北京奥运与竞技成绩/193

5. 机遇和挑战/194

　（1）机遇/194

　（2）挑战/195

附　录

附录1　《奥林匹克宪章》的主要内容/203

附录2　国际奥委会现任委员/205

附录3　历届夏季奥运会参赛信息/209

附录4　历届冬季奥运会参赛信息/211

附录5　女性参与夏季奥运会的情况/213

附录6　女性参与冬季奥运会的情况/214

附录7　北京奥运会场馆/215

参考文献/218

致　谢

　　随着2008年奥运会的临近,北京成为世界瞩目的中心,奥林匹克文化成为脍炙人口的热门话题。《奥林匹克文化论》一书是在北京大学自2002年起开设的面对全校学生的《奥林匹克文化》通选课的基础上,经过不断修改、补充和完善而形成的一本中、英文双语教材。因此,本书的完成首先要感谢北京大学教务部对本课程的扶持、支持和帮助,要感谢北京大学选修该课的同学们。此书的出版,更要感谢本书的责任编辑田炜女士。她严谨、一丝不苟的作风和耐心细致、温文尔雅而又不厌其烦的态度,鼓励和鞭策作者克服种种困难去不断完善该书的内容和表达,使该书成型并最终面世。

董进霞　J. A. 曼根
2008年4月

风中舞动的稻草
（代序）

2007年我在韩国召开的东南亚会议的致辞中提到，要承认这样一个事实：因历史的偶然和环境原因，英语是学术界的全球性语言。最近，著名的遗传学家斯蒂夫·琼斯教授也提及这一点。他说当他是一个学生时被迫学习德语，其原因是德语是科学的语言。他评论道："全世界的科学家当时及以后的数十年都不是用英语写作和交流的。"

然而，即使我说我意识到政治上、文化上和语言上正在发生一个地震性的从西向东的全球构造运动，我认为在未来三个主要的全球性语言依次是英语、中文和西班牙语。这些不会一夜之间出现，但最终会出现，且不可避免。

在过去十年，中国已进入世界重要位置，这仅仅只是开始。上升的证据到处可见。几乎没有一天不会看到新的增加点。这里，仅举一例：国际投资银行高盛公司最近预测到2049年中国将成为世界头号经济强国。英国闻名的商业记者马克·克莱曼不久前告诉他的一些读者："……我们教育系统实施中文（普通话）教学的努力是值得称赞的，可以绝对正确地说，中文将成为21世纪新的商业语言。"这种状况可能还不甚明了，但有远见的企业中产阶层早已觉悟到这一趋势。他们已经注意到这根稻草（象征意义的）在向哪个方向吹动——东方。有品位且读者群最广的英语报刊《每日电讯报》最近刊登了一篇文章，其主标题是"就像1、2、3一样容易"，副标题是"望子成龙的父母急忙签约说中文的保姆"。值得注意的一些评论是"忘了……法语课吧，从决定给孩子们一切机会的那些父母们那里得到的最新趋势是为孩子雇一个说中文的保姆"。这些父母是些什么人？商业精英、大权在握的国际生意人,他们要为自己子女的未来投资。他们已经明白中文是下一代极其重要的语言,他们想要自己的子女领先于人。

对中国人来讲,英语是同样重要的。这也是毫无疑问的。英语目前是、将来也是一门主要的外交、商业和学术领域的全球语言（如果不是唯一重要的语言的话）。任何国际外交家、商业人士和学者都不能不会英语。数百万中国人在学英语这一事实也说明英语比以往任何时候都更为重要。

上面的这些是要说明出版这本双语教材的必要性。该书是一个创举。它开创了一条他人将要跟随的道路,因为东方的学生热衷于英语,西方的学生欢迎中文,双方都逐步认识到双语读物有助于他们语言能力的发展。

出版这本书还有一个更迫切和直接的原因:北京奥运会。成千上万的中国学生在学习奥林匹克运动。在北京奥运会后,中国领军的东方会越来越多地介入奥林匹克运动,并对它产生更多的影响。很可能英语是奥林匹克运动中相互交流的首选语言,但人们在洛桑和其他地方将会越来越多地听到中文。从这个角度讲,该书的出版预示着未来的发展。

J. A. 曼根

前　言

> 请求全世界的人们相互爱戴只是一种幼稚的形式。请求他们相互尊重也多是不切实际的想法;但为了相互尊重,首先需要相互认识。
>
> （顾拜旦，1934）[1]

今日的奥林匹克运动已成为一个全球性的社会现象。它以友好、友谊和公平竞争的精神寻求国家之间的合作,寻求人类身体、心理和意志的和谐发展。奥林匹克运动具有众多不同的功能：

奥林匹克运动的功能

- 建立国家形象和声望；
- 推进社区团结、合作和稳固；
- 发展商业、创造就业机会和繁荣经济,包括促进城市经济增长；
- 提高个人和社区参与体育和享受体育的程度；
- 发展有益的技能和娱乐机会；
- 促进不同国家、民族和种族之间的跨文化理解。

为期两周左右的奥运会是奥林匹克运动的亮点。奥运会是运动项目、参赛人数和参赛国最多、支持力度最大的一个大型体育赛事。通过体育这一媒介,奥运会把世界人民连接在一起,为人们提供一个展示人类文化相似性和差异性的最好途径,提供一个极好的跨文化和国际间

理解和宽容的机会。奥运会揭示出人类可以借助体育来克服政治、经济、宗教和种族间的隔阂。通过运动员的进取、奉献和持之以恒的精神，奥运会激发人们通过努力去实现个人的梦想。从理想的角度来说，奥林匹克运动和奥运会的重要性就在于它们将竞争与合作、心理与身体、纪律与自由、民族主义和国际主义有机地结合在一起。因此，奥林匹克运动是一种独特的文化现象。它不仅仅有体育比赛，还有引导体育运动的价值体系。因此，从文化视角来探讨奥林匹克运动是十分必要的，它可以让人们全面地理解奥林匹克运动的性质，向人们展示奥林匹克运动与教育、艺术等其他社会表现方式之间的相似性。[2]

随着2008年奥运会的临近，奥林匹克运动在中国备受关注。国际奥委会和国家奥委会委员都成为公众人物，大众传媒对奥运会的关注远远高于其他体育赛事；体育专业院校有奥林匹克专业的教师和研究员，中小学也开设了奥运历史和人文奥运的课程；奥林匹克研究中心在不少大学挂牌[3]；有关奥运的学术书籍和通俗读物也不断涌现。结果有越来越多的人对奥林匹克文化产生了浓厚的兴趣。

奥林匹克文化涉及象征、神话、仪式、价值以及围绕和渗透奥运会的艺术品等众多方面。奥林匹克文化课的目的是深入分析现代奥运会和奥林匹克主义的方方面面，以全面理解现代奥林匹克文化的历史进程、当前的主要特征、对今日变革有重要影响的各种冲突及其性质等。

框　架

本书共有13章。每一章都力图展示多种观点，但不特别倾向于某一观点。相反，提出了对现代奥林匹克文化的多种不同解释，读者可批判性地来对它们做出评价。

关键点

每一章自成体系，可单独学习。然而，为了提高对奥林匹克文化复杂性的理解，章节之间互有提及。

补　充

教师指导手册和试题库、PPT课件、录像带和VCD等用做辅助教学资料。

注 释

[1] De Coubertin P (1934), "Forty Yerars of Olympism, 1894/1934", in Car-Diem-Institut (ed.)(1966), *The Olympic Idea: Pierre de Coubertin—Discourses and Essays*, Stuttgart: Olympischedr Sportverlag, pp. 126-130.

[2] 卢先吾:《奥林匹克文化现象的特征》,载谢亚龙主编《奥林匹克研究》,北京体育大学出版社,1994年,第118—120页。

[3] 例如,2002年人民大学成立了"人文奥运研究中心",北京联合大学设立了"奥林匹克文化研究中心"。

第一部分
社会视角

第一章
奥林匹克文化概述

本章要点
* 奥林匹克文化概念
* 奥林匹克文化内容
* 奥林匹克文化特点

1. 概念和分类

要理解奥林匹克文化,我们首先要浏览一下文化的概念。

(1) 文 化

文化的定义难以简单地做出,不同学者看法各异。目前,对文化的定义多达 100 多种。概括地说,文化有广义与狭义之分。

广义的"文化",在对人类与其他生命体进行比较的基础上,文化强调人类所具有的独特、复杂的特性。其涵盖面非常广泛,涉及政治、经济、社会、文化和精神。

狭义的文化,正如爱德华·B.泰勒在 1871 年所下的定义:"从文化人类学的角度来讲,文化是一个复杂的整体,它包括知识、信念、艺术、道德、法律、习俗,以及作为社会的成员而获得的其他能力和习惯。"[1] 总之,文化是人类所共有的,不同群体又有其独特性。

目前,关于文化的分类也有不同的观点。有些人把文化分为物质文化和精神文化两大类。也许将文化分为物质和非物质两类的做法不十分妥当,因为物质产品是人类思想的产物——是长期精神活动的结果。有些人把文化分为物质、制度、精神三个层次;有些人甚至建议将文化分为物质、社会关系、精神、艺术、语言符号、风俗习惯六大子系统。[2]当然,在现实中,所有的文化成分是互为交织、难以分离出来的。

(2) 奥林匹克文化

什么是奥林匹克文化?正如文化有多种不同的定义一样,奥林匹克文化也有多种不同的解释。本书暂且将其定义为起源于奥林匹克运动的一切事物。奥林匹克文化不仅仅涵盖奥运会,还包括理念、理想、具体活动和围绕奥林匹克运动的现实状况。它包括过去和现在,长处和不足,成功和失败,美德和恶行。

鉴于奥林匹克文化是奥林匹克运动在实践过程中所创造的物质、制度和精神财富的总和,奥林匹克文化可以下分为三部分:物质、制度和精神。

* 物质文化

从奥林匹克运动看,物质文化主要指各类场馆、器材等物质设施和由此产生的文化形态。[3]体育场馆、奥运村、奥林匹克博物馆、国际奥委会主楼和出版刊物以及大量的摄影、绘画、邮票、吉祥物和媒体宣传和广告等均属于物质文化的内容。

* 制度文化

它主要指在奥林匹克运动的发展过程中所建立起的各种规定、法规和管理结构——《奥林匹克宪章》、奥运会申办体制、比赛项目和程序,以及各种仪式如开幕式、闭幕式、点火仪式、火炬接力和发奖仪式等。

* 精神文化

它主要是指通过明确的目标和理想来体现的奥林匹克运动理念以及与之相关的各项文化艺术活动。[4]奥林匹克理想、口号和宗旨是其具体体现。它们构成了有别于其他文化现象的奥林匹克运动特征。

2．内容

如前所述，奥林匹克文化不仅指奥运会，它还包括以下的成分：

（1）开/闭幕式——它们包括了奥林匹克全部的象征意义和价值，如五环、点火和鸽子。

（2）发奖仪式——庆祝个人和国家的成就。

（3）文化活动——包括来自世界各地的艺术、音乐、舞蹈和民族活动。

（4）体育赛事——包括许多全世界都进行的现代游戏和体育活动。

（5）器材设备——奥运会是新器材的展示窗口，展示器材在提高运动成绩方面的贡献。

（6）技术——奥运会是一个理想的技术检测场，尤其是在媒体革新方面。

（7）建筑——奥运建筑展示了从体育设施到综合的城市设计等方面的最新建筑成就。

（8）环境——自20世纪90年代早期起，奥运会就开始探索解决大型体育赛事所带来的最棘手环境问题的方案和途径。

（9）收藏——奥运会为体育收藏家提供了一个最大的交流场所，他们进行纪念币、邮票、证章和其他东西的收集和交换。

（10）教育活动——通常情况下，奥运举办城市举行一系列针对青年人的体育和学术活动。

（11）奥林匹克的价值和规范——《奥林匹克宪章》所列出的整套价值。

（12）旅游——奥运会推进地方、全国和国际旅游的发展。

（13）博彩——这是一个涉及许多人和钱、但又常常被忽视的一个方面。

（14）商业——奥运会刺激了众多的商业活动，提供大量的服务和产品，如棒球帽和T恤衫。

上述这些成分构成了奥运会的形象。

3. 特征

（1）共性文化特征

* 当个体归属某个特定群体时所学到的文化价值。
* 文化是可以与他人分享的习得行为的一部分。
* 文化是适应特定的自然和社会环境的一组规范。
* 文化是一个完整的统一体，由整个过程组成。任一要素的变化都会对其他部分带来影响。[5]
* 文化具有一定的稳定性和连续性，但又是不断变化和发展的。

奥林匹克文化具有上述所有的特征。[6]这有可能给奥林匹克运动的和谐及世界的和谐带来一定的问题。

> **案例 1　美国和希腊之间的误解**
>
> 　　1984年美国洛杉矶奥组委将奥运火炬接力权出卖，每公里3000美元。对大多数希腊人而言，这一做法无疑是对其所钟爱的奥运会——神圣象征物——的商业侵蚀。而希腊人的态度让美国人无法理解，因为他们将大部分集资款项用于青年慈善事业。在希腊，很少有私人的慈善机构，国家负责青年发展事务。因此，希腊官员和记者把美国的这一理由想成是赤裸裸的市场营销的借口，何况洛杉矶的领导人物在这方面早已臭名昭著。对这样的态度美国方面显得无能为力，究其原因是对希腊文化没能充分理解。洛杉矶官员认为希腊奥委会只是想借此向美国索要昂贵的点火仪式费。这一文化认识上的差异导致了1984年美国和希腊在点燃火炬上发生的一场"战争"……（资料来源：《大英百科全书》，2002年）

（2）独特性

奥林匹克文化还具有其独特性：
* 象征性

通过奥运会会旗、会歌、会标、吉祥物等来体现奥林匹克的价值取向和文化内涵,使得抽象的概念变为可视、可听和可触的物质文化。

* 艺术性

奥林匹克运动不仅展示世界一流的人体美,还运用其他多种文化艺术形式创造出具有独特审美价值的作品,如开幕式和闭幕式的大型团体操表演,各种道具和灯光变化所产生的扑朔迷离感,歌唱、舞蹈和体育的综合表演,这些都创造出了奥运会所特有的艺术形式。

* 整合性

奥林匹克文化的内涵极为丰富,涉及从物质到精神、从个体到社会、从具体到抽象等多个方面。

* 仪式化

四年一个周期的奥林匹克运动包括众多的仪式,如会旗的交接、千万人参加的圣火传递、开幕式的入场式、点燃圣火、释放和平鸽等。

* 本土和全球的对立统一

奥林匹克主义是世界主题,但其表现方式却是民族的。历届奥运会都在标志等形象设计中充分体现国家的形象。如在美国举办的亚特兰大奥运会,在标志设计中将星条旗的元素融合进来;20 世纪 60 年代的日本东京奥运会和 1988 年的汉城奥运会也是如此。因此,只有是民族的,才能是世界的。

4. 奥林匹克运动的哲学基础

(1) 人生哲学

奥林匹克主义是奥林匹克运动的哲学基础,它是基于国际性和民主性、体育平等基础上的一种心理状态。这个哲学是由现代奥运会奠基人顾拜旦(1863—1937)发展起来的(尽管他没有对这一概念做出明确的定义);他在 1896 年到 1935 年间的好几个不同场合都对奥林匹克主义进行了解释。他在《现代奥林匹克主义的哲学基础》(1935 年)一文中[7],列出了奥林匹克主义的构成成分:

* 宗教的——强调道德。

* 杰出的——但又是平等的,以成就来决定。
* 勇士气概——在友好竞争下的同志关系,去除极端的民族主义情感。
* 韵律的——参考古代奥运周期,它是"自然"的时间周期,是反复出现的,就像收获和月亮的相位一样。
* 男性的——顾拜旦不允许女性参加公开比赛。在他的奥运会中,正如过去的比赛那样,主要作用是给男性胜利者加冕。
* 美学的——顾拜旦倡导并组织了奥运会期间的艺术比赛。
* 和平的——顾拜旦倡导在相互理解上做到相互尊重。
* 参与——顾拜旦在1908年奥运会的闭幕式上说了一段著名的话:"上星期天,在圣·保罗教堂欢迎运动员的仪式中,宾夕法尼亚大主教用极富感染力的词语回忆道:'在这些奥运周期中,重要的事情不是取胜,而是参与,……生命中重要的事情不是胜利而是奋斗;最重要的不是赢,而是打得漂亮。'"[8]

奥林匹克主义包含完整的人生哲学——提倡身、心和精神各种品质的均衡发展;它由强调体育在世界发展、国际理解、和平共处和社会道德教育方面可起建设性作用的社会哲学构成。

奥林匹克主义是要完善个人和社会,要开创以在奋斗中体验乐趣、优秀榜样的教育作用和尊重体育普遍伦理原则为基础的生活方式。

因此,一个奥运选手应该是:
* 全面发展的,
* 自我完善的,
* 具有领导能力(通过例子来体现),
* 具有道德责任感,
* 尊重和尊敬他人。

奥林匹克主义是建立在以下五个基本的人类价值之上的:
* 身体、心理和意志的和谐,
* 追求卓越,
* 行为端正,
* 尊重他人,

* 奋斗的快乐。

奥林匹克主义关注生命的全部过程;它包容,不排外;它不仅关注取胜,还关注参与;它认为体育不只是一个令人愉快的活动,还是影响个人和社会的一种力量。在参加奥运会的数千人中,只有一小部分运动员和运动队能进入决赛。对大多数竞赛者而言,参加奥运会就是一个荣耀。他们有机会代表国家,与优秀运动员同场竞技,并有机会去展示自己的拿手好戏。这些是理想奥运会的本质所在!

费利西安(Perdita Felicien)是参加悉尼奥运会的一名加拿大运动员,她的话抓住了这一本质:"……即使我在100米跨栏的预赛中被淘汰出局,我还是会全力以赴地去比赛。即使数月的大强度训练和到悉尼经历的30个小时漫长疲惫的飞行换来的只是在世界最热的跑道上跑13秒21。这一切都是值得的。"[9]

(2) 普世性的社会哲学

奥林匹克主义的目的是让体育服务于人类的发展,鼓励通过体育来创造一个和平的、关注人类尊严的全球社会,通过体育来教育年轻人学会相互理解。总之,奥林匹克主义的理想是建立一个更美好、更和平的世界。用顾拜旦的话来讲:

> 奥林匹克理想使体育运动能够将人类教育成为有良知的世界公民。奥林匹克理想是榜样性的原则,它表达了体育作为一个真正教育过程这一更深层的本质问题,这种教育是通过不断奋斗的奥运冠军和运动员形象来创造高规格、健康和高尚的人来实现的。[10]

总之,顾拜旦是19世纪后期自由主义的产物,是现代奥运会之父,他强调在奥运会中要体现平等、公平、尊严、理性、和谐和卓越这些价值,这些是奥林匹克哲学的必要条件。

结　论

自顾拜旦以后，奥运会变成了一个重要的文化现象。本章试图对奥林匹克文化进行定义，描述它的主要内容和特征，分析奥林匹克运动的哲学基础和基本成分，为后面章节的讨论奠定基础。

思考题
1. 奥林匹克文化主要有哪些内容？
2. 奥林匹克文化有什么特点？

注　释

〔1〕 Tylor, Edward B. (1871), *Primitive Culture: Researches into the Development of Mythology, Philosophy, Religion, Art and Custom*, vol. 1: Origins of Culture, Gloucester, Mass: Smith, 1958, p. 1.

〔2〕 张岱年、方克立主编：《中国文化论》，北京师范大学出版社，1994 年，第 4—5 页。

〔3〕 孔繁敏：《略论奥林匹克文化》，人文奥运建设座谈会发言材料，2002 年。

〔4〕 同上。

〔5〕 Kendall Blanchard, et al. (1985) *The Anthropology of Sport: An Introduction*. Massachusetts: Bergin & Garvey Publishers.

〔6〕 同上。

〔7〕 Baron Pierre de Coubertin (1935), "The Philosophical Foundations of Modern Olympism", Carl-Diem-Institut (ed.), *The Olympic Ideal: Pierre de Coubertin—Discourses and Essays*, Stuttgart Olympischer Sportverlag, 1966, pp. 130-134.

〔8〕 Revue Olympique, July 1908, p. 110 (from a speech given during the London Olympic Games in 1908)

〔9〕 2000 年 11 月 27 日她在田径队网页上所作的评论。

〔10〕 Nissiotis, N (1987), L'Actualité de Pierre de Coubertin du Point de Vue Philosophique, in Müller, N. (ed.) *The Relevance of Pierre de. Coubertin Today*. CIPC, Niedernhausen, pp. 125-161.

第二章
奥林匹克文化:制度

本章要点
* 奥林匹克家庭的构成
* 奥林匹克家庭成员之间的关系

1. 奥运大家庭的构成

国际奥林匹克委员会(国际奥委会)建立于1894年,是一个非盈利、非政府、自我选举和自我管理的国际组织,拥有自己的合法地位和继承权。奥运大家庭主要由5大成员构成:国际奥委会(IOC)、国际单项体育联合会(IFs)、国家奥委会(NOCs)、奥林匹克运动会组织委员会(OCOGs)、各国单项体育协会、俱乐部和属于这些机构的人员,特别是运动员。每个成员都有其自身的职责和利益,同时他们相互作用,以确保奥林匹克运动的健康发展。因此,奥林匹克家庭成员为有限的资源和控制权而竞争的局面恰好是权力关系的体现。

(1) 国际奥委会

国际奥委会(IOC)是奥林匹克运动的最高权力机构,拥有所有关于奥运会的权力。它的作用是推广奥林匹克理想、精神和规范。更确切地说,所有重大事情的决定都由奥委会来做出,比如哪些项目可以纳入奥运会比赛方案中,哪个城市来举办奥运会,怎样安排奥运家庭中的财富分配等。国际奥委会的功能详见《奥林匹克宪章》(见附录1)。

从 1915 年起,国际奥委会的总部就在瑞士的洛桑安了家。1981年瑞士联邦政务会法令授予国际奥委会有言论自由、聚会自由、免付国防税和雇佣外国员工不受配额限制等特殊的地位。国际奥委会的行政部门雇有 100 名左右的长期员工。

· 结构

国际奥委会由最高集体决策制定机构和操作机构组成。决策机构包括 IOC 年会和代表大会;操作机构包括由主席、副主席和执行委员组成的执行委员会、IOC 委员和许多其他的委员会组成(见图 2-1)。

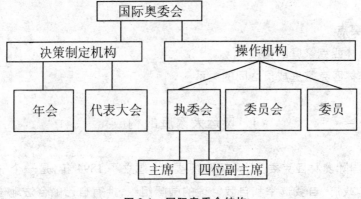

图 2-1　国际奥委会结构

* 年会和代表大会

年会是国际奥委会的最高机构。它采纳、修订和解释《奥林匹克宪章》。年会做出的决定是最终决定。根据执委会的建议,在年会上选出国际奥委会委员。他们每年召开一次年会,并做出重要决定。但是,当超过 1/3 的国际奥委会委员要求增开年会时,可以增开。2002年就举行了两届年会:在盐湖城(美国)举行的第 113 届年会和在墨西哥城(墨西哥)举行的第 114 届年会。

奥林匹克代表大会原则上每八年举行一次,主要解决战略性的长期问题。代表大会由国际奥委会的委员、荣誉委员,单项体育组织的代表,各国奥委会代表,国际奥委会承认的组织的代表,运动员和特邀人士参加。[1] 庆祝现代奥林匹克运动诞生 100 周年的奥林匹克代表大会是 1994 年在巴黎召开的,其口号是"团结的大会",大会确定了 21 世纪现代奥林匹克运动的基本作用。

* **执委会**

执委会由主席、四位副主席和另外十名委员组成。执委会委员在年会上选出。执委会有许多权力和义务,比如在与国际单项体育组织和国家奥委会协商后决定代表大会的日程;负责国际奥委会的财务管理并准备年度报告;推荐国际奥委会委员候选人;监督奥运会举办城市的选拔和接纳程序。

表 2-1　目前执委会成员

主席	雅克·罗格(比利时)
副主席	古尼拉·林德伯格(瑞典) 拉姆比斯·V.尼克劳(希腊) 猪谷千春(日本) 托马斯·巴赫(德国)
委员	格哈特·海伯格(挪威) 丹尼斯·奥斯瓦尔德(瑞士) 马里奥·瓦泽奎兹·雷纳(墨西哥) 奥塔维·辛奎塔(意大利) 瑟盖·布勃卡(乌克兰) 于再清(中国) 理查德·L.卡里翁(波多黎各) 黄思绵(新加坡) 马里奥·佩斯坎特(意大利) 萨姆·拉姆萨米(南非)

国际奥委会的主席由其委员投票选举,任期为八年,可续任 4 年。然而,自 1894 年国际奥委会成立之日起,只有八人担任过主席一职(见表 2-2)。

表 2-2　国际奥委会历任主席名单

姓名	时期	国籍
泽麦特里乌斯·维凯拉斯	1894—1896	希腊
皮埃尔·德·顾拜旦男爵	1896—1925	法国
亨利·德·巴耶-拉图尔	1925—1942	比利时
西格弗里德·埃德斯特隆	1946—1952	瑞典
艾弗里·布伦戴奇	1952—1972	美国

续表

迈克尔·莫里斯·基拉宁	1972—1980	爱尔兰
姓名	时期	国籍
胡安·安东尼奥·萨马兰奇	1980—2001	西班牙
雅克·罗格	2001—	比利时

国际奥委会主席拥有巨大的权力,从监督日常事务到选举新委员、设立或解散委员会等。主席在执委会的选举和决定方面也有很大的影响力,尽管他不能简单地把个人意愿强加上去。因此,主席在引导奥林匹克运动方面起着至关重要的作用。他的个性、经验和价值都会对奥林匹克运动的发展产生重大的影响。下面是国际奥委会历史上极具影响的几位人物。

国际奥委会主席皮埃尔·德·顾拜旦(1863—1938)

1863年出生于法国一个贵族家庭的皮埃尔·德·顾拜旦,在一个很有教养和地位的家庭中长大。他对古希腊史和教育有浓厚的兴趣,拒绝家庭为他安排的部队生涯,并放弃了很有前途的政治道路。他把教育看做是通向未来社会的关键,是振兴法国的一个手段(1870年法国被德国打败)。受英国公立学校的体育传统的影响,他希望改革法国的教育体制,改变法国人的形象。1887年前后,他就想复兴古代奥运会。为宣传这一想法,他在杂志上撰文,在公共场合演讲,与国内外知名人士交谈。1892年他公开倡议恢复现代奥运会。意识到体育将成为全球流行的运动,他接受了美国业余体育联合会一名委员提出的组织一次国际大会来研讨业余主义问题的建议。1894年6月该大会在巴黎召开,提出了"恢复奥运会"的设想,并得到了与会人员的积极响应。大会决定第一届国际奥林匹克运动会将于1896年在希腊雅典举行,而不是顾拜旦提议的1900在法国巴黎举行。

为确保第一届奥运会的成功,1894年7月顾拜旦创建了一本新杂志《奥林匹克评论》。他还前往雅典劝说希腊皇室成员和其他希腊人来支持奥运会,并在希腊诗坛文学社发表了激动人心的演讲。这一演讲被认为是奥林匹克运动史上的一个里程碑。可以说,顾拜旦的远见卓识、精力、热情和决心使得现代奥运会得以产生。

国际奥委会主席艾弗里·布伦戴奇(1887—1975)

他与顾拜旦有一个共同之处。业余主义思想构成了布伦戴奇奥林匹克主义概念的核心。他坚持"奥运会如果要想持续的话,必须保持业余性"。为成为一个奥运业余选手或获得参加奥运会的资格,一个竞赛者常常是把体育当作爱好来练,不会获得任何形式的物质收获。一个奥运业余选手把体育道德看得重于技术,高贵重于名望,荣誉重于成功。他年轻时曾参加过1912年斯德哥尔摩第5届奥运会,获田径五项全能第5名。1914年、1916年、1918年3次获美国田径全能冠军。他连任5届奥委会主席(1952—1972),共20年。

除上述这点外,他与顾拜旦是极为不同的。布伦戴奇是个很有争议的人物。他被不同的人描绘成一个孤立主义者、帝国主义分子、法西斯主义者。他自己则认为他是一个道教徒。

在社会背景方面,顾拜旦和布伦戴奇大相径庭。布伦戴奇来自工薪阶层,出生在底特律的一个工人家庭,5岁时移居芝加哥。不久,他的父亲抛弃了家庭。12岁时,他成为芝加哥的一名报童。他在克雷恩手工艺培训学校学习之时,每天要骑车7英里往返于学校,在那从9点到5点上课,之后进行田径训练。在黎明前要抓紧时间送两小时的报纸。后来,他在伊利诺斯大学学习市政工程。1912年他参加了斯德哥尔摩奥运会,在五项全能中获得第五名。他是一个杰出的运动员。在1914年、1916年和1918年他都是美国全能冠军。在这一阶段,他创建了自己的公司,从战后的房地产热中获利并成为百万富翁。顾拜旦是一个拥有特权的贵族,布伦戴奇则是一个靠自我奋斗取得成功的资本家。1925年他成为美国田径联合会的第二副主席,1928年升为主席。1936年他当选国际奥委会委员,1944年被任命为副主席。从1952年起,他作为主席领导国际奥委会达20年之久。

资料来自奥托·尚茨,《艾弗里·布伦戴奇的任期(1952—1972)》,在《1894—1994年国际奥委会——100年:理想—主席—成就》,洛桑:国际奥委会,1995年,第65—90页。

> **国际奥委会主席胡安·安东尼奥·萨马兰奇（1920— ）**
>
> 胡安·安东尼奥·萨马兰奇是一个纺织业主的儿子，曾是一个中产阶级实业家。他升至奥林匹克运动巅峰位置的道路起始于他那不同寻常的旱冰球运动生涯——他带领西班牙队获得世界冠军。
>
> 1966年当选国际奥委会委员，1968年担任协议起草官，他那不知疲倦的能力很快在各个委员会工作中派上用场。1970年，他成为执委会委员，1974—1978年任副主席。在1977年西班牙与前苏联恢复了外交关系后，他被西班牙政府任命为驻莫斯科大使（1977—1980）。1979年他作为协议起草官重新回到国际奥委会执委会，第二年当选国际奥委会主席。
>
> 从接管国际奥委会那一刻起，他就努力为受到莫斯科奥运会政治困境重创的奥林匹克运动指引一个新的方向，他在世界各地巡游，与各国领导人和体育负责人建立各种联系，捍卫奥林匹克事业。他确保了国际奥委会作为一个国际非政府组织的地位，调整它的财务状况（电视转播权，赞助方案）。在奥运会出现抵制事件的危机年代（1980年的莫斯科和1984年的洛杉矶），他让奥林匹克的精神生生不息。正是在他的努力之下，奥林匹克博物馆得以在洛桑奠基（1993）。
>
> 当国际奥委会发现因一些委员滥用信义而使组织处在危机之中时，他大刀阔斧地进行机构改革。萨马兰奇在2001年6月于莫斯科卸任，被选为终身名誉主席。

上面的每一任主席都有不同的背景，因各自的侧重点不同，他们服务于奥林匹克运动的方式也就不同；因生活的时代不同，每个人面对的挑战也不同；由于个人价值和所面对的困境有所差异，每个人的工作重点也有所不同。然而，所有人都表现出坚定的信念、推动事物发展的不折不饶精神和确保成功的技巧。顾拜旦让世界相信复兴奥运会的重要性；布伦戴奇在二战后的混乱中很快就恢复奥运会。萨马兰奇保证了国际奥委会作为一个国际非政府组织的地位，重组了不断增长的奥委会财政状况。

世上没有十全十美的事情。顾拜旦坚持将女性关在奥运大门之外，布伦戴奇是一个固执己见的独裁者；萨马兰奇没能阻止腐败和兴奋剂滥用的现象。然而，他们都确保了奥林匹克运动的前进动力，使它在现代体育中占居独特的地位。这三个人尽管不十全十美,但传承了作为奥林匹克运动核心的理想主义精神。

- **国际奥委会委员**

国际奥委会委员每年在全会上见面一次。所有委员的任期都是八年,八年后可续任。他们在年满70岁时退休(1999年12月11日前当选者例外,他们可在80岁退休)。

国际奥委会委员是从合格的候选人中选拔出来的,他们必须是国际奥委会所承认的国家奥委会所在国的公民,并在该国居住。与大多数国际组织不一样,国际奥委会委员是国际奥委会派往各国的代表,而不是这些国家在国际奥委会内的代表。这意味着这些委员政治上应该是独立于各国政府的。然而,现实远非如此。在国际奥委会中有许多人是外交官、皇室成员或国家领导人。这样,国际奥委会委员很难(如果不是不可能的话)不受各国政府的影响。

国际奥委会委员在各国的名额分配一直是争议不断的话题,因为目前202个会员国中有一大半国家没有奥委会委员,而举办过奥运会的大多数国家,如英国、美国、瑞士或俄罗斯都分得两个委员名额。这很容易导致那些没有奥委会委员的国家的不满。

- **国际奥委会专业委员会**

国际奥委会主席建立专业委员会来解决相关问题,并就相关问题向执委会提出建议。

* **团结委员会**确保所有的运动员有同样的机会参加奥运会。该委员会建立了许多方案来改善不同国家的体育基础设施,通过授予奖学金的形式来给参加奥运会的运动员提供财务资助。这笔资金可用于高水平运动设施的使用、专门的训练指导或医务监督以及参加奥运会资格赛。

* **医务委员会**支持体育科学的研究,包括运动医学、生物力学、运动生理学和营养。其重点是反兴奋剂。

* **女子体育工作委员会**关注在各级水平上增加女子参加体育的人数,增加女性在教练和管理位置的人数。

* **文化和教育委员会**促进体育和文化之间的关系。为庆祝奥林匹克运动的文化多样性,该委员会与各国奥委会合作,组织文化和教育活动,如文学、绘画和雕塑展览,奥林匹克艺术节和文化活动。

* **体育和环境委员会**关注生态问题并确保体育与环境和谐、持续性发展的需要。

此外,还有其他的一些委员会,如奥运会协调委员会,财务委员会,国际关系委员会,道德委员会,国际奥委会司法委员会,提名委员会,奥运会研究委员会,奥林匹克邮票、纪念币和纪念品委员会,奥林匹克项目委员会等。

(2) 国际单项体育联合会——奥林匹克运动的专家

奥林匹克大家庭中的一个重要成员是国际单项体育联合会。他们负责各自体育项目的发展、管理和组织。在奥运会期间,国际单项体育联合会管理奥运会比赛方案中的体育项目。目前,有35个国际单项体育联合会(28个是夏季体育项目,7个是冬季体育项目)负责各自体育项目的所有技术方面的问题,例如,规则、设备、场馆和裁判。国际单项体育联合会从1921年起才正式负责奥运会上各自项目的组织工作。每一个国际单项体育联合会都有100个以上的会员国。

表 2-3 国际单项体育联合会名单

夏季	冬季
国际田径联合会(国际田联)	国际两项联合会
国际自行车联合会(国际自联)	国际长撬和乘撬滑雪联合会
国际游泳联合会(国际泳联)	世界冰壶球联合会(国际壶联)
国际射箭联合会	国际冰球联合会
国际羽毛球联合会	国际小型撬联合会
	国际滑冰联合会
国际棒球联合会	国际滑雪联合会
国际篮球联合会(国际篮联)	
国际拳击联合会(国际拳联)	
国际皮划艇联合会(国际皮联)	
国际马术联合会	
国际击剑联合会	
国际足球联合会(国际足联)	
国际体操联合会(国际体联)	

续表

夏季	冬季
国际手球联合会(国际手联)	
国际曲棍球联合会(国际曲联)	
国际柔道联合会(国际柔联)	
国际现代五项联合会(五项)	
国际赛艇联合会	
国际航海联合会	
国际射击运动联合会	
国际垒球联合会	
国际乒乓球联合会	
世界跆拳道联合会	
国际网球联合会(国际网联)	
国际铁人三项联合会	
国际排球联合会(国际排联)	
国际举重联合会(国际举联)	
国际摔跤联合会	

资料来源：国际奥委会网站。

值得注意的是，并非所有的单项联合会都享有平等的地位和特权。有些联合会，如拥有 211 个会员国的国际田联和拥有 204 个会员国的国际足联比其他单项组织的地位要高[2]，也更富有。国际田联在 1992 年就与欧洲广播公司签订了价值 9100 万美元的为期四年的合同，而国际足联管理着一个全球性的运动，2003 年的收入达 7.12 亿瑞士法郎（约 5.88673 亿美元）。这两个组织的主席都是国际奥委会委员，在奥运会的配额、电视收入分配和对参赛者的控制等方面常与国际奥委会讨价还价。

（3）国家奥委会

奥林匹克家庭中的另一个重要成员是国家奥委会。一个国家要参加奥运会，就必须有一个得到国际奥委会认可的国家奥委会。它们的主要责任是确保各自国家的运动员参加奥运会。国家奥委会要给该国参加奥运会的代表提供装备、交通和食宿。根据《奥林匹克宪章》，国家奥委会不能是盈利的组织，不能与带有政治和商业性质的事务连在一起；必须是完全独立和自治的，要抵抗各种政治、宗教和商业的压力。

国家奥委会在各自国家要行使多种功能,从促进各级水平的体育发展到制定教育方案,到体育管理人员的培训。他们还要负责派遣运动员代表团参加奥运会。最后,他们还要确保所有全国性的方案要与《奥林匹克宪章》的原则相一致。

总之,国家奥委会要负责运动员的招聘、监督和担保。没有国家奥委会的证明,一个运动员就不能参加奥运会的比赛。随着奥运营销TOP计划的发展,全世界的国家奥委会被授权成为奥运五环在各自国家的独家经营者,在促进奥林匹克运动上是政府的合作伙伴和利益分享者。

要成为被认可的国家奥委会,一个国家必须有5个全国性的体育联合会加入国际单项体育联合会。目前全球共有202个国家奥委会:非洲53个,美洲42个,亚洲44个,欧洲48个,大洋洲15个。

国家奥委会有不同的类型:负责该国所有体育事务的国家奥委会;与其他国家体育组织合作的国家奥委会;每四年工作一次的国家奥委会。

此外,还有国家奥委会协会,它每两年至少有一次将各国的国家奥委会聚集在一起,目的是巩固他们在奥林匹克运动中的作用。国家奥委会协会又进一步分为五大洲协会:非洲国家奥委会协会,亚洲奥林匹克理事会,泛美体育组织,欧洲奥林匹克委员会和大洋洲国家奥委会。这些机构都努力发展他们自身的利益,获得更多的结构和财务上的特权,如参加奥运会的名额或赞助及电视转播收入的分配。

(4) 奥运会组织委员会(奥组委)

奥运大家庭中的另一个重要成员是组委会,它是在一个城市得到举办奥运会的权力后建立起来的。每个奥组委存在8年左右的时间:6—7年的准备工作,以及奥运会后1—2年的材料整理和给国际奥委会与其他相关机构书写总结报告。

到目前为止,夏季奥运会只有17个国家举办过,6个国家举办过一次以上。其中,美国举办了5次,另外有5个国家各举办过2次。有7个国家举办过冬季奥运会,法国和美国各举办过4次。

奥组委要与国际奥委会、国家奥委会和国际单项体育组织以及地方官员和其他重要人士密切合作,为比赛和来访者做好准备。主要责任有以下六方面:

(1) 要选择在什么地方和怎样建立比赛场馆,包括比赛馆、训练馆、奥运村等,总之它要负责奥运会顺利进行所需的一切基础设施。

(2) 提供高效方便的交通服务。

(3) 提供适宜的现场医疗服务。

(4) 举办文化活动——音乐会、戏剧、芭蕾和展览等。

(5) 告知大众所有的奥运准备工作,回答媒体提出的问题。

(6) 从国内外招聘和培训服务人员。奥组委能从上千名自愿服务人员的帮助中受益,自愿者对奥运会的成功可起到重要的作用。自愿者的活动包括很多方面,如交通、接待和管理。

(5) 奥林匹克运动员

奥运大家庭中最后一个重要成员是运动员。每个国家最多只能有3名运动员参加奥运会的每一个小项比赛。然而,国际奥委会与有关单项体育联合会商量后可以改变参赛的人数。在集体项目比赛中,一个国家只能有一个队。一般而言,国家奥委会只会选派本国公民参赛。

拥有双重国籍的运动员可以代表他选择的国家比赛,但是如果他已经代表一个国家参加过奥运会或其他大型体育比赛,在三年以内他就不能再代表另一个国家比赛。参加奥运会没有年龄限制,但为了健康原因,有些单项体育联合会设定了一定的年龄规定。如,参加奥运会的女子体操运动员必须年满16岁。

运动员到达举办城市后就住进奥运村。在奥运会期间,他们的时间并非全部用在比赛上。奥运会也是他们与其他运动员相识的一个机会。所有奥运村的居住者都认为:重要的不是环境的舒适和服务的质量,而是全世界运动员之间建立的这种关系。国际奥委会委员、前奥林匹克选手安妮塔·L.德弗朗兹谈到她在奥运村的经历时说:"两到四周内,奥运村变成了全世界优秀运动员的家。在那里我明白了每种形态、大小、种族和性别都可以创造卓越的成就。在那我明白了为成为奥运选手而付出努力后,一个奥运选手会尊重每一个人。在那我了解了每一个体育项目都要有特殊的技能和决心才能达到顶峰。"[3]

不管比赛是否取胜,参加奥运会的每一个人都将奥运村和比赛场地的特殊经历的记忆带回家去。为加强现役运动员和国际奥委会之间的联系,运动员委员会于 1981 年 10 月成立。该委员会由现役和退役的运动员组成,每年至少开一次会,定期与国际奥委会执委会见面,并提出建议。此外,该委员会形成工作组,与奥组委密切合作,确保运动员的需要得到满足。目前,委员的组成是夏季奥运会选出 8 名运动员、冬季奥运会选出 4 名、国际奥委会为平衡性别、地理分布和项目任命 7 名。

2. 奥林匹克家庭成员之间的相互关系

国际奥委会是世界最昂贵的文化产品——奥运会——的唯一拥有者。然而,不像其他的商业组织,国际奥委会不负责产品的生产、营销或销售价格,但对从销售得到的收入分配拥有绝对的控制。这样,国际奥委会拥有巨大的影响,但没有什么责任。为此,在国际奥委会、国际单项体育联合会和国家奥委会之间争执不断。近来有一种说法,国际奥委会是多余的,没有国际奥委会,国际单项体育联合会和国家奥委会也可以很好地运作奥林匹克运动。国际奥委会则回答道,尽管从短期讲没有它国际单项体育联合会可能会得利,但从长远来看,因为没有一个最高的调节机构,奥林匹克运动就会陷入一片混乱。[4] 为向国际奥委会提供一个集体的声音,一个游说组织:国际单项体育联合会总会在 1967 年诞生。为减低国际单项体育联合会日益增长的权力,国际奥委会在 1983 年成立了夏季奥林匹克国际联合会协会和国际冬季体育联合会协会。

国家奥委会和国际单项体育联合会要求在国际奥委会的决定中发挥更大影响。在这样的压力下,国际奥委会在 2000 年新版的《奥林匹克宪章》中规定了新的委员组成安排:15 名国际单项体育联合会的主席,15 名国家奥委会代表,15 现役运动员和 70 名个人代表。这样,国际奥委会与国际单项体育联合会和国家奥委会的协商不得不比过去多很多。

随着20世纪80年代以来奥林匹克运动在财务运作上的成功,每个成员都想从国际奥委会的TOP计划和转播的营销收入中分得更多的一份。为平衡潜在的利益冲突,在80年代末,国际奥委会开始给每位成员提供一定份额的奥林匹克收入(见表2-4)。

表2-4 国家奥委会,国际夏季和冬季联合会从国际奥委会获得的收入(百万美元)

奥林匹克周期	国家奥委会	国际夏季联合会	国际冬季联合会	总 数
1989—1992(阿伯特维尔/巴塞罗那)	86.6	37.6	17	141.2
1993—1996(利勒哈默尔/亚特兰大)	137.9	86.6	20.3	244.8
1997—2000(长野/悉尼)	211.7	190	49.4	451.1
2001—2004(盐湖城/雅典)	319.5		85.8	

资料来源:《IOC 2005 营销事实档案》:www.olyrnpic.org

这样,从1997起国际奥委会将营销收入的93%再投回到体育上,与国家奥委会、国际单项体育联合会和奥组委分享,只截留7%用于日常运作。例如,国际奥委会给长野奥组委提供了10亿多美元,比他们在申办时预期能从国际奥委会得到的多很多。[5] 2000—2004年周期的电视收入40%分给了奥林匹克运动,60%给奥组委,但在2004年后这一分配比例发生了改变,49%给奥组委,51%给奥林匹克运动。显然,国家奥委会和国际单项体育联合会是营销和电视收入的两个主要受益者。

总之,奥林匹克运动中的构成、结构、资金分配和关系表明了一个复杂的权力平衡,参与其中的各方都努力保证自己的专有利益。

结　论

　　国际奥委会在 1894 年建立。它是一个非盈利、非政府、自我调节的国际组织。它是一个由五个主要成员构成的家庭：国际奥委会、国际单项体育联合会、国家奥委会、奥运会组委会和运动员。国际奥委会的主要作用是推广奥林匹克理想。它的主席、副主席和委员都由选举产生。委员在每年的全会上见面。它还有针对独特问题的专门委员会。奥运大家庭中的一个重要成员是国际单项体育联合会。每个联合会负责其运动项目的组织、管理和发展。另一个重要的家庭成员是国家奥委会。他们是非盈利组织，负责该国奥林匹克队的选派、装备、交通和食宿。还有一个重要的成员是奥运会组委会。一旦一个城市获得奥运会的举办权，组委会就协助它为奥运会做准备，奥运会后还要做出运动会的评价报告。奥林匹克运动员集合起来成为奥运家庭的一个重要成员。

　　奥运大家庭中的关系并非始终和睦。国际奥委会、国际单项体育联合会和国家奥委会之间的紧张关系时常可见。无一例外，问题的核心是权力分配。为实现一个复杂的权力平衡，不得不进行及时的调整。

思考题

1. 你认为上面描述的最近几位杰出的主席中，哪一位对奥林匹克运动最重要？给出你的理由。
2. 有没有你要向国际奥委会推荐的其他委员会？如果有，请解释为什么；如果没有，给出你满意目前委员会的理由。
3. 你是否同意运动员（退役和现役）应该向国际奥委会提建议？不论是否同意，都请给出理由。

注　释

〔1〕　国际奥委会，《奥林匹克宪章》，2000 年 9 月 11 日，第一章。
〔2〕　国际奥委会三人主席拉图尔、埃德斯特隆和布伦戴奇都有田径运动的背景，

一个国家想要在国际奥委会中占有一席之地,成为国际田径联合会的会员被认为是极其重要的一步。详见 Alfred E. Senn (1999), *Power, Politics, and the Olympic Games—History of the Power Brokers, Events, and Controversies That Shaped the Games*, Human Kinetics, p.11。

[3] 2003年国际足联财务报告,国际足联常规代表大会,巴黎,2004年5月20—21日。

[4] 《奥林匹克讯息》,第33期,1992年7月。

[5] Christopher R. Hill (1996), *Olympic Politics: Athens to Atlanta 1896-1996* (Second edition), Manchester and New York: Manchester University Press, pp.69-70.

[6] 《XXVII届奥运会的终结报告》,第21页。

第三章
举办奥运会

本章要点
* 申办奥运会
* 举办奥运会
* 过去和现在的举办模式
* 举办奥运会可能出现的有利和不利影响

1. 申办奥运会

当顾拜旦和他的同僚在一个多世纪前恢复奥运会时,他们完全意识到了这一活动所需的工作量及资源。他们当时就决定要轮换奥运会的举办地点,以便更多的国家和人民能够经历奥运会并分担举办运动会的责任。[1] 自 1908 年以来,举办城市是通过竞选过程来选择,唯一的例外是 1948 年战后的伦敦奥运会。

通常,一个城市至少要提前八年提出举办奥运会的申请。比如,希腊在 1996 年 8 月 15 日提出举办 2004 年奥运会的申请,1997 年获得举办权。北京申请举办 2008 年奥运会也是如此。1998 年 11 月,党中央、国务院批准北京再次(前次申办 2000 年奥运会失利)申办奥运会以后,北京市市长刘淇于 1999 年 4 月向国际奥委会主席萨马兰奇递交了北京承办 2008 年奥运会的申请书。2000 年 6 月,北京奥申委向国际奥委会递交了包括 6 个方面、22 个问题的《申请报告》(见表 3-1)。2001 年 7 月 13 日,北京以压倒性多数战胜其他竞争对手,赢得了 2008

年奥运会的举办权。

表 3-1 北京 2008 年奥运会申办报告纲要

第一卷	第二卷	第三卷
前言 * 江泽民主席的支持信 * 朱镕基总理的支持信 * 北京市市长刘淇的信 * 中国奥委会主席袁伟民的信 简介 1. 国家、地区和候选城市的特征 2. 法律 3. 海关和入境手续 4. 环境保护和气象 5. 财政 6. 市场开发	简介 7. 比赛项目总体设想 8. 比赛项目 田径、赛艇、羽毛球、棒球、拳击、皮划艇、自行车、马术、击剑、足球、体操、举重、手球、曲棍球、柔道、摔跤、游泳、现代五项、跆拳道、垒球、网球、乒乓球、射击、射箭、铁人三项、帆船、排球 9. 残疾人奥运会 10. 奥运村	简介 11. 医疗/卫生服务 12. 安全保卫 13. 住宿 14. 交通 15. 技术 16. 新闻宣传与媒体服务 17. 奥林匹克主义和文化 18. 保证书 结论

获得举办奥运会荣誉的是一个城市,而不是一个国家。城市的选择完全在于国际奥委会。市长递交举办奥运会的申请前要得到国家政府的支持。申请中必须说明不会在体育馆或其他体育场所或奥运村举行政治集会或示威,必须承诺每个参赛者都可以自由入境,不会因宗教、肤色或政治信仰而受到歧视。这就保证了国家政府不会拒绝任何参赛者的签证申请。在 1976 年的蒙特利尔奥运会上,加拿大政府却拒绝给台湾代表发放签证,因为他们不愿意放弃中华民国的名称,当时台湾的奥委会是以这一名称进入国际奥委会的。强制性的保证很难进行,即使国际奥委会使用严厉的惩罚措施也不能确保消除摩擦。

所有的候选城市必须回答一个内容十分全面的问卷,展示其有利于申办的证据,政府还要保证给予市政、社会和商业上的支持。申办奥运的决定绝不是由单个体育或公共组织所能做出的,而是要由该市的政府官员与商业合作伙伴及政府一起来做出决定。在提出申办时各方需要合作,但并不一定需要听取民众意见。

从北京申办 2008 年奥运会的案例来看,以政府为主导的决策和领导机制起了很大的作用。提出申办奥运的最初想法是想利用这一活动来刺激北京的社会和经济发展，加速北京进入世界先进城市的进程，把奥运会当做展示中国文化和日益增长的影响力的窗口。与此相应，奥运会的预算和提议的场馆及配置都反映了这一目标。直接用于奥运场馆和相关设施的新增固定资产投资约1349亿元（约170亿美元）。在国际奥委会提出过度开支的警告后，这一切都被重新加以认真考虑。国家体育馆"鸟巢"的最初预算是40亿元（约5.06亿美元），后来不得不减少到20亿元（约2.503亿美元），[2]但实际花费为35亿元（4.86亿美元）。

由于奥运会对举办城市和国家具有很大的吸引力和潜在好处，在奥运会的申办过程中，各候选城市常采取各种措施，从传统的游说到收集每个成员的秘密档案，到单独走访关键人物，甚至采取一些心理上的把戏，如在投票的前一夜，为了给国际奥委会委员留下深刻印象，将他们下榻的饭店的枕套换成印有该城市主要赞助商名字的枕套。运用激情洋溢的明星是目前常见的做法。北京申办2008年奥运会时，就邀请了影视和体育明星如成龙、刘璇、莫慧兰、杨澜、巩俐、桑兰、邓亚萍等担任形象大使。

尽管国际奥委会加强了对候选城市和国际奥委会委员行为的规定和规范，但营私舞弊现象时被曝光。最突出的一个例子是盐湖城申办2002年冬奥会的丑闻，该丑闻导致了6名国际奥委会委员被开除、3名委员辞职。这一事件使得国际奥委会不得不在1999年对举办城市的选择程序进行改革。改革方案包括改善奥运会举办地之选择过程的一系列规定，明确了国际奥委会、申办城市和国家奥委会应遵循下列职责：

* 有意申办的城市须通过申办接纳程序，即在接纳它们作为候选城市之前评价它们的组织能力。

* 经过执委会选拔以后，一个城市才能作为候选城市。

* 被接纳为候选城市后，这些城市必须与它们的国家奥委会签订合同。

* 候选城市要递交它们的候选档案，准备国际奥委会评定委员会的来访。

* 不允许国际奥委会委员的个人来访或访问他们个人。

2. 举办奥运会:程序

获得奥运会的举办权以后,国家奥委会就要与市政官员、政府机构和商业人士一起组建一个组委会来负责操办该运动会。通常,组委会由参与了申办委员会的主要人士和机构组成。然而,申办奥运会多少是地方性的事务,如果成功的话,它就自动变成一个具有全国性和国际性意义的事务,在2000年悉尼奥运会和2004年雅典奥运会的例子中,好几个城市的主要人物,在成功申办后不得不退位,被更具有全国性和国际性影响的人物所替代。

(1) 组委会结构

一旦申办成功,奥组委就必须设计一个合适的组织结构。以北京为例,在申奥成功5个月之后,北京奥组委于2001年12月13日成立。该委员会要负责从场馆计划到环境管理的所有事情。现在,北京奥组委有23个部门[3],600多名工作人员,至2008年,奥组委有30多个部门,4000多名工作人员。

(2) 组委会的职责

组委会必须提供运动会所需的全部基础设施和服务:

* 提供物资及后勤基础设施、设备和训练场地。

* 为运动员、教练员和官员以及媒体工作人员的提供食宿。例如,雅典奥组委给1.6万名运动员和随队官员提供住宿和免费的服务。

* 为新闻和广播中心和媒体提供所需的设备和服务。在2004年雅典奥运会上,大约有2.15万名媒体人员报道奥运会(1.6万名转播人员,5500名摄影和文字记者)。

* 保证在奥运会前、奥运会期间和奥运会之后提供所需的信息(文件、邀请、认证信、比赛时刻表、标记、成绩、报道等)。

此外,奥组委还必须遵守35个国际单项体育联合会(28个夏季运动联合会,7个冬季运动联合会)的规则和要求;确保奥运会期间不会出现社会或政治暴乱。奥组委必须组织一些文化活动,如青年营、艺术节、音乐节和舞蹈节,来配合奥林匹克周期的庆典活动。

3. 举办奥运会的模式

随着奥运会的流行和壮大,全球出现了多种不同的奥运会组织模式。1896 年在雅典举行的第一届奥运会跟 100 年后的亚特兰大奥运会相比,无论从规模、经费预算和工作人员结构来讲,都只能算一个很小的工程(见表3-2)。

表 3-2 1896 年和 1996 年奥运会的比较

	奥运会比较				经费来源				
	天数	大项/小项	国家	运动员	私人捐助	赞助	电视	门票/纪念币/奖牌	特许经营	广告/邮票
雅典 1896	5	9/32	13	311	67%			11%		22%
亚特兰大 1996	17	26/271	200	10000		32%	34%	26%	8%	

资料来源:《奥林匹克主题:举办奥运会》

1912 年的斯德哥尔摩奥运会在设施、组织、电子计时和营销方面都为现代奥运会奠定了基础。该运动会的经费只有 68.1 万美元,由不拿工资的委员会成员运作。现在组织奥运会是专业人士的事情。亚特兰大奥组委雇佣了 4000 名员工,在 1991—1997 年的 7 年中,组委会支出 14 亿多美元。

对以往奥运会的分析表明,共有三种不同的组织模式:国家领导式,私人发起式和合作式。在 1984 年以前奥运会的组织模式是以国家驱动式为主,政府资助的经费占据总经费的 80% 左右。莫斯科奥运会是最典型的例子。前苏联政府担负了绝大多数建设、举办和行政支出的费用,给纳税人带来了很大的经济负担。这次奥运会成了一场财政灾难。由于1972年和1976年的奥运会出现了财务困境,许多城市都不愿意举办奥运会。为此,必须创造新的奥运组织模式来挽救奥林匹克运动的命运。在这样的情况下,1984年由私人运作的洛杉矶奥运会模式应运而生。

洛杉矶运动会是由美国奥委会和一个商业联合体构成的一个非盈利社团来组织的。通过引进赞助和电视转播权的概念,该组织最终获得1.5亿美元的利润。其他"新的"的商业安排使得洛杉矶奥组委又提取了1.17亿美元用于"服务设施"。1996年的亚特兰大奥运会重复了洛杉矶模式,但并不那么成功,而且参赛人员和观众对糟糕的交通和住宿以及没有新的基础设施表示了许多不满。

第三种举办奥运会的模式是公私部门的合作,反映了从政府和纯私人途径向合作途径的转变。这一模式的最好例子是1992年的巴塞罗那奥运会。这届奥运会是由HOLSA公司来负责的,该公司51%股份归联邦政府所有,49%归包括许多商业伙伴作为投资商和赞助商的城市所有。巴塞罗那的公共权力部门非常活跃,他们投资的股份达77.6%。这种途径带来了对公共工程和改善项目的大量投资。然而,在体育设施上的投资只占总投资的很小一部分(9.1%)。1988年的汉城奥运会和2000年的悉尼奥运会都见证了类似的做法。

4. 举办奥运会:有利和不利影响

(1) 社会影响

正如巴塞罗那、亚特兰大和悉尼等城市所显示的,举办奥运会有许多有形和无形的长期益处。主办奥运会能激励组织者去关注体育、教育和机会平等的问题,提出战略来建立身心和谐发展的公共意识,并突显体育在促进世界和平、国家地位和社团团结方面的作用。

奥运会是促进社会变化的一个重要要素,因为它有利于提高民族自豪感,动员全社会来支持较难完成的国家工程。最后,通过操办那些要求综合计划和密切合作的大型复杂工程,主办国各行各业的劳动力的培训和专业化程度都可以得到改善。

(2) 城市重建

通过改变外部环境、更新和建造设施、公园、娱乐区和交通设施,奥运会在城市重建上可起到极重要的作用。这很合一些政治家的胃口,他们把奥运会看做是推动城市变化的手段,是提升城市形象和吸引力的手段。为此,许多城市现在为举办大型体育赛事展开激烈的竞争。自 1984 年以来,每一届奥运会都吸引了七个以上的城市提出申办。申办奥运会不仅给那些取得举办权的城市带来好处,也给那些提出申办但未成功的竞争城市带来好处。1992 年和 1996 年都提出申办的英国曼彻斯特市就体现了这一点。政府给该城市补贴了 5000 万英镑用于建造一个用于自行车和其他项目的新的室内体育馆,通过更新交通设施、电讯系统和环境,曼城的形象发生了改变,而这只是各种有形和无形影响的一部分。

在一项关于奥运会对举办城市影响的比较研究中[4],从城市影响来讲,有三种类型的奥运会举办城市(见表 3-3)。

表 3-3 1896—2000 年奥运会城市影响

影 响	奥运会	工 程
第一类 影响不大	雅典 1896	新建 Parathenean 体育馆
	巴黎 1900	没有新建设施
	圣路易斯 1904	没有新建设施
	伦敦 1948	没有新建设施
	墨西哥城 1968	投资极少——没有新建设施
	洛杉矶 1984	投资极少——没有新建设施
第二类 体育设施变化 较大	伦敦 1908	白色城市体育场(一个多功能体育馆)
	斯德哥尔摩 1912	新的体育场馆及独立的专项设施
	洛杉矶 1932	新的体育场馆,奥运村,专项比赛的体育场馆
	柏林 1936	新建能容纳 10 万观众的体育馆、德国体育论坛、奥林匹克体育场、奥运村
	赫尔辛基 1952	新体育馆、奥运村
	墨尔本 1956	奥林匹克公园体育场、奥运村
	亚特兰大 1996	新建奥林匹克体育场、水上运动中心、篮球场、马术馆和曲棍球馆

续 表

影 响	奥运会	工 程
第三类 促进环境转变	罗马 1960	改善奥林匹克公路沿线的基础设施,新建现代化的市政供水系统、机场
	东京 1964	新公路,22条高速网络,2条地铁线及各种设施
	慕尼黑 1972	重新开发名胜古迹,修葺剧院区的步行街,改善公共交通,新建地下停车场、购物中心、酒店和高速公路
	蒙特利尔 1976	奥林匹克公园,20公里的地铁系统,新的飞机场、酒店和道路
	莫斯科 1980	新建12个新体育场馆、新饭店、机场,奥林匹克电视与广播中心,奥林匹克通讯中心,俄新社的建筑群
	汉城 1988	兴建体育设施和奥运村、清理汉江、3条地铁线、47条公交线路、汉城艺术中心、国家古典音乐学院、清州博物馆、翻新寺庙,车库控制和整体卫生改善
	巴塞罗那 1992	新建15个体育场馆,奥运村、沿海环路、新的码头,改造下水道系统,重建海岸线与滨水设施,根据环保原则改善通讯技术和条件,建设配备太阳能和水循环系统的新奥运场馆和奥运村
	悉尼 2000	奥运会工程建设投资为25亿美元

资料来源:S.艾塞克斯,B.恰克雷,(1998)《奥运会:城市变化的催化剂》,《余暇研究》总17,第3期,第187—207页。

表3-3从建筑和投资工程规模总结了该研究的主要结果。第一类(影响较小)包括那些努力将支出最小化、没建什么新的体育设施或对体育设施投资很少的城市。第二类包括那些建立了大型体育设施,但城市环境和基础设施建设变化不大的城市。第三类包括这样的城市,即组织者利用奥运会来发起大规模的城市开发和更新项目,远远超出了建造新体育设施的基本需要。

(3)奥运会的经济影响

奥运会的经济影响一直被定义为"举办社团因在体育赛事或设施

上的开销而产生的净经济变化"[5]。奥运会因其具有创造就业机会和推动旅游和其他工业发展的潜力,现在被看做是经济增长的催化剂。然而,正如前面指出的,直到1984年洛杉矶为止,大多数奥运会是以债务累累而告终。例如,1976年蒙特利尔奥运会给该城市留下了巨额债务。当地纳税人直到2006年还在支付奥运会的账单。首次由私人运作的洛杉矶奥运会才结束了这一状态——至少在一段时间内。1984年奥运会以2.25亿美元的赢利取得了商业成功。近五届奥运会的经济影响见下面的表3-4。

表3-4 奥运会的经济影响

奥运会	利润	经济	就业（获得举办权到奥运会召开的几年内）
汉城1988	获得3亿美元的利润	到1988增长了12%	191341个就业机会
巴塞罗那1992	500万美元	1986—1993年间增加了166亿美元	281231个就业机会,失业率由18.4%跌至9.6%
亚特兰大1996	获得1000万美元利润	为乔治亚州带来了51亿美元的收入	77026个就业机会
悉尼2000	17.56亿美元	使澳大利亚GDP增加0.27个百分点,即15.5亿美元(1995—1996年美元价格)	1994—2006年间创造了10万个全职工作机会
雅典2004	背上了80亿美元的债务,纳税人要花20年方能还清	旅游的增长,公共部门税收增长13亿美元,增长率35%	65000个新的长期工作机会

1992年及以前的数据来源:霍尔格·普鲁厄斯:《奥运会的经济学:胜者和败者》,巴里·霍利汗(编):《体育和社会:学生入门指导》,London: Thousand Oaks, New Delhi: Sage Publication,第262页;1992年以后的数据:《北京奥运会:赢利还是亏损?》,《今日中国》,2004年11月5日。

有证据表明,举办奥运会可促进旅游业的发展。澳大利亚在2000年接待的游客增加了11%。有趣的是,12月份,即奥运会后的第三个月,是最忙碌的一个月,有56.5万游客。

由于使用了不恰当的销售或就业系数,没计算成本或把本来就要到该城市访问的游客支出计算了进去,某些奥运会经济影响研究的结果是不可靠的。在1996年的一项研究指出了测量经济影响的两个基本的方法——支出—收益分析或计划、资产负债表,这两个方法各有长短。[6] 1996年的另一项研究开发出了一个计算奥运会影响的简化模式,它是以直接或再生需求为基础的。在这个模式的基础上,洛杉矶、汉城和巴塞罗那奥运会的全面影响被计算了出来(见表3-5)。

表3-5　1984—1992奥运会全面影响的比较(美元)

标准	洛杉矶1984	汉城1988	巴塞罗那1992
系数	K=3	K=2.99	K=2.66
净直接投入	7.92亿	31亿	98亿
创造效应	15.84亿	62亿	162亿
总效应	23.76亿	93亿	260亿

资料来源:C.达比,《一个大型体育赛事的经济效应》,《奥林匹克通讯》,1996年第3期,第89页。

然而,奥运会对经济的影响不一定全是好的,负面影响也时常可见。[7] 主办城市市内或周边的地产、房产和房屋租金和价格常常上涨。另外,一个主办国的主要收入不可避免地会流向奥运举办城市和地区,在一定程度上剥夺了那些需要改进的其他地方的机会。

谈论经济影响时,一个常被忽视的问题是,奥运会规模的扩大和费用的不断上涨对参赛国的影响以及为取胜而付出的代价。例如,选派更多更好的运动员参加奥运会是每个国家奥委会的目标,但这需要付出代价。

(4) 奥运会的环境影响

根据联合国粮农组织2005年发布的《全球森林资源评估报告》,全球每年的森林采伐达1300万公顷。[8] 自然环境和持续发展的问题得到人们的日益关注。奥运会面对的一个挑战就是在日益扩展的奥运会规模和资源保护之间求得平衡。

早在20世纪70年代体育和大自然冲突的问题就被严肃地提了出来。1972年慕尼黑奥运会组织者带头在环保上采取行动,邀请所有参赛的国家奥委会在奥林匹克公园种植一颗来自其国家的灌木,并刻上了"在完好的环境中健康比赛"的口号。这些早期的做法逐渐被国际奥委会转变为详细说明的战略和行动,目的在于阻止体育对环境的有害影响。

国际奥委会1992年参加了在里约热内卢举行的联合国环境和发展大会,提出了让奥林匹克运动为持续发展的这一理念服务(全球计划第21个议程)。在其他方针中,国际奥委会列出了对奥运申办城市的环境要求。它要求奥组委承担更多的责任和义务,与有关机构合作、计划和实施环保合格的工程。

为解决体育和自然界之间的冲突,国际奥委会和其他的一些权力部门采取了多种策略。一个契约性的战略是在奥组委、政府、地方社团和私人企业之间达成协议,来应对问题、解决问题。第二个策略是环境破坏的标准化监控。悉尼奥组委吸取了环境持续发展的概念,通过坚持一致同意的原则和实践范例来提高环境意识和环保的革新技术。奥运会的组织者们正不断地在环境保护方面做出努力,为未来的体育事业提供更好的对话条件。

结 论

每个希望举办奥运会的城市在获得本国政府同意以后,必须向国际奥委会递交申请。为避免玩忽职守、腐败和操纵行为,国际奥委会制定了申办程序的原则和规定。申办过程很复杂,市政官员、商业部门和政府机构之间的合作十分重要。一旦一个城市被授予举办权,国家奥委会要与市政权力部门、政府机构和有意参与的商业团体一起组建奥组委,来负责奥运会的举办。

随着奥运会的发展,出现了不同的组织模式。举办奥运会可得到有形和无形的长期益处,奥运会现在是社会变化的积极媒介,它还可成为经济增长的催化剂,尽管并非一定如此。最近国际奥委会努力保证奥运会要保护环境,提供有所改善的体育环境。

思考题

1. 为什么不久前国际奥委会严格了关于申办奥运会的标准和规定?
2. 请给出一个主要原因,说明为什么一个申办城市必须得到政府的支持?
3. 北京在举办 2008 年奥运会上采取了哪种组织模式?为什么?
4. 你认为举办奥运会可带来的有形和无形好处中哪些最有益?请给出理由。

注　释

〔1〕 www.olympic.org/ioc/facts/cities/candidate city intro e.html.
〔2〕 王军华:《携奥运经济提速北京现代化进程》,《北京晚报》,2003 年 2 月 25 日。
〔3〕 这些机构包括秘书处、国际联络部、体育部、新闻和宣传部、工程部、奥运会服务部、法律事务部、监督和审计部、文化活动部、安全保卫部、医疗服务部和信息中心等。
〔4〕 S. Essex, & B. Chalkley, (1998), "Olympic Games: Catalyst of Urban Change", *Leisure Studies*, vol. 17, no. 3, pp. 187-207.
〔5〕 同上。
〔6〕 J. Crompton, (1996), "Economic Impact Analysis of Sports Facilities and Events: Eleven Sources of Misapplication", *Journal of Sport Management*, 9, 14-35.
〔7〕 C. Dubi, (1996), "The Economic Impact of A Major Sports Event", *Olympic Message*, 3, 88.
〔8〕 世界森林开伐率和森林覆盖统计:2000—2005, http://news.mongabay.com/2005/1115-forests.html.

第四章
奥林匹克物质文化

本章要点
* 体育建筑
* 设备和技术

奥林匹克运动在全世界的流行在一定程度上离不开建筑上的进步和技术的革新。建筑和技术又是现代奥林匹克运动的主要组成部分。

1. 建筑

"建筑主要是一门为服务于人类各种需要、满足他们在特定建造环境下的特殊需求而设计空间的艺术和科学。当各种各样的工程服务与建筑学的基本成分——空间、结构和形式合理组合时,人类功能的实施和机械效用的操作变得有效、令人愉快和有成就感。"[1] 上述话语表明体育建筑包含许多东西,现代体育馆、露天体育场、游泳池、赛马场和游艇俱乐部是其中的一部分。体育建筑为奥运会提供建筑结构的基础,起到实用和美学的双重目的。

(1) 希腊体育场

全世界的古代文明都有不朽的体育建筑场所。古希腊人是真正的建筑革新者。他们建立了体育场、体操馆、剧院和跑马场等。这些建筑说明,早在古代体育、竞赛和建筑之间就有着紧密的联系。[2]

奥林匹亚是一个文化中心。在那里,体育和文化建筑极巧妙地与

图 4-1 宙斯庙

绘画和雕塑结合在一起。宙斯庙是古代最伟大的建筑物之一。作为希腊最大的一个多利安式寺庙,它由建筑师李班(Libon)设计,李班试图按理想的比例体系来建该庙,即每个柱子之间的距离与它们的高度成和谐的比例,其他的建筑成分大小比例也合适。

潘纳德奈运动场是以泛雅典娜节而著称,它建于公元前330年,古代体育比赛就在那里举行。有趣的是,它的跑道是一个罕见的细长形状,弯度很大,赛跑者不得不将速度明显放慢下来才能保持在跑道内。2000年后,经过翻新、铺上白色的大理石,该场地在1896年的第一届现代奥运会上用于田径比赛。

(2)罗马圆形剧场

罗马人也创造了他们的建筑艺术,如用于体育比赛的斗兽场。其正式名称是弗拉维圆形剧场,建于公元前1世纪,是角斗士比赛、动物捕捉和海军战斗的场所。附近是罗马著名的古竞技场,充满血腥和暴力的大型战车比赛就在此地举行。[3] 罗马大竞技场是个拥有凸起的座位供观众使用的大型椭圆形建筑,在罗马管辖的土地上时常可见这些剧场。最著名的建筑之一是奥运冠军宫。它是由尼禄国王在公元67年资助建立的,可为成千上万的观众提供食宿。罗马的公共浴池、竞技场和圆形剧场是世界最著名的一些建筑。竞技场和跑道的设计从罗马

图 4-2 罗马圆形大剧场

圆形大剧场和古竞技场时代起一直变化不大。现今的体育比赛场、跑道和公共游泳池大多数是起源于古罗马时代(尽管可以在克里特岛和古希腊找到先例)。2000 年前的摔跤比赛场所马克森提长方形大厅,1960 年被用做现代奥运会的摔跤比赛场所。同时,另一个古代场地卡拉卡浴池则被用做体操比赛,而康士坦丁拱门被用做马拉松比赛的终点。希腊和罗马的体育建筑给世界留下了深远的影响。

(3) 现代奥运建筑

* **体育馆**

奥运会为现代体育馆的发展提供了动力。从第一个现代奥运周期起,每四年举办国常常会耸起一个永久性的体育馆,标志奥运会的召

开。在现代奥林匹克运动一个多世纪的发展中,体育场馆的发展可概述为三个不同的阶段:

第一阶段(1896—1968年)的特征可概括为设备简陋、功能单一。体育馆的结构远谈不上复杂。第一个现代体育馆出现在1908年的伦敦奥运会。在白城建立的这个运动场可容纳5万多观众席,部分看台有屋顶。场内铺设了长为536.45米的煤渣跑道,在运动场周围还修建了一个自行车赛车场和游泳池,加上原有的击剑场等老设施,基本构成了一个大型综合运动场的雏形。

二战前兴建了有特色的奥林匹克体育馆的运动会有1912年的斯德哥尔摩、1924年的巴黎、1928年的阿姆斯特丹和1936年的柏林奥运会。1912年斯德哥尔摩奥运会标志着奥运建筑的一个新起点。从那时起,人们一直努力使建筑更适合奥林匹克的理想和不断变化的奥林匹克运动。1932年洛杉矶的大剧场式的奥林匹克体育馆以其比例让全世界震惊。该体育馆的座位达10万多个,一条由碾碎的泥煤铺成的跑道让人跑得特别快,结果在田径竞赛项目上创造了10项世界纪录。

图4-3 阿姆斯特丹体育馆

图 4-4　柏林体育馆

为举办 1936 年奥运会,一个综合体育馆——德意志体育场——在柏林西部拔地而起。该体育场占地 325 英亩(131 公顷),包括四个体育馆。建于 1935 年的柏林奥林匹克体育馆,面积为 7000 平方米,设有 70 层看台,共 27 米高。它可容纳 9 万多观众,座位达 6 万多个。[4]

为 1940 年奥运会而建立的赫尔辛基体育馆直到 1952 年奥运会才启用,因为二战的爆发使得 1940 年的奥运会被取消。该体育馆可容纳 7 万名观众,由建筑师约里奥·林德格瑞(Yrjö Lindegren)和托伊沃·詹蒂(Toivo Jäntti)设计,他们曾以功能主义风格在建筑比赛中取胜。该体育馆完工后经历了八个阶段的改造,以适应体育和建筑的发展。

为准备 1960 年的罗马奥运会,一流的意大利建筑工程师皮埃尔·奈尔维(Pier Luigi Nervi)创建了罗马大体育馆,它包括带有绫纹圆屋顶的体育广场。这个像"天文观测舱"的建筑相当大,可为 6.2 万名观众提供座位,有一个很大的运动场。由网状钢支撑的透明塑料板的圆顶横跨 642 英尺(196 米),高 208 英尺(63 米)。内部装有空调。自 1960 年奥运会以后,这个体育场被用于田径运动会和足球比赛,常常被罗马两个重要的足球俱乐部罗马和拉齐奥使用。[5]

1964 年首次见证了奥运会在亚洲的举行。日本政府为在三个公园里修建一批比较现代化的体育设施投资了 30 亿美元。大的体育场

图 4-5　罗马奥林匹克体育馆

计划采取两个半圆形的形式,根据相互关系稍微有些变动,不相连的两端伸长至尖端。入口坐落在凹陷的两边。屋顶是由钢索系统构成,涂以瓷釉的钢板焊接在钢索上。它靠两个钢筋混凝土柱子支撑,这种柱子使得以前在结构上不可能的大胆的新设计成为可能。弧线型屋顶更具抗风的能力,在该地风力可达到飓风的程度。

第二阶段(1972—1999年)与电视的出现紧密相连。由于电视直播的出现,照明灯的装置、记者和新闻设施、所有全程电子测量和显示装置、电脑化的播音系统等都成为体育场馆建造要考虑的因素。体育馆的座位和环境变得更加舒适,设计更加灵活以适应举行多种活动的需要。此外,现代化的管理方式也使得场馆收入的来源发生了变化,观看体育比赛成为家庭的一项活动;体育场馆的使用率也在增加,每年可用200—300天。

1972年为第20届奥运会而建的慕尼黑奥林匹克公园,以289米高的广播电视塔及独一无二的透明天篷而引人注目。它于1969年动工,1971年完工。坐落在公园内的奥林匹克体育馆包括准备活动设施、游泳设施、主体育厅,可容纳69256名观众(57456个坐席,11800个站席)。

为1976年奥运会而建的蒙特利尔体育馆值得特别注意。它的问

图 4-6　1972 年慕尼黑奥林匹克公园全景

图 4-7　坐落在公园里的慕尼黑奥运会体育馆

题比 2004 年雅典奥运会的出现得早,且更为严重。当奥运会开始时,那个具有开创性的可开启的屋顶还没有完工,其原因是与体育馆相邻的一个 556 英尺高的塔只完成了计划的四分之一。事实上,这个由 60696 平方英尺、重 50 顿的凯夫拉尔纤维构成的屋顶直到 1987 年才完成,又用了两年才使屋顶可收起。而开收屋顶方面的问题导致它的永久关闭。1998 年春,这个橙色的凯夫拉尔屋顶被去除,当年晚些时候,安上了一个造价 2600 万加元、不透明的蓝色屋顶。该体育馆的总支出超过 10 亿加元。[6]

1988 年的大型汉城综合体育场是沿汉江而建,汉江将韩国的首都

图 4-8　蒙特利尔体育馆顶部

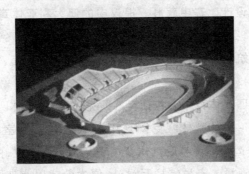

图 4-9　蒙特利尔体育馆不带顶

一分为二。占地 32 公顷、可容纳 10 万人的主体育场就坐落在汉城综合体育场内。开幕式、闭幕式、田径比赛、足球决赛和障碍赛都是在这个体育场内举行的。汉城奥委会建造了蚕室奥林匹克体育馆和含有体操、击剑、游泳、举重、网球和自行车 6 个场馆的奥林匹克公园。影响是当时考虑的核心，实用性在某些情况下摆到了次要位置。建在美沙里（Misari）的皮划艇比赛场花费了巨额资金，但奥运会后却搁置多年。室内自行车场维护费用很高，但一年中只有几次业余比赛在使用，且总共只用了 15 天。而自行车跑道更是难以维护，因为它是由一种特殊的非洲木料制成，难以经受韩国冬天的考验。[7]

1992 年的巴塞罗那奥运会建立了一个电讯塔，该塔覆盖了圣乔尔迪体育馆前的大广场,这是另一个技术革新。

从上述内容可看到,希望不断改进、比前一届奥运会做得更好的愿望激励着人们去寻找更好的材料和建筑技术。

21世纪迎来了以运用高科技、数字技术和环保设施以及计算机化的座位安置来实现观众与运动员互动为特征的第三阶段。2000年澳大利亚体育馆在这方面是个很好的例子。用前国际奥委会主席萨马兰奇的话说,该体育馆"是我今生看到的最出色的体育馆"。悉尼组委会要求竞标的建筑师设计一个漂亮的大型体育馆来容纳奥运观众,该体育馆在奥运会后要能缩小规模(不必重建)并符合生态上持续发展的需要。它不会破坏环境资源,能反映出将要举行的这一赛事的重要性和庄严性。知名的澳大利亚公司布莱佛勒·涅德和来自伦敦的劳布合伙企业在建筑设计比赛中获胜。提议中的澳大利亚体育馆形状奇异。对某些人而言,突然下降的半透明的屋顶看起来像回飞镖。并非人人都欣赏这一建筑,对著名的建筑师菲利浦·考克斯而言,它就像一块品客薯片!

雅典奥林匹克体育中心包括奥林匹克体育馆、奥林匹克室内大厅、奥林匹克水上中心、奥林匹克网球中心和奥林匹克室内自行车场。2004年雅典奥运会的奥林匹克体育馆有74767个座位,由著名的西班牙建筑师圣地亚哥·卡拉特拉瓦设计,原本希望以此来展现一个现代的雅典,但该体育馆由于费用超支过大和建筑延期而成为人们担心奥运会能否按期举行的焦点问题。延期的主要原因是屋顶,为使观众免于雅典太阳的暴晒就一定要有玻璃钢覆盖物。到2004年5月,支撑1.8万顿重的屋顶所必需的拱形结构还没到位,这促使国际奥委会提出彻底放弃这一屋顶工程的建议。然而,这个大型的屋顶在6月4日最终完工了,刚好用于希腊田径锦标赛。该体育馆的造价是1.7亿欧元,是希腊政府最初预算的三倍。[8]

从上述内容可见,体育馆随着时间的推移而不断变化:有些是矩形带弧形拐角;有些是椭圆形或U形的。体育馆的设计变得越来越灵活、功能越来越复杂、规模也越来越庞大,同时也更加现代化,注重技术和环保。

图 4-10　2000 年悉尼奥运会体育馆

* 奥运村

今日的奥运村几乎就是一个小城市，运动员和随队官员可以在那里吃住。例如，2004 年雅典奥运村在奥运会期间接纳了 1.6 万名运动员和随队官员，在残奥会期间接待了 6000 人。[9] 在奥运村运动员享有很多便利。他们一天 24 小时都可以在奥运村的饭店中就餐、理发，在电影院看电影或在酒吧和迪厅里放松。

然而，运动员并不总是享有这么好的住所。1932 年以前，没有专为运动员设置的奥运村。运动员居住在不同的地方：饭店、汽车旅馆、廉价的学校或军营住所。某些人甚至住在自己带到奥运城市来的船上。例如，1928 年阿姆斯特丹奥运会期间，美国、意大利和芬兰人住在港湾里。

第一个奥运村出现在 1932 年的洛杉矶奥运会上。它坐落在洛杉矶郊区的鲍尔温山丘上，占地 321 英亩（130 公顷）。来自 37 个国家的男运动员住在 500 个带走廊的平房内，村内有医院、图书馆、邮局以及供应多种风味的 40 个厨房。这是首次在奥运村提供医院、消防队和邮局服务。然而，女性则住在饭店，而不是奥运村内。直到 1956 年墨尔本奥运会，奥运村才对男女两性都开放。有趣的是，1952 年奥运会特为东欧国家在奥塔涅米区另建了一个奥运村,它是美国和前苏联这两个超级大国之间冷战的结果。

现在,奥运村的建设是组委会在筹备奥运会期间十分重视的问题。奥运村的位置与主体育馆和其他设施要尽可能靠近,住宿男女分开。只有参加比赛运动员和官员才可以住进奥运村。

(4) 与体育建筑相关的问题

为了赢得尽可能多的国际关注,主办国和城市通常要建一些"橱窗"设施。奥运建筑师应多注意场馆的功能,尽可能强调体育和艺术双重特性。此外,建筑外观必须与周围景观相协调,并充分利用周围的风景。[10] 一般而言,体育建筑必须考虑下列因素:

* 地点

制定确保主要政府设施和公共场馆的战略,需要对地理位置本身和周围地理环境进行深入的分析。这样的分析需要对包括建筑、公路和交通状况在内的整个地段进行评估和介绍。分析的关键是理解该地点周围的三维空间环境。

人类和自然的密切协作是现代奥林匹克设计的最重要特征之一。[11] 地点的选择必然影响到建筑的概念。日内瓦河或旧金山海湾,泰晤士河岸或北京平原显然是不同的。每一种风景都会激发不同的设计方案。

奥运场馆的选址还应注意社会标准。它应鼓励城市中不够发达和不太富裕区域的发展,这样能起到平稳发展的作用。[12]

* 技术

现在,技术创造出了十分复杂的设备,从整个建筑到桌椅,从视频长廊到商店、博物馆等,这些都是构成一个新体育场馆的基本部分。如下方面需细致考虑科技的运用:

* 规模

观众规模需要仔细估算。随着电视观众的增加,未来体育馆的尺寸也许可减小。

* **服务**

为吸引顾客,需要细心考虑设施的安全性和便利性,从高质量、舒适的座位到安全的站台,再加上优质的饮食安排。

* **考虑残疾人需要**

便于残疾人通行的道路和设备对各级水平的参与是至关重要的。

* **维护能力**

维护能力需要考虑。奥运会结束后,场馆以后的费用支出,包括早期投资的偿还,每年的日常运作、维护和翻新会远远超过最初的资本支出。对这些都必须有所认识,并做好计划。

* **平衡性**

现代奥运场馆是一项重要的基础设施投资。因此,平衡发展的重要性要求,要充分利用已有和新建的设施。持续发展(社会、财政、生态和物理)和环境保护是选址、计划、设计和新设施建造及与已有设施的关系等方面极为重要的成分。

奥运设施可分为永久性和暂时性两种。永久性设施可长期使用,给社区带来益处。然而,不言而喻,仅用永久性设施而不使用暂时性设施是难以举办大型赛事的。暂时性设施只满足一个赛事的需求,补充永久性设施的短缺以达到举办赛事所必须达到的标准。因此,关于永久性和暂时性场馆的决定显然要在计划的开始阶段就做出。

2. 技术

在奥林匹克历史上,奥林匹克文化、设备和技术一直是相互辉映、相互影响的。现代技术和设备的快速发展对奥林匹克运动产生了巨大的影响,下面是一些例子。

(1) 设备

在第一次世界大战前,体育器械和设施主要是由竹子、金属、橡胶和羽毛等自然材料制成。将橡胶硬化的过程改变了网球和其他的运动用球及其运动项目。其他的技术革新也紧跟而上,例如,在网球项目上,20世纪80年代铝合金的革新象征着木质球拍时代的结束。制造商试用不同材料,如玻璃纤维、硼、镁、陶和石墨来制造球拍。这些轻型材料让人们能够引进更大球端的球拍,让球手有更大的爆发力和控制力。与此同时,在自行车项目上,出现了"超级自行车",它是以碳素轮胎制成的无辐条自行车。作为奥运会项目的网球和自行车在设备和成绩上都彻底革新了。

(2)更准确的成绩测量

技术革新还带来了更准确的成绩测量。1912年瑞典斯德哥尔摩奥运会,安装了电动计时器,前6名运动员的成绩时间精确到1/10秒。电动计时器开创了体育测量仪器的新时代。由于使用了这一设备,一些运动成绩后来被相应的国际单项体育组织承认为正式的世界纪录。这样,首次官方奥运纪录诞生了。然而,由于电子计时设施昂贵,直到1932年奥运会才采纳它们。终点摄像机也出现在1912年的奥运会上。1964年精工创造了石英计时技术,它提供了到当时为止最准确的记时系统,到20世纪70年代,它成为大型体育赛事最重要的设施。国际田联规定世界锦标赛和奥运会必须使用自动计时系统来测量成绩,最小测量单位是百分之一秒。

(3)监督裁判

在北美,及时回放裁判过程是冰球和橄榄球比赛常见的一个做法,尽管裁判员最初对引进及时回放来协助或代替他们的决定不是十分热心。场上主裁判的决定可以被坐在场边观看回放以决定场上判罚是否准确的及时回放裁判员所推翻,即"鹰眼技术"。

此外,还有一些可协助像网球这样的项目进行仲裁的技术,如出界报告,但目前还不清楚这些技术能否发展到完全代替裁判的地步。

在未来,可通过动漫三维模型和那些用多角度拍摄的实际比赛胶片来开发仿真设施,这些设施允许裁判员做出决定,并从不同角度来回顾和重新评价他们的决定,评价他们相对于其他职业人士所做出的反应状况。[13]

(4) 技术和成绩

新技术现在还被用来分析成绩。例如,被称做"数据服装"的橡胶套装有分布在身体每个关节的感应器,能在在计算机绘制的图表中标出相应的位置。这样的套装在监控跳高、体操和其他技术性很高的项目中的身体运动上有明显的用途。

目前,计算机广泛被用于运动员的训练上。训练受技术的影响越来越大,比如生物反馈,想象训练和虚拟现实训练。此外,新材料用在船只、服装和运动器材上。激光加速器甚至用在短跑训练中。拳击教练在击打袋中装入测量加速度的设施,教会拳击选手更快、更狠地击倒对手。撑杆跳的垂直杆可用发光二极管来测量运动员跳了多高。最后,在希望根除兴奋剂、确保公平竞争的管理者和希望运用生物技术来提高成绩的人之间的斗争中,人们还竞相使用对抗的技术进行博弈。

(5) 技术和观众的更多选择

20 世纪 80 年代和 90 年代,新的通讯技术的出现拉开了全球体育重新定位的过程。[14]付费电视和卫星电视的出现,尤其是按次计费电视的出现,给电视和体育的关系增添了新的维度。按次计费在 1980 年出现,当时雷伊·伦纳德(Ray Leonard)和罗伯特·杜兰(Robert Duran)的对抗吸引了 17 万名顾客,每人支付了 15 美元。到 90 年代后期,按次计费成为大型拳击赛事推广活动的主要形式。

Sky Sport 采纳了一项最初用在海湾战争的技术,它是以色列的傲威高技术系统有限公司为追踪萨达姆·侯赛因的飞毛腿导弹而开发的。这一技术把运动行为数字化地转换成电子游戏一样的图像形式,可让电视分析者从各个角度来重建主要的事件。

总之,科技已经深刻地影响了奥林匹克运动的发展。合成材料跑道已经代替了煤渣跑道,数码和视频技术的结合给运动员和教练员提供了监控比赛成绩的生物力学方面的手段。运动员和教练员欢迎那些有助于他们取得更好成绩的新的特殊设施,裁判员也充分利用这些新技术来帮助他们做出决定,最后,媒体评论员、分析员和观众也得益于这些技术进步。今后还会有更多这样的进步。技术目前是、将来也会是奥运会的重要组成部分。

结 论

体育建筑是奥运会的建筑基础。建筑及其影响可追溯到许多世纪以前。古希腊和罗马的建筑给现代奥运和其他体育建筑留下了它们的印记。然而，在过去的一个世纪，体育场馆的结构、风格和基本要素都在一定程度上随着现代奥运会的发展而变化。环保是其中的一个，它在促进体育场馆设计和结构变化上起到越来越重要的作用。在过去100多年中，由于技术革新，体育设备变得越来越复杂。但是，近年来媒体技术对奥运会的影响才算最大。很可能，在未来也会如此。

思考题

1. 现代体育场馆应有什么特征？为什么？
2. 在奥运建筑和地理环境之间的理想关系是什么？
3. 现代技术在哪些方面影响了奥运会的性质？你认为最近的技术革新那个最重要？

注 释

〔1〕 建筑理事会，《建筑的实践》，http://www.coa-india.org/practice/practice.html.
〔2〕 Martin Wimmer(1976), *Olympic Buildings*, Edition Leipzig.
〔3〕 David Levinson and Karen Christensen (eds.) (1996), *Encyclopaedia of World Sport: From Ancient Times to the Present*, Oxford: ABC-CLIO Ltd., 21.
〔4〕 John Arlott (ed.) (1975), *The Oxford Companion to Sports & Games*, Oxford University Press, p. 735.
〔5〕 同上。
〔6〕 http://www.ballparks.com/baseball/national/olympi.html.
〔7〕 http://www.cyclerace.or.kr/e_cra/launching02_a.html.
〔8〕 http://www.cbc.ca/olympics/venues/olympic_stadium.html.

〔9〕 http://www.olympic.org/uk/games/athens/index_uk.asp.

〔10〕 Coubertin, P. de (1976), "A Modern Olympia", in Martin Wimmer, *Olympic Buildings*, Edition Leipzig, 210.

〔11〕 Coubertin, P. de, 1976, op. cit., 209.

〔12〕《建筑和国际体育赛事——未来计划和发展》,国际奥委会和国际建筑联盟联合会议,2002年5月,http://multimedia.olympic.org/pdf/en_report_644.pdf.

〔13〕 Mike Laflin, Sport and the Internet—The Impact and the Future, http://multimedia.olympic.org/pdf/en_report_60.pdf.

〔14〕 Ellis Cashmore (2002), *Sports Culture: An A-Z Guide*, London and New York: Routledge, pp. 402-405.

第五章
奥运会与大众传媒

本章要点
* 国际奥委会与媒体日益密切的联系
* 电视对国际奥委会日益增长的影响
* 国际奥委会不断增加的"媒体财富"

1. 媒体的力量

　　本章将讨论奥运会和大众传媒之间的关系,重点是电视在转变现代奥运会中所起的作用。参与转播2004年雅典奥运会比赛的媒体人员大约有2.15万人,其中电视转播工作人员1.6万名,摄影、文字媒体人员5500。[1] 很明显,奥运会与大众媒体已密不可分。大众传媒是一个具有多重身份的机构。"它是……一个经济机构,一个文化机构,……它是制造利润的行当,……是意义的生产者,社会意识的创造者"。[2] 因此,大众传媒可以被看成是一个传播社会信息的设备,一个追求财富的组织,负责建构现实的人和他们的方针,以及控制团体意识的来源。

　　奥运会是全世界观看的最大的体育节目。据估计有来自220多个国家的37亿多人观看了2000年悉尼奥运会的转播。因此,奥运会是一个独特的广告媒介。它有一个重要的优势,即奥运会转播人可以在比赛的中断时间内插播广告,且不会引起观看者的愤怒。此外,奥运会包括了吸引不同观众的众多体育项目。足球和拳击最吸引年轻的男性,艺术体操和花样游泳最吸引女性,但奥运会还包括对两性都有吸引力的体育项目,如田径。

广告潜力只是一个方面。大多数人没有机会现场观看奥运会,媒体架起了奥运会和观众之间桥梁。它向全球观众传递奥林匹克的价值,同时提供运动成绩、记录和得分方面的背景信息。它起着娱乐和教育的作用,也起着控制的作用。媒体的影响力巨大,它向国内外观众解释奥运事件的意义和重要性,同时也影响着他们的观点。媒体选择要转播的赛事和故事,从而确定奥林匹克的事实。

奥运会是一出伟大的国际性戏剧———一个全球性的戏剧表演,运动员就是演员。他们包含了人类情绪的所有方面。他们有当众流下痛苦和快乐的眼泪的时刻;他们有展示成功和失败的场所;他们见证人类的伟大、勇气、决心和耐心;他们展现身体的优雅、美丽和力量。他们集娱乐、电影、芭蕾和戏剧为一体,是为全球数亿观众演出的剧目。媒体则是传递的手段。

此外,奥运会给体育英雄们的丰功伟绩提供经久不衰的记忆。媒体将这些记忆储存在胶片、磁带和纸张上,而且为了日后反复使用还将它们一一复制。这样,媒体使运动员和运动成绩变得不朽。

2. 大众传媒的主要形式

所有形式的大众传媒——文字媒体、广播和电视都会转播奥运会(见表5-1)。

表 5-1 奥运会注册媒体代表

奥运会	文字媒体	广播和电视	媒体代表总数
罗马 1960	1146	296	1442
东京 1964	1507	2477	3984
慕尼黑 1972	3300	4700	8000
洛杉矶 1984	4000	4200	8200
巴塞罗那 1992	4880	10360	15740
亚特兰大 1996	5000	12000	17000
悉尼 2000	5298	10735	16033
雅典 2004	5500	16000	21500

资料来源:《奥林匹克营销事实文件》(1996至2005年),国际奥委会网页。

(1) 文字媒体

印刷文字是将奥运会的有关事实和数据向国际观众传送的传统方法。体育报纸和杂志首先出现在 19 世纪早期，当时英国的皮尔斯·艾根开始用多彩的词汇和丰富的行话写作，这种方法是现在体育作家常用的方法。报纸和杂志在 20 世纪早期首先遇到广播的竞争。第二次世界大战后，它们又遇到了与其争夺市场的电视。目前出版的有关体育和奥运会的专业杂志和报纸达数千种，许多国家都有体育日报。关于奥运会的书籍、杂志和学术刊物也层出不穷，形成了自己独特的类型，报纸也用相当的版面报道奥林匹克运动。尽管遇到了广播、电视和因特网的激烈竞争，文字媒体仍成功地生存下来，由早期体育作家奠定的风格在许多方面依然可见。

(2) 广播

在 20 世纪早期美国广播开创了体育直播的方式。体育爱好者打开广播，收听体育（包括奥运会）的直播。广播电台给体育转播分配了大量的时间。1920 年只有几千人有广播接收装置，十年后该数据升到了 2400 万，而 1940 年则上升到 4400 万。[3] 第二次世界大战后，奥运会的广播转播遇到了电视的挑战，但广播评论并未被完全取代。事实上，许多体育爱好者今天还会关闭电视来听广播播音，因为它更生动、详细和全面。

(3) 电影

由哈维·马克·泽克和劳伦斯·J.巴比奇在 1987 年剪辑的《体育电影》列出了 2042 部电影，分为 17 类，奥林匹克运动是其中的一类。在该领域最著名的导演者是雷妮·瑞芬斯塔尔。她拍摄的 1936 年柏林奥运会《奥林匹亚》堪称经典。她首创慢动作、特写镜头和全新剪辑的手法，创造了令人难以忘怀的生龙活虎的运动员形象。

雷尼·瑞芬斯塔尔

1932年雷妮·瑞芬斯塔尔参加了一个德国的政治集会,主讲人阿道夫·希特勒给她留下了深刻的印象。为此,她写信给他,告知实情。碰巧,希特勒是她刚执导的新片《蓝色之光》的影迷,于是决定由她来拍摄1933年在纽伦堡举行的纳粹大会。她拍得极为成功,并为她赢得了两年后拍摄奥运会的邀请。她让人挖坑,以静止的天空为背景,用广角来拍摄运动员。当国际奥委会反对时,她哭着大闹。她把摄像镜头捆在气球上,这些气球携带返程标志,以便在它漂浮到柏林郊区后能把他们拉回来。摄像镜头还放在马鞍上来拍摄三天的比赛。雷妮拍摄出了一个漂亮的电影,而不仅仅是一个运动会的记录,为此她不惜造假。例如,撑杆跳比赛持续到天黑,而天黑后无法拍摄,她就让运动员第二天回来再拍摄。而游泳运动员的特写镜头是在训练中拍摄的,然后再插入到最后的电影中。最为著名的是,在艺术性跳水的系列动作中,一些胶片是从后往前放的,因为这样看起来更好。

以奥运会为主题的电影不少。每一届奥运会几乎都拍摄了纪录片。市川昆在1964年拍摄了《东京世运会》,这一杰作接近《奥林匹亚》的制作水平。1972年慕尼黑奥运会是《慕尼黑运动会》(1973年)的创作源泉,该片把八个知名的导演集合到一起,每一个人侧重一个项目或一个运动员。例如,拍《邦妮和克莱德》的阿瑟·潘拍摄了撑竿跳高;梅伊·塞特灵的重点是举重;市川昆分析了男子100米短跑;约翰·施莱辛格把巴勒斯坦恐怖分子人质劫持死亡事件与英国马拉松选手罗恩·希尔的运动故事联系在一起。[4]

自20世纪20年代以来,以奥林匹克人物为核心的电影拍摄了不少(见下表)。1981年《烈火战车》戏剧性地叙述了在1924年巴黎奥运会中苏格兰的埃里克·利德尔和英格兰的哈洛德·亚伯拉罕之间的竞争,该片赢得了三项奥斯卡奖——最佳影片奖、最佳服装设计和最佳原创音乐奖。

奥林匹克人物电影

年份	影片名称	出品地	导演
1925	9秒6	美国	劳埃德·B.卡尔顿
1928	奥林匹克英雄	美国	R.威廉姆·内尔
1936	万里挑一	美国	西德尼·兰菲尔德
1937	陈查理在奥运会	美国	赫.布鲁斯·亨伯斯通

续表

年	影片名称	出品地	导演
1951	吉姆·索普——美国的代表	美国	迈克尔·柯蒂兹
1954	鲍勃·马西亚斯的故事	美国	弗朗西斯·D.莱昂
1955	威·乔迪	英国	弗兰克·朗德
1962	它发生在雅典	美国	安德鲁·马顿
1966	走,不要跑	美国	查尔斯·瓦尔克斯
1969	下半生赛跑者	美国	迈克尔·里奇
1970	世运铁人	美国	迈克尔·温纳
1974	我的方式	南非	约瑟夫·布伦纳
1975	梦断天涯	美国	拉里·皮尔斯
1976	慕尼黑二十一小时	美国	(为福布斯电视而摄制)
1977	2076年奥运会	美国	詹姆斯·P.马丁
1977	胜者为王之拳王阿里	美国/英国	汤姆·格里尔
1977	奥运情结	西德	斯蒂芬·卢克斯基
1977	维尔玛	美国	巴德·格林斯潘
1979	道恩·弗莱泽	澳大利亚	肯汉南
1979	金女郎	美国	约瑟夫·萨金特
1979	花逢月满永不残	美国	唐纳德·怀尔
1979	强人	美国	斯蒂芬·希利亚德·斯泰姆
1980	第40个奥运周期	波兰	安德泽奇·克特寇斯基
1981	冰上奇迹	美国	斯蒂芬·希利亚德·斯泰姆
1981	烈火战车	英国	休·赫德森
1982	私人最佳	美国	罗伯特·唐纳
1983	勇敢地跑	加	D.S.艾弗雷德
1984	第一届奥运会:雅典1896	美国	阿尔文·寇夫
1984	杰西·欧文斯的故事	美国	理查德·欧文
1985	奔金牌而去:比尔·约翰逊的故事	美国	唐·泰勒
1986	登峰造极	美国	艾伯特·马尼奥利
1986	血债	加/美国	迈克尔·安德森
1988	勇气	美国	兰迪·布拉德肖
1992	冰上浪漫曲	美国	保罗·迈克尔·格拉泽
1993	凉快的跑道	美国	乔恩·图泰尔泰博
1994	死亡五项	美国	布鲁斯·马尔毛斯
1996	破浪而出	美国	斯蒂芬·希利亚德·斯泰姆
1996	引爆亚特兰大	美国	艾·佩恩
1996	追梦	美国	尼曼·伯纳特

续 表

年	影片名称	出品地	导演
1996	光荣与疯狂	加/日	原田真人
1996	阿普正传	美国	史蒂夫·詹姆斯
1998	永无止境	美国	罗伯特·唐纳
2000	奔向终点	美国	李·格兰特

资料来源:《现代奥林匹克运动百科大全》,第527页。

当提到奥林匹克电影时,有一个人必须提到,那就是巴德·格林斯潘,目前他是奥运会官方纪录片制作人。

传奇的电影制片人巴德·格林斯潘

巴德·格林斯潘出生于1926年9月18日,21岁时在纽约开始了体育播音员的生涯。他播出的节目包括 Warm-up time、Sports Extra、布鲁克林广告赛前和赛后报道、曲棍球、篮球、田径、网球比赛等。后来,格林斯潘改为杂志撰稿人。从此以后,他向美国和国外的主要出版商出售了数百篇小说和非小说文章。1967年在他成立自己的公司之前,格林斯潘为劳伦斯·冈巴比内中介公司、舞蹈家—费茨杰拉德—样品有限公司和纽约城的 SSC&B 等公司制作电视商业片。

在专门报道奥运之后,他拍摄的22集电视系列剧《奥林匹亚》(1976—1977年)和为 ABC 公司的1980年冬奥会电视转播而制作的历史图像赢得了艾美奖,1994年他因编辑利勒哈默尔冬奥会而再次获得艾美奖。1997年他被授予广播和电视业最高荣誉的乔治·福斯特·皮博迪终身成就奖。格林斯潘是最著名的体育电影作家、制作人和导演,是世界最重要的体育史学家之一。

资料来源:http://www.goodmanspeakersbureau.com/biographies/greenspan_bud.htm。

从1964年以来他制作了数十部涉及奥林匹克运动不同方面的电影。《杰西·欧文斯重返柏林》(1964),《马拉松》(1974),《澳大利亚人》(1975),《东欧人》(1980),《奥运会中的美国》(1984),《奥林匹克梦想》(1988)。1988年出品的22集系列片《奥林匹亚》,其中包括《冬奥会中的伟大时刻》、《忍耐之人》和《不朽》。他继续制作奥运电影,比如《他们国家的荣誉》(1991年)、《测量伟大》(1992)[5]、《奥林匹克百年辉煌》和《伟大的美国奥林匹克选手》(1996)以及《冬奥会最精彩的瞬间》(1997)。

（4）电视

电视转播对于成功举办奥运会是极为重要的。它是奥运财务的支柱。1936年奥运会首次开始奥运会转播。在柏林架起的25个大屏幕，让居民能够免费观看奥运会。第二次世界大战后，电视成为主要的媒介。在美国，1949年大约只有2%的家庭拥有电视机；一年后，大约10%的家庭拥有电视机[6]，到1965年该数据升到93%[7]。1964年美国广播公司（NBC）转播了东京奥运会的开幕式，尽管直到夏末才肯定通过第三号同步通信卫星定位的图像会有较高的网络质量。1968年墨西哥奥运会首次采用彩色转播，引入现场慢动作胶片。之后的10年电视转播呈爆炸式增长。悉尼奥运会转播组织提供了3500小时的奥运节目，转播了300场比赛和开/闭幕式，220个国家的观看人数达到创纪录的37亿人；而NBC用441个小时转播悉尼奥运会，1210小时转播2004年雅典奥运会（7个频道每天70个小时的转播）。[8]

除作为连接全球观众的桥梁以推广奥林匹克主义外，电视还通过出售奥运会的电视转播权来给奥运大家庭提供巨额资金（详细情况如下）。悉尼奥运会转播就获得了所有收入的45%。这笔数目在2004年上升到52%。国际奥委会从1984年到2008年间的奥运会电视转播合同中获得100多亿美元。[9]然而，这一局面不是轻而易举就出现的。奥运会和电视发展史充满了冲突和控制。

为电视转播费而斗争

1960年奥运会电视转播权出售以后，奥运会组委会，国际体育单项联合会和国家奥委会以及国际奥委会都想从该收入中多分得一份。国际奥委会面对着一个又一个的挑战。为此，在20世纪60年代，当时的国际奥委会主席布伦戴奇建立了一个分配公式，该公式将给奥林匹克运动带来和平，同时维护它的理想境界，并满足奥组委的财务需要。1966年国际奥委会的第一个电视收入分配公式是67%给奥组委，剩余的33%由国际奥委会，国际单项体育联合会和国家奥委会来平分。然而，刚开始时，此公式很难实施。慕尼黑想要从与美国电视转播谈判得到的费用中扣除技术服务费。国际奥委会做出让步，让其从与美国广播公司（ABC）的1350万美元合同中扣去600万。以后的奥运会中再没有出现这样的问题。国际奥委会禁止给想要举办奥运会的城市任何折扣。1977年在主席基拉宁领导下的国际奥委会决定,它将与1984年和以后的组委会一起谈判电视合同事宜。

然而,在后来的十年中,该协商方针问题不断。洛杉矶奥组委主席皮特·尤伯罗斯对它发起了挑战,要求独自控制谈判过程。得知欧洲转播联盟过去一直没有被要求支付电视转播费,尤伯罗斯赢得了国际奥委会的支持去与欧洲转播联盟谈判。结果,欧洲转播联盟付费转播1988年的汉城奥运会。由有关城市直接谈判是目前普遍采纳的做法。

资料来源:《现代奥运会百科全书》,第509—519页。

电视对奥运会有着深远的影响。例如,它导致了对比赛时间安排的干涉。[10]此外,目前的比赛安排和展示风格也充分体现出电视转播的要求。[11]

(5)因特网

因特网在奥运会转播中起着越来越重要的作用。1996年奥运会官方网页的点击率达1.86亿次;1998年长野冬奥会的点击率达6.34亿次。近几年因特网的使用更是变化多端。因特网成为日常生活的一部分,而体育是因特网的最爱,它吸引全世界数以亿计的观众查询各自所喜爱的运动、队伍和运动员的信息。受大众喜欢的以信息为基础的体育服务提供体育赛事的现场描述。"体育地带"有足球"进球表"和篮球"投篮表"。这些图表形象地展示赛事的即时进展情况。如此详细的信息对版面有限的报纸而言是不可能的,对信息着迷的球迷十分喜欢它,但必须为此支付每月的会员费。新闻、统计数据、分析、日常安排和价格等都可以在网上找到。

出售体育"统计数据"现在是数百万美元的产业。[12]许多大的报纸和转播组织都有网页,有专门的包括奥运会在内的体育栏目。体育变成路透社的一大收入来源,其中因特网起了很大的作用。路透社的"体育反馈"网址每月平均费用是5000美元,你只要算一算有多少网站需要其内容(目前有2500多个体育相关的网页),就知道这是一个多大的市场。[13]路透社还新设立了一个由80人组成的部门来专门开发体育内容市场,他们被很多人认为是因特网上体育信息的主要来源。[14]像斯泰兹这样的公司提供持球跑卫数量和裁判吹哨趋势等细节信息,注册费30美元,上网每分钟25美分。[15]所有这些大的体育服务机构都有大量的统计信息;ESPN分数栏每分钟收费95美分。摩托罗拉的报道棒球进展情况的体育BP机每月成本50美元。现在,网上服务提供顾客所需要的、及时的滚动积分板。

网上发出的信息量就像滚雪球一样。成千上万的体育爱好者开始进入3W建立自己的信息库。大多数职业体育组织有情报网址,想用它来增加收入或巩固他们的球迷基础。运动队把队员的信息、比赛安排和票务情况等放到网上。与其他的网上专门体育商店一起,运动队也展示并出售比赛用品。

电子邮件、邮件列表、新闻群和聊天服务给体育狂热者提供了一种新的交流形式。这些服务致力于满足人们与他人对话和联系的基本需要。他们主要的缺点是要求使用者做过多的工作,谈话常常是被迫的、难以令人鼓舞的或让人争论不休的。由于电子邮件、新闻群和聊天室的互动频率和结构不能让人们完全地投入,致使体育最诱人的一些东西丧失了。

根据体育商业网2001年1月10日的统计,哥伦比亚广播系统(CBS)网体育在线的时事栏目在2000年第四季度的点击率约28亿次,平均每天的点击率3020万次。体育商业网每天向它的所有顾客发送包括体育事物的时事报道,主持体育新闻和体育商业年会,包括在2000年12月与国际奥委会一起举办的一个会议。[16]

网上的信息服务能提供其他地方得不到的信息。现行系统用多媒体可以提供比其他媒体更快的信息,但它们受终端设施的限制,这些设施不能像纸张那样方便和有吸引力。

因特网直接影响着奥林匹克运动的发展。由于对即时信息和奥运会网络服务之需要的增长,奥运会组织所面临的技术挑战也随之激增。国际奥委会成立了工作组来帮助奥组委和国际奥委会的技术供应商确定对硬件安装、系统和应用软件开发和网络设计方面的要求。该工作组也指导所有技术工程的实施和操作。国际奥委会开发了它的全球技术模式来指导所有相关方的互动。与奥组委和所有合作伙伴一起工作的最重要的工具之一是奥林匹克成绩和信息服务(ORIS)。该手册列出了对每一个大项和各小项的技术要求,以便每个人都清楚在每一个地方必须提供什么东西。[17]

互联网与一般媒体有一些共同之处。互联网的目的是赢利;其理想是提供服务;其目标是建立作为一个可靠信息源的信誉;其愿望是以独特的艺术形式来表示自己。最后,它还负责消息的生产和传递。

3. 转播权

转播权的问题对奥运会极其重要,值得详细讨论。早在1954年,当时的国际奥委会主席布伦戴奇(1952—1972年担任主席)就看到了电视可作为国际奥委会长久的收入来源。

国际奥委会最初开始收取电视转播费是在1960年夏季和冬季奥运会,CBS为在加利福尼亚斯阔谷举行的冬奥会和在罗马举行的夏奥会分别支付了5万美元和39.4万美元。1960年以后,美国电视网络公司ABC、CBS和NBC为获得转播奥运会的权利而展开了激烈的竞争(见表5-2)。

表5-2 美国转播权费用

夏季奥运会		转播公司	百万美元
1976	蒙特利尔	ABC	25
1980	莫斯科	NBC	85
1984	洛杉矶	ABC	225.6
1988	汉城	NBC	300
1992	巴塞罗那	NBC	401
1996	亚特兰大	NBC	456*
2000	悉尼	NBC	705
2004	雅典	NBC	739.5*
2008	北京	NBC	834*

*加上利润分享(资料来源:《奥运营销2005事实档案》:IOC网站)

结果,1964年美国转播权的费用直线上升,超过了200万美元,然后进一步盘旋上升,1996年NBC为转播百年奥运会支付了4.56亿美元,2000年奥运会达到了7.05亿美元,2004年为7.39亿美元。从下表中可见,美国公司占领了奥运会的转播市场。

表 5-3 2004 年雅典奥运会转播公司和转播费

洲	公司	转播费(百万美元)
美洲	美国国家广播公司(NBC)	793.0
	加拿大广播公司(CBC)	37.0
	拉丁美电视广播组织(OTI)	17.0
	波多黎各电视(WKAQ)	1.25
亚洲	加勒比海广播联盟(CBU)	0.35
	亚太广播联盟(ABU)	14.5
	日本雅典奥运会协会(AOJC)	155.0
	阿拉伯国际广播联盟(ASBU)	5.5
	中国台北雅典联营(CTAP)	3.65
	韩国雅典奥运联营(AOKP)	15.5
欧洲大洋洲	欧洲广播联盟(EBU)	394.0
	澳大利亚七网络(Seven)	50.5
	电视新西兰(TVNZ)	3.5
非洲	非洲广播、电视联盟(URTNA)/南非广播公司(SABC)	9.25
	国际超级体育(SSI)	3.0
总计		1476.9

电视体育赛事的流行确保了电视网络会继续提供一笔巨大的转播费用,商业赞助商或政府代理也会继续支付这些费用。的确,2003 年 6 月,NBC 将其与国际奥委会的转播合同延长到 2012 年(见下)。

NBC 为转播到 2012 年为止的奥运会的总费用是 22.01 亿美元
* 这 22.01 亿美元可分成以下四个部分:
—2010 年冬奥会 8.2 亿 (2006 年在都灵是 6.14 亿美元)
—2012 年夏季奥运会 11.81 亿美元(北京 2008 是 8.94 亿美元)
* NBC 的母公司通用电器在国际奥委会的 TOP 6 和 TOP 7 营销方案中对奥运会的赞助至少达 1.6 亿美元,高则达 2 亿美元;
* 对美国奥林匹克选拔赛的转播费达 1200 万美元;建立数字电视图书馆和档案系统估计在 1000 万美元;
* 此外,NBC 还花了数亿美元在奥运会前和奥运会期间来推广奥林匹克这一名词。

资料来源:《IOC 官方新闻发布》,2003 年 6 月 6 日。

上面的 NBC 套餐意味着 32.6% 的总增长率（冬奥会 34%，夏奥会 32%），冬奥会的综合年增长率是 7.5%，夏奥会的综合年增长率是 7.2%。[18]

与日益增长的转播权费用并肩而行的是转播时间的增加。1996年，NBC 用 171 个小时转播奥运会；2000 年转播了 441 小时；2004 年该数字升到了 806 个小时（几乎是四年前悉尼奥运会的两倍）。[19]

大的电视网络公司投资得到的回报也是十分可观的。估计 NBC 转播 1988 年汉城奥运会的赢利达 8200 万美元[20]，2004 年夏季奥运会估计可带来 10 亿美元的广告收入——悉尼奥运会是 9 亿。[21]重要时段和主要地点的广告费用更加昂贵。NBC 在奥运会期间对 30 秒商业广告时段的收费是 73 万美元。因此，人们对该公司最终可能从广告中赢利 5000 万美元这一说法毫不感到奇怪。

奥运电视权的出售成为保护 IOC 收入的主要来源。表 5-4 反映出了从 1980 年到 2008 年间的电视收入。从悉尼转播权的出售中，IOC 至少就集资了 13.32 亿。比 8.98 亿美元的亚特兰大奥运会转播费增长了近 50%。[22]在 1996—2000 年四年的周期中，IOC 仅从奥林匹克转播权的营销和世界范围的赞助中就得到了 24 亿美元，比 1993—1996 年间获得的财富多出近 9 亿美元。[23]

表 5-4　不同时期全球电视收入

夏季奥运会		百万美元	冬季奥运会		百万美元
1960	罗马	1.178	1960	斯阔谷	0.05
1964	东京	1.578	1964	因斯布鲁克	0.937
1968	墨西哥城	9.750	1968	格勒诺布尔	2.613
1972	慕尼黑	17.792	1972	札幌	8.475
1976	蒙特利尔	34.862	1976	因斯布鲁克	11.627
1980	莫斯科	87.984	1980	普莱西德湖	20.726
1984	洛杉矶	286.914	1984	萨拉热窝	102.682
1988	汉城	402.595	1988	加尔加里	324.897
1992	巴塞罗那	636.06	1992	阿伯特维尔	291.928
1996	亚特兰大	898.276	1994	利勒哈默尔	352.911
2000	悉尼	1331.550	1998	长野	531.485
2004	雅典	1494.028	2002	盐湖城	736.135
2008	北京	1697*	2006	都灵	833

* 到目前为止协商的转播费（资料来源：《IOC 2005 营销事实文档》见 www.olympic.org）

大多数的收入是通过奥林匹克运动来进行分配的。IOC 现在给奥组委、国际单项体育组织、国家奥委会和其他机构或组织（如世界反兴奋剂机构和国际残疾人奥委会）的支持比以往任何时候都多。[24]尽管从 20 世纪 80 年代开始通过奥林匹克合作伙伴方案集资的企业赞助费使得 IOC 的收入来源更加多样化，但电视收入仍提供了一半的奥林匹克运动所需的财务资源。

与媒体联系在一起意味着奥运会对其自身活动和命运的控制程度在削弱。在得到好处的同时也付出了一定的代价。随着媒体对奥运会参与和控制的增加，它们在对比赛有关事项的决定上处于一个强势的位置。为了提高媒体的覆盖率，有些奥运项目的规则作了修订，比赛环境也发生了改变。比如体操，在过去，在同一个时间段内常常有 4—6 名运动员在不同项目上进行比赛。为了保证几乎所有的运动员都能被摄像镜头捕捉到，现在一般是在比赛时只有 1—2 名运动员上器械表演。汉城奥运会比赛时刻表的改变（某些比赛在一大早就进行）是为了满足北美观众的要求。毫无疑问，大众传媒在重新定位奥运会。

然而，有一件事是有利于国际奥委会的。为推广奥林匹克主义，尽量降低商业化对奥运会的负面影响，国际奥委会决定奥运会的转播权只卖给那些保证在它们转播的国家内，能让人们免费地看到尽可能多的奥运会实况的转播商。国际奥委会拒绝了一些转播商提议的更高价位的奥运会转播权申请，因为它只面对有限的人群。奥运会是世界上仍保持免费收看方针的为数不多的主要体育赛事之一。

结　论

奥运会与媒体被一种复杂的关系紧紧地捆绑在一起。报纸、杂志、广播、电视和因特网在推广并影响着奥运会。今天，电视占统治地位，但在未来因特网将起越来越重要的作用。总之，媒体对奥林匹克运动的特色和发展的影响力在不断上升,然而奥运会的管理机构似乎没有阻挡这一趋势。

思考题

1. 奥运会和大众传媒的本质关系是什么?
2. 你认为电视公司应该决定比赛的时机和结构吗?
3. 你是否把因特网或电视看成是国际奥委会未来的一个主要影响力量?
4. 美国电视观众对奥运会比赛项目的安排有如此大的影响是否合理?

注 释

[1] http://www.olympic.org/uk/games/athens/index_uk.asp.
[2] D. C. Hallin, "The American Media: A Critical Theory Perspective", in H. Forester (ed.) (1985), *Critical Theory and Political Life*, Cambridge, MA: MIT, p. 141.
[3] Ellis Cashmore, (2000), *Sports Culture: An A-Z Guide*, London and New York: Routledge, 138.
[4] 同上。
[5] John E. Findling and Kimberly D. Pelle (2004), *Encyclopedia of the Modern Olympic Movement*, London: Greenwood Press, 563.
[6] Ellis Cashmore (2000), ibid., pp. 405-406.
[7] David Levinson and Karen Chritensen (eds.) (1996), *Encyclopaedia of World Sport*, Oxford: ABC-CLIO, p. 244.
[8] 《国际奥委会将2010年和2012年的奥运会的转播权授予NBC》,国际奥委会官方新闻披露,2003年6月6日。
[9] 《国际奥委会005营销档案》,www.olympic.org.
[10] 例如,汉城奥运会100米短跑就安排在当地时间上午而不是通常的下午或晚上举行。
[11] 以体操为例。运动员必须一个一个地上器械表演而不是像过去那样,好几个运动员在不同的器械上同时比赛,同时,取消了赛前准备活动时间。
[12] P. H. Lewis, "In Cyberspace, a High-Tech League of Their Own", *The New York Times*, April 5, 1994.

〔13〕 Yahoo Sports. http://www.yahoo.com/Recreation/Sports/.

〔14〕 Mike Laflin, "Sport and the Internet—The Impact and the Future", http://multimedia.olympic.org/pdf/en_report_60.pdf.

〔15〕 D. Katz (1995), "Welcome to the Electronic Arena", from Sports Illustrated Online—no longer available. Can find at http://www-white.media.mit.edu/~intille/st/electronic-arena.html.

〔16〕 Mike Laflin, 见上。

〔17〕《XXVI 奥运会的终结报告》, 第 17 页。

〔18〕《国际奥委会将 2010 和 2012 年奥运会的美国电视权授予 NBC》, 见上。

〔19〕 Associated Press, "TV Will Nearly Double Sydney's Coverage", http://espn.go.com/oly/news/2003/0205/1504525.html.

〔20〕 George H. Sage, (1990), *Power and Ideology in American Sport*, Human Kinetics Europe Ltd, 124.

〔21〕 George Raine, "2004 Athens Games: Advertising Sporting a Profit: NBC Sells Expansive Olympic Coverage", *Chronicle Research*, August 12, 2004.

〔22〕《XXVII 奥运会的终结报告》, 第 21 页。

〔23〕 同上引, 第 5 页。

〔24〕 同上。

第六章
奥运会仪式

本章要点
* 奥林匹克仪式
* 国际奥委会详细的仪式礼节：开幕式的方方面面

自 1896 年第一届现代奥运会起，奥林匹克仪式就成了奥运会的一个部分。奥运会仪式随着时间的推移而不断增加。现在，主要的奥运仪式包括火炬接力、点火、开幕式、发奖仪式和闭幕式。这些仪式使得奥运会有别于其他的体育赛事。他们揭示出奥林匹克运动的文化特性和举办国的文化特征，大多数仪式都有固定的模式。

1. 点 火

火焰象征着追求完美、力争胜利、追求和平和培养友谊。也许奥运会最振奋人心的一个仪式就是点火。奥运圣火在开幕式上点燃，然后整个奥运会期间在奥林匹克体育馆和其他的比赛馆日夜燃烧。在闭幕式结束、奥运会旗降下之时，奥运火焰才会熄灭。

现代奥运会第一次点燃奥运火炬是 1928 年阿姆斯特丹运动会。奥运会期间在主体育馆入口处燃烧。奥运会期间点燃火炬这一想法来自于古希腊人，他们在奥运会发祥地奥林匹亚，借助太阳光束来点燃火焰。1932 年奥运圣火在洛杉矶点燃，奥运会期间在大体育馆的顶端熊熊燃烧，这是最后一次在奥运会场地点燃奥运火炬。1934 年国际奥委会决定火焰要从奥林匹亚传递到举办城市。奥林匹亚便成为奥运火焰点燃之地。

> **奥林匹亚点火**
>
> 在赫拉神庙前使用凹透镜，利用太阳光线来点燃火焰。为此，一个专门的仪式性火炬被用来进行实际点火。火焰然后转换到一个瓮内，由一个高级女祭司带到古代体育馆。在一个简短的仪式后，正式的火炬点燃，并由第一个火炬接力手带走。

图 6-1　借助太阳光束来点燃火焰

图 6-2　女祭司手举火焰

2. 圣火传递仪式

现代火炬接力的做法是从 1936 年奥运会开始的。从那以后，火炬接力变成了奥运仪式的一个固定成分。它不只是一个胜利者的跑步，而是拥抱世界、庆祝人类文明和普世性的奥林匹克主义的一个旅途。火炬接力手通常来自各行各业，包括政治家、艺术家、商人、运动员、残疾人、年轻人和年长者。能当选为火炬接力手是一个巨大的荣誉。因此毫不奇怪，当悉尼奥组委副主席让其 11 岁的女儿代替 15 岁的澳籍希腊学生,成为2000年奥运会第一个火炬接力手的澳大利亚人时,引起了大众的不满。[1]

通常,最后一名火炬接力手用火炬的火焰来点燃体育馆的大火炉。该名选手要绕田径场一周,登上台阶,点燃奥运会期间日夜燃烧的奥运之火。1992年西班牙残疾奥运射手安东尼奥第一次在奥运会上用燃烧的箭点燃体育馆上方的火炉,该火焰直冲到3米高,令人叹为观止。

由于多种原因,每届奥运会火炬接力的路线和规模有所不同(见表6-1)。

表6-1 现代奥运会火炬接力信息

	接力人数	持续天数	总距离	最后一棒的姓名
2004	10000	141	78000多公里	尼可劳斯·卡克拉马纳基斯
2000	11000	126	27000公里	卡西·弗里曼
1996	800多人在希腊,12467人在美国	84	2141公里(希腊),26875公里(美国)	穆罕默德·阿里
1992	9849人,加上599位自行车手	51	大约6300公里	篮球运动员胡安·安东尼奥·桑·埃皮番尼奥
1988	1467	26	大约4700公里	1936年柏林马拉松金牌得主孙基祯
1984	3636	82	15000公里	拉菲尔·约翰逊
1980	大约5000	30	4915公里	谢尔盖·贝洛夫
1976	大约1200	4	775公里	斯蒂芬尼·普里芳泰涅,桑德拉·亨德森
1972	6000	30	5532公里	冈瑟·扎恩
1968	2778	50	13620公里	诺玛·恩里奎塔·巴西里奥
1964	870(日本境外),4374	50	15508公里(日本境外空中接力),地面接力732公里,	坂井义则

续表

	接力人数	持续天数	总距离	最后一棒的姓名
1960	1529	13	1863公里	吉安卡罗·佩雷斯
1956	3118（澳大利亚2830人）	20	4912公里	罗纳德·威廉姆·克拉克
1952	3372	25	4725公里	帕沃·努米
1948	1416	12	3160公里	约翰·马克
1936	3331	12	3187公里	弗里兹·希尔根

1952年奥运火焰从希腊飞到丹麦，然后由人举起火炬接力，经瑞典到达芬兰边境。另一个地方火炬是在拉普兰的帕拉斯吞图瑞山顶上借助半夜的太阳光点燃。这两个火焰汇合，传递到赫尔辛基。四分之一的芬兰人观看了沿途的火炬接力。火炬由前著名的芬兰运动员、当年55岁的帕沃·努米携带到体育馆。到1956年火炬接力已经变得十分规范，组织严密，引人关注，火炬接力手人数达到3500人之多。

各个举办国都在火炬接力上竭尽全力，力图有所创新。1968年墨西哥奥运会上，火炬接力计划按哥伦布首次航海发现新大陆的路线进行，以象征古老世界的一流文化与新世界的杰出文化的结合。火炬接力路线的主要中途停留站是意大利的热那亚（克里斯托弗·哥伦布的诞生地）、西班牙的帕罗斯（从那里他开始了发现新世界的首次航程）和圣萨尔瓦多岛（他接触新世界的第一个岛屿）。20岁的跨栏选手诺玛·恩里奎塔·巴西里奥成为奥运史上第一个携带火炬进入体育馆、点燃火炉的女性。

1976年出现了一个技术革新，象征着奥林匹克运动愿意迎接变革。奥运火焰从希腊带到加拿大的火焰祭坛后，用一个火炬转换到一个能捕捉火焰中离子的传感器，它按顺序传递电子脉冲。通过通讯卫星Intelsat，这些脉冲传递到位于渥太华的议会山，在那里他们通过激光束和反射镜再转变成火焰。加拿大首相皮埃尔·埃利奥特·特鲁多从来自渥太华的运动员莱斯·利兹手中接过火焰，再递给象征着加拿大10个省及育空和西北地区的12个火炬接力手，他们跑完1公里后再传给第一个单个奔跑者。

图 6-3　1952 年帕沃·努米点燃奥运火距

在开幕式的那一天,16 个火炬手接力跑进入奥林匹克体育馆。斯蒂芬尼·普里芳泰涅和桑德拉·亨德森跑最后的一段路程,并点燃奥运之火。这是第一次男女共点奥运之火。这一事件把他们俩紧密地连在一起。他们后来喜结良缘,成为火炬接力史上的"梦之侣"。

1984 年出现了另一个现代做法,洛杉矶奥组委将火炬接力权按每公里 3000 美元的价格出售。这一做法激怒了希腊人。3 万希腊示威者试图阻止美国人从奥林匹亚点燃圣火,1.5 万希腊军人不得不封锁进入奥林匹亚的通道。希腊总统康斯坦丁·卡拉曼利斯躲到灌木丛中,准备在必要时出来为士兵和示威者进行调解。美国奥运官员乘直升飞机直接进入封锁的地带,拿走由女祭司长点燃的火焰(该女祭司因此而受到死

图 6-4　火炬接力

亡威胁），省去了在顾拜旦纪念碑前的常规仪式,在人群的咒骂声中起飞,飞到雅典附近的一个军用机场,美国政府的飞机在那里等候。[2]

　　2000 年火炬从奥林匹亚点燃之后,传到雅典,然后在大洋洲的 12 个国家各停留一会,绕澳大利亚传递了 100 天。本届奥运会的火炬接力为最大限度地实现社区参与而进行了仔细的安排,1.1 万名火炬手有一半人是由社区委员会选出,火炬的中途停留站有社区的火炉点火,且常常安排在午餐时间和晚上。最后的 7 名火炬手全是女性,庆祝女性参加奥运会一百周年。

　　2004 年雅典奥运会火炬接力是一个 21 世纪风格的"旅游者"之旅。它到达了以往每一届夏季奥运会的举办城市,以及 2008 年的举办城市北京,并选择了一些其他的城市,如印度的新德里,埃及的开罗,南非的开普敦,巴西的里约热内卢,美国的纽约,比利时的布鲁塞尔,瑞士的日内瓦和洛桑,乌克兰的基辅,土耳其的伊斯坦布尔,保加利亚的索菲亚,塞浦路斯的尼科西亚,总共 27 个国家、34 个城市。全世界的路线是澳洲、亚洲、非洲、南美、北美,最后是欧洲。这是有史以来规模最大的一次奥运火炬接力,首次将非洲和拉丁美洲包括在内。

从上面的描述可看出,火炬接力自 1936 年以来持续时间和跨越的距离不断扩展。它已经变成一个真正的全世界参与的全球活动。

3. 开幕式

每一届运动会都有开幕式,届时体育馆内充满了音乐、歌声、舞蹈和烟花。开幕式是世界上关注度最高的体育活动。仅在英国,2004 年雅典奥运会的开幕式就吸引了 850 万人观看(比悉尼开幕式增加了 2.5 倍)。在法国,730 万人在法国 2 频道观看了雅典的开幕式。在德国,1295 万多人通过 ZTF 观看了这个开幕式(比悉尼的开幕式增加了 3.5 倍)。在美国,5600 多万人通过 NBC 观看了 2004 年的开幕式。[3]

正如前面所提到的一样,开幕式也是随着时间的推移而不断发展、壮大的。1908 年伦敦奥运会首次举行开幕式。参加的运动员在各自国旗后进入白城体育馆,没有穿统一的服装。然而,运动员入场受到政治争论的影响。芬兰队进场时对俄罗斯统治芬兰表示抗议。许多爱尔兰运动员因拒绝作为英王旗下的臣民参加比赛而缺席开幕式,美国铅球运动员拉尔夫·罗斯没有倾斜国旗向英国国王爱德华七世致意而拉开了美国和英国之间长时间不和的序幕。这一拒绝的方式后来成为美国运动员在开幕式行进中的标准做法。

1932 年洛杉矶奥运会的开幕式开创了壮观场面和表演技巧的先河,建立了特定的模式。数百面旗子在大体育馆上方飘扬。国旗和奥运五环旗点缀着东端由圆柱构成的院子。这一结构本身体现了顾拜旦的经典名言:"奥运会中重要的不是取胜,而是参与;本质不是征服,而是很好地战斗。"一个由 250 个乐器组成的乐队和 1200 人的合唱队表演了热情洋溢的音乐。希腊代表团走在最前面,运动员队伍走过大体育馆的主要通道,沿横跨场地的柱子而立,十分引人注目。[4]

1936 年德国组织者不同寻常地从意识形态上改造了开幕式。由迪艾姆为开幕式而写作的"奥林匹克艺术"表演充分反映出体育与国家社会主义死亡礼拜的结合。开始是欢快的青年人运动会,接着的第四幕是主题为"英雄的战斗和死亡的哀悼"。在"青年男性的剑舞"中，出现了年轻士兵间的英雄般的战斗,而结局是他们牺牲生命,妇女哀悼——舞蹈者是德国舞蹈先驱玛丽·魏格曼[5]。在这些英雄的生命牺牲之时,一个巨大的圆顶聚光灯在体育馆上方弯成一个由特殊光线创造的弓形,1.5万名歌手唱着席勒和贝多芬的《死亡颂》[6]。

1996年亚特兰大奥运会的开幕式长达5个小时,以歌颂美国文化为特征。而悉尼的开幕式则与汉城和巴塞罗那展示本国文化的模式相似:展示土地和它的原始居民,体现火和水对这个岛屿陆地的重要性,表现移民的到来和一个充满活力和技术先进国家。开始的片段十分激动人心,"深海之梦"介绍了土著人对黄金时代的看法,以及海洋对澳大利亚岛民的重要性。

雅典2004年开幕式更为突出,以让人震撼的希腊3000年历史和文化的生动场面赢得了全世界的称赞。在火焰沿着体育馆80米高的屋顶穿行,去点燃位于体育馆内象征爱琴海的人造湖上的现代奥运会标志之前,四百名鼓手模仿着人的心跳。一条载有一个男孩的船只划过湖面,去接受总统斯特凡诺普洛斯、国际奥委会主席罗格和雅典2004年奥组委主席安娜·安杰罗普洛斯·扎斯卡拉基的祝福。然后是像梦一般的开幕式的核心部分和描写固定风格人物的多姿多彩的入场式,这些人物看起来就像是复活了的希腊壁画、嵌镶图、雕塑和绘画。这个表演按时代顺序展示了从史前到现代的图像。这个演出不仅是为了娱乐,还要达到教育的目的,给观众上一堂关于奥运会和希腊的历史课。雅典开幕式把过去的历史与现代技术结合在一起。注满200万升水的体育场在三分钟内就被抽干,准备下一场演出。随着演出的进行,时机恰好的焰火点亮了体育馆周围的上空。人们翘望北京奥运会的开幕式的精彩表演。

4. 发奖仪式

发奖仪式是一个古老的奥林匹克习俗,获胜者被授予奖牌、证书和橄榄枝或桂冠。在古代奥运会,用简单的野橄榄花冠来纪念胜利者、其家庭和城市就足以。用橄榄枝做成的花冠来自阿提斯的野橄榄树，它被称为美丽花冠的橄榄。希腊气候干燥，岩石很多，橄榄树是他们的重要资源，橄榄油可食用、可洗浴，也是制作香水的基础材料。据希腊的一个传说，是大力英雄赫拉克勒斯将橄榄树引入希腊。

在1896年第一届现代奥运会上，胜利者的奖励是橄榄花冠和一块银牌，而亚军则获得铜牌和桂冠。直到1904年才授予金、银、铜牌。1932年奥运会在发奖仪式上见证了获胜者的国歌被奏响和国旗升起的场面。从这以后，这些仪式是在每一项比赛结束后马上进行，而不是所有比赛的发奖仪式都在闭幕式的那天进行。1932冬奥会后（美国），奖牌的授予是在一个台上进行的。

图6-5　早期发奖仪式

每项比赛的前八名获得奖状，他们的名字被宣读。2004奥运会上，在16天内共进行了301场发奖仪式。

奖牌的设计

奖牌的设计每届奥运会均有所不同,它们由举办城市的组委会负责。坚固的金牌最初出现在 1912 年。从 1928 起奖牌变得标准化。奥运奖牌直径至少为 60 毫米,厚度为 3 毫米。金银牌必须由 92.5% 的纯银制成,金牌必须镀金至少 6 克。奖牌正面呈现的是一个一手持花冠、另一手持棕榈叶的胜利者的形象。反面则展示一个获胜的运动员在一群人的肩上。从 1972 起,只有奖牌的正面保持没变,反面则每一届奥运会都有所变化。

然而,冬季奥运会的奖牌就没有这么多限制。没有什么规则规定特定的形状或设计。除金、银、铜以外,其他的材料也被用来制作奖牌。阿尔贝维尔(法国)运动会就引进了水晶盘。利勒哈默尔(挪威)的奖牌有花岗岩成分,长野(日本)运动会的奖牌有一部分是漆器制造的。事实上,每一届冬奥会的奖牌设计都不尽相同。

图 6-6　北京 2008 年奖牌

感受奥林匹克荣誉胜利的那一刻是运动员走上领奖台去领取奖牌之时,这通常在每一项比赛结束后,在不同的比赛场馆进行。金牌获得者站在最高层的中央,银牌得主站在他/她的右边,铜牌得主站在左边。

国际奥委会的一名委员把由链子或缎带相连的奖牌挂到胜利者的脖子上,他们的国旗升至旗杆顶端,同时冠军所在国的国歌(缩简版)被演奏。此时,观众也应像这三个成功的运动员一样:起立、面向国旗。

5. 闭幕式

闭幕式在奥运会最后一天的最后一项比赛结束后进行,通常最后一项是马术。在1932年奥运会的闭幕式上,国旗列队行进代替了运动员列队行进。喇叭和礼炮伴随着五环奥运旗的徐徐落下,洛杉矶市长接过旗子,保管到1936年它在柏林升起为止。大群人加入到大型的乐队中,一个由千人组成的合唱团在这个激动人心的时刻,伴随着太阳落至地平线唱起了《再见歌》。在以后的几届奥运会的闭幕式上,运动员都是按国家列队入场。但1956年墨尔本奥运会打破了这一习以为常的做法。根据一个澳籍华人学生的建议,不同国家的运动员并肩行进,共同庆贺,增进友谊。[7] 从此,闭幕式不再那么正规、刻板了。2004年雅典奥运会的闭幕式有3691名来自15个国家的自愿者参加了演出,另有来自32个国家的2200名自愿者参与了辅助性的工作。在一些著名的希腊歌手演唱了多首歌曲以后,紧跟着的是男子马拉松的发奖仪式,这在奥运历史上还是首次。

在雅典组委会主席和国际奥委会主席进行简短的讲话后,希腊和中国的国歌奏起,奥运会旗递到下一届奥运会举办城市北京市市长王岐山的手中。最后,国际奥委会主席雅克·罗格宣布雅典2004年奥运会闭幕。大约170名中国艺术家呈现了8分钟的表演,该节目是由著名电影导演张艺谋编导。

概括起来,闭幕式包括:
* 运动员入场,每个国家6名,混合在一起,8—10人一排,象征奥林匹克运动的友好团结。
* 奥运会旗递交给下一届奥运会主办城市。然后,国际奥委会主席号召全世界的年轻人四年后在下一届奥运会再相聚。
* 运动员在体育馆内自由组合(象征友谊)。
* 火炬熄灭,号角声响起,奥运圣火熄灭。

* 国际奥委会主席宣布奥运会闭幕。在奥运会会歌的伴奏下,奥运会旗降下,运动会结束。

6. 国际奥委会仪式礼节:开幕式的详细情况

国际奥委会详细规定了开幕式的一些内容——从国际奥委会和奥组委主席在体育馆的入口处等候举办国的元首到最后一个队退场、入场式结束等。

* 运动员随所在的代表团进入体育场

按字母顺序,除第一个入场的希腊和走在最后的举办国以外。

每个列队都穿着它的官方制服走在写有该国国名的引导牌后,一名运动员高举国旗走在前面。

1924年巴黎奥运会后,当运动员走进体育场时,把双臂伸向右侧变成了常见的做法。在柏林,德国运动员走过主席台时以德国礼进入体育场:一臂放在身体前,奥地利人也是如此。当法国队以奥林匹克问候的方式进入体育场时,10万名观众欢呼起来,因为他们以为法国人在行德国礼。这一场面在瑞芬斯塔尔的奥林匹克电影中可看到。1980年夏季奥运会上,一些国家抗议苏联插手阿富汗事件,而用奥运会旗来代替他们的国旗。

* 举办国元首宣布奥运会开始

在国家元首宣布奥运会开始之前,组委会主席致简短欢迎词,国际奥委会主席做简短发言。

* 奥运会旗进入体育场

当奥运会旗缓缓升旗时,喇叭吹奏声响起。

奥运会旗

奥运会旗与参赛国国旗一起在体育馆和它的周围高高飘扬。奥运会旗的原型是顾拜旦在1914年呈送的：白底，中心是五个交错的环形——蓝、黄、黑、绿、红。蓝色的环在最左边，靠近旗杆。五环体现了奥运会的国际性。该旗是顾拜旦于1913年设计的，在1914年6月庆祝奥运会重建20周年的期间，首次在巴黎展出，但直到1920年才在奥运会上展出。根据顾拜旦的设想，白底、五环交织的多色环象征世界五大洲在奥林匹克主义指导下团结在一起，同时重现每个国家的颜色。[8]

奥运五环被看成是全球最具活力的营销符号。国际赞助研究公司在1996年进行的一个调查指出，78%的世界人口能识别奥运五环和它们对奥林匹克运动的重要性。这一比例排在调查列表的最上方，在壳牌、麦当劳、奔驰和国际红十字协会这些符号之前。

奥运会旗在1920年成为奥运会的正式象征，在整个奥运会期间，会旗在体育馆上方和体育场内飘扬。

图 6-7　奥林匹克会旗

*《奥林匹克颂歌》

奥林匹克圣歌表达了奥林匹克精神。由希腊人斯皮罗斯·萨马拉斯作曲，其友科斯蒂斯·帕拉马斯作词的《奥林匹克颂歌》，在1896年第一届现代奥运会上演奏。之后,不同的音乐作品为开幕式提供了背景伴奏。直到1960年,萨马拉斯/帕拉马斯的颂歌才被当做正式的奥林匹克颂歌。[9]

> **奥林匹克颂歌**
>
> 古代不朽的精神,
> 美丽、伟大而正直的圣洁之父,
> 降临、彰现,给我们带来光明,
> 在这大地苍穹中,
> 见证了不易熄灭的火焰。
>
> 赠与这些高贵的比赛以生命和活力吧!
> 向赛跑和竞争中的胜利者投掷永不褪色的花环吧!
> 在我们的胸中创造钢铁般的心脏!
>
> 在阳光、平原、高山和大海,
> 辉映着玫瑰的色彩,形成一个巨大的神殿,
> 世界各地都赶来这神殿膜拜你,
> 啊,不朽的古老精神!

* 放飞和平鸽(和平的象征)

在1920年安特卫普奥运会,开幕式上首次放飞了和平鸽。时至今日,这仍是仪式的一个组成部分。

* 举办国的一名运动员和一名官员宣誓

在古代,运动员要与他们的父亲、兄弟和其他男性亲戚一起与裁判相见,到宙斯神庙前发誓他们具有参赛资格,是希腊臣民,没有犯罪记录。1920年,比利时击剑和水球运动员维克托·博因做了现代奥运会上的第一个宣誓。从那以后,奥林匹克誓言一直是奥林匹克仪式的一个部分。常规的做法是,一名运动员代表所有的运动员许诺在奥运会期间遵守规章制度。第一个官员誓言出现在1972年慕尼黑奥运会上。

图 6-8　放飞和平鸽

> **2000 年悉尼奥运会誓言**
>
> 运动员誓言："我，谨代表全体运动员，誓以至诚，我们将以真正的体育精神参加奥林匹克运动会，恪遵大会一切规章，发扬运动光辉，争取队誉，致力于远离毒品的体育。"
>
> 裁判员誓言："我，谨代表全体裁判员和官员，誓以至诚，我们将以真正的体育精神，公正无私地执法奥运会，恪遵大会一切规章。"

结　论

　　火炬接力、点火、开幕式、发奖仪式和闭幕式是已确定的奥林匹克礼仪，是奥林匹克庆典的精彩内容。随着时间的推移，它们在不断发展、扩充和变化。它们从地方事件变成了全球性的事件。音乐、歌舞融入这些仪式中，创造出一种友好节日的气氛。由于具有全球性的意义和影响，这些仪式由国际奥委会来管理，同时举办城市也被鼓励去努力创造不同寻常的、独特的一些场景或表演来给世界留下深刻印象。政治、技术、教育和娱乐是这些仪式的构成成分。先进的技术是它们推广自身的手段。

思考题

1. 你想给北京奥运会的开幕式带来一些变化吗？如果是，为什么？
2. 你赞同在闭幕式上，参赛者像四海为家的一群人那样一同进场这样的变化吗？
3. 北京奥运会怎样在开/闭幕式上把中国传统元素与现代先进技术手段有机结合起来，充分展示中国文化？你有什么建议？
4. 你对现在盛行的这些仪式想做出什么改变吗？如果是，为什么？什么变化？

注　释

〔1〕 John Pye,"Olympic Ceremony Sparks uproar Gosper under Fire for Giving Daughter Torch", *The Associated Press Sydney*, *Australia*(AP), Thursday, May 11, 2000.
〔2〕《大不列颠百科全书》，2002年。
〔3〕《雅典奥运会开幕式创电视收视新纪录》，http://english.people.com.cn/200408/23/eng20040823_154349.html.
〔4〕 John E. Findling and Kimberly D. Pelle (eds.) (2004), *Encyclopaedia of the Modern Olympic Movement*, London: Greenwood Press.
〔5〕 玛丽·威格曼，生于1886年11月3日，1973年9月18日去世，是德国现代舞蹈的主要创始人。
〔6〕 John E. Findling and Kimberly D. Pelle (eds.)(2004)，见上。
〔7〕 John E. Findling and Kimberly D. Pelle (eds.)(2004)，见上，第152页。
〔8〕 Roland Renson, "Antwerp 1920", in John E. Findling and Kimberly D. Pelle, (2004), *op. cit.*, 74.
〔9〕 Charles Beck (ed.), *Oi Olympiakoi Agones, 776 PX-1896* (*The Olympic Games, 776BC-1896*), Athens, 1896.

第七章
艺术和奥运会

本章要点
* 艺术和古代奥运会
* 奥运会、艺术比赛、文化节和文化奥林匹克周期
* 音乐和现代奥运会

1. 简要的历史回顾

体育应被看做是艺术的制作者和一个艺术机会。它制造美,因为它创造活雕塑般的运动员。它是一个艺术机会,体现在为体育而建立的建筑、景观和它所激起的庆典活动。(顾拜旦,1919)[1]

顾拜旦认为,现代奥林匹主义的基本成分之一是由艺术带来的美的愉悦。对他而言,艺术是现代奥林匹克运动的不可分割的一部分。

古代埃及、苏门(古巴比伦的一个地区)、希腊和罗马文明留下了大量的体育艺术例子。在古希腊,艺术和体育被看做是体现身体和心灵和谐的完美合作伙伴。与体育相关联的最早期的造型艺术作品是由公元前6世纪中期前的一个伟大的雅典艺术家所创造的"狂奔的骑师"[2]。希腊陶瓷花瓶上绘有非常精致的摔跤、拳击、跑、跳等体育项目的图案,从希腊到纽约的数十个博物馆的展室有大量这类作品。仅雅典彩绘花瓶就有 1571 个展示体育场景的图案。[3]的确,"整个古希腊的历史和它那无数的艺术形式和知识生活都可从奥林匹亚看

图 7-1 狂奔的骑师(公元前 550 年)

图 7-2 花瓶上的绘画

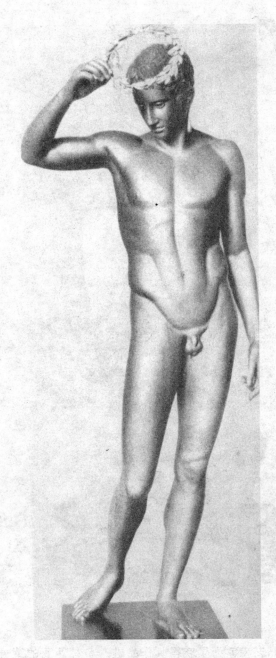

图 7-3　奥运冠军（公元前 5 世纪）

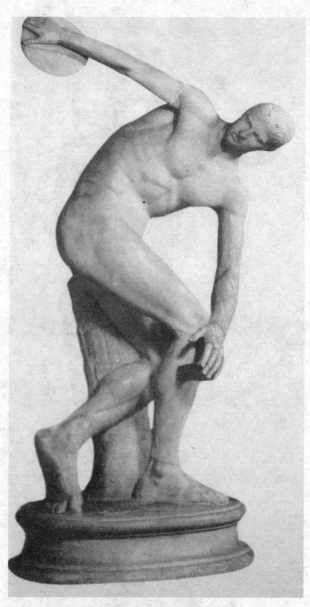

图 7-4 掷铁饼者

到"[4]。所以,艺术家为了获得其作品进入奥林匹亚的荣誉而展开激烈的竞争。

这些艺术品能够存在是因为这些胜利者的形象是对神的纪念和

图 7-5　大力神

供奉。而神本身的存在则是通过他们的礼仪雕像来体现。最著名的宙斯塑像在古奥林匹亚遗址至今仍可见到。

　　罗马人用铜或大理石复制了希腊铜塑。但是,他们要保守多了,当他们复制希腊艺术作品时,他们用无花果叶遮盖了男性生殖器(这是区分希腊作品与罗马复制品的一种方法)。然而,与希腊作品相反,罗马人更喜欢表现武装男性在致命的对抗中充满血腥味搏斗的艺术作品,以及与野兽搏斗的男性和在洪水泛滥地方进行的伟大海战这一类的艺术作品,它们是残酷体育的反映。

图 7-6　齐默曼和他的自行车（劳特累克，1895）

在现代奥运会复兴和现代体育的启蒙时期，各种类型的体育竞赛吸引了艺术家。网球、竞走和自行车尤其受到他们的青睐。后印象派画家之一的劳特累克，不仅画了自行车比赛，而且还画了许多冠军的肖像画，如齐默曼、"多变"的沃伯顿、迈克尔和福尼耶。结果，体育作为绘画对象变得十分流行，1885 年乔治·珀蒂美术馆办了题为"艺术中的体育"画展。顾拜旦一定感受到了这些艺术发展趋势，在 1906 年于巴黎举行的艺术、科学和体育咨询会议上，顾拜旦建议把艺术纳入到奥运会中。[5]他建议奥运会应包括那些围绕体育而构思的、尚未公开发表的建筑、雕塑、绘画、音乐和文学作品的比赛。他期望这些比赛会吸引当时的伟大艺术家来参与。

1912 年斯德哥尔摩奥运会是通过引入艺术比赛来实现体育和艺

图 7-7　自行车手迈克尔（劳特累克，1896）

术长久结合的起点。[6]直到 1948 年为止,被称为"缪斯五项"的艺术竞赛都是与体育比赛并肩举行。不同的时期具体安排有所不同。如 1924 年巴黎奥运会包括了国际性的艺术和文学竞赛。奖牌的设置分为五类:建筑、文学、音乐、绘画和雕塑。法国知识分子对奥运会十分热衷。小说家、诗人和散文家在报纸和杂志上发表了大量的体育赞美诗。诺贝尔奖获得者塞尔玛·拉格芙和莫里斯·梅特林克担任了文学评委。

1932 年洛杉矶奥林匹克美术比赛暨展览包含了由 32 个国家的艺术家创作的 1100 幅作品,内容涵盖绘画、雕塑、建筑、形象艺术、文学和音乐等。包括水彩画、印刷品和素描在内的获奖画作有《斗争》、《折叠刀》和《体育馆》等标题。荣誉奖授予了由美国土著艺术家布卢·伊格尔所创作的《印第安球类游戏》。雕塑的一等奖授给了美国的马洪瑞·杨,他创作了《击倒》。受人尊敬的加拿大雕塑家 R. 泰特·麦肯齐创作的《运动员的保护网》获得第三名。建筑设计奖中有位于康涅狄格州纽黑文市的耶鲁大学佩恩·惠特尼体育馆,而加利福尼亚帕洛·阿尔托的斯坦福体育馆获得荣誉奖。像体育比赛一样,美术比赛的获奖也在体育馆宣布。美国的两名文学巨匠威廉姆·里昂·费尔浦斯和桑顿·怀尔德担任文学评委。艾弗里·布伦戴奇的散文《业余体育的重要性》获得荣誉奖。

图 7-8 "印第安球类游戏"(布卢·伊格尔)

与以前的奥运举办城市不十分注重奥林匹克艺术有所不同,1936年柏林举行的"纳粹奥运会"举办了规模空前、具有明显的宣传性质的文化节。然而,由于宣传力度不够和参与国家的数量有限,加之裁判之争,运输作品困难,对业余艺术家的多重标准,更主要的是公众对这些事件缺乏兴趣和了解,因而几乎没有非西方人在艺术比赛中获得奖牌。[7]

奥运会期间的艺术比赛在 1948 年后停办,取而代之的是与体育比赛完全分开进行的艺术奥林匹克周期或文化奥林匹克周期,并产生了多种艺术和文化活动的节日。

2. 现代奥林匹克文化活动方案

1952 年赫尔辛基奥运会上,艺术比赛正式被展览、文化节和表演所取代。在它之后的墨尔本奥运会第一次组织了包括视觉艺术、文学、音乐和戏剧四部分的艺术节。视觉艺术包括建筑和雕塑展、油画和素描展以及形象艺术。文学展包括早期的澳大利亚历史重要性的案例,由澳大利亚作家写作的书籍和在澳大利亚极为出色的生产书籍的例子。音乐和戏剧被进一步分成三部分：戏剧、管弦乐和室内音乐。[8]

自墨尔本以后，举办体现举办国艺术的展览成为一种趋势。然而，墨西哥和慕尼黑的文化方案则是国际性的。同样是自墨尔本以后，每一个举办城市在奥运会的文化活动安排上有不同的做法。在慕尼黑，从许多国家来的戏剧公司、音乐团体、艺术家、舞蹈家和其他的表演家在斯皮尔斯特拉斯(Spielstrasse)进行表演，并举行了其他展览，如在德国博物馆专为古奥林匹亚艺术举行的展览。艺术中的体育在露天以复制品的形式展出，并为它出版了一本专辑。这些活动的宣传画极其诱人，这里应特别提到受这次运动会委任的那些具有国际声望的艺术家，如柯克施卡、瓦瑟热里、哈屯、波利亚科夫、霍克尼、琼斯和伍德里奇。

1960年罗马组委会举行了一个题为"历史和艺术中的体育"大型展览，该展览持续了6个月，吸纳了2300幅作品。1968年墨西哥举行了长达一年的文化节，它包括国际电影节、民间艺术、雕塑和诗歌等活动；还组织了各种各样的展览，从奥运集邮、奥运会的历史和艺术到体育研究等。这些活动在博物馆、大礼堂、繁华大道的两侧和城市绿色、空旷的恰普尔特派克(Chapultepec)公园举行。这一文化节的一个要素是时至今日在该城市仍可见到的一群包括19个抽象而有纪念意义的混凝土雕塑，它们沿被称为"友谊之路"的环型高速公路17公里的延长带而立，在奥运村的两侧。这群雕塑由一支国际团队所创造。国际奥委会主席艾弗里·布伦戴奇表达了他的一个希望，即墨西哥具有想象力的文化方案标志着"纯洁、美和朴素"的奥林匹克传统得以恢复。

奥林匹克文化方案的主题从强烈的民族节日转变成国际性节日，从对大众活动的关注到对精英活动的关注——下面是一些例子。

前面提到的慕尼黑(1972年)文化节完全纳入到奥林匹克体育赛事之中。把奥运会本身看做是一个文化活动，慕尼黑用即兴的方式展示艺术成分。这在人们称为"娱乐大道"的街道上得到体现，该大道的街边有戏剧表演、小丑和杂技。这在一定程度上，从结构和运作上为以后的艺术节奠定了基础。蒙特利尔(1976年)展示了一个小规模但极受欢迎、具有明显的民族特点的即兴节日。洛杉矶(1984年)举行了一个大型的、宣传得很好的一个文化节，其重点是国内和国际的精英事件,几乎没有户外的大众活动。汉城(1988年)则把国际精英和大众活动结合在一起。

值得注意的是在20世纪60年代和70年代,某些艺术形式试图把美术与流行文化融合在一起。像那些在日常生活中的陶器上绘有美丽运动员的古希腊艺术一样,更多的"流行"艺术作品开始歌颂那个时代的体育英雄。

巴塞罗那奥运会(1992年)见证了文化奥林匹克周期概念的建立,它是一个在奥运会之间、持续四年的文化庆典方案,从1988年的"文化通路"、1989年的"文化和体育年"、1990年"艺术年"到1992年"奥林匹克文化节"。亚特兰大以在国家层次上的"南部连接"和"国际连接"这两个主题,也组织了四年的文化节活动。悉尼通过举办多种活动,如致力于多元文化群体的1997土著文化节,1998年的移民浪潮,1999年和2000年的国际节,让人们了解澳大利亚众多不同的文化社群。[9] "2000年奥林匹克艺术和体育竞赛"在悉尼举行。竞赛分为两类艺术家:学艺术的学生和属于国家奥委会、其从事的运动是奥运比赛项目的运动员。所有的作品都必须与体育主题相关。在1998年6月至1999年11月之间,由来自全世界艺术界的知名人士组成、由国际奥委会主席和国际奥委会文化和教育委员会主席共同主持的评委会进行了大量的工作。该活动接到了来自54个国家奥委会的68件雕塑作品和113幅绘画作品。2000年3月举行了发奖仪式(见表7-1)。[10]

表7-1   2000奥林匹克艺术与体育竞赛获奖名单

	雕塑			绘画		
	名称	艺术家姓名	国家	名称	艺术家姓名	国家或地区
一等奖	速度	康斯坦丁·科斯图申科	白俄罗斯	坚持	陈麒任	中国台北
二等奖	范围	黛博拉·C.V.韦斯特	澳大利亚	解除权力	钟大富	中国香港
三等奖	竞争者	格泽戈雷兹·韦特克	波兰	奥林匹斯山之火	达雅·墨洛茨	白俄罗斯
				奥林匹克体育	扎克利亚·穆罕迈德·索里曼	埃及

艺术家个人的作品也得到了国际奥委会的认可。2001年,墨西哥艺术家尼托画了三个动物——野兔、山狗和熊——来表现奥林匹克的宗旨:更快、更高和更强。这幅画被称为"奥林匹克的力量"。他还为2002年的盐湖城冬奥会创作了一幅作品,叫做"和平与忠诚"[11]。

3. 现代奥林匹克音乐

在过去两千年中时尚已经发生了很大的变化,但音乐仍是最能在一群人中传递情感、与伟大奇观气氛最吻合的一个因素。(顾拜旦,1919)

顾拜旦认为音乐对奥运会有极其重要的意义。为此,他确保音乐在现代奥运会中占有一席之地。时至今日,它的地位仍不容动摇。

在古希腊,音乐竞赛与体育竞赛同时在奥运会上举行。在20世纪早期的希腊,音乐是第一届现代奥运会的一部分。今天它仍然在继续着,是21世纪奥运会的一部分。因此,音乐一直是奥运会不可或缺的内容。1896年科孚交响乐队走在行进队伍的前列,一群歌手唱着《水手少年》的歌曲,接着是一个乐队演奏瓦格纳的《罗恩格林》。这支队伍实际上是由9支管弦乐队组成。同样是在1896年,第一首官方的奥运圣歌被演唱,该圣歌是由希腊作曲家斯皮罗斯·萨马拉斯作曲、科斯蒂斯·帕拉马斯作词的。萨马拉斯的版本一直到1912年都是正式的奥林匹克圣歌。此后,新的圣歌在各种不同的场合出现。萨马拉斯的圣歌在1960年奥运会重新被启用,并延续至今。在开、闭幕式上都能听到它。

音乐不仅是仪式的一部分,也是公共场合和娱乐的一部分。例如在1932年的洛杉矶奥运会上,一个由1200人组成的合唱团在奥运会前排练了好几个月。该合唱团还与由1000名成员、250个乐器组成的奥林匹克乐队一起出现在开、闭幕式和足球表演赛上。除了乐队和合唱团以外,一群号手在马拉松赛、开/闭幕式上吹奏,在奥运村和奥运会期间的其他场合吹奏,以娱乐气氛。在伦敦奥运会(1948年)开幕式上,警卫队的集合乐队(200人)进行了演奏。该乐队还演奏了国歌。在释放象征和平的和平鸽仪式上号角被吹响。大型合唱团由1200名歌手组成。赫尔辛基奥运会(1952年)演奏了一首新的奥运圣歌,526名成员组成的一个合唱团表演了一首新的奥运圣歌,由塔讷里·库希斯托创作的清唱剧(一种芬兰式的祈祷)。在奥运会的开幕盛宴上,上演了男声四重唱。之后,2500人的男子合唱团奉献了一台音乐会。在国王的开幕演讲后,身着中世纪服装的号手站在高高的塔上吹起奥运的号角。来自瑞典合唱协会的合唱团在对国王的欢呼之后唱了一支民族歌曲。运动员在奥运会胜利进行曲的伴奏下入场,该曲是由H.亚历山德森博士创作,在瑞典奥委会举办的一个比赛中获得一等奖。其他的音乐盛会还包括Lynyrd Skynyrd乐队、The Giants of Jazz乐队、Travis Tritt乐队、著名音乐指挥家列维(Yoel Levi)和威廉·弗里德·斯科特(William Fred Scott)等的演出。同样具有影响的是澳大利亚青年管弦乐队和亚特兰大青年管弦乐队的合作演出,其中包括马勒的第二交响曲《复苏》的演奏。这些艺术家多数都参与了开、闭幕式的演出。[12]

1984年、1988年《手拉手》和1996年《召唤英雄》的奥运会主题曲是由美国最著名的作曲家约翰·威廉姆斯创作。凭借为《星球大战三部曲》、《侏罗纪公园》、《犹太人》、《超人》、《小鬼当家》等多部电影作曲,威廉姆斯享誉全球。

从上述介绍中可看到音乐在奥林匹克历史中能产生巨大作用,是有其原因的。奥林匹克音乐有一些共同的特点。几乎所有在奥运会上出现的音乐都旨在宣传友谊、和平和正义这些理想,同时展示主办国的民族文化传统。在二战前,西方古典音乐、歌剧甚至宗教音乐等是奥林匹克音乐的主要来源。二战后,尤其是20世纪70年代以来,随着亚洲、美洲等新兴国家承办奥运会,音乐表演带有更强烈的民族气息,同时采用了更易为大众所接受的通俗流行音乐形式。不管音乐的性质如何,音乐与奥运会的其他文化活动一起,分担了将全世界人们在这个世界各民族的大聚会上实现团结的目的。

结 论

奥林匹克运动与文化活动方案一直有着密切的关系,而文化活动方案随着时间的推移从规模、组织和内容上都在不断地变化和发展。不论是在古代还是现代奥林匹克历史上,艺术一直被用来表达奥林匹克体育项目的戏剧性变化和运动员的情绪体验。艺术与奥运会相联系的主要形式是绘画、雕塑和音乐,后者尤为重要。

顾拜旦倡导通过建筑、雕塑、绘画、音乐和文学比赛的形式实现艺术与奥运会的结合。这样的比赛在1912年至1948年间的确存在过,后来被艺术奥林匹克周期或文化奥林匹克周期所取代,但曾经是古代奥运会一部分的艺术仍是现代奥林匹克主义的重要部分。

思考题

1. 你认为在奥运会中是否有必要重新引进艺术比赛?请说出是或不是的理由。
2. 北京奥林匹克文化周期应包括哪些常见的文化活动?这些活动应该是国内的还是国际的?
3. 你倾向于艺术比赛、节日还是展览?请给出理由。

注 释

[1] Durry, J. (1998), "The Cultural Events at the Olympic Games and Pierre de Coubertin's Thinking", *Proceedings of the 38th Session of the International Olympic Academy*, p. & J.

[2] 《狂奔的骑师》是古老艺术的一个杰作,它把雅典的严肃性与希腊东部的丰富装饰传统融合在一起。在1877年雅典卫城发现的这个男性头塑是公元前550年左右雕刻的(古代希腊、伊特鲁尼亚和罗马:古希腊雕塑艺术[公元前7—6世纪] http://www.louvre.fr/llv/oeuvres/detail_notice.jsp?)。

[3] D. W. Masterton, "The Contribution of the Fine Arts to the Olympic Games", http://www.ioa.leeds.ac.uk/1970s/73200.htm.

[4] Yalouris, N. (1971), "The Art in the Sanctuary of Olympia", *Report of the E-*

leventh Session of the International Olympic Academy, Athens, 90.

[5] 顾拜旦:《奥林匹克理想》,第16页。

[6] Martin Wimmer (1976), *Olympic Buildings*, Edition Leipzig, 27.

[7] Beatriz Garcia Garcia, *The Concept of Olympic Cultural Programmes: Origins, Evolution and Projection*, Centre d'Estudis Olympics I de'Estport (UAB), International Chair in Olympism.

[8] John E. Findling and Kimberly D. Pelle (eds.) (2004), *Encyclopaedia of the Modern Olympic Movement*, London: Greenwood Press.

[9] Beatriz Garcia Garcia, op. cit.

[10] Art & Sport 2000 Olympic contest, http://www.olympic.org/uk/passion/museum/temporary/exhibition_uk.asp?id=17&type=0.

[11] 这幅画描绘一个美国印第安首领脚边的一匹狼,该首领头戴毡帽、手握鹰的羽毛。尼托声称鹰的羽毛是一个拥有很高价值的全球性的象征物,而狼体现了人和犬之间的关系和与宗族相关的忠诚。

[12] William K. Guegold (1996), *100 Years of Olympic Music: Music and Musicians of the Modern Olympic Games 1896-1996*, Golden Clef Publisher.

第二部分
历史视角

第二部分

历史科论

第八章
古代奥运会

本章要点
* 古希腊文明和古代奥运会
* 古代奥运会的历史、规定和比赛项目
* 古代奥运会的衰落

早在公元前776年古代奥运会就在希腊举行。为什么奥运会会出现在希腊而不是在其他一些文明古国如中国和埃及呢?要回答这一问题,就必须在古希腊文明的背景下来分析古奥运会。

1. 古希腊文明

希腊是位于欧洲南部巴尔干半岛顶端的一个地中海国家,其海岸线蜿蜒曲折,高山岩石陡峭。在古代,这些地形特点造就了独立的城邦小国。

古希腊人很重视教育。对他们而言,它有特殊的意义。"教育"一词意指"整个人的培养,不能硬性地分割为身体和心理教育,因为智力不能脱离身体而存在;没有智力,身体也就没有意义"[1]。因此,身体和智力同样重要,只有共同发展,人的潜力才能得以实现。

奥运会诞生地的古希腊,以民主和西方文化的摇篮而著称。世人皆知的大哲学家苏格拉底、柏拉图和亚里士多德对希腊民主教育原则和实践的发展起到了重要的作用。著名哲学家苏格拉底(公元前

470—公元前399)指出:"从体育训练的角度讲,任何一个公民都不能是业余级选手;一个人到老都没能看到他身体的力量和优美是很丢人的事情。"[2]柏拉图(公元前427—公元前347)本人曾是一个优秀的运动员。他的摔跤教练将其名字从亚里斯多克勒斯改为柏拉图(为肩宽体阔之意)。他当时就提倡男女孩都参加体育活动。亚里士多德(公元前384—公元前327)对身体发展不均衡者极尽批评之词。他说:"一开始,立法者就得保证年轻男性的身体健康发展。"[3]这些思想家的影响不容质疑,而为战争做好准备的需要也是一个重要因素。结果,身体练习非常普及。据说全希腊每年正式的体育比赛就达173次之多。[4]

美丽的身体是社会推崇的对象。古希腊人甚至把他们中的许多神描绘成理想的人体,正如在奥林匹亚的半神大力士的雕像所展示的。神的雕像和画作反映了完美男性的裸体身体形象:精干、强健和活力。体育和裸体是古希腊不可分割的两个概念。体育馆和体操两词取自同一词根 yuuvos,意为"裸体的"。在体育馆中,运动员裸体训练,在体育馆外,纪念最伟大的运动员的塑像也是裸体的。

(1) 宗教

正如在白天天空中没有一颗星星比太阳更温暖、更明亮一样,没有一个比赛比奥运会更宏伟壮观。(品达,希腊抒情诗人,公元前518—公元前438)

古希腊的各种体育节日随着时间的演进而不断发展。这些节日还包括希腊人祭祀他们尊敬的神灵,并祈求得到他们恩惠的宗教仪式。这样,希腊的运动会与宗教仪式密切地联系在一起,宗教仪式构成了神灵礼拜的一部分。在古希腊,没有一个著名的宗教节日和祭祀地不把对神的礼拜与举办运动会联系在一起。的确,运动会最初的比赛地点都是在神殿的前院或周围的地方,神作为主要的观众。

希腊的神居住在山顶上,与人生活在一起,享受着各种活动。对希腊人而言,神是参与者,以最美丽的男人(和女人)形象出现。

奥运会就这样把人与神联系在一起,这就是为什么运动会总是在奥林匹亚、德尔菲、伊斯特摩斯和尼米亚这些最神圣的祭祀地,在神的监护下进行。奥运会是为纪念希腊众神之王宙斯而在伊利斯城邦的奥林匹亚举行的运动会。在运动会的中间一天,人们要烧烤100头牛来祭祀宙斯。[5]

随着时间的推移,奥运会开始繁荣起来,奥林匹亚变成祭祀宙斯的主要地。一些个人和社区给神捐献房子、雕塑、祭坛等贡物。在奥林匹亚最壮观的场景是宙斯登基的黄金和象牙膜拜塑像,它是由雕塑家菲迪亚斯创作,放在神殿内。该塑像是古代世界七大奇迹之一,高度达42英尺。

图 8-1　宙斯塑像

奥运会保持了它早期在宗教习俗上的功能达数世纪之久,后来它们发生了渐进性的变化,变成了真正的体育活动。

(2) 战争和奥林匹克文化

正如前面提到的,在基督前的数世纪,希腊由许多小的城邦组成,它们被自然的屏障分割开来。这些城邦强烈地捍卫着它们的自由。由于连年不断的战争,每个希腊臣民都必须时刻准备战斗。这样,参加体育活动被看做是希腊人的一种生活方式。地方冲突时常中断庆典活动和运动会。在公元前884年,地方君主,如伊利斯国王伊菲图斯,斯巴达的莱库格斯和皮萨的克莱奥斯西奈斯执政官在奥林匹亚签订了休战条约。[6]描述这一条约的铭文写在一个展于奥林匹亚的铜盘上。在奥运会期间的休战中,战争停止,武器不允许带进伊利斯,禁止司法诉讼和死刑的执行。这样,胜利者可以安全地往返于奥林匹亚。违反这一休战条约的惩罚可至死刑。奥林匹亚圣地的政治和军事中立是古代奥运会得以持续下去的原因之一。神圣的休战条约每年要持续三个月,以让人们安全地参加奥运会。

2. 古代奥运会的发展变化

(1) 节日、运动会和奥林匹亚

在古希腊,生死、婚姻和葬礼、农作物丰收、赢得比赛、战争的胜利等都要以节日来庆祝。像奥运会这样的运动会就起自于非正式的餐后竞赛和葬礼游戏。体育比赛与葬礼习俗相联系是基于这样的一种信念:生与死是一种辩证的关系——死去的地球会生长出新芽,参加比赛的年轻人从逝去的英雄那里汲取力量,他们为纪念这些英雄而比赛。

到公元前6世纪,最具影响的希腊体育节日至少有4个:在奥林匹亚举行的奥运会,在德尔斐举行的皮托运动会,在尼米亚举行的尼米亚运动会以及在科林斯举行的依斯米安竞技会。奥运会被认为是整个希腊世界最具有意义的一个运动会。

图 8-2　奥林匹亚

图 8-3　奥林匹亚体育场

> **奥林匹亚**
>
> 奥林匹克坐落在伊利斯的领土上,位于伯罗奔尼撒半岛的最西端,在崎岖的阿卡迪亚山脉和不宜居住的爱奥尼亚海岸之间。与大多数希腊地点不一样,奥林匹亚置身于一大片树林之中,郁郁葱葱。
>
> 奥林匹亚有史前铁器时代,即在来自北方的多利安式侵略后的公元前12世纪,遗迹揭示出奥林匹亚在古代麻烦不断的历史中起到了重要的政治和军事作用,在整个希腊世界具有极大的权威性。人们在那里发现的成千上万的贡品就是最好的说明,这些贡品至少是公元前10世纪的东西。奥林匹亚祭祀地一直把竞赛精神的培养作为它的使命。[7]一千多年中,不论是和平还是战争,希腊人都在这相聚,庆祝这个伟大的节日。"在奥林匹亚,伟大的地米斯托克利被欢呼,希罗多德朗读一部分他的历史作品,柏拉图发表演讲,德莫斯梯尼(雄辩家)、希皮亚斯、普罗迪克斯、阿那克西米尼、品达、西蒙尼提斯、修昔底德、波鲁斯、高尔吉亚、阿那克萨哥拉、第欧根尼和琉善都来充当观众。"[8]

古代奥运会至少持续了1168年之久(公元前776—公元393)。人们通常接受这样一种说法,在公元前776年奥运会就已经持续了至少500年。在奥林匹亚记录有从公元前776年到公元217年的冠军的名字。第一个被记录的奥运冠军是伊利斯的科洛布斯。

奥运会每四年举行一次,在夏末、初秋时的8月6日至9月19日,此时正是农作休闲时节。奥运会在希腊人的生活中占有非常重要的地位,以至于他们的时间都是用两次奥运会之间的间隔——奥林匹克周期来衡量。奥林匹亚的名气极大,大批的人群每四年都到此来祭祀神灵,欣赏伟大的艺术作品,聆听历史学家、诗人和散文家朗诵,观摩像雕塑般的男人、健壮的少年和飞奔的马匹在令人眼花缭乱的比赛中对抗。奥林匹亚变成了全希腊世界的聚集点。正如已经指出的,这些泛希腊节日不仅仅是体育赛事。在很早的时候,各国,其中许多是海外的殖民地,都力图确保自己在该圣地拥有永久的一席之地,而奉献寺庙或财宝。这样,奥林匹亚变得十分富有,远超出其地方资源本身所能提供的。

奥运会从希腊的这个伟大中心繁荣开来。然而,正如上面提到的,奥运会是如此闻名,它不仅吸引了最好的运动员,还有最好的雕塑家、诗人、作家、演说家和政治家。

（2）规定

古代奥运会不同于今日的奥运会，下面是几个例子。奥运会最初只限于那些具有自由身份的希腊人。参赛者要旅行上百英里，因为他们来自大陆和希腊城邦的殖民地，这些殖民地远至今日的西班牙、意大利、利比亚、埃及、乌克兰和土耳其。[9]

图8-4　古希腊城邦地图

运动员是业余选手，唯一的奖品是花冠或花环，但各城邦会对成绩优异的运动员给予奖励。运动员要进行一段时间的高强度、有指导的训练，这样他们最终也变成了真正的职业选手。取胜不仅有相当的奖励，奥运冠军还从他所代表的城市中能得到许多好处和赞扬。结果，运动员最终变成了全日制的专业选手，这是现代奥运会的一个趋势，并引发了对业余主义长久而又艰苦的争论。

(3) 比赛安排

奥运会包括预选赛,选拔最好的运动员来参加决赛。在奥运会的第一天,运动员和裁判员宣誓他们会诚实地进行比赛和裁判。在第二至第四天,分别进行不同项目的比赛。奥林匹亚的主要项目是短跑或"场地跑",这一项目的胜利者的名字将是该奥运周期的名字。第五天,在奥运会的闭幕式上,每个胜利者会得到用野生橄榄树叶做成的花冠作为奖品。

橄榄花冠

橄榄花冠对参赛者、他的家庭和城市而言是最高的荣誉。它是金钱或官位都不能超越的一种荣誉。胜利者与不朽的人连在一起,被诗人和雕塑家所赞赏,通常在公共拨款下度过他们的余生。

公元前776年时只有一项比赛,即场地跑,在以后的几十年中逐步添加了一些项目,如公元前724年中距离跑(两个场地跑),公元前720年的长跑(相当于现代的1500甚或5000米比赛)。因此,在奥林匹亚有不同类型的比赛项目。赛跑者可以进行一个场地(192米)的冲刺跑,两个场地跑(384米)和7—24个场地跑的长距离赛跑(1344米—3608米)。

摔跤和由跳远、标枪、铁饼、竞走和摔跤构成的五项全能比赛出现在公元前708年。跟现代的摔跤类似,摔跤运动员需要把对手摔到地上,臀、肩或背直接落地。要赢一场比赛必须把对手摔倒3次,不允许咬人,抓生殖器也是非法的;但允许折断对手的手指。

拳击在公元前688年引进。拳击手的对抗,不分轮次,直到一个人被打倒或承认他败了为止。跟现代拳击不一样的是,没有规定禁止击打一个倒下的对手。在成人和少年组中不分重量级别,一场比赛的对手是随机抽选的。古代拳击手不戴手套,而是用皮带缠绕手和手腕,手指留在外面。

战车赛是公元前680年纳入的。有两匹马和四匹马的战车赛。另一种比赛是在由两匹骡子驱赶的战车之间进行。跑程是绕体育馆跑道

图 8-5 摔 跤

图 8-6 古代拳击

12圈(9英里)。

公元前648年角斗——一项极度紧张的拳击和摔跤混合而产生的比赛项目——添加到奥运会中。这一比赛允许运动员拳打脚踢、任意搏击,但运动员在比赛时两手不缠拳击皮带。规则只禁止口咬和用指甲挖眼、鼻或嘴。踢对手的肚子,在现代比赛是违反规则的,但在当时却是完全合法的。角斗与拳击、摔跤一样,也分成人和少年组。

当时没有跑表记录赛跑的时间,对跳远、标枪或铁饼的长度也没有准确的测量。没有集体项目比赛,也没有水上项目,女性不允许参赛。

(4) 竞争和欺骗

在第77个奥运周期(公元前472年)之前,所有的比赛都在一天进行;后来,比赛分散到四天进行,也许中间有中断,第五天则是闭幕式的发奖和冠军的宴会。除了得墨忒耳女祭司外,女性作为观众也不允许。

正如上面提到的,古代运动员只是作为个体参赛,而不像现代奥运会是作为一个队的一部分。通过当众比赛来强调个人成绩的做法与希腊追求个人卓越的理想相关的。不论是通过文字还是行动来达到这一理想的男人,就赢得了永久的荣誉。而没能实现这一理想的人会感到当众受辱和丢脸。

这样的压力可能导致激烈的竞争,为此有些人采取不诚实的做法来取胜。被发现有欺骗行为的人会被罚款,所罚的钱被用来制作宙斯铜像,铜像立在通向体育馆的路上。塑像上记下描述这一违规行为的话语,警告其他人不要欺骗,提醒运动员胜利是靠能力取得,强调奥林匹克公平竞争的精神和对神灵的尊重。

最早有记录的欺骗是塞萨利的欧波洛斯,他在第98个奥林匹克周期中贿赂了拳击手。雅典的卡利普斯在第112届奥运会的五项全能比赛中买通了他的竞争对手。两个埃及拳击手,迪达斯和萨拉帕蒙因在第226届奥运会中预先安排比赛结果而被罚款。所有这些人都是因欺骗而被作家鲍萨尼亚斯记录在公元2世纪的《希腊指南》之中,以告诫子孙后代。

3. 古代奥运文化的衰亡

希腊在公元前 2 世纪中期失去了独立地位,成为罗马的殖民地。之后的一个世纪,对奥林匹亚和其他地方的体育竞技活动的支持显著下降。罗马人认为希腊体育毫无意义,他们更欣赏伊特拉斯坎人的剑斗体育。希腊人教育他们的年轻人去追求完美,罗马人则教育他们的年轻人去征服。[10] 罗马人以轻蔑的眼光看待竞技体育——赤身裸体地当众比赛在罗马人的眼中是低级下流的。然而,罗马人很欣赏希腊节日的价值。酷爱体育的奥古斯都国王(公元前 68—公元 14 年)在大竞技场附近建立了一个临时的木质体育馆,在那里举行体育比赛。而尼禄(公元 37—68 年)国王一直是希腊节日的资助者。

罗马人至少是跟希腊人一样喜欢他们的运动会。到公元 4 世纪,拥有 100 万人口的罗马,有 150 多个体育节日。在古希腊竞技场有战车比赛,在可容纳 25 万观众的大马戏场有赛马比赛(见图 8—7)。在可为 5 万人提供住宿的圆形剧场内,动物和人被以体育的名义残杀。尽管公共体育比赛数量繁多,对罗马人来讲体育比赛只占次要位置。最使他们感兴趣的打斗项目是摔跤、拳击和角斗。可以说,希腊人和罗马人在态度上的主要差异表现在:希腊人为参赛者组织比赛,罗马人为大众组织比赛。一个主要是竞赛,另一个则是娱乐。希腊节日被描绘成竞赛,罗马则为游戏。

公元前 146 年希腊被罗马统治后的这个阶段对奥林匹亚产生了重要影响。地震留下了大片的废墟,希腊人之间接连不断的战争,再加上在希腊土地上罗马人发动的内战产生了可怕的洗劫和破坏。在此阶段,经济、道德和社会崩溃,大多数的地方运动会不再举行,泛希腊运动会只能勉强维持生存。

在这个极度困难的时期,泛希腊运动会能够继续存在主要得益于两个因素。首先,这些运动会给希腊人带来极大的声望。其次,体育馆作为一个社会机构对希腊人而言是极其重要的。体育馆在希腊城市生活中占有重要的一席之地。在罗马征服后,被征服的希腊人利用他们

图 8-7　罗马大竞技场外景

有限的自治在体育馆相聚。它成为希腊人民族认同的中心,他们在体育馆中继续从事得到允许的体育、知识和社会活动。因此,由于合理的政治原因,罗马人尽管对竞技体育和希腊体育传统漠不关心,但也没有镇压奥运会或体育馆。那样做会激怒希腊人,尽管罗马人让体育馆作为一个机构继续存在,他们也时常干涉它的管理,以确保对希腊的控制。

在公元前 1 世纪米特立达战争期间,奥林匹亚遭受了疯狂的袭抢,泛希腊运动会,尤其是奥林匹克运动会的存在遭遇致命的威胁。最终,狄奥多西一世皇帝(第一个基督教皇帝)在公元 394 年下令禁止奥运会。这是由于因为宗教的原因,他反对希腊神的概念。最后一届奥运会是公元 393 年的第 293 届。[11]

概言之,古代奥运会经历了三个发展阶段:

(1)开始阶段(公元前 800—公元前 600 年)

此时正值奴隶制出现(自由身份的运动员需要奴隶制给他们自

由,以便为奥运会进行训练),社会生产力相当低下,交通不发达,这样,不同城邦之间的交流非常困难。为此,奥运会起初只限于伯罗奔尼撒半岛的城邦参加,后来才把希腊的其他城邦包括进来。

(2) 鼎盛阶段(公元前 600—公元前 400 年)

这一阶段,雅典经历了它的黄金时期:在雅典政治家伯里克利领导下的民主管理体制成熟;在雅典卫城建立帕台农神庙,索福克勒斯、埃斯库罗斯和欧里庇得斯三大悲剧作家的创造;苏格拉底和柏拉图哲学体系的建立。在这样的背景下,奥运会不断发展,形成了其特有的文化传统。

(3) 衰落阶段(公元前 400—公元 394 年)

这是一个社会动荡不安的阶段。奴隶起义、各城邦之间战争不断。终于在雅典和斯巴达之间爆发了一场持续 29 年之久的伯罗奔尼撒战争(公元前 431—公元前 404 年)。之后,罗马控制了希腊,再后来罗马帝国经历了内部斗争,最终基督教统治了罗马。这些事件对奥运会造成了负面的影响,正如前面所说的,奥运会最终在公元 394 年被罗马皇帝狄奥多西所镇压。

结 论

古代奥运会与古希腊的政治、经济和社会环境密不可分。城邦之间连续不断的对峙使得作为战争培训的身体活动成为日常生活不可缺少的一部分。城邦之间的频繁冲突要求身体健壮的战士。体育比赛因而得到重视。为确保奥运会的连续性,当时战争中的各城邦签订了休战条约。古奥运会还是具有重要意义的宗教节日,它是为纪念宙斯神而设立的。

希腊人被罗马人征服后,奥运会走向衰落。罗马人总的说来是蔑视希腊竞技体育,通常并不支持奥运会。战争、地震和基督教最终导致古奥运会在公元 394 年消亡。

古奥运会持续了 12 个多世纪,它不同于现代奥运会。比赛项目比现在少很多,只有说希腊语的自由男人可以参赛。奥运会一直是在奥林匹亚举行,从没落脚他乡。然而,古奥运会给世界留下了一笔文化遗产,对现代世界体育产生了深远的影响。具体说来,古代奥林匹克理想强调和平、友谊、公平竞争和卓越,对现代奥运会影响至深。

思考题

1. 为什么身体活动对希腊各城邦的公民是那么重要?
2. 为什么这么多的古奥运项目都是涉及武器和极端身体攻击的准军事化项目?
3. 古奥运会衰落和灭亡的确切原因是什么?
4. 古代奥运会是业余的运动吗?

注 释

[1] Douskou, Iris (1982), *The Olympic Games In Ancient Greece*, Athens: Ekdotike Athenon.

[2] John T. Powell (1994), *Origins and Aspects of Olympism*, Champaign, Illinois: Stipes Publishing Company, 37.

[3] Aristoles (1878), *The Rhetoric of Aristotle*, London: G. Bell, Translated by J. S. Walson Book Ⅲ, 13.

[4] John T. Powell (1984), "Ancient Greek Athletic Festivals", *Olympic Review*, 63.

[5] Gray Poole (1963), *The Ancient Olympic Games*, London: Vision Press, 17.

[6] C. Palaeologos, (1964), "The Ancient Olympics", Paper Presented at the Proceedings of the International Olympic Academy, University of Leeds. (www.greekembassy.org/press/pressreleases/truce/TRUCE.html)

[7] Nicolaos Yalouris, ed., (1979) *The Eternal Olympics: The Art and History of Sport*, New Rochelle, New York: Caratzas Brothers, Publishers, 77.

[8] C. Paleologos, (1964), op. cit.

[9] http://www.perseus.tufts.edu/Olympics/site.html.

[10] David Levinson and Karen Christensen (eds.) (1996), *Encyclopaedia of World Sport: From Ancient Times to the Present*, Oxford: ABC-CLIO Ltd., 21.

[11] Diane L. Dupuis, Marie J. MacNee, Christan Brelin, Martin Connors (1993), *The Olympics Factbook*, Detroit: Visible Ink Press.

第九章
现代奥运会：苏醒与复活

本章要点
* 奥运会的苏醒
* 奥运会的复活
* 对奥运会的挑战

由于自然灾难破坏并掩埋了奥林匹亚圣地，古代奥运会被人们忘却了 13 个多世纪，直到 1896 年现代奥运会才得以出现。为什么奥运会会苏醒过来？奥运会的复活有什么样的特性？

1. 现代奥运会的创建

奥运会的复兴是后中世纪时期欧洲在政治、经济、文化和社会等方面长期变化的结果。

（1）意识形态背景

15 世纪到 18 世纪这段时间见证了欧洲三大运动——文艺复兴、宗教改革和启蒙运动。它们引起了根本性的变化。这些运动为资本主义、民主、科学和技术的发展铺平了道路。

> **概念：文艺复兴、宗教改革和启蒙运动**
>
> 15世纪的文艺复兴见证了与中世纪集体主义相对应的现代个人主义的成长，古典文学的复苏以及在欧洲遗失了千年的古典雕塑、绘画和建筑的重新发现。
>
> 16世纪的宗教改革是一场宗教运动，它表面上的目的是内部更新占统治地位的罗马天主教堂，但实际上导致了对教会的极度反感和教会权力的削弱。
>
> 18世纪的启蒙运动是一次重要的知识运动。有影响的思想家和作家相信：可运用人类的理性来战胜无知、迷信和暴政，从而建立一个更美好的世界。他们的主要靶子是宗教迷信和世袭权力统治。

渐渐地，个人主义和自由主义代替了集体主义和专制，变成了欧洲的重要价值。宗教幸存了下来，但被削弱了，常常变得难以相认。事实证明政治与宗教的分离有利于学术自由思想的发展，世袭的君主制和贵族统治的作用明显削弱。对后来复兴奥运会尤为重要的事情是，文艺复兴时期的人道主义者提出对神的适当崇拜包括对它的创造物——人——的赞美。他们试图再次体验古希腊人和罗马人的骄傲、热情和创造力，复制他们的成功并超越他们。文艺复兴时期的画家、建筑师、音乐家和学者都在一个新的自由氛围内中施展他们的才能。古希腊因其人道主义价值而受到崇拜。这些运动以不同的方式为奥运会的复活铺平了道路。

（2）工业革命

始于18世纪末期英国的工业革命对社会和体育的属性产生了重要的影响。蒸汽机[1]的发明极大地推动了工业化进程，给英国带来了巨大的财富。

工业革命激起的巨大社会变化先后改变了英国、欧洲和北美洲等全世界大多数地方的体育。起初在英国，新财富、"新"的(扩展的)中产阶级、"新"的(扩展的)教育机构、新余暇活动和新技术带来了对待体育的新态度和让人享受的新体育项目。[2]以蒸汽火车和蒸汽船形式出现的蒸汽机这一伟大发明极大地缩短了地区或国家之间距离，把体育运动广泛地传播开来。这样，国内、国际性的比赛对世界上许多国家而言都变得愈加可能。

(3) 资产阶级教育改革

在工业革命的后期,英国和其他欧洲国家的教育发生了许多变化。欧洲的中产阶级逐渐拥护古典世界的教育价值。智慧和身体成为教育的主要关注点。然而,大多数现代体育起源于英格兰是由于完全不同的原因。在 19 世纪后半期,工业革命和帝国主义扩张使得英格兰拥有一个十分兴旺的中产阶级。结果,为中产阶级开设的学校数量迅速增长。他们大多数是以"公立学校"而著称的男子寄宿学校。在 1850 年前只有为数不多的寄宿学校,这些学校非常严酷,没有什么有组织的体育活动,学生的自由度很大。结果,无纪律现象十分泛滥。

现代体育被系统地开发出来,其目的是控制这些男孩子,让他们精疲力竭,把他们维持在学校校园内。当时,学术标准低,而体育标准高;体育奖励多于对学习成绩的奖励。这样的制度为领导帝国造就了强壮、健康和自信的男学生。[3] "体育似乎发展的不仅仅是男孩子那让人羡慕的身体能力,还有他们的性格。他们折射出坚定的自信,他们的老师认为这是把许多时间花在板球、足球和橄榄球上的结果。"[4] 这种自信引起了顾拜旦的注意,他对 1870 年法国败在普鲁士人手中的军事耻辱耿耿于怀,而英国帝国主义的成功则给他留下了深刻印象。在他看来,英格兰中产阶级的体育有许多让人称赞的地方。因此,英格兰为现代体育的盛行奠定了直接的基础,为奥运会的复活起到了间接的作用。

(4) 体育的国际化

中产阶级拥护体育的一个结果是体育俱乐部和协会首先在欧洲和美国相继出现。到 19 世纪末期,高尔夫、足球、网球和体操等体育项目逐步发展起来。体育开始超越国界,国际体育比赛和交流应运而生。在这种情况下,不同体育项目的国际体育组织相继诞生。1881 年第一个国际单项体育组织——国际体操联合会成立,1892 年另外两个组织:国际赛艇联合会和滑冰联盟先后成立。这些国际体育组织的产生,使运动竞赛摆脱了原来的地方传统,具有了国际性。到 19 世纪末期,体育国际化成为一个不可阻挡的趋势。随着单项体育组织的增多和国际单项体育竞赛的蓬勃开展,人们呼唤大规模、包含所有项目的综合性运动会。因此,19世纪末期的体育国际化为现代奥运会的产生创造了条件。

(5) 考古发掘

在1766年以前,英国、法国和德国的考古学家探测古奥林匹亚遗址的想法被土耳其人所阻挡。奥林匹亚当时是土耳其帝国的一部分。然而,英国学者理查德·钱德勒在1766年被允许进入希腊进行科学考察。他发现了古代奥林匹亚的遗址,引起了许多考古学家的兴趣。在以后的岁月中,英国人、法国人和德国人都前去勘测,但直到100多年后,德国科学家库尔提乌斯等人在1875年至1881年间才使得掩藏在泥土下的遗迹重见天日。到1876年时,考古学家在奥林匹亚遗址已经发现了50个建筑物、130座塑像。这些发现激起了欧洲知识界极大的兴趣。1887年,柏林展览了从奥林匹亚发掘出的大量文物,进一步激发了人们对古代奥运会的好奇。

(6) 复兴奥运会的尝试

在17世纪到19世纪之间,世界各地恢复奥运会的尝试比比皆是(见表9-1)。

表9-1 1896年以前重建奥运会的17个尝试

年份	尝试
1604	罗伯特·多佛在英格兰的科茨沃尔德发起了"奥运会",它断断续续地举行,直至1857年。中断95年后,于1952年又重新举行。
1819	在苏格兰的圣费兰斯,起源于凯尔特人的高地运动会被人们重新拾起,之后由苏格兰移民传播到澳大利亚、加拿大、南非和美国。
1839	在瑞典也举行了一个"奥运会"。瑞典伦德大学的J.斯卡图教授曾组织过两次被当地报纸称之为"奥运会"的比赛活动。
1844	1844年在德国组织了一个"旅行奥运会",还顺访了当时被普鲁士占领的波兰西部。
1849	在英格兰的斯罗普郡,由一个名叫威廉·彭尼·布鲁克斯的医生发起了一个奥运会。

续　表

年份	尝试
1853	美国纽约的富兰克林竞技场,举行了许多古希腊和罗马最吸引人的运动会。
1859	扎巴斯试图在希腊恢复奥运会
1862	英格兰利物浦首届奥林匹克节由利物浦田径(体育)俱乐部组织。
1863	第二届利物浦奥林匹克节
1864	第三届利物浦奥林匹克节
1866	英国体育协会在威尔士的小镇兰迪德诺组织了第一届奥林匹克节。
1867	英国体育协会在利物浦举行了第二届奥林匹克节。
1870	希腊第二次尝试复兴奥运会(雅典)
1873	在德国占领下的波兰城镇克洛德兹克·维尔科珀尔斯基举行了地方奥运会。
1875	雅典第三届奥运会
1888	雅典第四届奥运会
1892	J.阿斯特里·库珀建议举办"盎格鲁—撒克逊奥林匹克运动会",没有成功,但激起了大英帝国运动会的想法,后来这一运动会被称为英联邦运动会。

尽管这些尝试大多数都没有成功,但它们在古代和现代奥运会之间建立了桥梁。在上述的这些尝试中,最引人注目的是1859年到1889年间在雅典举行的运动会——由于慈善家伊万杰里斯·扎巴斯的慷慨资助,该运动会举办了四次。然而,由于这一运动会只对希腊参赛者开放,在国际上没有引起什么关注。对现代奥运会奠基人顾拜旦产生直接影响的是文拉克运动会,它是1850年由英国斯罗普郡的医生威廉·彭尼·布鲁克斯发起,每年在马齐·文拉克的菩萨树场地举行,比赛的项目是传统的英国体育项目。布鲁克斯邀请顾拜旦参加了1890年的文拉克运动会。

2. 国际奥委会的诞生

现代奥运会的产生是深受英国公立学校体育至上影响的法国贵族皮埃尔·德·顾拜旦伯爵的智慧产物。他力图通过引进在当时法国学校课程中所没有的运动训练和比赛来鼓舞法国年轻人。

皮埃尔·德·顾拜旦伯爵

现代奥运会的设计师是皮埃尔·德·顾拜旦伯爵。他于1863年1月1日出生在巴黎,其父亲是一个艺术家,母亲是音乐家,在一个很有教养的贵族环境中长大。1870年法国在普法战争中惨败之后,他开始寻思让法国重新站立起来的各种手段。受英国中产阶级教育体制的鼓舞,他看到了体育的作用。作为一个活跃体育分子,他参加拳击、击剑、骑马和划船等运动。他相信体育是培养国家能量的首要手段。像大多数的法国人一样,年轻的顾拜旦心中燃烧着复仇和收复失去省份(两个东部省份:阿尔萨斯和洛林)的愿望。随着年龄的增长,他不像以前那样盲目地爱国,更加关心具有人文主义的和平世界,坚信体育在建立国际关系方面拥有独特的价值。

他的贵族地位不允许他从事资产阶级的职业。家庭传统职业是军队生涯或政治,但24岁的顾拜旦坚持他的未来职业是教育,他认为教育是社会未来发展的关键,应该通过改革法国毫无想象力的过时教育体制来恢复法国的高贵。受英国公立学校中体育地位的鼓舞,在彭尼·布鲁克斯和希腊的复兴人士如维凯拉斯的友谊驱动下,顾拜旦想把奥运会改造成一个国际性的、综合性体育节日。1892年,在法国体育运动协会联合会的一次会议上,作为秘书长的他宣布要复兴奥林匹克运动会。尽管他的声明没有得到积极的响应,但他没有就此放弃。经过两年的不懈努力,他聚集了足够的公众支持,最终在巴黎举办了1894年国际体育大会。49个体育组织(来自九个国家)的79名代表参加了1894年6月举行的这个会议,在会上,顾拜旦陈述了复兴奥运会可能性的问题。尽管只有少数对复兴奥运会真正感兴趣,但在会议结束时,这一建议通过无记名投票表决通过了。这次会议后来被看做是第一次奥林匹克大会,该会还成立了由15名委员组成的国际奥委会,并同意奥运会将于1896年4月在雅典首次举行。它的如期举办标志着现代奥运会的诞生。皮埃尔·德·顾拜旦致力于奥林匹克运动,直到1925年他才从国际奥委会退休。之后,他献身于教育工作,他称之为"没有完成的交响曲"。

1931年69岁时,顾拜旦出版了他的《奥林匹克论文集》,在文集中他强调奥林匹克事业的知识性和哲学性,他希望"从一开始就把国际奥委会的作用放在单个体育协会之上"。皮埃尔·德·顾拜旦于1937年9月2日在日内瓦的一个公园里因心脏病发作而突然去世,他的"交响乐"未能完成。洛桑城早先就决定授予他荣誉公民,但在举行仪式前他却辞世了。根据顾拜旦最后的遗愿,他被埋葬在洛桑,他的心脏放在奥林匹亚一个为他建立的石碑内。

图 9-1　首届国际奥委会委员

从左至右：吉普哈德、顾拜旦、顾斯、维凯拉斯、凯米尼、布托夫斯基、巴尔克

选择古代奥运会作为现代体育的启示，顾拜旦发现了唤起希腊理想主义原则的一个方法，而希腊理想主义在欧洲一直被传承，自文艺复兴起就在欧洲文化中占统治地位。奥运会要歌颂体育，但同时它又服从于这种理想主义。

3．现代奥运会的发展

应当指明的是"当现代奥运会在 1896 年首次举行时，它并不想成为古代奥运会的一个历史翻版"[5]，"奥林匹克"这一名词被用来强调综合多项比赛的现代需要。在一个多世纪的历程中，奥运会无论从规模上还是普及程度上都不断地发展以满足这一需要（见表 9-2）。

表 9-2 不同时期夏季奥运会概况

	日期	城市	国家	国家数	运动员		项目数量	
					总数	女性	小项	大项
1	4.6—4.15 1896	雅典	希腊	14	241	0	43	9
2	5.20—10.28 1900	巴黎	法国	19	997	19	166	24
3	7.1—11.23 1904	圣路易斯	美国	12	651	6	104	6
4	4.27—10.31 1908	伦敦	英国	22	2008	36	110	21
5	5.5—7.22 1912	斯德哥尔摩	瑞典	28	2407	57	102	13
7	4.20—9.12 1920	安特卫普	比利时	29	2626	77	154	21
8	5.4—7.27 1924	巴黎	法国	44	3089	136	126	17
9	5.17—8.12 1928	阿姆斯特丹	荷兰	46	2883	290	109	14
10	7.30—8.14 1932	洛杉矶	美国	37	1332	127	117	14
11	8.1—8.16 1936	柏林	德国	49	3963	328	129	19
14	7.29—8.14 1948	伦敦	英国	59	4104	385	136	17
15	7.19—8.3 1952	赫尔辛基	芬兰	69	4955	518	149	17
16	11.22—12.8 1956	墨尔本	澳大利亚	72	3314	371	151	17
17	8.25—9.11 1960	罗马	意大利	83	5383	610	150	17
18	10.10—10.24 1964	东京	日本	93	5151	683	163	19
19	10.12—10.27 1968	墨西哥城	墨西哥	112	5516	781	172	18
20	8.26—9.11 1972	慕尼黑	德国	121	7134	1058	195	21

续 表

	日期	城市	国家	国家数	运动员		项目数量	
					总数	女性	小项	大项
21	7.17—8.1 1976	蒙特利尔	加拿大	92	6084	1247	198	21
22	7.19—8.3 1980	莫斯科	前苏联	80	5179	1124	204	21
23	7.28—8.12 1984	洛杉矶	美国	140	6829	1567	221	21
24	9.17—10.2 1988	汉城	韩国	159	8391	2186	237	23
25	7.15—8.9 1992	巴塞罗那	西班牙	169	9364	2707	257	24
26	7.19—8.4 1996	亚特兰大	美国	197	10318	3516	271	26
27	9.15—10.1 2000	悉尼	澳大利亚	199	10735	4069	300	28
28	8.13—8.29 2004	雅典	希腊	201	10625	4412	301	28

资料来源：DK, *The Olympic Games: Athens 1896-Athens 2004*, London: Dorling Kindersley Limited, 2004, pp.253-367.

表 9-3　不同时期冬奥会概况

	日期	城市	国家数	运动员		项目数量	
				总数	女性	大项	小项
1	1924.1.24—2.5	夏蒙尼(法国)	16	258	13	5	14
2	1928.2.11—2.19	圣莫里兹(瑞士)	25	464	26	6	14
3	1932.2.4—2.13	普莱西德湖(美国)	17	252	21	5	14
4	1936.2.6—2.16	加米施—帕腾基兴(德国)	28	646	80	6	17
5	1948.1.30—2.8	圣莫里兹(瑞士)	28	669	77	7	22
6	1952.2.14—2.25	奥斯陆(挪威)	30	694	109	6	22
7	1956.1.26—2.5	科蒂纳丹佩佐(意大利)	32	821	132	6	24
8	1960.2.18—2.28	斯阔谷(美国)	30	665	143	6	27

续　表

	日期	城市	国家数	运动员		项目数量	
				总数	女性	大项	小项
9	1964.1.29—2.9	因斯布鲁克(奥地利)	36	1091	200	8	34
10	1968.2.6—2.18	格勒诺布尔(法国)	37	1158	211	8	35
11	1972.2.3—2.13	札幌(日本)	35	1006	206	8	35
12	1976.2.4—2.15	因斯布鲁克(奥地利)	37	1123	231	8	37
13	1980.2.13—2.24	普莱西德湖(奥地利)	37	1072	233	8	38
14	1984.2.8—2.19	萨拉热窝(南斯拉夫)	49	1272	274	8	39
15	1988.2.13—2.28	卡尔加里(加拿大)	57	1823	313	8	46
16	1992.2.8—2.23	阿伯特维尔(法国)	64	1801	488	10	37
17	1994.2.12—2.27	利勒哈默尔(挪威)	67	1737	520	10	61
18	1998.1.7—1.22	长野(日本)	72	2176	787	14	68
19	2002.2.8—2.24	盐湖城(美国)	77	2399	886	7	78
20	2006.2.10—2.26	都灵(意大利)	80	2508	960	7	84

资料来源：DK, *The Olympic Games: Athens 1896-Athens 2004*, London: Dorling Kindersley Limited, 2004, pp.267-367.

从以上两个表格中可得到以下启示。

(1) 组织模式的逐渐建立

上述两表揭示出现代奥运会随着时间的推移而逐渐发展。起初，国际奥委会没有什么权威性。相反,主办国在决定比赛项目和诸多其他事务上有较大的自主性。结果，早期奥运会的组织和者运作都相当灵活。例如，第一届奥运会任何人想要参加比赛都可报名,结果好几个参赛者竟是毫无准备的旅游者。1900 年巴黎奥运会持续时间达 5 个月之久,大多数比赛是在不太合适的场所里进行的。这届奥运会和接下来的一届分别是巴黎世界博览会和路易斯世界博览会[6]的一个附属部分。由于组织松散,市场营销效果不佳,宣传力度不够,不少官员和运动员甚至不知道他们在参加奥运会。总之,最初的三届奥运会总的说来是组织涣散、比赛规定和规则很不完善、器材设施落后。

1908年奥运会是首次由众多体育机构来组织的一届运动会。1912年奥运会采取了更为理性的途径,更关注大众需求和细致的计划。1924年起,国际单项协会对各自的体育项目拥有更多的控制力,使比赛规则和规定向标准化方向发展。同时,大多数国家的国家奥林匹克组织开始组织选拔赛,以确保最优秀的运动员被选送到奥运会。这样,运动成绩提高显著。

奥运会的结构也是逐渐建立起来的。1920年奥运会旗首次在安特卫普运动会上引进,奥运圣火则在1928年的阿姆斯特丹运动会出现。冬奥会从1924年开始与夏季奥运会同年举行。奥运村在1932年建立,同时奥运会的持续天数固定在两周左右。1936年人们看到一个携带奥运火炬的奔跑者进入体育场、点燃奥林匹克圣火。二十年后的墨尔本奥运会引进了更为自由和非正式性的闭幕式入场形式。面对日益增长的兴奋剂事件和对性别身份的争议,1968年奥运会首次进行兴奋剂检测和女性性别检测。从20世纪60年代起,随着现代技术的发展,媒体尤其是电视报道变得越来越普遍和重要。电视广播权变成国际奥委会最重要的收入来源。

(2) 世界大战对奥运会的影响

由于两次世界大战的爆发,原计划在柏林、赫尔辛基和伦敦举行的1916年、1940年和1944年奥运会不得不取消。为了激励遭受战争破坏严重的比利时进行战后重建,一战后的奥运会被授予安特卫普市。由于没有足够的时间来清理战争留下的废墟、建造新的运动设施,当奥运会开始时田径场还未完工,运动员住在安有折叠小床的拥挤的房间内。战败国德国、奥地利、匈牙利、保加利亚和土耳其没有被邀请参赛。

二战后,伦敦得到举办1948年奥运会的通知时只有两年的时间来准备,这届奥运会帮助人们从战争的阴影中走出来。但战败国德国和日本又一次没被邀请参赛。

(3) 奥运会规模的不断扩展

自 1896 年雅典奥运会复兴以来,现代奥林匹克运动经过了一个多世纪的洗礼,不断地发展壮大,尽管道路崎岖不平。首先,参赛人数在 1960 年、1972 年和 1996 年出现了显著性的增长(见图 9-2)。

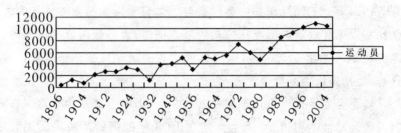

图 9-2 奥运会参赛人数

其次,作为国际奥委会会员的国家奥委会数量持续增加。到 1968 年它超过 100 个,到 2000 年超过 200 个(见图 9-3)。

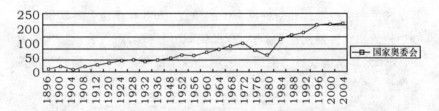

图 9-3 国际奥委会接纳的国家奥委会数量

再者,奥运会由世界不同国家来举办。在二战前,大多数举办城市位于欧洲国家,大多数参赛者是西方人。1945 年后这一情形开始变化。例如,1956 年奥运会被授予澳大利亚——第一个举办奥运会的南半球国家。第 18 届奥运会于 1964 年东京举行。到目前为止,非洲是唯一一个没有举办过奥运会的洲。

(4) 举办城市的地理位置和它对奥运会的影响

从表 9-1 中很清楚地看到有三届奥运会,即 1904 年的圣路易斯、

1932年的洛杉矶和1956年的墨尔本,参赛人数比前一届少。这可能与举办城市的位置有关。在20世纪早期欧洲是奥林匹克运动的主力军。当时要到洛杉矶去,欧洲运动员必须先坐船到纽约,然后乘火车穿越美洲大陆,需要三周的时间。一些参赛者为了得到参加奥运会所需的10周时间,不得不把三年的假日积攒起来。此外,美洲对欧洲人而言是一个遥远的、未开垦的地方,许多人不愿到美国去参加奥运会。这样,1904年大约76%的参赛者是美国人。1904年和1932年在美国举行的奥运会因而出现了参赛人数下降的局面。同样的情况出现在澳大利亚举行的1956年奥运会上。由于澳大利亚远离欧洲和美洲,加之当时出现了两次国际危机[7]以及由于澳大利亚的检疫限制导致马术比赛移至斯德哥尔摩,1956年奥运会的运动员人数比前一届要少。

1968年奥运会在墨西哥城举行,其高原位置对田径运动员既有好处也有不利。在稀薄的空气中,短跑和田赛运动员的成绩十分突出。例如,美国的鲍勃·比蒙(跳远)和雷·伊万斯(400米)创造了新的世界纪录,大大地超过以前的纪录。但大多数长跑运动员却没有那么幸运。只有在高原进行过训练的非洲运动员例外。最为突出的是肯尼亚运动员基普·凯诺,赢得金银牌各一枚。

(5) 现代的改革变化

现代奥运会已经历了好几次大的转变:

第一,奥运会从宗教(古代)特点向非宗教(现代)特点的转变。随着现代技术的使用,如1912年电子计时设施和公共宣告系统,1936年的电视转播奥运会,20世纪60年代记录成绩的计算机系统,20世纪90年代有线电视和卫星电视的征订,奥林匹克运动已经变成世界上最流行、最现代化的体育赛事。[8]

第二,奥运会从欧洲的活动变成了一个全球性事件。从国际奥委会和第一届奥运会诞生之日起,大多数国际奥委会的委员是欧洲人。现在的116名委员来自79个国家和地区(见附件)。在总共举行过的25届夏季奥运会中,17次都是在欧洲举行,4次在美国,在亚洲和澳洲各2次。尽管欧洲仍占统治地位,奥运会已走出欧洲。

图 9-4　鲍勃·比蒙的"世纪之跳"

第三,一些关键的原则,如只有男性参加和业余主义,已经被放弃。在 1896 年首届奥运会中,没有女性参加。1900 年女性开始参加奥运会,但只有 19 名女运动员参加了网球和高尔夫比赛。一个世纪后,4069 名女性参加了在悉尼举行的夏季奥运会的 25 个大项、132 个小项的比赛。在雅典奥运会上,女性参加了 26 个大项、135 个小项的比赛。

然而,这些转变并非轻而易举、毫无困难就实现的。女性进入奥运会就非常不易。她们用了 28 年才将田径和体操变成奥运会女子比赛项目,用了 72 年才使女性参赛人数达到四位数。

在新千年中,奥林匹克运动已经发生了许多变化,并将继续发生变化。盐湖城申办 2002 年冬奥会引发的贿赂丑闻是近期变化的一个催化剂。在 1998 年以前对国际奥委会的腐败问题批评声不断,但一名电视记者在 1998 年 11 月揭露出来的盐湖城申奥丑闻还是让全世界震惊。据称有数名国际奥委会委员接受了贿赂——以现金、礼物、娱乐、商业好处、旅游支出、医疗支出甚至子女的大学学费的形式,来换取他们投盐湖城成为 2002 年冬奥会场所的一票。[9] 以前几个申办委员会的行为也受到了违规的谴责。悉尼奥申委就是其中之一。

国际奥委会委员中存在着普遍的腐败现象这一说法迫使国际奥委会迅速地做出反应。首先,国际奥委会在自行调查之后,在奥运史上首次将 6 名成员开除出局——4 名在决定宣布之前已经辞职,1 名已去世。另外还有 10 名委员受到警告。此外,国际奥委会决定改革奥运会举办城市选拔的方针、结构和过程。例如,不允许国际奥委会委员到奥运申办城市访问。此外,运动员在决策中将发挥更大的作用,对国际奥委会的重要问题将发表自己的意见。人们希望这些变化能对奥林匹克运动产生深远的影响。支撑奥林匹克精神的基本伦理价值将会比以往更得到强调,责任、包容、透明、合理和民主将更受关注,以确保一个"纯洁"的奥林匹克运动。

4. 奥林匹克运动的未来

在 21 世纪奥林匹克运动面临着一系列的挑战:

第一,随着政府和企业介入的增多,国际奥委会的独立性日益受到威胁。

国际奥委会通常反对把奥运会作为实现政治目的的工具,但这并没有完全实现。在过去时常出现的制裁和在最近的举办城市选票竞争期间国家元首们的公开演讲就充分反映了这一点。国际奥委会处在进退两难的困境之中——要依靠奥运会的商业化来全球性地推广奥林匹克运动,但同时要努力将商业化对奥运会的干涉降低到最小的程度。为此,时常要做一些妥协,在比赛场地和时间的变化上就体现了这一点。[10] 甚至有这样一种说法,即国际奥委会把1996年的奥运会卖给了总部在亚特兰大的多国公司,如可口可乐和有线新闻网络(CNN)。[11]

第二,奥运官员的腐败导致了对奥林匹克运动的信任危机。

在选拔奥运会举办城市上反复出现的丑闻导致对国际奥委会委员行为的质问,国际奥委会的信誉岌岌可危。赞助商对于是否继续他们对奥林匹克运动的财务支持变得十分谨慎。怎样洗刷它的名声、恢复大众对国际奥委会的信任将是该组织期面对的一个困难任务。

第三,滥用兴奋剂的运动员威胁到奥林匹克运动的未来。

奥运会是公开与公平竞争理想联系在一起的,兴奋剂问题仍是"体育可信性的头号威胁"(雅克·罗格,2001)。为了消除使用兴奋剂的现象,国际奥委会增设了日益严厉的惩罚措施,引进了最先进的检测手段,检测频率加大。然而,"反兴奋剂之战是一个复杂的事情,涉及到科学、法律和伦理"[12]。兴奋剂检测耗资巨大,经常引起争议和官司,正如下面的雷洛兹案所反映出来的。[13]

雷洛兹案

1992年俄亥俄州的一个美国联邦法官认为国际田联给"男孩"哈里·雷洛兹因兴奋剂阳性而禁赛两年的决定是错误的,并裁定这个当时的400米世界纪录的保持者应得到2600万美元的补偿。国际田联认为俄亥俄法庭的这一裁定不合适,在任何命令都不能被强迫实施这一设想的基础上,选择不为这一案件辩护。

雷洛兹的律师在国际田联有资产的好几个州都获得了命令,去追要这一罚款。于是国际田联被迫做出反应,对早先的判决提出申诉。最终,这个案子到达了美国最高法院。1993年美国上诉院推翻了给雷洛兹补偿的判决,裁定俄亥俄法官对总部在伦敦的国际田联没有裁定权。

这个案子促使国际田联决定对任何案子建立法律辩护。在 1996 年亚特兰大夏季奥运会之前，所有的参赛者被要求签订一份申明在对兴奋剂检测有争议的情况下，他们不会在体育仲裁法庭外寻求法律补偿。[14]

上面涉及的雷洛兹事件生动地表明生物技术方面的商业公司介入到奥运会中。体育商业化使得兴奋剂的铲除变得很困难，如果不是不可能的话。当国际奥委会希望根除兴奋剂、保持"公平"竞争之时，不少人，包括某些国家和地区的政治家、教练、科学家和运动员在内，都想要运用生物技术来提高成绩。因而，反兴奋剂战变得愈发困难。

第四，规模庞大使得奥运会很难操办。

随着奥运会的不断扩展，巨型规模已经变成了一个问题。现在举办夏季奥运会的运作费用达到 20 亿美元左右，举办冬奥会也达到 15 亿美元左右。举办奥运会的要求变得越来越苛刻和困难，尤其是对小国家和发展中国家来讲。这将会对奥运会的普遍性原则带来挑战。怎样缩减奥运会的规模和复杂性成为雅克·罗格领导下的国际奥委会关心的问题。然而，这不是一个容易的过程，因为越来越多的体育项目想要成为奥林匹克比赛项目，已经加入进来的项目不想被踢出去。罗格自 2001 年起不断号召缩减奥运会的规模，但还没看到具体的成果。减少运动项目的难度是很大的。这场斗争还在继续。

第五，安全变成所有各方——奥运会的申办和组织委员会、赞助商、参赛者和观众——都关注的中心问题。

1972 年以色列运动员被巴勒斯坦恐怖分子杀害后，安全问题开始引起国际奥委会和奥运会组委会的注意。安全是奥运会预算的一个专项开支，并在不断上升。更多的资源和更复杂的技术也被运用进来。例如，1988 年大约 10 万安全人员被招募，因为汉城到朝鲜很近（30 英里），而且学生可能为统一问题举行示威。尽管在 1996 年亚特兰大奥运会上采取了严格的安全防范措施，在奥林匹克百年纪念公园还是出现了管道炸弹爆炸，导致两名人员死亡。2001 年 9 月 11 日在纽约世贸中心和华盛顿五角大楼的恐怖分子袭击使得安全成为更令人焦虑的问题。举办 2002 年冬奥会的盐湖城在安全费用上花费了 3.1 亿美元。[15] 2004 年雅典的安全费用达 12 亿美元左右，远远超出 7.5 亿美元的安全预算。大约

7.1万名受过专门训练的安全人士,七国的奥林匹克顾问组和北约盟国都被调用。[16]也许因为安全支出巨大,雅典在2004年奥运会后身负巨债。[17]安全费用的上涨,复杂性的增加带来了一些重要的问题:小国家以后能负担起这些安全保障措施并有能力实施安全防卫吗?不断上升的费用会让奥运会进一步远离发展中国家吗?大城市还愿意冒险来举办奥运会吗?运动员、官员和观众还会来看奥运会比赛吗?如果答案是"不",那会给以后的媒体和商业利益带来什么样的影响?奥运会的未来会是怎样——体育景观还是军事演习?无疑,安全问题将对奥运会的未来产生明显的直接和间接的影响。

结 论

现代奥运会在19世纪末期的诞生是许多因素,如政治、经济、文化和社会等综合作用的结果。文艺复兴、宗教改革、启蒙运动、工业革命、欧洲强调身心和谐发展的资产阶级教育改革、希腊古奥林匹亚遗址的发现、英国中产阶级教育理念和实践、体育的国际化和顾拜旦不倦的努力,都在确保现代奥运会的出现上起到了各自的作用。

现代奥运会的性质随着时间的推移而逐步建立起来。出现了一些主要的变化。现代奥运会在100多年的时间内从一个地区为中心的体育赛事转变为一个以全球为中心的体育赛事。变化还在继续。在21世纪,国际奥委会一直处在要求其改革方针、结构和实践以遏制奥委会委员中腐化泛滥的压力之下。结果是是一揽子改革方案的出现。然而,怎样面对政治干预、奥运会的商业化、兴奋剂、腐败、规模巨大和安全等问题仍然是目前和未来的挑战。人们将拭目以待奥运会更多的变化。

思考题

1. 欧洲导致了奥运会最终复活的重大历史事件的顺序是什么?你认为哪一个影响最大?
2. 为什么皮埃尔·顾拜旦想要复兴古代奥运会?
3. 你认为在过去的100多年中奥运会的那些变化是最重要的?请给

出理由。

4. 未来奥运会将面临哪些最严重的挑战？请给出理由。

注　释

〔1〕 1705年，工程师汤姆斯·纽科门制造了首台现代蒸汽机，以改进泵的设备，排除锡、铜矿的渗漏问题。1763年，詹姆士·瓦特，格拉斯哥大学的一个工具师，开始对纽科门的蒸汽机进行改良，使它成为一个复式发动机，这样将它从一个气体机变成一个真正的"蒸汽"机。

〔2〕 David Levinson and Karen Christensen（eds.）（1996），*Encyclopaedia of World Sport：From Ancient Times to the Present*，Oxford：ABC-CLIO Ltd.，p.391.

〔3〕 关于体育在公立学校中的作用的全面和最新的讨论，参考 J. A. Mangan (1981)，《维多利亚和爱德华时代公立学校的运动竞赛》，剑桥大学出版社。

〔4〕 Allen Guttmann (1992)，*The Olympics：A History of the Modern Games*，Chicago：University of Illinois Press, p. 9.

〔5〕 Joachim K. Ruhl (2004)，"Olympic Games before Coubertin", John E. Findling and Kimberly D. Pelle, *Encyclopaedia of the Modern Olympic Movement*，London：Greenwood Press, p. 3.

〔6〕 该届奥运会起初计划在芝加哥举办，后移师路易斯。国际奥委会官员决定将奥运会与路易斯购物展一起举办，该展览是庆祝美国获得路易斯版图100周年的一个大型集会。

〔7〕 埃及、黎巴嫩、伊拉克因抗议以色列入侵西奈半岛在十月宣布抵制奥运会。在奥运会开始前的一周，苏联部队进入匈牙利的布达佩斯，镇压大规模的反政府学生起义。荷兰、西班牙、瑞士因抗议苏联侵略而抵制奥运会。

〔8〕 Ellis Cashmore (2002)，*Sports Culture：An A-Z Guide*，Routledge, pp. 402-405.

〔9〕 详细信息可参见 Lex Hemphill, "Salt Lake City 2002", in John E. Findling and Kimberly D. Pelle (eds.) (2004), op. cit., pp. 424-427。

〔10〕 为满足美国电视转播商的要求，汉城奥运会不少项目的比赛时间不得不从下午移到运动员很不习惯的一大早，因为大多数的电视观众是美国人。

〔11〕 Alfred E. Senn (1999)，*Power, Politics, and the Olympic Games：A History of the Power Brokers, Events, and Controversies that Shaped the Games*，Human Kinetics, p. 249.

〔12〕 Jacques Rogge, 2001.

〔13〕 Michael Janofsky, "Track And Field; Reynolds Case Spotlights Battle of the Regulators", *The New York Times*, October 11, 1991.

〔14〕 Ellis Cashmore (2002), op. cit., pp. 356-357.

〔15〕 第十九届冬季奥运会隆重开幕, http://61.135.180.163/xwzx/tpxw/5945.shtm.

〔16〕 Gianna Angelopoulos Daskalaki, "We Are Ready to Compete on the World Stage Again", *The Daily Telegraph*, August 12, 2004.

〔17〕《雅典奥运几项财务数据带给北京的启示》,《体育产业信息》,2004年第10期。

第十章
奥林匹克运动:理想主义与现实主义的冲撞

本章要点
* 业余主义与职业主义
* 慈善与商业化
* 远离政治与亲近政治
* 公平竞争与暗箱操作
* 男性统治与性别平等

现代奥林匹克运动已有 100 多年历史,但还没有一个明确的或隐喻的奥林匹克主义价值得到完全实现。业余主义与职业主义之间、慈善和商业主义之间、政治亲善关系和政治敌意之间、各种形式的暗箱操作和公平竞争之间、男性统治和性别平等之间的紧张关系十分明显。然而,通过处理这些紧张关系,奥林匹克运动得到发展壮大,并成为全世界最大的体育盛会。因此,有必要理解为解决这些冲突而做出的努力,以便抓住奥林匹克运动成功的本质属性。

1. 业余主义与职业主义

业余主义与职业主义一直是现代奥运会争论不休的话题。这些问题在古代奥运会就存在。从公元前 5 世纪起,对获胜运动员的物质奖励变得越来越多。尽管表面上泛希腊运动会的奖品只是简单的一个橄榄枝花冠,这在前面已经提到,但许多城市开始给他们的胜利者提供物质或金钱或可以用金钱来衡量的特权来表彰他们。在希腊文化时期（公元前323—公元前331年），某些运动员只是为钱而比赛，某些人甚至接受对手的钱，把胜利拱手让人。[1]

自现代体育诞生起，业余主义和职业主义就是相互对立的思想观念。一个业余选手参加体育不为物质奖励，而是为了乐趣。而职业选手则是为了奖励去参赛，旨在取胜。

现代体育在19世纪后期的英格兰开展起来后，业余主义就被强调。大多数现代体育是在英国特权阶层的学校开始的。这些学校的许多学生在离开学校后组建体育俱乐部。这些俱乐部都是业余的。会员为了快乐而不是为了物质奖励来从事体育。简言之，这就是现代业余主义的起源。现代体育的职业主义是与业余主义同时出现的。职业选手为金钱而比赛，职业主义随着日益上涨的商业主义、观赏性的增加和运动成绩的提高而逐渐升温。

在1970年以前，奥运会只限于业余选手参加，明文规定：

一个曾经作为职业选手参赛的人，曾经训练过运动员并获取报酬的人，或为个人利益而从事体育或与体育有联系的人都没有资格在一个国家级委员会就职。该原则规定在有关国家奥委会的建议下，国际奥委会执委会可对这几类提出异议。没有遵守国际奥委会原则和规定的国家奥委会将丧失国际奥委会的认可，没有权力选派运动员参加奥运会。[2]

吉米·索普的奖牌

在1912年瑞典斯德哥尔摩奥运会上，美国运动员索普一举夺得男子五项、十项两枚金牌。在发奖仪式上，瑞典国王告诉索普："先生，你是世界上最伟大的运动员。"但次年因有人告发他以前参加过一场职业棒球比赛，他的名字被从奥运冠军名单中删去，国际奥委会追回了他的金牌。当时涉及到的钱数是微不足道的（一星期15美元）。直到1982年，国际奥委会才为这一冤案平反，在相隔70年后，奖牌才返回到其主人的家属手中。

这样规定的结果是,某些体育项目和运动员被扔出了奥运会。例如,1924年,奥运会取消了网球项目的比赛,因为许多非业余选手参加这一项目。网球直到1988年才重回奥运会。

自20世纪70年代以来,关于运动员资格的一些规定逐步放松。1971年国际奥委会决定从宪章中去掉"业余选手"这一说法;接着修改了关于参赛资格的一些规定,允许运动员因参加训练和比赛活动而离开工作的这段时间得到"中断时间"的工资。国际奥委会还使得国家奥委会、体育组织和私人公司的赞助合法化。在有些运动项目,包括田径、花样滑冰、滑雪,运动员必须把从商业代理和赞助得来的收入放在有限信托基金,由他们的国家协会来控制。

要求参赛选手是业余身份的奥林匹克规定最终在1986年被推翻,职业选手能否参赛的决定由各单项管理机构来决定。冰球、网球、足球和马术的职业选手被允许参加1988年的奥运会,尽管他们的资格还是受到一定的限制;来自于非田径项目的职业选手有资格参加奥运会田径比赛。

规定的变化与公众对娱乐的要求密切相关。例如,1992年被称为"梦之队"的美国篮球队打败所有的对手,轻松地获得金牌。该队由美国篮球协会(NBA)的11名明星组成,包括迈克尔·乔丹("飞人")、斯科蒂·皮蓬、艾文·约翰逊("魔术师")、拉里·伯德("大鸟"),全都是引人注目的人物。在20世纪早期,98%的奥运会参赛者没有从他们的参赛中得到金钱;到21世纪早期,奥运会的参赛者大多不再是业余选手。[3]

2. 慈善与商业化

最初,国际奥委会的经费来源完全来自私人捐款。在1896年第一届奥运会上,60%的经费来自富裕的希腊慈善家乔治·阿维罗夫的个人捐赠,剩余部分则是政府拨款和发售纪念邮票筹集资金。但是,在1981年前,国际奥委会很难负担得起它的运作费用或支付其会员的花销。

这样,自80年代初期起,奥运会向商业主义靠拢。商业主义可用商品化——物品和人在市场中转变为商品——这个术语来很好地解释。商品化是资本主义社会以消费者为基础的经济出现的结果。它孕育了一种只要有机会,就去做贸易并获得盈利的商业文化。例如,1984年奥运会,火炬接力跑每公里收费3000美元。[4]

作为商品化的一个结果,企业赞助成为国际奥委会收入的主要来源。国际奥委会的经费预算明显上升,从1972—1976年的1410万美元到1992—1996年的17亿美元。从软饮料生产商到汽车公司的私人企业,现在竞相成为奥运会的官方赞助商。例如,可口可乐支付了2200万美元以确保竞争对手的软饮料在汉城奥运会中不能使用奥林匹克标志。[5]

在寻求商业支持得到广泛认同的同时,人们日益关心这一支持的程度,对奥运会的过渡商业化现象已经发出了批评之声。有人甚至声称国际奥委会把1996年奥运会卖给了落户亚特兰大的多国公司,如可口可乐和有线新闻网络(CNN)[6]。

为遏制缺乏控制的商业化,国际奥委会坚持以下主要的方针:

* 不允许场地广告,奥运会不允许在体育场地或运动员身上做广告,这在世界大型体育赛事中是独一无二的;

* 奥运会转播商进行"干净的"转播;

* 控制主要赞助企业的数量,从更少的合作伙伴那里得到更多的支持!例如,盐湖城组委会和国际奥委会为2002年盐湖城开发的营销支持和收入比规模大得多的1996年百年奥运会要大、要多。这一事实表明奥运营销伙伴的价值得到提高,也表明国际奥委会努力控制对举办奥运会起支撑作用的商业主义。

3. 远离政治与亲近政治

《奥林匹克宪章》规定:"国际奥委会反对政治上滥用体育和运动员。"前国际奥委会主席布伦戴奇(1952—1972)曾宣称:"体育与政治毫无关系。"然而,奥运会时常受到政治事件的影响,也不时地被当做一个有力的政治工具。在一个多世纪的历程中,奥林匹克运动经历了各种各样的政府和政治运动的干涉。三届奥运会因世界大战而被迫取消。奥地利、保加利亚、德国、匈牙利和土耳其因为在第一次世界大战中的作用而没有受到参加1920年奥运会的邀请。政治影响最明显的一届奥运会是1936年柏林奥运会。奥运会在1931年被授予柏林时,没人能猜想到鲁道夫·希特勒和纳粹德国会控制奥运会。尽管希特勒把这次奥运会当做一次政治力量的展示,他没能"证明"他的种族优越理论,因为美国黑人运动员杰西·欧文斯在田径100米、200米、跳远和4×100米接力比赛中获得4枚金牌。

在第二战世界大战以后,1948年的伦敦奥运会见证了共产主义国家的第一次参赛,但战败国德国和日本却被拒于奥运会的大门之外。埃及、伊拉克和黎巴嫩因抗议以以色列为首的国家管制苏伊士运河而没有参加1956年的墨尔本奥运会。西班牙和瑞士也因抗议苏联入侵匈牙利而抵制此届奥运会。1960年,南非因实行种族隔离政策而被禁止参加奥运会。国际奥委会直到1991年才重新接纳南非奥委会,1992年南非重回奥运会。

1968年在墨西哥城举行的奥运会是自1936年柏林奥运会以来政治色彩最浓的一届奥运会。在奥运会开始前10天,学生抗议墨西哥政府把钱花在奥运会上而不是用在社会方案上。在三文化广场军队包围了学生,并开枪射击。250多名抗议者被杀,1000多人受伤。在男子200米跑的发奖仪式上,当国歌奏起时,美国运动员托米·史密斯和约翰·卡洛斯(分别为金牌和铜牌得住)光脚站立在领奖台上,低头、举起一个带着黑手套的拳头。这两名运动员把这一姿势说成是对他们美国黑人遗产的致意和对美国少数民族生存条件的抗议。国际奥委会和美国奥委会裁定这一行为与奥运会理想背道而驰,禁止这两名运动员进入奥运村,并将其遣送回家。

与奥运会相关的最恐怖的一次政治事件发生在1972年慕尼黑奥运会上。9月5日,8名阿拉伯恐怖分子冲进以色列队总部,杀害2人,后来又有9人在德国警察尝试在飞机场营救人质失败后被杀。这一事件使全世界都为之震惊。第二天早上在人山人海的奥林匹克体育馆内举行了悼念仪式。当天以色列队被允许立刻回家,之后比赛重新开始。在以后的数日和数月中,对国际奥委会主席艾弗里·布伦戴奇在恐怖袭击发生后作出继续进行比赛的决定一直争议不断。

图 10-1　黑拳

抵制

抵制——为了施加压力,一个政府不允许其运动员参加奥运会,故意恶化与某个人、国家或群体关系的做法。例如,1979 年 12 月苏联入侵阿富汗破坏了 1980 年和 1984 年奥运会。许多非共产主义国家决定抵制 1980 年莫斯科奥运会。接着针锋相对的政治出现在 1984 年洛杉矶奥运会,前苏联和其他共产主义国家在最后一分钟抵制奥运会。这两届奥运会的比赛质量因此而受到影响。抵制并未马上停止——朝鲜、古巴、埃塞俄比亚和尼加拉瓜因为政治原因没有参加 1988 年汉城奥运会。

因其国际影响力,奥运会作为政治工具有相当的潜力。反之亦然,

图 10-2　1972 年奥运会降半旗

奥运会可被用来改善国家之间、社团之间的关系。事实上,从它致力于平等的全球机会和全世界参与体育、实现国际间理解和和平的角度讲,奥运会表现为一个政治工程,要求有政治性决策和行动,包括建设性的折衷。在胡安·萨马兰奇 1980 年成为国际奥委会主席以后,国际奥委会采纳了一个务实的立场:"奥林匹克运动是社会的一个组成部分,它有义务与公众人物达成协议。"但是,如果奥运会被用来服务于负面的政治目的的话,奥林匹克理想主义就会受到威胁。

4. 公平竞争与暗箱操作

奥林匹克传统强调公平竞争。公平竞争是一组期望,包括遵守规则、尊重他人、胜不骄败不馁、宽容待人,目的是在体育中创造持久、积极的人际关系。

然而,在奥林匹克运动中,违规操作时常可见,使用兴奋剂就是一例。

(1) 兴奋剂

使用兴奋剂是欺骗。使用兴奋剂与死亡联系在一起。生理上死亡是通过不合理的操纵来根本地,有时是不可逆转地,改变正常的过程。身体上的死亡,正如近年某些悲剧案例所表现出来的那样。还有是精神上和智力上死亡,即通过同意欺骗和隐瞒个人的能力,通过承认自己无能或不愿意接受自己、超越自己的局限。最后是道德死亡,事实上把自己放在所有人类社会都要求的行为规范之外。(胡安·安东尼奥·萨马兰奇,国际奥委会主席,1980—2001)

* 国际上的兴奋剂

体育中滥用兴奋剂的问题——运动员有意或不小心使用可以提高成绩的物质或方法——有很长的历史。[7]然而,直到 20 世纪 50 年代中期,当自行车运动员被发现兴奋剂阳性后,滥用兴奋剂的问题才引起国际注意。[8]使用兴奋剂的运动员人数不断上升这一问题向国际奥委会发出了警告,国际奥委会在 1962 年通过了一项反兴奋剂决议,在 1968 年的冬、夏季奥运会上进行兴奋剂检查。1967 年,国际奥委会成立了医学委员会,为 1968 年的冬、夏季奥运会提供医务控制服务。自 1972 年起全面的兴奋剂检测开始实施。

在汉城奥运会(1988 年)本·约翰逊检测阳性后,加拿大政府着手进行了调查,这个调查是全世界讨伐体育界滥用兴奋剂现象的一个重要事件。在约翰逊报告公布 13 年后,在反兴奋剂战争中的一个主要突破是结束了保持缄默的协定,这样的协定涉及运动员、教练员、体能训练师、医生和管理人员。

本·约翰逊案例

在1988年汉城奥运会上,本·约翰逊跑出了100米9.79秒的成绩,使他成为历史上跑得最快的人。但这个在加拿大运动史上令人骄傲的成绩很快就成了一场噩梦。62个小时后,奥运官员走进约翰逊的房间,出来时拿走了他的金牌。本·约翰逊被查出类固醇阳性。他因此失去了数百万的形象代理和赞助费,并被禁赛两年。

约翰逊早在汉城奥运会前6年就开始使用类固醇。在汉城奥运会前的一次休整课上,他在杰米·阿斯塔范医生的指导下用药。据说该医生警告了约翰逊和他的教练现在用药可能会在奥运会上查出阳性,他索要了100万加元保守秘密。约翰逊的教练没做任何事情,让他继续比赛。

20世纪90年代初期,约翰逊试图再次攀上顶峰。不幸的是,在1993年蒙特利尔田径比赛后,他又一次被查出兴奋剂阳性,被国际田联终身禁赛。这一次,约翰逊坚持自己是干净的。记录表明他在1月15、17和21日测试了三次,只有1月17日的样本检测呈阳性。约翰逊声称不可能在两天前和四天后都是干净的(中间一次却是阳性),但他没有钱到法庭去申诉。他辉煌的田径生涯最终结束。

他继续训练,1999年一名加拿大仲裁人裁决约翰逊在1993年没有受到正常程序的对待,他将被允许在加拿大比赛。然而,国际田联维持终身禁赛的决定。这意味着尽管约翰逊现在可以在加拿大跑步,但不能比赛。他的竞争对手后来被认为染指兴奋剂,也被禁止参加国际比赛。1999年10月他在一个慈善活动中与良种动物、溜蹄的马和运牲口的车赛跑。在运牲口的车陷入泥潭中后,约翰逊排名第三。

约翰逊2000年夏天接受了一个为期三个月的工作,训练利比亚领导人穆阿玛尔·卡扎菲的儿子,一个足球运动员。这让他再次出现在新闻头条中。

本·约翰逊仍在多伦多居住。他从没有持续干过一份工作,靠一周几百美元的收入维生。他在约克大学与他的第一任教练珀西·邓肯一起训练,为可能永不会出现的比赛而准备。本·约翰逊坚持认为他是历史上最棒的短跑选手,尽管使用了药物来提高成绩。他说:"大多数人喜爱娱乐,他们知道这个游戏。体育绝不能保持干净。"

(资料来源:《尽全力取胜:本·约翰逊的故事》,www.tv.cbc.ca/witness/doping/dopmain.htm,Feb.21,2001.)

某些运动员和官员声称:"比赛中药检只能抓到那些大意的、没有受到有效指导的人。"这是因为运动员、他们的教练和医务顾问常常确信在他们必须上交尿样之前,荷尔蒙药的所有痕迹已经离开了运动员的身体。约翰逊是大意还是指导不当是不得而知的问题。对于加拿大,一个其人民感到生活在美国影响下的国家而言,约翰逊战胜美国的著名运动员卡尔·刘易斯,是头顶奥林匹克光环让全球瞩目的一个机会。在一定程度上,这是导致一个愚蠢行动的动机。

许多体育机构没能严肃地对待滥用兴奋剂的问题,并采取有效措施来检测出非法使用药物的现象,也助长了大量运动员使用药物来提高成绩这一毒瘤。另一个问题是当运动员被查出使用了提高成绩的药物后,只有运动员受到处罚;教练员、医生或相关的体育组织却没有责任。

2003年夏天美国户外全国锦标赛提取的药样以及赛外检测表明一种新的药物THG(一种专门设计的类固醇)被广泛使用。THG以食物补充剂的伪装形式被售出。由于THG是新药,人们对它的特定效果还知之甚少,但它与其他已知类固醇十分相似的化学作用,意味着它会带来像合成类固醇一样的风险,合成类固醇的副作用包括肝脏损害、心脏病、焦虑和暴躁。

在因处理悉尼奥运会前兴奋剂阳性事件不当而遭致批评之后(让查出兴奋剂阳性的运动员参加奥运会),美国田协同意把此事交给美国反兴奋剂协会来处理。然而,这样的行动来得太迟,没能阻止过去的一切在2003年8月的巴黎世界田径锦标赛上重演。有人揭露美国获胜的4×400米接力赛的一个成员杰罗姆·杨,早在1999年就被查出兴奋剂阳性,但仍被美国田协允许参赛。美国田协的形象同一年再次被凯莉·怀特事件所损。怀特是巴黎比赛的短跑双料冠军,没能通过兴奋剂检测。还有其他一些美国运动员在兴奋剂检测中也翻车了。[9]

事实上,多年以来国际奥委会已经知道赛中检测并不足以探测和提取残留物,并这样说了,但干净、公平比赛的这一理想形象仍一直被维持着,而直接参与体育比赛的人都知道事实真相。

世界反兴奋剂组织已经建立起来,并拥有行为规范,得到了大多数国家和国际联合会的支持。这个机构一直在努力确保好几个政府许诺的经费能够到位。[10]

* **兴奋剂在中国**

兴奋剂的出现促使中国在1989年宣布了严厉禁止、严格检查、严厉处罚的"反兴奋剂三严方针"。接着,在国内大型比赛中都引进了兴奋剂检测。[11]1990年165名运动员接受了检查,有3人为阳性(占总人数的1.82%)。然而,这些违禁者并没有受到处罚和公开点名。相反,误服中药常被当成借口。

1998年1月中国游泳运动员成为滥用兴奋剂的谴责对象。1998年1月8日在悉尼机场,中国游泳运动员原媛的行李中被发现有一个水杯,其中装有生长荷尔蒙。[12]一周后,在珀斯世界游泳锦标赛期间,另有四名运动员在赛前的药检中呈现阳性。[13]这些事件强化了很久以来的一个怀疑:中国人参与了一个系统化的全国性用药方案。中国体育官员对此进行了迅速反击。

新华社引用当时的国家奥委会副主席袁伟民的话说:"我们不仅要不遗余力地反对兴奋剂,还要抵制少数体育官员用双重标准对我们进行带有偏见的攻击。"尽管情绪激昂地做出快速反应,来自其他国家的不少运动员和官员仍觉得不够,建议将整个中国游泳队从世界锦标赛中开除出去,号召抵制一个月后在中国举行的游泳世界杯赛。

对此感到十分羞辱的中国体育官员发誓要加大对兴奋剂控制的力度。在悉尼奥运会前夕采取了坚决的行动。他们对即将参加奥运会的队员进行血检,将不合格的40名运动员和官员,包括14名田径运动员、4名游泳运动员、2名皮划艇和7名赛艇运动员,从代表团的名单中删除。[14]结果,中国运动员在悉尼奥运会上没有出现一例兴奋剂阳性。2004年雅典奥运会上也是如此。

* **国际奥委会反兴奋剂方针**

参加奥运会的选手受《资格规定》的管理。该规定强调选手必须遵守国际奥委会的医学规定。这个规定禁止使用兴奋剂,列出了可使用药物的清单,建立了禁药和程序的分类清单,让运动员有义务服从医务控制和检查,制定了对违反规定进行制裁的办法。国际奥委会在奥运会前向所有的国际联合会、国家奥林匹克委员会、运动员、教练员和随队医生提供全面的、最新的清单。

表 10-1　国际奥委会列出的违禁物质分类一览表(1994 年 2 月)

药物种类	功　能
刺激物	直接对运动员的神经系统起作用,加速大脑和身体工作。它可以增加反应速度并减缓疲劳。
麻醉止痛剂	止痛药或镇定剂。运动员服用它们以便在痛苦和伤病的情况下仍能比赛。
合成代谢类	包括荷尔蒙睾丸激素这样的物质,使运动员的肌肉增大。
β-受体阻止药	这些药使运动员不颤抖,降低他们的血压,使他们的心律减慢,有镇定的作用。
利尿药	这些药增加运动员的排尿量。因此,它们被按重量分级运动项目、很难把体重降到级别所要求的运动员使用。
缩氨酸荷尔蒙和类似物	这些药帮助身体生长肌肉并影响身高。生长荷尔蒙催发肌肉增长,提高速度和力量。

通过血液注射,实施药理、化学和物理操纵的药物都受限制。酒精、局部麻醉剂和皮质类固醇这些物质在一定程度内是允许的。

不服从医疗控制(药检/尿样)或被发现药物滥用者会被国际奥委会从当时和以后的奥运会中开除出去。如果一个选手是某个队的成员,出现违规时的那场比赛或项目的全队成绩可以被取消。如果违反医务规定,奖牌可以被收回。

国际奥委会医学委员会负责尿样的收集、密封和标号,并把它们交给国际奥委会认可的实验室。国际奥委会有 24 个认可的实验室检测非法物质。

从 1968 到 1992 年,尿样的提取和分析是根据医学规定进行的。然而,在 1994 利勒哈默尔冬奥会上,在国际滑雪联合会的全权控制下,对北欧滑雪项目上进行了血液检测。

在长野冬奥会上,国际奥委会—长野组委会的医学队进行了 700 例兴奋剂控制测试,没有出现阳性案例。在悉尼奥运会期间,国际奥委会—悉尼组委会医学队进行了 2076 例赛中检测,404 例赛外检测和 307

例血液（EPO）检测。国际奥委会发现 11 名运动员兴奋剂违规。[15]

国际奥委会通过医学规定,并要求国际单项联合会在所有的国际比赛中遵守医学规定。2003 年 12 月,国际奥委会执委会做出重要决定要重新测试在盐湖城冬奥会收集到的样本,看是否有新设计出来的药物 THG，这是在征得专家建议的基础上做出的决定,因为专家肯定这么做是合法的和科学的。国际奥委会执委会在 2004 年 2 月决定,盐湖城奥运会的米莱格和黛尼洛娃不合格,他们的奖牌要被收回。国际奥委会还同意把从奥运村开始到奥运会闭幕这段时间看做是赛中测试阶段。[16]

运动员要参加奥运会,就要尊重奥林匹克价值,同意进行药检。在整个奥运会期间,药检是在国际奥委会和它的医学委员会的授权下进行。药检也可以在奥运会前的一个时间段进行。在每个项目比赛后,前四名运动员要与另外两名随机抽取的运动员一起接受检查。

（2）其他违规操作

其他类型的违规操作在奥林匹克家庭中同样存在。前面已经提到的 1998 年盐湖城申奥官员和国际奥委会委员的不道德行为就是最突出的一个例子。某些国际奥委会官员被指控从 2002 年冬奥会盐湖城奥申委接受贿赂,采取从现金、礼物、娱乐、生意照顾、旅游开支、医药费到给其子女的大学学费等不同形式。[17] 1998 年 12 月 11 日,国际奥委会执委会任命了一个特别委员会来调查所有可能的确凿证据。后来,盐湖城组委会和美国奥林匹克委员会发起了调查。国际奥委会调查后的一个结果是,国际奥委会委员投票表决,开除了 6 名委员。在该决定公布之前,受到调查的 4 名委员辞职,1 名去世。另有 10 名委员受到警告。

这一事件导致了对奥林匹克运动的信任危机。为保持和恢复国际奥委会的纯洁形象,国际奥委会不得不采取措施来阻止腐化的泛滥。很快,国际奥委会 2000 改革委员会建立。1999 年 12 月,出台了 50 条改革的一揽子方案,包括从国际奥委会委员的选拔和行为、申奥过程、财务交易的透明度、奥运会的规模和实施到兴奋剂规定等多方面。一个独立的国际奥委会道德委员会也得以成立。

5. 男性统治与男女平等

正如前面提到的,古代奥运会禁止女子参加比赛。已婚女性进入赛场观看比赛也是不被允许。如果她们因此而被抓住,就会被从当地最陡峭的悬崖上扔下去。卡利帕忒拉伪装成一个教练,带她的儿子到奥林匹亚比赛。她看比赛时被抓,但因她的儿子、兄弟和父亲都是奥林匹克冠军,她才被免于惩罚。但这之后就出现了一项法律:所有的教练在进入比赛场前必须脱去衣服。

在这种情况下,女性创造了她们自己的纪念女神赫拉的运动会。赫拉是宙斯的妻子和妹妹。据说,西珀达米亚为了感谢赫拉安排了她和珀罗普斯的幸福婚姻,选择了16名女性,与她们一起开创了运动会,并把她们献给女神赫拉。选择16个女性的想法产生于皮萨暴君达马佛恩对伊利斯人十分残酷的时代。在他死后,皮萨和伊利斯希望在他们之间建立友谊。因此,16个伊利斯城中各选1名选手参赛。后来,这16人受命来管理运动会。

现代奥运会于1896年复兴时,顾拜旦不同意女性参加奥运会。"在我看来,真正的奥运英雄是一个男性。"[18]这样,第一届现代奥运会是彻头彻尾的男子运动会。四年后的巴黎奥运会,女性首次参赛,但只有网球和高尔夫球两项对她们开放。在20世纪早期的社会中,女运动员必须面对许多偏见。当时,一些人担忧她们会失去女性的特点,变得满身肌肉、毫不诱人或不能生育。早期的女运动员必须面对这些偏见。

在1908年的伦敦奥运会上,36名女选手参加了花样滑冰和网球比赛。在这届运动会后,英国奥林匹克协会建议女子游泳、跳水和体操运动员应被允许参加未来的奥运会比赛。结果,瑞典奥组委在1912年的斯德哥尔摩奥运会上为女子加入了两个游泳比赛和一个跳水比赛,在这届奥运会上,澳大利亚的范妮·杜拉克在100米自由泳比赛中获胜,成为第一个女冠军;令人难以忘怀的是,她的时间跟男性胜利者几乎相同。

图 10-3　早期的网球运动

由于对女性开放的比赛项目极少,1919 年第一届女性运动会在巴黎召开,在一天之内,2 万名观众看到了田径场上的 18 项纪录被打破。1921 年第一次"全女性奥运会"在摩纳哥举行,来自 5 个国家的 300 名女性就奥运会上不允许的项目,如田径和篮球进行了竞争。该比赛是如此成功,以至于在 1922 年和 1923 年又举行了两次。1924 年国际奥委会决定允许更多的女性参加奥运会。1926 年第二届女子运动会在瑞典的哥德堡举行,有 10 个国家的运动员参赛。1936 年奥运会为女性设立了 9 个项目,以后女子运动会取消。

然而,女性参与奥林匹克的道路并非一帆风顺。1928 年,好几个女运动员在 800 米跑的终点瘫倒在地。这一现象导致一些人认为该项目对女性而言是危险的,从此它被关在奥运会大门之外直至 1960 年。为了抗议女子奥林匹克项目的稀少,这一年英国女性发起了抵制 1928 年奥运会的行动。这一行动创造了奥运史上的唯一一次女权主义抵抗运动的历史。

女性一个项目接一个项目地逐渐在奥运会上赢得了自己的位置。然而,到1948年伦敦奥运会时只有5个女性项目。在这以后,全世界女性参加体育的人数显著上升。在20世纪70年代,女性参加奥运会的人数增长更迅猛,反映出人们日益认识到体育在促进女性生活上的积极作用。1976年奥运会后,向女性开放的项目数量开始迅速增加。1991年国际奥委会决定任何想要加入奥运会的项目必须包括有女子参与的小项。这样,在奥运会的比赛中,有越来越多的项目对女性敞开了大门。1996年亚特兰大奥运会,有26个大项、97个小项对女性开放,而对男性开放的小项是163项。在2000年悉尼奥运会上,女性参加了28个大项中的25个项目、132个小项的比赛,占小项总数的44%。这些数据在2004年奥运会上继续升高(135个小项)。在雅典奥运会上,女性参加了除棒球(女子是垒球)和拳击以外的所有项目的比赛。在摔跤、击剑和航海项目中还为女性增加了好几个新的小项目。[19]最后,参加奥运会的女运动员比例随着时间的推移不断增长。例如,在亚特兰大(1996年)女性比例是34.2%,在悉尼(2000年)是38.2%,在雅典(2004年)是40.6%。

  女性不仅作为运动员,还作为教练员、裁判员、官员参加奥运会。1981年首次有两名女性当选为国际奥委会委员。女性开始进入国际奥委会的领导层。1994年,《奥林匹克宪章》被修订,加入了需要提升女性参与领导的词句。"通过相应的途径,国际奥委会极力鼓励提升在各级水平上的体育女性,尤其是在国家和国际体育组织的执行机构,严格遵守男女平等的原则。"[20]妇女体育工作组在1995年成立,它由运动员和国际单项体育联合会、国家奥委会和专家组成,给国际奥委会执委就提升女性在体育执行的地位方面应采取的措施提出建议。该工作组还与奥林匹克团结基金会一起举办培训班和研讨会。每四年召开一次世界性的大会,评估在奥林匹克运动中取得的进步,分享经验,确定未来的工作重点。女子工作组在2004年更名为女子体育委员会。

  1995年国际奥委会决定为国家奥委会和国际单项体育联合会制定了一个目标:到2000年12月,所有的决策部门至少有10%的女性,到2005年这一比例应达到20%。

图10-4　21世纪的网球运动

通过持续和共同的努力,在提高女性在领导层的代表率上取得了一定的进步。1996年美国的安妮塔·黛芙冉兹成为国际奥委会的第一个女副主席(1997—2001年)。到2001年,大约有66%的国家奥委会和43%的国际单项联合会实现了女性在决策位置上达到10%的目标。到2003年12月1日,奥运家庭中的32个单项体育联合会(91%)的执行机构中至少有一名女性。瑞典的格尼拉·林德伯格在2004年当选为国际奥委会副主席。同一年,纳瓦尔·埃尔·穆塔瓦科尔成为第一个领导国际奥委会评定委员会工作的女性(负责至2012年奥运会候选程序)。然而,走向女性平等之路并非一帆风顺。至2003年12月1日,35个单项体育联合会中只有20个(57%)实现了10%的目标,只有8个(23%)奥运会的单项联合会在其执行机构有20%以上的女性。[21]

结 论

理想主义是现代奥林匹克主义值得赞赏的一个组成部分,但它常常不得不与现实主义共存。在现代奥林匹克运动的 100 多年历史中,业余主义与职业主义的冲突、慈善与商业主义的冲突、政治和谐与不和谐的冲突、公平竞争与违规操作的冲突、男性统治和性别平等的冲突是奥林匹克历史的主要特征。然而,理想主义依旧存在,奥林匹克运动在降低有关的冲突、坚持全球体育理想主义方面的努力和热情不减,它们应得到称颂。

思考题

1. 职业主义对奥运会产生了有害的影响吗?
2. 未来的商业化会对奥运会产生什么影响?
3. 国际政治会继续妨碍奥林匹克理想主义吗?
4. 你认为兴奋剂现象能根除吗?
5. 你认为女性在奥运会中的未来前景是什么?

注 释

〔1〕《体育运动中的专业主义》,www.athens2004.com。
〔2〕 国际奥委会,《奥林匹克宪章》,1964 年。
〔3〕 David Levinson and Karen Christensen (eds.) (1996), *Encyclopaedia of World Sport: From Ancient Times to the Present*, Oxford: ABC-CLIO Ltd., p. 81.
〔4〕《大不列颠百科全书》,2002 年。
〔5〕 David Levinson and Karen Christensen (eds.) (1996), op. cit., p. 81.
〔6〕《大不列颠百科全书》,http://www.britannica.com/eb/article? eu = 137628
〔7〕 现代体育是在 1865 年最初出现兴奋剂的报道。1879 年以后自行车选手喜欢用乙醚和咖啡因来延迟疲劳症状的出现。20 世纪 30 年代一些自行车选手使用士的宁和其他的刺激物,后来被健美运动员、足球和径赛运动员所采纳。详见 Ellis Cashmore (1996), *Making Sense of Sports* (Second Edition), London and New York: Routledge, p. 150。

[8] The Sports Council,"History of Doping in Modern Sport",Craig Donnellan (ed.) (1995),*Drugs and Violence in Sport: Issues for the Nineties*,No. 26,Cambridge: Independence Educational Publishers, p. 27.

[9] David Powell,"Americans Stand Accused of Doping Conspiracy",*Times Online—Sport*,October 17,2003.

[10] John Goodbody, "Inquiry into Drug Use Created Long-term Positive Effects", *Times Online—Sport*,September 24,2003.

[11] 1989年国家体委颁布了《全国性体育竞赛检查禁用药物的暂行规定》。

[12] 根据有关医疗方面的消息,中国人所携带的兴奋剂、促生长素,足够全队23人在澳大利亚期间所用。运动员原媛被禁赛4年,教练员则被禁赛15年。(Crag Lord, "Caught Red-Handed—Amid Global Cries Of 'I Told You So', China Awaits Its Fate In The Great Doping Scandal",*Sunday Times*,11 January 1998)

[13] 女运动员王璐娜、蔡慧珏、张怡和男运动员王炜的尿样中含有利尿剂氨苯蝶啶成份。该药可用来掩盖违禁药物,使用它可解释成试图操纵药物检测,因此被当做阳性对待。

[14] http://www.guardian.co.uk/print/0,3858,4060177-105268,00.html. 2005年5月21日。

[15] Final Report on the XXVIIth Olympiad, p. 37.

[16] IOC Executive Board Concludes Last Meeting Of The Year, International Olympic Committee Press Release, Friday 05 December 2003.

[17] 详见王晋军:《悉尼2000》,作家出版社,第33—40页。

[18] *Le Sport Suisse*, *31st year*,7 August 1935, p. 1.

[19] "New Record Participation of Women at the Olympic Games", http://www.olympic.org/uk/organisation/commissions/women/full_story_uk.asp?id=1017, August 19,2004.

[20] 《奥林匹克宪章》,第五段,第二条,1994年。

[21] 《奥林匹克运动中的女性》(2004年7月更新),http://multimedia.olympic.org/pdf/en_report_846.pdf.

第十一章
奥林匹克营销:作为商业的奥林匹克运动

本章要点
* 奥林匹克营销的历史、特点和渠道
* 奥林匹克营销的管理
* 营销收入的分配
* 营销(知识)产权的保护
* 营销和过分商业主义

今天的体育没有钱是行不通的。奥运会当然是一种商业,但它还没有变成人可以消费的产品。(萨马兰奇,前国际奥委会主席,1986)

前面的章节一次又一次地提到,奥林匹克运动的目的是要通过鼓励平等的体育参与和机会,追求卓越和国际间的理解及公平竞争来使世界变得更美好。要实现上述使命,需要巨大的资源。因此,奥林匹克营销是十分重要的。作为一个引起媒体关注和全世界都感兴趣的现象,奥运会提供了一个世界上最有效的国际性商业营销的机会。根据中国的零点调查公司在2004年进行的一项调查,79.9%的回答者更倾向于已经赞助了奥运会的公司;75.1%的被调查者会购买或使用带有奥运五环标志的产品。这两项指标在18—25岁的年龄组内分别达到了87.7%和80.1%。[1]在其他国家也见到了类似的情况(见表11-1)。这表明赞助奥运会可有效地提高公司产品的品牌形象,增加对顾客的吸引力,使利润增长。

表 11-1　奥运赞助商品牌调查数据

	总数 (n = 3200)	美国 (n = 1274)	中国 (n = 724)	独联体 (n = 199)	印度 (n = 338)	英国 (n = 193)	德国 (n = 277)	法国 (n = 195)
增加的附加形象	79	78	91	91	94	70	39	64
更加肯定的形象	78	78	92	88	96	68	34	60
更多的注意力和意识	77	77	89	81	97	67	36	53
通过促销获得的购买机会	75	77	90	83	83	69	36	55
想要购买赞助商的产品	66	65	74	80	95	46	28	44

* 资料来源：三星公司（中国）

毫无疑问，奥运五环是世界上最具认可度的符号。作为五环的唯一拥有者，国际奥委会掌控具有赢利潜力的营销标识。奥运营销是一个在全球范围内推广奥运会和增强奥林匹克运动的财务稳定性的活动方案。这种营销与体育营销直接相关，与多国和其他公司的消费产品的营销间接相关。

1. 从历史的视角看奥运营销

奥运营销可追溯到 1896 年第一届现代奥运会，当时一些公司通过在纪念品中加入广告来提供一定的经济支持。其中的一个广告客户就是柯达，它今天作为 TOP 方案的合作伙伴继续支持奥运会（详情见后）。1912 年大约有 10 家瑞典公司购买了"独家权"，主要是拍照和出售斯德哥尔摩奥运会的纪念品。一个公司购买了在场馆内为观众放置体重机的权力。1920 年安特卫普运动会的官方方案充斥着广告。1924 年奥运会允许场地广告——奥运历史上第一次，也是唯一的一次。四年后，国际奥委会规定体育馆、体育场和建筑物不能因招贴画而破坏外形,但允许秩序册中做广告。目前的 TOP 方案合作伙伴之一的可口可乐公司,在 1928 年就开始了与奥运会的长期联系。1932 年的奥组委通过提供免费的商品广告别针来接近商业组织和零售商店。1952 年国际奥委会的一个销售部门出售了多种在奥运会现场做生意的权力。来自 11 个国家的公司捐赠了从给运动员的食品到奖牌获得者的鲜花等具有某种价值的产品,这是国际营销方案的首次尝试。到 1964 年,与奥运会有联系的公司数量增加到 250 家。一个叫做"奥林匹亚"的新的香烟品牌为东京奥组委增加了 100 万美元的收入(香烟类广告后被取消)。1972 年慕尼黑运动会一个私人广告公司首次作为特许经营来使用奥运标识。使用奥运会所拥有的官方徽章的权力被出售,当时有好几类的特许经营和广告合同。该运动会第一次出现了奥运吉祥物"沃尔迪",私人公司获得特许来销售这个形象。[2]

尽管 1976 年蒙特利尔运动会有 628 个赞助商和供应商,官方的赞助方案进一步分为官方赞助商、官方支持商和官方促销商,该方案只为组委会征集到了 700 万美元。当萨马兰奇当选国际奥委会主席后,他认识到如果奥林匹克运动不开发自己独立的财政基础和收入渠道的话,它就难以生存下去。1984 年奥运会标志着成功的公司赞助的开始,它进一步强化了萨马兰奇对奥运营销的看法。1984 年洛杉矶奥组委第一次把赞助分成三种类型:官方赞助商、"官方供应商"和特许经销商。本次奥运会赢利 2.15 亿美元。可以说洛杉矶奥运会是奥运营销的分水岭,尽管营销活动主要针对主办国和美国的公司。在 1984 年以前,没有真正意义上的国际性奥运营销,能从营销活动中挣得一些收入的国家奥委会不到 10 个。在 1984 年奥运会后,奥运营销变成一个全球范围的协同活动,1985 年国际奥委会的奥林匹克合作伙伴方案(TOP 方案)建立。1996 年达成了到 2008 年为止的长期奥运转播和赞助协议[3],它保证未来的奥林匹克运动有稳定的财务收入。通过门票出售、特许经营和转播权的出售以及赞助,从营销中得到的收入自 1980 年以来节节上升(见表 11-2)。

表 11-2　1980—2004 奥运周期中的奥运营销收入变化

	莫斯科/普莱西德湖	洛杉矶/萨拉热窝	汉城/卡尔加里	巴塞罗那/阿伯特维尔	利勒哈默尔/亚特兰大	长野/悉尼	盐湖城/雅典
收入（百万美元）	350	790	1150	1870	2630	3770	4264

资料来源：《奥运营销 1980—2001：史无前例的对体育长达 20 年的支持》

表 11-3　奥运营销收入途径：过去三个奥运周期（单位：百万美元）

途径	1993—1996	1997—2000	2001—2004
转播	1251	1845	2236
TOP 方案	279	579	603
国内赞助	534	655	736
票务	451	625	608
特许经营	115	66	81
总计	2630	3770	4264

资料来源：《奥运营销事实文件，2005》，第 17 页，www.olympic.org

2. 独特性

奥运会是最昂贵的全球文化产品。例如，举办 2004 年雅典奥运会花费了 116 亿美元。[4]作为一个非盈利性组织，国际奥委会与两个主要的市场有联系：给该组织提供现金或服务的贡献者（用奥运术语说是合作伙伴）和它的顾客，即奥运大家庭成员，包括国家奥委会、国际单项体育联合会、组委会、运动员。国际奥委会营销方案必须兼顾奥林匹克运动的贡献者和它的顾客。国际奥委会与商业或生意企业打交道，以达到双赢的目的。国际奥委会的顾客既是金钱和服务的接受者，又是他们的产品——奥运会——的生产者和消费者。这一独特性使得奥运营销充满挑战，奥运家庭中就财富分配和国际奥委会构成问题时常出现的争吵就反映了这一特点。[5]

不像一般的生意，国际奥委会对奥运会的生产、销售和营销费用不负什么责任。运动员的准备主要由他们的俱乐部、国家协会和政府负责。主办奥运会则主要是主办城市和国家的任务(尽管很大一部分经费是由国际奥委会通过赞助和电视转播权的出让来解决的)。

3. 奥林匹克营销收入的主要来源

总的说来,奥运收入来自电视转播权、赞助、票务、特许经营和纪念币/邮票。下图体现了 2001—2004 年间不同财务渠道对奥运营销收入的贡献率。在过去 20 年中,随着新的财务渠道的开拓,电视转播权收入的贡献率下降到 50% 左右。

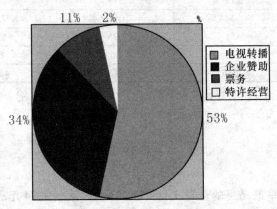

图 11-1 2001-2004 年奥运营销收入的组成示意图

(1) 赞助

赞助是奥运财务的第二大来源。赞助大约占总营销收入的 30%—40%。赞助的目的是确保有一个独立的财务稳定性,对奥运大家庭给予持续性的支持,并平等地分配收入。所有的赞助方案是由国际奥委会来协调,并在三个水平上来操作:

* 国际水平,被称做 TOP(奥林匹克合作伙伴)的全世界方案;
* 举办国,组委会的地方方案;
* 国家水平,国家奥委会方案。

表 11-4　1976 到 2000 年通过奥运会做广告的企业数量

	1976 蒙特利尔	1980 莫斯科	1984 洛杉矶	1988 汉城	1992 巴塞罗那	1996 亚特兰大	2000 悉尼
企业数	742	325	98	80	107	119	109

资料来源:《奥运营销事实文件（1976—2001）》

表 11-5　组委会从赞助奥运会中得到的收入（非特许经营者）（百万美元）

	1976 蒙特利尔	1980 莫斯科	1984 洛杉矶	1988 汉城	1992 巴塞罗那	1996 亚特兰大	2000 悉尼
收入	40	80	219	215	550	588	588

资料来源:《奥运营销事实文件（1976—2001）》

赞助不仅为奥林匹克运动提供重要的财务支持,还提供产品、技术支持和员工培训等方面的服务。此外,通过赞助商的促销活动,对奥林匹克运动的公共意识和支持度可得到提高。

*奥林匹克合作伙伴方案

为使奥林匹克运动的收入基数多样化,获得更多的赞助,国际奥委会在 1985 年创建了奥林匹克合作伙伴（TOP）方案。TOP 的合作伙伴公司是由能够为奥运会的举办提供直接的资助、赞助服务或专门技术的跨国公司组成。此外,这些合作伙伴以提供现金和某些价值的支持来资助国家奥委会和参加奥运会的奥运队伍。作为对他们财务奉献的回报,TOP 合作伙伴拥有在世界范围内就协议规定的某类产品,如软饮料、电视和收音、办公设备等进行独家经营的保证。这就是说他们的竞争对手在世界的任何一个地方都不能将自己与奥运队伍或奥运会联系起来。除了排他性以外,TOP 合作伙伴还有机会在他们的产品上使用奥运标识和奥运胶片,在奥运会上受到款待的机会,优先获得转播广告、现场特许经营、奥运会期间销售或展示产品的机会。因此,成为 TOP 赞助方案的一部分可以提高品牌形象。韩国的三星公司就是一个很好的例子。20 世纪 80 年代早期,三星是一个很不起眼的地方企业。1988 年夏季奥运会在汉城举行时它加入了 TOP 方案。这一行动将三星转变成了一个全球性品牌。2001 年三星品牌的价值达 64 亿美元,全球排名第 43 名,一年后上升到 34 名,品牌价值达 83 亿美元。由于赞助奥运会可以带来显而易见的好处,为了成为 TOP 合作伙伴,公司之间的竞争十分激烈。

每一期TOP都有一个给定的数字,如TOPI(1985—1988),TOPII(1989—1992)等。加入TOPIV(2005—2008)方案的国际公司有12个(包括可口可乐、源讯、通用电气、恒康公司、柯达、联想、麦当劳、松下、三星、欧米加手表、强生和维萨卡等)。联想是第一个加入TOP方案的中国公司。[6]

自1985年引入TOP方案后,每一期的TOP合作伙伴数固定在10个左右,但加入费却随时间的推移而稳步上涨。结果,TOP方案给国际奥委会的财务稳定起到了很好的作用(表11-6)。

表11-6 不同时期TOP合作伙伴的数量和贡献

	TOP I (1985—1988)	TOP II (1989—1992)	TOP III (1993—1996)	TOP VI (1997—2000)	TOP V (2001—2004)	TOP IV (2005—2008)
TOP合作伙伴的数量	9	12	10	11	10	11
总贡献(百万美元)	96	172	279	579	663	866

资料来源:《奥运营销事实文件》,2005。

奥运赞助还可在国家一级进行。国家级赞助方案由各国的国家奥委会和奥组委来运作,但国家级的赞助商必须与国际赞助商的产品类型不同。

表11-7 国内赞助收入(百万美元)

	亚特兰大 1996	长野 1998	悉尼 2000	盐湖城 2002	雅典 2004
数量	111	26	93	53	38
赞助额	426	163	492	494	242

* **奥林匹克供应商方案**

奥林匹克供应商方案是另一种类型的商业关系。它比TOP赞助的经营权和机会要少。供应商的经营权受到的限制要多些,通常不包括对奥运会举办的直接资助。供应商的设定是为了协助国际奥委会对奥林匹克运动的管理和对运动员的资助。

* 奥林匹克特许经营方案

国际奥委会特许经营方案是国际奥委会、国家奥委会或奥组委和商业企业之间就商品使用奥运会徽章、吉祥物达成的一种协议,它通常包括纪念性的东西,如T恤衫、别针或棒球帽。作为回报,这些公司支付10%—15%的产权费。特许经营方案是在品牌的驱动下,在有控制的商业环境中来推广奥林匹克形象和传达主办国的文化。下表的数据展示了最近一些特许经营方案的情况以及由它所带来的并用于夏季和冬季奥运会的收入。

表11-8 奥运会特许经营(百万美元)

奥运会	1988 汉城	1992 巴塞罗那	1996 亚特兰大	2000 悉尼	2004 雅典
特许经营商数	62	61	125	100	23
给奥组委带来的收入	18.8	17.2	91	52	56

资料来源:1988至2005年之间的《奥林匹克营销事实文件》

奥运特许经营方案是在保持高商业标准以提高奥运形象、给公众提供高质量物品的同时,创造性地主动管理奥运品牌,作为能唤起消费者消费欲望的奥运会的视觉窗口。

这些特许经营方案包括:奥组委、国家奥委会和国际奥委会特许的产品。这些产品印有奥运会或奥运队伍的徽章和吉祥物,是专门设计用于纪念奥运会和奥运队伍的。在奥林匹克运动中有三个等级的特许经营。

(2) 奥运票务

奥运票务大概是所有活动中最复杂的票务实践。国际奥委会希望奥组委向所有的会员国提供一个可买到、透明和公平的票务分配。同时,奥组委又必须通过票务来获得预期的收入。从下面两表中可见,奥组委的票务及分配是不断变化的。

表 11-9　1976 到 2008 年奥运会门票出售比较(百万张)

		1976	1980	1984	1988	1992	1996	2000	2004	2008＊
门票	总数	5	6.1	6.9	4.4	3.9	11	7.6	5.3	9
	出售	3.2	5.3	5.7	3.3	3.021	8.318	6.7	3.8	7
	所占百分比	74	90	80.6	75	80	82.3	88	72	77
收入(百万美元)		56.56	6.1	156	36	79	425	551	228	166.4

＊ 北京奥申委的估计值(2000)

资料来源：Preuss（2002）；"2005 Marketing Fact File"；Bidding Committee Beijing (2000)

上表体现出了票务的财政潜力。由于以相对较高的票价出售了大量的门票，1984 年洛杉矶、1996 年亚特兰大和 2000 年悉尼这三届奥运会取得了很高的收入。[7]雅典 2004 的平均票价要比悉尼的票价低 34%，因此 2004 年奥运会的票务收入比 2000 年奥运会少。

(3) 奥林匹克纪念币

胡奥特写道："今天一个硬币的价值是由它表面的价值所决定，这个表面价值几乎与它的内在价值毫无关系。内在和表面价值的差异，正如货币铸造税所指，是所有国家政府的一个非常重要的收入来源。"[8]纪念币也是国际奥委会的一个重要的收入来源。

第一个使用奥运纪念币来纪念现代奥运会的政府是 1951 年的赫尔辛基政府(500 马克银币)。估计在两年的时间内，它发行了 60.5 万枚纪念币，给芬兰铸造厂带来了 100 万美元的利润，其中一部分被用来支付举办奥运会的费用。

自 1951 年这一做法取得成功以后，全球卖出了 3.5 亿枚奥运纪念币，为政府和奥运家庭集资了 11 亿多美元。然而，这一收入的最高峰出现在 1972 年的慕尼黑奥运会，其收入支付了奥运会的大部分花销。1984 年奥运会来自奥运纪念币的收入只少于电视转播权费收入，为组委会和美国奥委会带来了 7350 万美元。1992 年国际奥委会引入了奥林匹克纪念币方案以庆祝国际奥委会成立百周年和第一届现代奥运会举办一百周年。这个国际纪念币方案是由国际奥委会来管理，使用五个国家造币厂的资源，它于 1996 年 12 月结束。世界范围内销售了 9

万枚金币、50万枚银币,获得4800万美元的收入,是至今为止最为成功的奥林匹克纪念币方案。[9]

(4) 奥林匹克邮票

来自奥林匹克邮票的收入是相当可观的。1896年,一个希腊集邮者建议发行纪念性的奥林匹克邮票来支持奥运场馆的建设。1912年,大约10个瑞典公司购买了独家拍照权和出售奥运会纪念品的权力。1928年阿姆斯特丹奥组委用集邮方案的收入支付了奥运开支的1.5%。葡萄牙发行了邮票来资助它的奥运队伍去参加阿姆斯特丹运动会,在三天中要求人们都购买邮票。1992年有137个国家发行了123万张拥有奥林匹克五环的邮票系列。1994年发行了4本邮票纪念奥林匹克运动百周年。1996年150多个国家共发行了1500万张奥林匹克邮票。1998年为纪念长野冬奥会发行了3本奥林匹克邮票。2000年发行了5本纪念奥运会的邮票,生产了4800多万张邮票和首日封。在奥运会期间卖出了1000多万张奥林匹克邮票。这是第一次,主办国在比赛的第二天发行纪念本国每一个金牌获得者的邮票。[10]

4. 奥林匹克营销的管理

在过去的20年内,奥林匹克营销做到了确保奥运会有健康、稳定的财务状况。支撑这份成功的管理结构如下所示。

(1) 管理结构

国际奥委会及其执委会和1989年建立的专门的营销部门负责管理奥运营销的总方向和各种方案。他们的工作得到以下专门机构的协助:

* 顶点管理公司(协调TOP方案的管理,作为国家奥委会的联络人);
* 奥林匹克电视档案局(协调奥运胶片、历史性的活动形象档案,并对其拥有独家所有权,专门的广播节目是由世界最大的体育电视制

造商 TWI 来管理);

* 奥林匹克照片档案局(管理奥林匹克运动的历史性照片档案,开发专门的摄影工程。它是由世界最大的照片图书馆 Allsport 来管理);
* 赞助研究国际(执行国际奥委会的全球市场调研工作);
* 体育营销调查公司(执行国际奥委会的转播数据分析)。

在追求"公平竞争"中,为确保商业和媒体伙伴的支持,1997年奥林匹克营销规则确立,体育产业的领头人如耐克、阿迪达斯、锐步、美津浓和爱世克斯签订了一项协议,同意他们的广告将与奥林匹克理想保持一致。另外,每一个与国际奥委会签约的转播者都有义务转播奥运会,并在全年365天中都要推动奥林匹克运动。

(2) 营销收入的分配

国际奥委会把约92%的奥运营销收入分配给奥林匹克运动中的所有组织,以支持奥运会的主办,推动全世界的体育发展。国际奥委会截留8%的奥运营销收入,用于奥林匹克运动的管理和运作费用。

表 11-10　奥运营销收入对国家奥委会的贡献(百万美元)

奥运四年周期	转播收入	TOP方案收入*	总收入对国家奥委会的贡献
阿尔贝尔特维拉/巴塞罗那 1989—1992	51.6	35	86.6
利勒哈默尔/亚特兰大 1993—1996	80.9	57	137.9
长野/悉尼 1997—2000	118.7	93	211.7
盐湖城/雅典 2001—2004	209.5	109	318.5

*上面表现的数据不包括对举办国国家奥委会的贡献。

表 11-11 奥运营销收入对国际单项体育联合会的贡献(百万美元)

	夏季奥运会				冬季奥运会			
	1992	1996	2000	2004	1992	1994	1998	2002
给国际单项体育联合会	37.6	86.6	190		17	20.3	49.4	85.8

表 11-12 奥运营销收入对奥组委的贡献(百万美元)

	夏季/冬季奥运会	
TOP 方案	50%	
转播	2004 年前 60%	2004 年后 49%

(3) 知识产权保护

正如前面已阐明的,环环相扣的五环和其他的奥运象征物是极有价值的知识产权。事实上,它们是奥运营销方案的基石,对开发收入是十分重要的。在过去四年中,国际奥委会使用那些与推广品牌相一致的策略和实践来提高和保护这些奥运财产的价值。例如,在澳大利亚,有两个详细和严格的条例:《奥林匹克勋章保护条例》(1987)和《悉尼奥运会(标记和形象)保护条例》(1996)。类似地,在英国有《奥林匹克象征(保护)条例》(1995)。用悉尼组委会营销主任约翰·摩尔的话来说:"奥运品牌是丰富和复杂的人类努力、体育和多元文化主义的现实综合体。"在确保持续增长上,它有一定的发展和调整空间,它的潜力远未耗竭。

(4) 过分商业化的挑战

随着赞助商作用的增加,国际奥委会面临着避免奥运会过于商业化的巨大挑战,尽管奥运会是唯一的在体育场馆内和运动员身上不让做广告的大型体育赛事。一直以来有人担心营销作为一种财务来源被过分强调了,其结果将是奥运会过分商业化的危险。悉尼奥运会期间所调查的一些数据(样本人数 1973 名)表明 53.4%的人把商业化看成是未来 20 年对奥运会的威胁。对德国和奥地利 518 名体育专业的大学生的调查也反映出了同样的担心(62.2%)。在另一项调查中,66%的德国旅游者(人数=212)和72.3%的体育专业学生(人数=628)意识到了这一威胁。[11]为了保护奥林匹克运动的形象,国际奥委会仍坚持场地没有广告这一做法,要求奥运会电视转播者要"干净"地转播,并细致地控制主要赞助企业的数量。但对未来而言,这是否足够了呢?

结　论

奥运营销对于确保奥林匹克运动未来的全球健康发展是极为重要的。奥运营销并非今日才有,但国际范围的奥运营销在1984年前并没出现。在1985年TOP方案推出以后,奥运营销变成了一个全球协同一致的活动。奥运收入主要来自电视转播权、票务、特许经营和硬币/邮票。在过去的20年,通过各种奥运营销手段确保了奥运会适宜的财务稳定状况。为促进奥运大家庭成员奥组委、国际单项体育联合会、国家奥委会的利益,国际奥委会在不断地建立和调整分配其收入的政策。但是,怎样不使奥运会过度商业化将是未来奥运营销面临的一个挑战。

思考题

1. 奥运营销有什么独特的特征?
2. 你认为限制进入TOP方案的公司数量是必要的吗?如果是,请给出你的理由。
3. 除了TOP方案以外,北京是否应吸引更多的赞助商?

注　释

〔1〕《体育营销是提升企业的品牌知名度与品牌形象的》,《中华工商时报》,2004年12月10日。

〔2〕国际奥委会,《2004年奥林匹克营销事实文件》,www.olympic.org。

〔3〕《1980—2001年奥林匹克营销:二十年对体育运动的史无前例的支持》,《奥林匹克营销通讯》,第19期,2001年7月。

〔4〕《雅典奥运会:历史上最昂贵的奥运会》,http://english.people.com.cn;2004年11月14日。

〔5〕 Girginov Vassil(2005),*The Olympic Games Explained*,London:Routledge.

〔6〕 联想集团是中国最大的计算机制造商。自1997年以来,该集团所拥有的PC机是中国和亚太地区(除日本外)最畅销的品牌。联想集团积极支持体育运动,曾在1999年赞助中国女子足球队,并为北京成功申办2008年奥运会提供资助。

〔7〕 Holger Preuss (2005), "Economic Dimension Of The Olympic Games", Centre d'Estudis Olímpics i de l'Esport(UAB), *International Chair in Olympism.*

〔8〕 Huot, R., *Letter*, June 20, 1997.

〔9〕 国际奥委会,《2005年奥林匹克营销事实档案》,www.olympic,org。

〔10〕 佚名,《2000年悉尼奥运会纪念邮票》,Coll.org.cn,2006年12月6日。

〔11〕 Preuss, H. (2001), "The Economic and Social Impact of the Sydney Olympic Games", in IOC, *Proceedings of the 41st Session of the International Olympic Academy*, Lausanne, pp. 94-109.

# 第三部分

中国与奥运会

第十二章
奥运会和中国:历史进程

本章要点
* 20世纪、21世纪中国参与奥林匹克运动的历程
* 中国的奥林匹克梦想、战略和成绩

中国在全世界推广奥林匹克运动上起着越来越重要的作用,这体现在其出色的体育成就上,如2004年奥运会金牌榜名列第二,越来越多的中国人在国际奥委会所属委员会任职以及北京成功地获得2008年奥运会的举办权等方面。所有这一切是中国人八十多年不懈地努力、争取世界认可的结果。这个过程充满了斗争、挑战,甚至是冲突。因此,有必要用一章来介绍奥林匹克运动在中国的历史进程,它可以揭示出国际政治和国家政治、体育方针和国家地位之间的复杂关系。

1. 建立关系

当现代奥运会在1896年诞生时,中国正处在因鸦片战争而导致的西方侵略和半殖民统治的苦海之中。鸦片战争使中国从一个封建统治、中央政治集权、地方经济自治的农业社会转变成了一个半封建、半殖民地社会。尽管国际奥委会给中国发出了邀请,但没落的清政府根本没有时间或精力来考虑奥运会。很显然,国家存亡先于体育发展。1922年,曾任外交高官的体育领导人王正廷[1]当选为国际奥委会委员,中国与奥林匹克运动的正式关系建立起来。

受西方侵略的羞辱,中国人决心实现民族复兴。洋务运动(1860—1890)和戊戌变法运动(1896)在全国发起。在众多的改革措施中有一项就是教育改革。西方模式的学校相继成立,包括体操、击剑、拳击、足球、田径、游泳、滑冰等内容的现代体育引入学校课程。[2]到20世纪20年代,体育已成为多数大、中、小学的一门必修课程,专门的体育学校和学院也陆续建立起来。此外,在20世纪初出现了地区性和全国性的现代体育比赛。省运动会和全国运动会从1910年起开始举行。另外,从1872年起,中国选派学生到英国、法国、德国、美国、日本学习。所有这些为中国进入奥运会铺平了道路。

1924年在法国巴黎奥运会上,中国有3名网球选手参加了表演赛。1928年在阿姆斯特丹奥运会上,中国国民政府派教育部官员宋如海[3]先生作为观察员出席。三年后,国际奥委会正式接纳了于1924年成立的中华全国体育协进会为其会员。1932年洛杉矶奥运会上,在由5人组成的中国代表团中,只有刘长春一名运动员,他参加了田径比赛。刘长春的参赛不仅仅是一个体育事件,更是一个政治事件——阻止了由日本侵略者在中国东北设立的傀儡国伪满洲国派代表团参加奥运会的企图。

随着现代体育在大、中、小学的不断发展,选派更多的运动员参加奥运会成为可能。1936年,在日本侵华战争爆发前夕,一个由69名运动员和34名官员组成的代表团参加了柏林奥运会。中国选手参加了足球、篮球、拳击、举重、田径、游泳、自行车的比赛及武术表演。但是,他们的成绩均远远落后于西方国家。

内战(1927—1937、1945—1949)和抗日战争(1937—1945)造成的混乱状况使中国人几乎不可能全力以赴地从事体育、参加奥运会。[4]1948年伦敦奥运会召开时,中国正陷在内战的炮火之中,但还是选派了33名运动员参加篮球、足球、田径、游泳和自行车的比赛。他们的成绩不尽人意是意料之中的事情,但国民政府不支付代表团回家的路费则令人难以置信。代表团不得不自筹经费,在经历了数月的艰辛之后,他们最终得以回国。

2. 中断关系(1949—1979)

1949年中华人民共和国的成立标志着中国历史上一个新纪元的到来。赢得国际认可和尊重、保持主权和领土完整是新政府的首要问题和迫切任务。1952年赫尔辛基奥运会被认为是新中国通过体育走向世界的一个机会。尽管国民党统治的台湾也被邀请参加该运动会(在最后一刻撤出奥运会),新中国还是派了41人的代表团奔赴芬兰首都,代表团中有24名男子篮球和足球队员、2名女游泳选手。然而,由于多数参赛选手到达芬兰太晚,只有游泳运动员吴传玉一人参加了比赛。而中国运动员晚到的原因在于,国际奥委会对"两个中国"的问题争执不下,很晚才给中国发出参赛的邀请。[5]在以后的28年内吴传玉是中华人民共和国唯一的一名奥运选手。[6]

中国人迫切希望在第十六届奥运会展示社会主义的优越性。为准备这届奥运会,中国在1956年10月举办了7个项目的选拔赛,来自27个省、市、自治区的1400多名运动员参加了比赛。92名运动员获得了参加在墨尔本举行的第16届奥运会的资格。然而,在布伦戴奇领导下的国际奥委会同时承认"北京和台湾的两个奥委会",违背了《奥林匹克宪章》规定的一个国家只能有一个国家奥委会的原则,中国对此提出抗议并抵制了第16届奥运会。[7]1958年,中国正式退出国际奥委会和另外8个国际组织。[8]这一行动体现了中国竞技体育受国家政治影响的程度。

尽管中国离开国际奥委会20多年,中国人要赢得奥运胜利的理想并未消失。竞技体育在全国稳定地开展。为激励广大教练员和运动员的训练热情,更为重要的是向世界展示中国体育的进步,全国运动会在1959年发起。

3. 关系正常化(1979—1992)

1979年是中国奥林匹克运动的一个重要转折点。在1972年当选主席的基拉宁的领导下,国际奥委会于1979年11月最终承认中国奥林匹克委员会的合法地位。[9]从此以后,中华人民共和国的国旗和国歌将在所有的仪式中使用;台湾奥委会的名称改为"中国台北奥林匹克委员会",台湾以前使用的旗、歌和会徽将不再使用。这种独特的"奥林匹克折衷方式"使得来自中国台湾和大陆的运动员可同时参加奥运会。

中国开始准备参加1980年的冬季和夏季奥运会。中国首次选派运动员和教练员到德国、美国和前苏联训练数月。26名男女运动员首次参加了1980年在普莱西德湖举行的冬奥会。然而,政治和体育仍紧密地纠缠在一起。为反对苏联入侵阿富汗,中国加入了美国和其他西方国家抵制莫斯科夏季奥运会的行动。遗憾的是,这一抵制残酷地剥夺了许多中国运动员一生中唯一一次参加奥运会的机会,也使中国人在这个最大的国际体育赛事上亮相的时间推迟了四年。

1984年构成了中国奥林匹克历史的分界点。中国第一次派出包括225名运动员在内的一个大型代表团参加奥运会。中国人不仅打破了奥运奖牌"零"的记录,还赢得了15枚金牌。这一出色成绩极大地改变了中国人在世界上的形象,激励着各行各业奋发图强,使中华民族尽早实现现代化。结果,一种强烈的爱国主义情感在海内外中国人心中被激发起来。[10]自1984年以后,中国持续稳定、全面地参与到奥林

图12-1　中国女排

图 12-2　1984 年获 6 块奖牌的李宁

匹克运动之中。

　　1985 年中国提出了奥运战略,该战略后来变成了中国竞技体育发展的蓝图。根据奥运战略,体育工作的重点转移到奥运项目上,即所有可能的资源都集中到少数有可能在奥运会上摘取奖牌的重点项目上。然而,走向世界体育强国的道路崎岖不平。在 1984 年奥运会辉煌成绩的鼓舞下,中国人对 1988 年汉城奥运会信心百倍。国家体委保守的目标是取得 8 到 10 枚金牌,进入奥运会前六名国家。[11]但大众的期望是中国摘取 15 到 20 枚金牌,进入前四名行列。[12]在这样的背景下,一个由 445 人组成的大型代表团,包括 298 名运动员(女性占 46%),被派往韩国。不幸的是,结果让人十分失望:中国运动员只赢得了 5 枚金

图 12-3　1992 年张山获金牌
在本届奥运会上她打败了男选手并创造了世界纪录

牌,排名第 11 位,甚至排在韩国之后。[13]对大多数中国人而言,这无疑是一个惨败——真可谓"兵败汉城"。[14]然而,这一失败并没有终止以奥运为导向的方针政策。相反,它进一步坚定了对奥运战略的追求。

1990 年北京成功地举办了亚运会。中国运动员在亚运会上获得了大量的奖牌,一扫 1988 年失败的阴影。亚运会后,中国的注意力很快转向了即将到来的巴塞罗那奥运会。1991 年,国家体委将田径、游泳和体操等 16 个项目确定为奥运会重点项目。这些项目从预算到训练安排等各个方面都享受优厚的待遇。[15]奥运成绩始终是国家体育机构的关注点。因此,为了保证奥运会的成绩,早在 90 年代国家体委就调整了有关全运会的政策。首先,全运会的时间由奥运会前一年改为奥运会后一年。这样,七运会由 1991 年延期至 1993 年。为了进一步激发各地对奥运会的热情,1991 年国家体委宣布,1992 年奥运会的成绩将记入 1993 年全运会的总分计算中。[16]这些政策的变化立见成效:在 1992 年巴塞罗那奥运会中,中国赢得了 16 枚金牌,在奖牌排行榜上名列第四。

除了参加奥运会外,中国人还通过在国际奥委会不同的委员会和所属的组织中任职参与到奥林匹克运动的管理之中。例如,1981 年何振梁[17]成为国际奥委会委员,1985 年他进入国际奥委会执委会,1989 年成为国际奥委会的副主席。担任国际羽毛球协会主席的吕圣荣[18]在 1992 年当选国际奥委会委员。在各种国际体育组织中还可见到更多的中国面孔。

4. 举办奥运会:雄心(1993—2001)

举办大型国际体育赛事的能力已经成为政治稳定和经济繁荣的象征。中国通过体育实现了政治宣言。北京亚运会的巨大成功使中国人对自己举办大型国际赛事能力的信心倍增。在亚运会的闭幕式上,看台上出现了一个巨大横幅,写着"亚运成功盼奥运"。1991 年 3 月 18 日,北京宣布 2000 奥运会申办委员会成立。12 月 4 日,北京在洛桑正式向国际奥委会主席萨马兰奇递交了申请书。

中国申办奥运会的想法可追溯到 1908 年。当时,《天津青年》杂志提出了这样几个问题:中国何时派运动员参加奥运会?中国运动员何时获得奥运奖牌或金牌?中国何时举办奥运会?事实上,早在 1945 年中国就打算申请举办 1952 年的第 15 届奥运会。[19]中国运动员在 1992 年巴塞罗那奥运会上的成功(16 枚金牌,奖牌总数位于第四)更是激发了北京申奥的热情。为配合奥运会的申办,1991 年到 1993 年间北京组织了各种与体育相关的活动。在"争办2000年奥运会"的主题下,北京把1992年6月命名为"体育月"。3万多人参与到123项活动之中,包括奥运知识竞赛和马拉松跑。同一个月中,申办口号:"开放的中国盼奥运"在人民日报刊出。此外,北京的基础设施得到了极大的改善。当时北京已经有举办奥运会所需的76%的体育场馆。1993年初,北京向国际奥委会递交了候选城市文件。1993年6月20日,国家主席江泽民给国际奥委会委员写信,再次表示中国政府对北京申办2000年奥运会的支持。应该指出的是,北京首次申办就赢得了大多数市民的支持(98.7%)。北京申办2000年奥运会激起了人们对奥林匹克运动的兴趣,有助于在全国范围内推广奥林匹克运动。在20世纪90年代早期,奥运研究成为体育院系的一个新兴学科,奥运研究中心在大学中建立。此外,各种出版物相继出现,从奥林匹克百科全书、奥运大众读物、小学生奥运故事、中学生奥运知识到大学生奥林匹克运动教材都纷纷涌现。[20]

尽管北京为申奥付出了很大的努力,投入了大量的人、财、物,不幸的是北京以两票之差惜败悉尼(澳大利亚)。[21]当这一消息在电视上播出后,全国陷入一片沉寂之中。然而,这一挫败并没有折断中国的奥林匹克梦想,反而增强了中国要通过出色的运动成绩来成为奥运强国的决心。为了减少国家和地方之间的冲突,国家体委在1993年规定,只有奥运会项目和中国的传统项目武术可以加入1997年的全运会。这一做法反映出国家在确保奥运胜利方面的决心。

以奥运为导向的国家政策还带来了全国各省市运动队的重组。非奥运项目的运动队明显减少。至1995年,非奥运项目的运动员只占全体运动员的7.34%。另外,比个人项目投资多、又没有取得奖牌潜力的团体项目,在大部分省市中已经被撤销。

为确保1996年亚特兰大奥运会的胜利,与奥运相关的体育设施、营养和研究的专项经费到达了6500万元(按当年比价,约781.79万美元)。有200多个研究员参与了56个奥运课题的研究。[22]此外,在1994到1996年间,中国集中了960名来自全国的运动员来备战这一全球性赛事,比实际参赛人数多出两倍多。[23]这无疑是一个耗资巨大的方案。尽管对1996年奥运会投入的具体数字不得而知,但有资料报道其费用比四年前的奥运会翻了一番。这些精心的努力在1996年奥运会上结出了可喜的成果——中国在金牌和奖牌总数上保持了第四的位置。在20世纪最后十年中国巩固了奥运排行第四的位置。

1992年市场经济得到鼓励之后,在对外开放的同时,国内经济和其他改革过程加速。在向市场经济快速转化的时刻,经济、政治、文化都在不断变化。到90年代中期,中国提前实现了到2000年国民生产总值翻两番的最初目标。人民的生活水平显著提高。作为首都的北京也表现出了经济增长的巨大潜力,1999年国内生产总值上升到2016亿元(240亿美元),相当于人均国内生产总值16800元(2000多美元)。1990年,北京的国内生产总值只有469.8亿元(54亿美元)。[24]

随着国民力量的增长,北京在1998年11月再次发起了申办奥运会的运动。"新北京、新奥运"的口号意味着北京在社会和经济改革的过程中发生了巨大的变化。值得注意的是,北京申奥的徽章是一个称作"中国结"的传统手工艺品;它看起来像一个在打太极的人,有着与奥运五环相同的颜色。这个优美、和谐和动态的徽章设计象征了全世界人民的团结、合作、交流和发展。

为了确保申奥成功,1998年到2001年间组织了一系列精心计划的活动。例如,奥运冠军刘璇、电影明星巩利、成龙等被任命为北京奥运的形象大使,来争取国际奥委会的投票;大约1100个来自不同领域的非政府群体,从高科技、商业、建筑、体育、教育、卫生到环境等,在给国际奥委会主席萨马兰奇的信上签名,支持北京申办奥运会。[25]1999年北京为环保工程投入了59.7亿元(合7.46亿美元)。盖洛普公司2000年11月在北京进行了一个民意调查,结果表明:94.9%的北京市民完全支持北京申办2008年奥运会,62.4%的人相信北京会赢得举办权。[26]

2001年,申奥活动不断升温。仅2月份,在一条高速公路上就挂出了一个长达1260米的彩色申奥广告牌;首辆申奥公交车开始在长安街上行使;澳大利亚奥运画家查尔斯·比利奇向北京奥申委员会呈送了一幅题为"北京千年城市景观"的画作,以表示他个人的支持;《北京2008》专刊杂志在北京到旧金山的CA985航班上供旅客阅读;百年奥运集邮展和中国体育展在中华世纪坛举行;大众奥林匹克读物和《奥林匹克宪章》中文版出版。北京体育总会下属的92个体育协会的1万名人士在天安门广场签名、骑车行进,表达他们对申奥的支持。[27]一句话,各行各业的人士多多少少都参与到这个申奥运动之中。下面是申奥过程的主要事件。

表12-1 北京申办2008年奥运会的主要事件

日期	事件
1998.11.25	北京宣布申办2008年奥运会。
1999.6.9	北京2008奥运会申办委员会在京成立。刘淇市长担任主席,中国奥委会主席袁伟民担任执行主席。
2000.1.2	北京2008奥运会申办委员会的标识、口号(新北京、新奥运)和网站正式亮相。
2000.8.28—29	洛桑——北京、伊斯坦布尔、大阪、巴黎和多伦多被国际奥委会执委会接受为候选城市(开罗、塞维利亚、吉隆坡、曼谷和哈瓦那被排除)。
2000.9.9	国家主席江泽民给国际奥委会主席萨马兰奇写信,表示中国政府对北京申奥的支持。
2000.12.13	洛桑——每个候选城市向国际奥委会执委会做10分钟陈述。
2001.1.17	候选城市文件递交国际奥委会。
2001.2.20—25	国际奥委会评估委员会访问北京,检查北京举办奥运会的能力
2001.5.15	国际奥委会评估委员向执委会递交报告。北京的申办被称赞为"极好的"。该报告说北京将举办一届极好的奥运会。国际奥委会执委会指定的候选城市递交到国际奥委会年会进行选举。
2001.7.13	国际奥委会第112届年会,莫斯科——选举2008年的第29届奥运会举办城市

当前国际奥委会主席萨马兰奇在2001年7月13日宣布北京击败大阪、巴黎、多伦多和伊斯坦布尔[28],赢得2008年第二十九届奥运会举办权的时候,北京及整个中国顿时沸腾了。成千上万的市民涌入市中心,加入到民族自豪的庆典活动之中。国家主席江泽民突然出现在现场,向兴奋的人群致以"最热烈的祝贺"。

中国成功地获得2008年奥运会举办权正好与中国进入世界贸易组织同步。这两个事件将在中国现代化过程中留下它们的印迹。这将在下一章中论述。

图 12-4 人们欢呼申奥胜利

结 论

当现代奥运会在 19 世纪末复活之时,中国正处在西方侵略和半殖民地的痛苦之中。很显然,清政府没有时间和精力去考虑奥运会,尽管一开始它就接到了国际奥委会的邀请。以后几十年的内战和抗日战争的混乱状态使得中国运动员很难(如果不是不可能的话)去参加奥运会。1949 年中华人民共和国的建立,彻底改变了这一景象。然而,这个新政府面对着复杂的政治局势,它影响了中国在世界体育中的位置。为抗议国际奥委会接纳"两个中国"的做法,中国在 1958 年脱离与国际奥委会的关系,这一做法无疑推迟了中国人在国际体育界亮相至少 20 年。直到 1979 年,中国奥委会的合法地位才重新得到恢复。自此以后,中国人稳步地加入到奥林匹克运动中。1984 年以来奥运的成功和失败极大地刺激着中国人要成为奥运强国的雄心,促使了奥运战略的实施,带来了体育方针、竞赛制度和投入结构方面的诸多变化。结果,中国在奥运奖牌榜的位置从 1992 年和 1996 年的第四名升到 2000 年的第三,在 2004 年金牌数还位于第二。最终中国赢得了举办 2008 年奥运会的权力。"奥运"现在是全国最流行的词汇。

思考题

1. 为什么中国在 1932 年前没有参加奥运会？
2. 是什么原因促使中国在 1958 年从国际奥委会中撤出？
3. 中国要成为奥运强国的动机是什么？
4. 为什么在过去 20 年中中国在奥运会中取得了巨大的进步？

注　释

〔1〕王正廷 1910 年获耶鲁大学博士学位，国民党政府期间曾任外交部长和驻美大使。自 1921 年起任北京中国大学校长。1922 年，王正廷被选为国际奥委会委员，成为中国第一位和远东第二位国际奥委会委员。1924 年，被推选为新成立的"中华全国体育协进会"名誉会长，1933 年任该会主席董事。1936 年和 1948 年作为中国体育代表团总领队，率团先后参加第 11 届和第 14 届奥运会。1952 年定居香港，1961 年逝世。

〔2〕《体育史料》，1980 年第 1—4 期。Jonathan Kolatach，*Sport, Politics and Ideology in China*，New York：Jonathon David，1972，pp.8-11.

〔3〕宋如海当时是中华全国体育协进会名誉干事，正在美国考察学习。受中华体育协进会的指派，由美国乘船前往荷兰，出席了赛会。这是中国首次正式派人参与奥运会。

〔4〕在中国参加 1936 年的第 11 届奥运会代表团中，李森是 22 名运动员中的唯一一位女性。

〔5〕台湾和大陆都要求其国家奥委会得到排他性的承认。台湾的中国人从法律的角度来辩论，而大陆的中国人则声称他们现在是 6 亿人民的实际代表。国际奥委会被双方的政治对骂搞得疲惫不堪，希望找到一种妥协的解决方案。详细情况见 Jonathan Kolatach（1972），*Sport, Politics and Ideology in China*，pp. 171-174。

〔6〕More detail see Jonathan Kolatach (1972), ibid., pp. 171-174.

〔7〕根据《奥林匹克宪章》，一个国家只能有一个奥委会得到承认。中国共产党领导的中华人民共和国和国民党领导的台湾当局展开了斗争。在以布伦戴奇为主席的国际奥委会中，对哪一个奥委会应得到承认展开了激烈的争论，最后的决定是双方都得到了参加奥运会的邀请。

〔8〕包括国际游泳、田径、篮球、举重、射击、摔跤、自行车联合会及亚洲乒乓球联合会。

〔9〕 1979年10月25日,国际奥委会执委会起草一项决议,决定中国奥委会是中国在国际奥委会的合法代表。台湾奥委会作为它的一个地方机构仍保留在国际奥委会中。这一决议一个月后被国际奥委会以62票赞成、17票反对而得到通过。

〔10〕 Susan Brownell (1995), *Training the Body for China: Sports in the Moral Order of the People's Republic*, Chicago and London: The University of Chicago Press.

〔11〕《体育界的一次对话》,《体育论坛》,1988年第1期,第9页。

〔12〕 根据由中国日报和美国柯达公司发起的一项民意测验:"中国能赢得多少块金牌",在20万回答者中只有1536人预测5块或少于5块(赵禹:《强国梦——当代中国体育的误区》,《当代》,1988年第二期,第9页)。

〔13〕 国家体委,《七五期间体育必须坚持改革扩充道路,执行分类指导以取得更大的成就》,《体育工作情况反映》,1986年第9期,第3页。

〔14〕 它是作家赵禹报告文学的一个书名。见《赵禹体育问题报告文学集》,北京:中国社会科学出版社,1988年。

〔15〕 陈金华:《1993年全国经济社会发展计划完成情况的报告及1994年全国经济社会发展计划的草案》,《人民日报》,1994年3月25日。

〔16〕 国家体委(编):《中国体育年鉴》49—91精华本(下册),北京:人民体育出版社,1993年,第202页。

〔17〕 何振梁现任国际奥委会委员,国际奥委会文化和奥林匹克教育委员会主席。他1950年毕业于上海复旦大学,1952年作为翻译参加在芬兰举行的第十五届奥林匹克运动会。1955年调到国家体委后一直在体育领域。1981年任国家体委国际联络司副司长的同时当选为国际奥委会委员。1985年任国家体委副主任之时,当选为国际奥委会执行委员会委员。1989—1993年任国际奥委会副主席,1994年和1999年又两次当选为国际奥委会执行委员会委员。为恢复中国在国际奥委会的合法席位、北京成功申办2008年奥运会做出了杰出的贡献。

〔18〕 吕圣荣1964年毕业于北京外国语大学英语系。1964—1972年在中华全国妇女联合会国际部工作。1972年以后在国家体委、国家体育总局外联司工作。自1980起她开始涉足全国和国际羽毛球管理工作。1993年当选为国际羽毛球联合会主席。三年后,当选为国际奥委会委员,第一个担任此职的中国女性。

〔19〕 1945年的全国体育工作会议上,就起草了一个方案并提交给与会代表。详细情况见《申奥:申办2000年奥运会》,中国奥委会官方网站,2003年。

〔20〕 任海:《中国和奥林匹克运动》(2002),体育奥林匹克研究中心。

〔21〕 北京在前三轮投票中都领先于悉尼,但最后一轮时,北京落后于悉尼两票。在 1999 年揭露出在这最后一轮投票前澳大利亚人贿赂了两名国际奥委会委员后,中国人十分气愤,质问这次申奥的有效性。

〔22〕 张天白:《第 26 届奥运会及中国体育代表团参赛情况》,《体育工作情况》1996 年第 16—17 期(总.624—625),第 14 页。

〔23〕 袁虹衡:《增强竞争,促进改革 —— 吴寿章在奥运选拔赛上的讲话》,《北京晚报》,1996 年 6 月 2 日。

〔24〕 佚名(2004):《申奥 ABC》,http://wjhsqxx.wjedu.net/web_ztwz/2008_beijing/2008/Article_Class2.asp?ClassID=28。

〔25〕 《人民日报》,2002 年 1 月 20 日。

〔26〕 赖海隆:《从紫禁城午门走向 2008》,中国新闻网,http://www.chinanews.com.cn/zhonghuawenzhai/2001-08-01/txt3/12.htm。

〔27〕 2001 年 2 月申奥大事,www.beijing-2008.org。

〔28〕 两轮的票数是:北京 44/56;伊斯坦布尔 17/9;大阪 6;巴黎 15/18;多伦多 20/22(http://olympic.sportsol.com.cn,July 7, 2002)。

第十三章
走向 2008 奥运会

本章要点
* 全面准备北京奥运会
* 北京奥运：机遇和挑战

北京 2008 奥运会对中国人的重要性是不言自明的事情。人们期待奥运会能推动中国的现代化进程，为中国全面走入世界、在世界事务中发挥更大的作用提供一个桥梁，为中国以一个现代国家的面貌屹立于世界、结束长达一个世纪的西方和日本侵略带来的羞辱提供一个平台。[1] 为把北京奥运会办成奥运历史上最好的一届运动会，中国上下一致，全力以赴。中央政府和北京市政府许诺在经费出现短缺时会提供资助。[2]

1. 基础设施建设

举办奥运会是一项复杂、艰巨的系统工程，要求有大量的场地设施、现代化的通讯网络、良好的交通系统、大量的旅店和令人放心的食品卫生。自 2001 年赢得举办 2008 夏季奥运会举办权以后，北京就拉开了一个令人叹为观止的为奥运会而准备的建筑和投资方案。为此，北京计划支出近 2800 亿元（350 亿美元）。[3]

（1）交通

交通堵塞是令北京深感头痛的一个问题。为解决这一难题，北京计划投入 900 亿元（大约 112.5 亿美元）来修建地铁、轻轨、高速路和

图 13-1　北京城市剪影

飞机场。到 2008 年,城市轨道系统年客运量将达 18—22 亿人次。为解决北京交通拥挤的问题,北京将对公交汽车的建设投入数十亿元。北京的公交汽车的年客运量将达 45 亿人次,运行车辆将达 1.8 万辆。此外,城区将新建 8 条地铁线,公共运输线的数量将达到 650 多条。为确保方便快捷地到达奥运会的比赛场馆,62 条公路和 4 座桥梁还需建造或改建。[4]在三环、四环上将设立专用奥运车道,在中心区等 16 个奥运比赛场馆(群)布设 38 条奥运专线。[5]这些专用车道和专线在奥运会开幕前14天起投入使用,残奥会闭幕后3天关闭。在奥运会期间,从居住地到比赛场地的行车时间将不超过30分钟。为保证奥运选手和官员的交通顺畅,通过采用以3S为基础的核心技术,一个高效的智能交通网络系统将建立起来,北京旅客和货物运输的有效性将赶上世界水平。在这些场馆和公路周围的环境也会得到改善。[6]

(2)体育场馆和公园

为了在2008年能举办历史上最好的一届奥运会,北京计划建立世界上最先进的体育场馆设施。在奥运会所要求的37个体育场馆中,31个坐落于北京,其中包括11个新建体育馆、9个临时赛场、11个改建的体育馆(详见附录5)。此外,还需要41个训练场馆和与奥运会直接有关的5个设施。直接用于奥运场馆和相关设施的费用约130亿元(约18亿美元)。[7]所有的体育场馆到2008年4月全部完工。

值得注意的是,为实施国际奥委会提出的"瘦身"计划,采用由不规则角度的金属梁柱构成的巨型网状结构的"鸟巢"国家体育馆[8],由原计划的40亿元(约5.06亿美元)减少到35亿元(约4.86亿美元),最初计划的可开启屋顶不得不放弃。[9]

图13-2　鸟巢体育馆

在奥运会期间将容纳1.6万名运动员和官员的奥运村,位于北京中轴路的北端,占地66公顷,在它的北部有奥林匹克森林公园,南部是主要的奥林匹克场馆。村内的居住区将包括22座6层楼的建筑、20座9层楼的建筑以及诊所、饭店、一个图书馆、一个娱乐中心、多个游泳池、网球场、篮球场和跑道。奥运会后,该奥运村将变成豪华的住宅楼。[10]

(3) 通讯网络

在信息时代,通讯网络对于奥运会的成功至关重要。2008奥运信息系统将由计时记分系统、成绩处理系统、Intranet/Internet综合信息查询系统、运动会管理系统、通信和网络系统这五大系统构成。在数字奥运信息投资预算上,北京原计划投资300亿元(37.97亿美元)进行信息化建设(该数字可能还会大幅增加),包括数字通讯系统,比赛软件和智能管理系统,记者或官员可收看到所有场馆比赛情况的光纤网络。

(4) 环境保护

1993年北京申奥失败的原因之一是中国当时糟糕的自然环境。从那以后,环境问题就得到了高度重视。公众对环境保护的热情在一定程度上帮助北京成功地赢得了2008年奥运会的举办权。根据"绿色奥运"——申办报告中提出的三大目标之一,北京准备用570亿元来治理环境,使北京的天变蓝、水变清、地变绿,未来将有更多的绿化带和公园。[11]为此,北京市在2002年内搬迁了40家污染比较严重的企业,2005年,约150家工业企业再一次搬迁。[12]

通过举办奥运会来促进人和环境的和谐是北京的目标之一。为实现这一目标,数字化、宽带网络、节能和节水技术来建造体育场馆,安置电讯和交通设施;环保技术如再生能源、太阳能、地热和风能将被运用;体育场馆还将安装高技术烟雾间,这些房间的精细空气过滤器将把烟雾分解成常规气体。奥运村和比赛场馆之间的交通将使用电动汽车以减少空气污染。2005年9月24日,北京奥运会的环保标志——"绿色奥运"正式向公众公布。该标志是以书法形式展示的由人和树构成的一个图案。

图 13-3　奥运环保标志

2. 组织建设

在赢得奥运会举办权后五个月,北京奥组委于 2001 年 12 月 13 日成立。2004 年 3 月,奥组委有 18 个部门、90 名委员和 240 名工作人员。到 2006 年 3 月,又增加了 5 个部门[13]和 389 名工作人员。[14]奥组委的部门数量和工作人员数量会逐渐增加,到 2008 年将达到 30 多个部门和 4000 多名工作人员。目前,奥组委执委会有 17 名委员,包括 3 名女性,北京市市委书记刘淇担任主席。

此外,与奥运会相关的委员会也相继成立。例如,2002 年 6 月第二十九届奥运会科学技术委员会成立。标志着宣传"新北京、新奥运"窗口的北京奥运新闻中心在 2004 年 11 月揭幕。北京奥林匹克广播有限公司于 2005 年建立。

为聘用能干的人才,北京奥组委 2002 年首次在全球公开招聘。在半个月内,应聘者就达到 3515 人,其中海外留学人员 301 人[15]。2004 年进行了第二次公开招聘。据称,北京奥组委已经建立了包括 10000 多人、27 个专项的人才档案库。

(1) 比赛管理

如通常所见,并非所有的奥运会比赛都在首都进行。2008 年奥运会足球比赛的资格赛将在天津、上海、沈阳、秦皇岛举行,航海比赛在青岛举行。马术比赛则从北京移师到香港。为确保 2008 奥运会的成功,比赛协调委员会、北京奥组委体育部和北京奥组委赛事委员会有责任确保这些不同地点赛事工作的通畅。

(2) 奥运营销

从 2002 年起北京奥组委开始与通讯、金融、保险、汽车、石油、电器和航空等行业的大型国内外企业进行赞助谈判。2004 年 4 月在北京召开了一个奥运推广会,会上推出了涉及基础建设、环保、高端技术、制造业和旅游业的 370 个项目,价值 1000 亿元。[16]到目前为止,北京奥组委已经与 11 个公司签订了协议,授予它们北京 2008 合作伙伴的地位。[17]其中一个就是阿迪达斯——德国运动服装和运动装备巨头,阿迪还给中国参加夏季奥运会和 2006 年都灵冬奥会队伍提供装备。阿迪将给北京奥运会的工作人员提供制服,价值 5000 万美元。[18]

此外,北京 2008 已有 11 个合作伙伴、10 个赞助商和 15 个独家供应商[19]。北京奥组委还通过了 300 多种奥运特许产品。

(3) 组织竞赛

北京奥组委组织了从体育场馆设计、雕塑、口号、吉祥物、奥运主题歌曲到开闭幕式设计等各种竞赛活动。北京奥运会和残奥会吉祥物征集设计大赛在 2004 年 8 月 1 日—12 月 1 日举行。参赛的作品中,大陆有 614 件(92.75%);港澳台有 11 件(1.66%);国外作品 37 件(5.59%)。2005 年 1 月 1—31 日进行了奥林匹克口号征集活动。2005 年 6 月 26 日在奥林匹克文化节期间发布了从 21 万条应征口号中挑选出来的口号:"同一个世界,同一个梦想。"该口号的书法和海报在全世界范围内征集。北京奥运会组织者在 2005 年 3 月 1 日到 7 月 31 日公开征集对北京奥运会大型开/闭幕式仪式的建议,获胜者将应邀加入到这些仪式的设计队伍之中。[20]奥运歌曲征集活动从 2003 年开始,每年评选出十首"北京 2008 奥运歌曲"(即"入围作品"),进行广泛推广,并从入围作品中遴选出 2008 年奥运会开幕式的主题歌。

（4）人才培训和教育

我国十分缺乏奥运组织与管理、高级体育经营管理等各方面的人才。[21]奥运人才培训提到了重要的议事日程,北京奥运培训工作协调小组于 2005 年成立。它提供四个层次的培训:专业人员培训(奥组委官员、职员,有关体育管理人员、运动员、教练员、裁判员);奥运志愿者,仪式官员和人员的培训;相关行业人员培训(媒体和传播行业、安保人员、窗口服务和相关行业人员等);大众、包括学生等。[22]为确保培训工作的成功,北京奥组要从国外聘请培训顾问。[23]

为培养北京 2008 年奥运会 28 个大项的赛事管理人员,提高和加强他们的赛事管理经验和外语运用和交流的能力,相应的培训行动已经开始,如奥组委选派一部分人到雅典奥组委实习半年;从 2006 年开始组织不同项目的裁判员和官员奥运知识和外语培训班等。北京从 2006 年开始对商业服务业、旅游业等 11 个行业近 20 万从业人员开展培训。

北京奥组委还鼓励教育机构开设奥运会和奥林匹克主义方面的课程。奥林匹克文化选修课和讲座在许多院校也定期开设。建立了多所奥林匹克示范校,以确保年轻人在北京奥运会之前熟悉与奥运相关的问题。在 2006 年全国有 356 所学校又被命名为"北京 2008 奥林匹克教育示范学校"。除北京奥组委负责奥运人才的培训工作之外,各运动项目管理中心也组织各自的奥运知识和英语人才培训班。200 余所中小学参加了北京 2008 奥林匹克教育"同心结"的交流活动,与世界其它国家的学校建立结对关系。[24]

（5）准备残疾人奥运会

除夏季奥运会外,北京还要负责组织 2008 残疾人奥运会。2005 年,在北京奥组委下设立了残奥会筹备办公室。2004 年 7 月 13 日北京残奥会纪念章公布。

3. 人文发展

人文奥运是北京申奥时提出的三个口号之一。它是指奥运会应该促进社会和人文的发展,应强调公平竞争、友谊和人与自然的和谐这些奥林匹克理想。为宣传北京奥运,中央电视台体育频道专设了《北京2008》节目,湖南卫视等地方台也增设了《我的2008》等奥运专题节目,报纸如《北京晚报》、《竞报》等开设奥运专门栏目。国际知名导演张艺谋执导了奥运宣传片"新北京,新奥运",该片2003年在"意大利米兰21世纪国际体育电影和电视节"上获得三项一等奖。[25]

中国历史悠久。中国人想借助北京奥运会来展示其灿烂的文化和传统。在2003年8月揭晓的2008奥运徽章:"中国印——舞动的北京"就是具体的体现。该徽章是以一个中文字的印章作为主体表现形式,用东方风格的毛笔书写"北京2008"。国际奥运会主席罗格说:"从这个徽章中,我看到了新北京、新奥运的希望和潜力。"[26]

北京2008年奥运会的吉祥物福娃是由五个小孩组成,他们分别体现了鱼、熊猫、藏羚羊和燕子这四种最受中国人喜爱的动物的自然属性和奥林匹克火焰。福娃将把友谊和和平的信息和来自中国的祝福带给全世界的儿童。[27]

开幕式和闭幕式是重要的文化象征,它们最能反映出中国文化的特性。雅典奥运会的开幕式以激动人心的3000年希腊历史和文化场面赢得了全世界的称赞,也给中国增加了压力:中国人能否创造出比雅典更精彩或至少一样精彩的开/闭幕式吗?

尽管开/闭幕式的方案还没确定下来,2008年奥运会的火炬接力已经确定,将从2008年3月开始,在8月8日奥运会开幕结束,经过五大洲、28个外国城市和70多个中国城市,火炬接力手将达1.5万人左右。值得一提的是,奥运圣火第一次登上了地球之巅——珠穆朗玛峰。[28]

中国人有很强的爱国主义情结。正如一位乒乓球选手所说:"在中国举行的奥运会将让外国人看到这是一个多么伟大和强大的国家。"[29]为此,北京奥运会收到了来自公众的许诺和支持。2005年7月的一项民意调查显示,95%的北京市民希望成为2008年奥运会志愿者。[30]

2005年6月5日北京奥运会志愿者项目启动仪式在北京饭店举行,同时发布了《北京奥运会志愿者行动计划》和北京奥运会志愿者标识,并举行了"志愿服务与人文奥运"国际论坛。估计10万名来自国内外的志愿者将担任奥运会的各种义务工作,如治安、媒体运营和翻译等。

2001年中国加入世界贸易组织和北京获得奥运会举办权以后,中国与国际社会的联系在不断增强,变得越来越开放。"同一个世界、同一个梦想"的口号反映了这一趋势。该口号从全世界征集到的21万条口号中脱颖而出的原因,就在于它反映了奥林匹克精神的本质特征和团结、友谊、进步、和谐、参与和梦想的全球价值。[31]的确,北京变得越来越开放,[32]奥运会促进了这一变化。北京奥组委通过竞赛的形式,向国内外征集奥运口号、主题歌、开闭幕式等建议。外国金融机构也可以参加通过与国内银行合作来参与项目融资。澳大利亚人鲍勃·埃尔芬斯顿[33]成为北京奥组委的体育顾问。[34]所有这些都表明,北京奥运会将促进中国走向世界的步伐。筹备奥运会加快了中国与西方世界互动的步伐,对中国社会、文化和生活方式都会带来重要的变化。

4. 北京奥运与竞技成绩

中国运动员的成绩将是判断北京奥运会是否成功的一个重要指标。而北京奥运会又将给中国实现奥运强国梦想提供一个极好的机会。作为东道主,中国在2008年将拥有天时、地利、人和等有利条件。为确保2008年取得好成绩,国家体育总局在2002年出台了《2008奥运争光计划》。根据该计划,中国运动员将参加所有的28个大项的比赛,希望获得比以往奥运会更多的奖牌,目标至少是前三名。具体来讲,中国人希望在298个小项上摘取180枚奖牌。为实现既定目标,女性将再次撑起大半边天,因为80%以上的奖牌将由她们获得。[35]为实现争光计划,各奥运项目管理中心都提出了各自的《2008年奥运争光计划实施方案》和具体的指标。例如,田径力争2枚金牌,水上项目力争拿2—3枚金牌。

为确保2008年的胜利,奥运会科研服务工作至关重要。为此,国家体育总局专设了奥运攻关科研课题经费。2002年度投入项目攻关的经费总计达1400万元,其中,其中对优势项目、潜优势项目共投入了470万元左右,田径、游泳、水上等涉及119块奥运金牌的科研项目,投入经费是600多万。[36]

为调动地方积极性,国家从体育总经费中划出300万元,对在冬季、夏季奥运会上取得前八名的省级体育部门予以奖励。全国有22个省(区、市)提出冲击2008年奥运会金牌的目标,有28个省(区、市)提出冲击奖牌的目标。[37]

5. 机遇和挑战

(1) 机遇

2007年中国的贸易总额到达2.137万亿美元,超过日本成为世界第三大市场[38]。北京奥运会将带来更多的海外投资。史无前例的全球关注和相应的投资,会推进中国经济的发展。奥运会上千亿美元的基础设施建造和相关活动会将中国的GDP向上拉动0.3%。一项研究表明,北京会比原计划提前两年实现人均GDP 6000美元的目标。[39]据推算,2002年至2007年,筹办奥运会将累计新增就业岗位约为194万个,平均每年新增就业岗位约为32万个左右[40](具体的就业机会见表13-1)。

表13-1 不同行业的就业机会

不同行业的就业机会
* 环保技术、产品和服务(废水处理,污染控制和降低设施,修正、再生和替代能源等);
* 能量、能量节省和再生能源(建筑技术,灯光发射二极管,再生能源,燃料电池技术等);
* 建筑服务,建筑设施和建筑材料;
* 信息技术和通讯;
* 多媒体;
* 安全、监视、X-光和安全扫描设备;

续 表

不同行业的就业机会
* 交通和交通管理设备;
* 建筑设计和项目设计;
* 项目管理;
* 医疗设备,应用和卫生保健基础设施;
* 旅游和接待,旅馆和饭店的供给和管理;
* 食品、饮料和酒类出口;
* 计算机、软件、硬件和相关产品;
* 专业性服务,包括银行、法律和财务;
* 电视转播和经营组织;
* 特许、品牌和赞助权;
* 工业机械、电子和电动设备。

北京奥运会将会带来1417亿元的直接投资,它会使北京的经济在2002年至2007年间增长87.83亿元,或年均增长2.07%。[41]此外,北京奥运会还会给北京的房地产市场注入巨大的活力。由于改善的基础设施和环境条件,房地产肯定会升值。一句话,举办2008年奥运会将会给北京提供一个向世界展示一个充满信心、文明和现代化的大都市新形象的机会,带来经济的繁荣。

(2) 挑战

作为人口众多的发展中国家的首都城市,北京面临着许多问题,如空气污染,水资源短缺,交通拥挤和居住条件的不尽人意,但更急迫的问题是缺乏高水平、熟悉国际规则和实践的合格的体育管理人员、体育营销代理、记者和律师。[42]

另一个问题是语言,尤其是英语。作为一个非英语国家,语言对中国人而言是一个巨大的挑战。尽管大多数北京人,包括出租车司机都在学习英语[43],语言障碍是很难克服的。说不同语言的人是很容易产生误解的。

此外,安全问题也是一个挑战,它会使得奥运会的经费预算升高。北京奥运会的预算比原计划要多。[44]阻止恐怖主义的代价是昂贵的,大型赛事的安保费用每年都在增加。

另外,鉴于日益上升的爱国主义情结,"如果奥运会不能令人满意的话或如果中国运动员的成绩不理想,可能会出现消极的后果,例如针对对手的暴力和对政府的批评"[45]。运动员、教练员以及官员将面临巨大的压力。

结　论

举办2008年奥运会具有广泛的社会和政治意义。史无前例的国际关注和资金流入会推动中国经济的发展,但中国希望更多的东西。由于当代奥运会具有重要的全球意义,成为一个奥运强国是中国长久以来的一个梦想。2008年北京奥运会将提供实现这个梦想的绝妙机会。举办一个"绿色奥运"、"科技奥运"和"人文奥运",北京将变成一个真正的具有自身特点的国际大都市。然而,挑战与机会并存。北京迫切需要高素质的体育专家。对英语的熟练性也令人有所担忧。恐怖主义和防恐的代价也让人感到不安。运动员比赛要顶住足以摧垮人的压力。尽管如此,北京和整个中国正充满信心地准备着历史上最好的一届奥运会。

思考题

1. 举办奥运会会给北京和中国带来哪些影响?
2. 北京在筹备2008年奥运会中应注意哪些问题?
3. 你认为中国运动员在2008年奥运会会取得什么样的成绩？请给出理由。

注　释

[1] John W. Garver (1993), *Foreign Policy of the People's Republic of China*, Englewood Cliffs, NJ: Prentice Hall, p. 20.

[2] Daniel Covell(eds.) (2003), *Managing Sports Organisations: Responsibility for Performance*, Thomson: South-western, p. 296.

[3] 王军华:《携奥运经济提速北京现代化进程》,《北京晚报》,2003年2月25

〔4〕 "Olympic Venue Construction Making Remarkable Headway", September 20, 2005, http://en.beijing-2008.org/19/82/article211668219.shtml。

〔5〕 谢永利:《2008奥运进行曲顺畅》,www.bjd.com.cn,2006年8月6日。

〔6〕 《奥运工程进展顺利》,beijing2008.com,2006年12月8日,http://www.china.org.cn/english/sports/191730.htm。

〔7〕 王军华:《携奥运经济提速北京现代化进程》,《北京晚报》,2003年2月25日。

〔8〕 "鸟巢"由2001年普利茨克奖(被誉为建筑界的诺贝尔奖)获得者瑞士建筑师赫尔佐格、德梅隆与中国建筑设计研究院合作完成,2003年3月从中外13个竞赛方案中胜出。

〔9〕 赵丽萍:《鸟巢瘦身缘于经济问题,要尽快复工以减低损失》,《京华时报》,2004年8月27日。

〔10〕 北京奥组委,《北京2008:北京奥运村开建》,北京奥组委官方网站,2005年6月29日。

〔11〕 《北京奥运投入300亿元用于信息化建设》,《第一财经日报》,2007年1月25日。

〔12〕 朱鹰:《为"绿色奥运"让路 北京四十家工厂迁出四环》,中新网,2002年10月30日。

〔13〕 23个部门分别是秘书行政部、总体策划部、国际联络部、体育部、新闻宣传部、工程和环境部、市场开发部、技术部、法律事务部、运动会服务部、监察审计部、人事部、财务部、文化活动部、安保部、媒体运行部、场馆运行部、物流中心、残奥会部、交通部、火炬接力中心、注册中心、开闭幕式工作部。

〔14〕 高鹏、汪涌:《北京奥组委今年工作人员数量将增加一倍》,www.xinhuanet.com,2006年3月16日。

〔15〕 汪涌:《北京奥组委确定首批公开招聘人员笔试名单》,新华网北京,2002年11月21日。

〔16〕 《北京寻找对2008年奥运会的投资》,CCTV.com,2004年3月24日。

〔17〕 这11个企业是中国银行、中国网通、中国石化、中国石油、中国移动通讯、大众汽车、阿迪达斯、强生、中国国际航空公司、中国人寿保险、中国电网。

〔18〕 《阿迪达斯提供北京奥运会工作人员制服》,http://www.tdctrade.com/imn/05020301/clothing162.htm,Feb 3,2005。

〔19〕 10个赞助商:UPS、海尔、百威、搜狐、青岛啤酒、伊利、燕京啤酒、必和必拓、

恒源祥、统一。15个独家供应商：皇朝家私、华帝股份、千喜鹤食品、爱芬食品、泰诺健、亚力克国际、中粮酒业、贝发文具、梦娜、歌华特玛捷票务有限公司、思念食品、亚都科技、Aggreko、史泰博、Schenker。

[20] 《北京奥组委征集奥运艺术》，2005年8月10日，http://www.olympic.org/uk/games/beijing/full_story_uk.asp?id=1449.

[21] 《北京征求奥运仪式建议》，2005年3月1日，CRIENGLISH.com.

[22] 《北京奥运人才"叫渴" 代表建议全面启动培训工程》，http://news.xinhuanet.com/newscenter/2005-03/06/content_2659524.htm，2005年3月6日。

[23] 《人民日报》，2002年7月5日。

[24] 刘昊：《北京近20万窗口行业从业人员参加奥运培训活动》，《首都之窗》，http://www.beijing2008.com/44/19/article212031944.shtml，2006年7月30日。

[25] 在奥运会开幕前，"同心结"学校学生将学习和了解结对国家或地区的语言、文化、历史、地理、风俗、礼仪等知识，开展与结对学校的交流活动；进入赛时阶段，"同心结"学校师生代表将参加奥运村欢迎仪式，到赛场为结对的国家或地区的体育代表团加油助威，邀请运动员到学校参观，开展联谊活动等。

[26] http://english.people.com.cn/200311/13/eng20031113_128200.shtml.

[27] 《罗格：2008奥运会徽体现"新北京新奥运"承诺》，http://www.china.com.cn/chinese/zhuanti/zgy/378582.htm，2003年8月4日。

[28] 《北京2008年奥运会吉祥物》，http://en.beijing2008.com/80/05/article211990580.shtml.

[29] 高鹏：《2008年奥运会火炬传递遍及五大洲》，http://news.xinhuanet.com/olympics/2006-04/18/content_4444401.htm，2006年4月18日。

[30] Daniel Covell(ed.)(2003), ibid., p.296.

[31] 《刘淇谈北京奥运"钱途" 挣钱同时要让民众得实惠》，http://www.tongxin.org/j-sys-news/page/2005/1116/17331_106.shtml，2005年11月16日。

[32] Getty/Guang Niu，《北京2008：同一个梦想，同一个世界》，http://www.olympic.org/uk/games/beijing/full_story_uk.asp?id=1370，2005年6月28日。

[33] 同上。

[34] 他连续担任悉尼2000奥运会体育官员、澳大利亚奥委会秘书长、国际奥委会体育顾问和国际篮球联合会副主席等职。他曾参加1984年到2000年的

四届夏季奥运会和1994年到2002年的三届冬奥会。

[35] Zhang Yu, "Bob Elphinston Becomes the Sports Consultant of BOCOG", http://en.beijing-2008.org/92/71/article211667192.shtml.

[36] 国家体育总局竞技体育司:《各省自治区直辖市备战2004年、2008年奥运会调研情况报告》,《全国竞技体育工作会议参考资料之一》,2003年。

[37] 林文:《备战奥运,144个科研攻关课题招标》,《市场报》,2003年2月26日。

[38] 国家体育总局竞技体育司(2003年),同上引。

[39] 《中国贸易总额今年可超2.1万亿美元》,www.chinaview.cn,2007年10月28日。

[40] 刘燕:《奥运大餐谁与争羹》,《北京现代商报》,2003年4月4日。

[41] 王军华:《携奥运经济提速北京现代化进程》,《北京晚报》,2003年2月25日。

[42] 《1417亿元奥运投资提速北京经济》,京报网,2005年3月24日。

[43] 杨润声:《奥运 催生多种新职业》,《竞报》,2005年8月29日。

[44] 出租司机要求能说出租服务常用的100句英语。因此,他们在获得驾驶许可之前必须通过英语考试。

[45] http://www.china.com.cn/chinese/2003/Aug/378176.htm.

[46] 董进霞:《女性、爱国主义和北京奥运会:为荣誉而准备》,"体育、社会和认同"国际会议上上的讲话,雅典,2004年。

附 录

附录 1
《奥林匹克宪章》的主要内容

一、性质和作用

《奥林匹克宪章》是国际奥委会制定的基本原则、规则和附则的汇总。它指导奥林匹克运动的组织和运行,规定相关组织之间的关系和职责,明确举办奥林匹克运动会的条件和规范等。不论以何种身份属于奥林匹克运动的人员或组织,都须受《奥林匹克宪章》条款的约束,并应遵守国际奥委会的决定。

二、宪章的演变

第一部宪章是由顾拜旦倡议和起草的,在 1894 年 6 月通过。在以后的 100 多年中,多次进行修改和补充。最新版的《奥林匹克宪章》于 2000 年 9 月国际奥委会地 111 次全会批准。

三、主要条款

《奥林匹克宪章》由基本原则和奥林匹克运动、国际奥林匹克委员会、国际单项体育联合会、国家奥林匹克委员会、奥林匹克运动会等 5 章组成。

第一章的内容包括奥林匹克运动的最高权力、国际奥委会的职能、奥林匹克运动的成员等,规定了国际奥委会承认和赞助的对象及程序,阐述了奥林匹克代表大会的召集和奥林匹克团结工作问题。第一章还有关于奥林匹克徽记、旗帜、格言、标志和火炬等的规定。

第二章包括关于国际奥委会的法律地位、成员的资格与产生等内容,规定了国际奥委会全体大会、执行委员会和主席以及道德委员会处置和处分的权力和职责,还规定了国际奥委会的工作程序、工作语言和经费来源等。

第三章是1992年增加的一章,内容包括国际奥委会对国际单项体育联合会的承认和国际单项体育联合会的作用。国际奥林匹克单项体育组织在奥运会和国际奥委会赞助的比赛中,对所管理的运动项目负有技术监督和指导的责任。

第四章的内容包括国家奥委会的使命和作用、组成和与本国单项体育组织的关系以及会旗、会徽和会歌等。国家奥委会的基本任务是根据《奥林匹克宪章》,在各自的国家发展奥林匹克运动。

第五章是内容最多的一章,内容包括奥运会的组织与管理、奥运城的选择、奥运会参赛条件和比赛项目、文化节目和奥运村的设立及礼仪等问题。奥林匹克礼仪包括奥运会邀请信的发送,各种奥林匹克证件及持证人的权利与待遇,奥运会开幕式、闭幕式与发奖仪式等。

附录2
国际奥委会现任委员

姓　名	国家奥委会	入选年	奥运会参加情况
若昂·阿维兰热	巴西	1963	1936/52
穆罕默德·姆扎利	突尼斯	1965	
维塔利·斯米尔诺夫	俄罗斯	1971	
彼得·塔尔伯格	芬兰	1976	1960/64/68/72/80
凯万·高斯帕	澳大利亚	1977	1956/60＊＊
夏格达尔扎布·马格万	蒙古	1977	
里查德·庞德	加拿大	1978	1960
何振梁	中国	1981	
佛朗哥·卡拉罗	意大利	1982	
菲利浦·沃尔特·科尔斯	澳大利亚	1982	1960/64/68
伊万·迪博斯	秘鲁	1982	
猪谷千春＊	日本	1982	1952/56/60＊＊
阿纳尼·马蒂亚	多哥	1983	
罗克·拿破伦·穆尼奥斯·培尼亚	多米尼加	1983	
帕尔·施密特	匈牙利	1983	1968/72/76＊＊
挪拉公主	列支敦士登	1984	
弗朗西斯科·埃利扎尔	菲律宾	1985	
阿尔贝二世亲王	摩洛哥	1985	1988/92/94/98/02
兰维斯·尼科劳.＊	希腊	1986	
阿妮塔·德弗朗兹	美国	1986	1976＊＊
安东·基辛克	荷兰	1987	1964＊＊
安妮公主	英国	1988	1976
吴经国	中国台北	1988	
拉姆·鲁希	毛里求斯	1988	

续表

姓　名	国家奥委会	入选年	奥运会参加情况
维利·卡尔特施米特·鲁坚	危地马拉	1988	
弗朗西斯·沃尔·尼扬维索	乌干达	1988	1960
费南多·F. 利马·贝罗	波兰	1989	1968/72
瓦尔特·特罗格	德国	1989	
冈野俊一郎	日本	1990	1968 **
因德拉帕纳	泰国	1990	
安东尼奥·罗德里格斯	阿根廷	1990	
德尼·奥斯瓦尔德 *	瑞士	1991	1968/72/76 **
雅克·罗格 *	比利时	1991	1968/72/76
马里奥·巴斯克斯·拉拉 *	墨西哥	1991	
托马斯·巴赫	德国	1991	1976 **
阿尔-沙巴赫	科威特	1992	
詹姆斯·伊斯顿 *	美国	1994	
克雷格·里迪	英国	1994	
马里奥·佩斯坎特	意大利	1994	
盖哈德·海贝格 *	挪威	1994	
阿尔内尤格维斯特	瑞典	1994	1952
奥斯汀·西利	巴巴多斯	1994	
罗宾·米切尔	斐济	1994	
阿尔法·易卜拉欣·迪亚洛 *	几内亚	1994	
阿莱克斯·吉拉迪	以色列	1994	
沙米利·塔尔皮斯切夫	俄罗斯	1994	
瓦列里·波尔佐夫	乌克兰	1994	1972/76 **
勒内·法塞尔	瑞士	1995	
让-克洛德·基利	法国	1995	1964/1968 **
萨姆·拉姆萨米	南非	1995	
雷纳尔多·冈萨雷斯·洛佩斯	古巴	1995	
马里奥·巴斯克斯·雷纳	墨西哥	1995	1964/68/72/76
安通·弗尔多贾克	克罗地亚	1995	
帕特里克·希凯	爱尔兰	1995	
托尼·霍里	黎巴嫩	1995	
穆斯塔法·拉法欧伊	阿及利欧伊	1995	
沙赫德-阿里	巴基斯坦	1996	
张雄	朝鲜	1996	
古尼拉·林德伯格 *	瑞典	1996	

续　表

姓　　名	国家奥委会	入选年	奥运会参加情况
胡里奥·塞萨尔·马格利奥尼	乌拉圭	1996	
李健熙	韩国	1996	
奥泰维·辛奎塔*	意大利	1996	
居伊·德鲁	法国	1996	1972/76 **
伊雷娜·茨文斯卡	波兰	1998	1964/68/72/76/80 **
卢森堡大公爵	卢森堡	1998	
穆尼尔·萨贝特	埃及	1998	
纳瓦勒·穆塔瓦基尔	摩洛哥	1998	1984 **
梅利顿·桑切斯·里瓦斯	巴拿马	1998	
利奥波德·瓦尔纳	奥地利	1998	
奥兰治王子	荷兰	1998	
黄思棉	新加坡	1998	
萨米·穆达拉尔	叙利亚	1998	
约瑟夫·布拉特	瑞士	1999	
拉米内·迪亚克	塞内加尔	1999	
谢尔盖·布勃卡*	乌克兰	1999	1988/92/96/00 **
罗伯特·克特夫特里克	美国	1999	1988/92/96 **
曼努埃拉·迪辛塔	意大利	1999	1984/88/92/94/98 **
亚历山大·波波夫	俄罗斯	1999	1992/96/00/04 **
塔马斯·阿贾恩	匈牙利	2000	
吉安·佛兰科·卡斯帕	瑞士	2000	
基普乔盖·凯诺	肯尼亚	2000	1964/68/72 **
卡洛斯·阿什·努兹曼	巴西	2000	1964
拉萨呐·帕伦弗	科特迪瓦	2000	
亨利·瑟兰德	法国	2000	
于再请*	中国	2000	
霍震霆	中国香港	2001	
拉迪·辛格	印度	2001	
约翰·D.科茨	澳大利亚	2001	
伊萨·哈亚图	喀麦隆	2001	
胡安·安东尼奥·小萨马兰奇	西班牙	2001	
布雷达·维里斯曼	荷兰	2001	
呐瓦夫·肥萨尔·法德·阿齐兹	沙特阿拉伯	2002	
帕特瑞克·钱姆达	赞比亚	2002	
塔米姆·本·哈马德·阿尔-泰尼	卡塔尔	2002	

续 表

姓　　名	国家奥委会	入选年	奥运会参加情况
凯·霍尔姆	丹麦	2002	
尤素法·恩戴耶	塞内加尔	2002	
帕尼拉·维贝格	瑞典	2002	1992/94/98/02＊＊
菲利普-克雷文	英国	2003	
简·泽莱兹尼	捷克	2004	1988/92/96/00/04＊＊
希克曼·埃尔·盖鲁伊	摩洛哥	2004	1996/00/04＊＊
佛朗克·弗雷德里克斯	纳米比亚	2004	1992/96/04＊＊
兰尼亚·埃尔瓦尼	埃及	2004	1992/96/00
巴巴拉·肯达尔	新西兰	2005	1992/96/00/04＊＊
佛朗西斯哥·里奇-比蒂	意大利	2006	
通克·依木兰王子	马来西亚	2006	
尼科尔·霍弗尔茨	阿鲁巴	2006	1984
比特瑞斯·艾伦	冈比亚	2006	
海因·维尔布鲁根	荷兰	2006	
里贝卡·斯考特	加拿大	2006	1998/02/06＊＊
萨库·科伊维	芬兰	2006	1994/98＊＊
安德列·波特洛·菲利浦斯伯恩	克罗地亚	2007	
帕特瑞克·鲍曼	瑞士	2007	
哈亚·宾特·埃尔·侯塞因公主	阿联酋	2007	
瑞塔·苏泊瓦	印度尼西亚	2007	

＊ 执委会委员
＊＊ 奥运奖牌得主

＊ 现任国际奥委会委员来自 79 个国家,瑞士、意大利各占有 5 个席位,荷兰有 4 席,俄罗斯、美国、澳大利亚、英国和法国各有 3 席,巴西、中国、匈牙利、乌克兰、墨西哥、芬兰、埃及、德国、日本、加拿大各有 2 席。

附录 3
历届夏季奥运会参赛信息

届数	举行日期	举行地点	国数	运动员人数
1	1896.4.6—4.15	雅典(希)	14	241
2	1900.5.14—10.28	巴黎(法)	24	997
3	1904.7.1—11.23	圣路易斯(美)	12	651
4	1908.4.27—10.31	伦敦(英)	22	2008
5	1912.5.5—7.22	斯德哥尔摩(瑞典)	28	2407
7	1920.4.20—9.12	安特卫普(比)	29	2626
8	1924.5.4—7.27	巴黎(法)	44	3089
9	1928.5.17—8.12	阿姆斯特丹(荷)	46	2883
10	1932.7.30—8.14	洛杉矶(美)	37	1332
11	1936.8.1—8.16	柏林(德)	49	3963
14	1948.7.29—8.14	伦敦(英)	59	4104
15	1952.7.19—8.3	赫尔辛基(芬)	69	4955
16	1956.11.22—12.8	墨尔本(澳)	72	3314
17	1960.8.25—9.11	罗马(意)	83	5338
18	1964.10.10—10.24	东京(日)	93	5151
19	1968.10.12—10.27	墨西哥城(墨)	112	5516
20	1972.8.26—9.11	慕尼黑(德)	121	7134
21	1976.7.17—8.1	蒙特利尔(加)	92	6084

续　表

届数	举行日期	举行地点	国数	运动员人数
22	1980.7.19—8.3	莫斯科(苏)	80	5179
23	1984.7.28—8.12	洛杉矶(美)	140	6829
24	1988.9.17—10.2	汉城(韩)	159	8391
25	1992.7.15—8.9	巴塞罗那(西)	169	9364
26	1996.7.19—8.4	亚特兰大(美)	197	10318
27	2000.9.15—10.1	悉尼(澳)	199	10735
28	2004.8.11—8.29	雅典(希腊)	201	10625

附录4
历届冬季奥运会参赛信息

届数	举行日期	举行地点	国数	运动员人数
1	1924.1.25—2.5	夏蒙尼(法)	16	258
2	1928.2.11—2.19	圣莫里兹(瑞士)	25	464
3	1932.2.4—2.13	普莱西德湖(美)	17	252
4	1936.2.6—2.16	加米施-帕滕基兴	28	646
5	1948.1.30—2.8	圣莫里兹(瑞)	28	669
6	1952.2.14—2.25	奥斯陆(挪)	30	694
7	1956.1.26—2.5	科蒂纳丹佩佐(意)	32	821
8	1960.2.18—2.28	斯阔谷(美)	30	665
9	1964.1.29—2.9	因斯布鲁克(奥地利)	36	1091
10	1968.2.6—2.18	格勒诺布尔(法)	37	1158
11	1972.2.3—2.13	札幌(日)	35	1006
12	1976.2.4—2.15	因斯布鲁克(奥地利)	37	1123
13	1980.2.13—2.24	普莱西德湖(美)	37	1072
14	1984.2.8—2.19	萨拉热窝(南斯拉夫)	49	1272
15	1988.2.13—2.28	卡尔加里(加)	57	1423
16	1992.2.8—2.23	阿尔贝维尔(法)	64	1801
17	1994.2.12—2.27	利勒哈默尔(挪)	67	1737
18	1998.2.7—2.22	长野(日)	72	2176

续　表

届数	举行日期	举行地点	国数	运动员人数
19	2002.2.8—2.24	盐湖城（美）	77	2399
20	2006.2.10—2.26	都灵（意）	80	2508

附录5
女性参与夏季奥运会的情况

年	大项	小项	国家	参赛者	%	年	大项	小项	国家	参赛者	%
1896	—	—	—	—		1956	6	26	39	384	16.1
1900	2	3	5	22	1.6	1960	6	29	45	610	11.4
1904	1	2	1	6	0.9	1964	7	33	53	683	13.3
1908	2	3	4	37	1.8	1968	7	39	54	781	14.2
1912	2	6	11	48	2.2	1972	8	43	65	1058	14.8
1920	2	6	13	77	2.9	1976	11	49	66	1247	20.7
1924	3	11	20	136	4.4	1980	12	50	54	1125	21.5
1928	4	14	25	290	9.6	1984	14	62	94	1567	23
1932	3	14	18	127	9	1988	17	86	117	2186	25.8
1936	4	15	26	328	8.1	1992	19	98	136	2708	28.8
1948	5	19	33	385	9.4	1996	21	108	169	3626	34.2
1952	6	25	41	518	10.5	2000	25	132	199	4069	38.2
						2004	26	135	201	4329	40.7

附录 6
女性参与冬季奥运会的情况

年	大项	小项	国家	参赛者	%	年	大项	小项	国家	参赛者	%
1924	1	2	7	13	5	1972	3	13	27	206	20.5
1928	1	2	10	26	5.6	1976	3	14	30	231	20.6
1932	1	2	7	21	8.3	1980	3	14	31	233	21.7
1936	2	3	15	80	12	1984	3	15	35	274	21.5
1948	2	5	12	77	11.5	1988	3	18	39	313	22
1952	2	6	17	109	15.7	1992	4	25	44	488	27.1
1956	2	7	18	132	17	1994	4	27	44	532	30
1960	2	11	22	143	21.5	1998	6	31	54	788	36.2
1964	3	13	28	200	18.3	2002	7	37	55	886	36.8
1968	3	13	29	211	18	2007	7	40	60	960	38.3

附录 7
北京奥运会场馆

一、北京

(一)新建的 12 个场馆

1. 国家体育场("鸟巢")
2. 国家游泳中心("水立方")
3. 北京射击馆
4. 老山自行车馆
5. 五棵松体育馆
6. 国家体育馆
7. 小轮车赛场铁人三项赛场
8. 奥林匹克森林公园网球场
9. 中国农业大学体育馆
10. 北京工业大学体育馆
11. 北京大学体育馆
12. 北京理工大学体育馆

(二)11 个改扩建场馆

1. 丰台垒球场
2. 工人体育场

3. 工人体育馆
4. 北京航空航天大学体育馆
5. 奥体中心体育场
6. 奥体中心体育馆
7. 英东游泳馆
8. 老山山地自行车场
9. 北京射击场飞碟靶场
10. 首都体育馆
11. 北京理工大学体育馆

(三) 8个临时场馆

1. 会议中心击剑馆
2. 五棵松棒球场
3. 奥林匹克森林公园曲棍球场
4. 沙滩排球场
5. 奥林匹克森林公园射箭场
6. 奥林匹克水上公园
7. 城区公路自行车赛场
8. 石景山自行车越野赛场

二、京外体育场馆

(一) 新建项目

1. 青岛国际帆船中心
2. 天津体育场
3. 秦皇岛体育场

（二）改造项目

1. 沈阳五里河体育场
2. 上海体育场
3. 香港沙田赛马场

参考文献

英文

1. 书籍

Alfred E. Senn, *Power, Politics, and the Olympic Games—A History of The Power Brokers, Events, and Controversies That Shaped the Games*, Human Kinetics, 1999.

Aristoles, *The Rhetoric of Aristotle*, London: G. Bell, 1878, Translated by J. S. Walson Book III, 13.

Allen Guttmann, *The Olympics: A History of the Modern Games*, Urbana and Chicago: University of Illinois Press, 1992.

Carl-Diem-Institut (ed.), *The Olympic Ideal: Pierre de Coubertin – Discourses and Essays*, Stuttgart Olympischer Sportverlag, 1966.

Charles Beck (ed.) *Oi Olympiakoi Agones, 776 p. X. -1896 (The Olympic Games, 776 BC-1896)*, Athens 1896.

Christopher R. Hill, *Olympic Politics: Athens to Atlanta 1896 – 1996 (Second edition)*, Manchester and New York: Manchester University Press, 1996.

Craig Donnellan (ed.), *Drugs and Violence in Sport: Issues for the Nine-*

ties, No. 26, Cambridge: Independence Educational Publishers, 1995.

Daniel Covell, eds., *Managing Sports Organisations: Responsibility for Performance*, Thomson: South-western, 2003.

David Levinson and Karen Christensen (eds.), *Encyclopedia of World Sport: From Ancient Times to The Present*, Oxford: ABC—CLIO Ltd., 1996.

Diane L. Dupuis, Marie J. MacNee, Christan Brelin, and Martin Connor, *The Olympics Factbook*. Detroit: Visible Ink Press, 1993.

Douskou, Iris, *The Olympic Games In Ancient Greece*. Athens: Ekdotike Athenon, 1982.

Dong Jinxia, "Women, Nationalism and the Beijing Olympics: Preparing for Glory", in Boria Majumdar and Fan Hong (eds.), *Modern Sport: The Global Obsession—Politics, Religion, Class, Gender; Essays in Honour of J. A. Mangan*, Lodon and New York: Routledge Taylor & Francis Group, 2007.

Ellis Cashmore, *Making Sense of Sports* (Second Edition), London and New York: Routledge, 1996.

Ellis Cashmore, *Sports Culture: An A—Z Guide*, Routledge, 2002.

FIFA Financial Report 2003, Ordinary FIFA Congress, Paris, 20 and 21 May 2004.

Olympic Message, No. 33, July 1992.

Girginov Vassil, The Olympic Games Explained, London: Routledge 2005.

Gray Poole, *The Ancient Olympic Games*, London: Vision Press, 1963.

H. Forester (ed.), *Critical Theory and Political Life*, Cambridge, MA: MIT., 1985.

Hai Ren, "China and the Olympic Movement", 2002 Centre d'Estudis Olímpics de'Esport (UAB). Holger Preuss, Economic Dimension Of The Olympic Games, Centre d'Estudis Olímpics i de l'Esport (UAB), International Chair in Olympism, 2002.

International Olympic Committee, *Olympic Charter*, 1964.

International Olympic Committee, *Olympic Charter*, Sept. 11, 2000.

John Arlott (ed.), *The Oxford Companion to Sports & Games*, Oxford University Press, 1975.

John E. Findling and Kimberly D. Pelle, *Encyclopedia of the Modern Olympic Movement*, London: Greenwood Press, 2004.

John T. Powell, *Orignins and Aspects of Olympism*, Champaign, Illinois: Stipes Publishing Company, 1994.

Jonathan Kolatach, *Sport, Politics and Ideology in China*, New York: Jonathon David, 1972.

John W. Garver, *Foreign Policy of the People's Republic of China*, Englewood Cliffs, NJ: Prentice Hall, 1993.

Kendall Blanchard (et al), The Anthropology of Sport: An Introduction. Massachusetts: Bergin & Garvey Publishers, 1985.

Martin Wimmer, *Olympic Buildings*, Edition Leipzing, 1976.

Nicolaos Yalouris ed., *The Eternal Olympics: The Art and History of Sport*, New Rochelle, New York: Caratzas Brothers, Publishers 1979.

Susan Brownell, *Training the Body for China: Sports in the Moral Order of the People's Republic*, Chicago and London: The University of Chicago Press, 1995.

Tylor, Edward B., *Primitive Culture: Researches into the Development of Mythology, Philosophy, Religion, Art and Custom*, vol. 1: Origins of Culture, Gloucester, Mass: Smith, (1871) 1958.

Yalouris, N. *The Art in The Sanctuary of Olympia*. Report of the Eleventh Session of the International Olympic Academy. 90. Athens 1971.

2. 杂志

Essex, S., & Chalkley, B., (1998), "Olympic Games Atalyst of Urban Change", *Leisure Studies*, Vol. 17, no. 3, 187-207.

J. Crompton, "Economic impact analysis of sports facilities and events: eleven sources of misapplication", Journal of Sport Management, 9, 1996, 14-35.

C. Dubi, "The Economic Impact of a Major Sports Event", Olympic Message, 1996, 3.

Coubertin, P. de: "A Modern Olympia", in Martin Wimmer, *Olympic Buildings*, Edition Leipzig, 1976.

George Raine, "2004 Athens Games: Advertising Sporting a Profit: NBC Sells Expansive Olympic Coverage", *Chronicle research*, August 12, 2004.

John T. Powell, "Ancient Greek Athletic Festivals", *Olympic Review*, 1984.

3. 报纸

P. H. Lewis, "In Cyberspace, a High-Tech League of Their Own", The New York Times, Tue Apr. 5, 1994.

Michael Janofsky, "Track and Field: Reynolds Case Spotlights Battle of the Regulators", *The New York Times*, October 11, 1991.

Gianna Angelopoulos Daskalaki, "We Are Ready to Compete on The World Stage Again", *The Daily Telegraph*, August 12, 2004.

John Pye, "Olympic Ceremony Sparks uproar Gosper under Fire for Giving Daughter Torch", The Associated Press, Sydney, Australia (AP), Thursday, May 11, 2000.

"Olympic Marketing 1980-2001: Two Decades of Unprecedented Support for Sport", *Marketing Matters* (The Olympic Marketing Newsletter), No. 19, July, 2001.

David Powell, "Americans Stand Accused of Doping Conspiracy", Times Online-Sport, October 17, 2003.

John Goodbody, "Inquiry into Drug Use Created Long-term Positive Effects", Times Online-Sport, September 24, 2003.

Crag Lord, "Caught Red-Handed—Amid Global Cries Of 'I Told You So,' China Awaits Its Fate In The Great Doping Scandal", *Sunday Times*, 11 January 1998.

C. Palaeologos, "The Ancient Olympics", Paper presented at the Proceedings of the International Olympic Academy, University of Leeds, 1964.

William K. Guegold, "Volunteerism and Olympic Music Venues", papers of the Symposium held in Lausanne, 24-26 Nov., 1999.

中文

1. 书籍

国家体委(编):《中国体育年鉴》49-91 精华本(第二卷),北京:人民体育出版社,1993年。

谢亚龙主编:《奥林匹克研究》,北京体育大学出版社,1994年。
张岱年,方克立主编:《中国文化论》,北京师范大学出版社,1994年。
赵禹:《赵禹体育问题报告文学集》,中国社会科学出版社,1988年。
孔繁敏:《略论奥林匹克文化》,人文奥运建设座谈会发言材料,2002年。
国家体育总局竞技体育司:《各省自治区直辖市备战2004年、2008年奥运会调研情况报告》全国竞技体育工作会议参考资料之一,2003年。

2. 杂志

《体育产业信息》,2004年第10期。
《体育史料》,1980年1—4期。
《体育论坛》,1988年第1期。
《当代》,1988年第2期。
《体育工作情况反映》,1986年第9期(4月)。
《体育工作情况》,1996年第16—17期(总.624—625)。

3. 报刊

《中华工商时报》,2004年12月10日。
《北京晚报》,2003年2月25日。
《市场报》,2003年2月26日。
《人民日报》,1994年3月25日;2002年1月2日;2002年7月5日。
《京华时报》,2004年8月27日。
《北京日报》,1996年6月2日
《北京现代商报》,2003年4月4日
《竞报》2005年8月29日

网　站

京报网
www.olympic.org

http://www.athens2004.com
http://news.mongabay.com/
http://www.coa-india.org
http://www.ballparks.com/baseball/national/olympi.htm
http://www.cyclerace.or.kr/e_cra/launching02_a.html
http://www.cbc.ca/olympics/venues/olympic_stadium.html
http://www.olympic.org/uk/games/athens/index_uk.asp
http://multimedia.olympic.org/pdf/en_report_644.pdf
http://multimedia.olympic.org/pdf/en_report_60.pdf
http://www.olympic.org/ 2005 Marketing File/
http://www.yahoo.com/Recreation/Sports/
http://multimedia.olympic.org/pdf/en_report_60.pdf.
http://www-white.media.mit.edu/~intille/st/electronic-arena.html
http://espn.go.com/oly
http://english.people.com.cn
http://www.olympic.org/uk
http://www.louvre.fr
http://www.ioa.leeds.ac.uk/
http://www.perseus.tufts.edu/Olympics/site.html
http://61.135.180.163/xwzx/tpxw/5945.shtm
www.athens2004.com
http://www.britannica.com/eb/article?eu=137628
http://www.sports.gov.cn.
http://www.guardian.co.uk/?
http://www.chinanews.com.cn/zhonghuawenzhai/2001-08-01/txt3/12.htm
www.beijing-2008.org
http://olympic.sportsol.com.cn
www.bjd.com.cn
http://www.china.org.cn/english/sports/191730.htm
www.xinhuanet.com

http://www.china.com.cn/chinese/2003/Aug/378176.htm

CCTV.com（2004-03-24）

http://www.tdctrade.com/imn/05020301/clothing162.htm

http://www.forbes.com/columnists/free_forbes/2004/0524/043.html

The Olympic Culture: An Introduction

(Bilingual Textbook)

Dong Jinxia   J. A. Mangan

The Olympic Culture: An Introduction

(Bilingual Textbook)

Dong Jinxia & J. A. Mangan

Introduction of the Authors

Dong Jinxia is a professor of Peking University, the Director of the Peking University Research Centre for Gender, Sports and Society; Deputy Director of the Peking University Research Centre for Sport, Society and Culture; member of Chinese Sports Science Association and FIG International Gymnastics Judge. She received her Bachelor and Master degrees from Beijing Sports University in the 1980s and Ph. D. from University of Strathclyde (UK) in 2001. She worked in Beijing Sports University between 1985 and 2001. Since 2001 she has been working at the Peking University, lecturing and researching in the fields of Olympic Culture, Gender and Sport, Sports Sociology and Physical Shaping.

In recent years she has been invited to universities and international conferences in the following countries and regions: Germany, Canada, USA, Greece, Denmark, Japan, Korea and Hong Kong in China to lecture at her research area of sport, women and society in China. She has authored hundreds of articles and books both in Chinese and English on sport, culture and gender, including the internationally acclaimed book *Women, Sport and Society in the New China* published by Cass Publisher, London in 2003.

J. A. Mangan is an emeritus professor of Strathclyde University, UK and Fellow of the Royal Historical Society. He is a scholar of the highest repute in the fields of sport history and cultural studies. He is the chief editor of the following journal: *The International Journal of the History of Sport*, and the founding editor of *Sport in Society* and *Soccer and Society*, He is also the founding editor of the internationally acclaimed Series *Sport in the Global Society*, which has one hundred published volumes. There are about 40 monographs and collections under his name, including the internationally acclaimed *Athleticism in Victorian and Edwardian Public School: the Emergence and Consolidation of an Educational Ideology*;

The Games Ethic and Imperialism, *Manliness and Morality: Middle Class Masculinity in Britain and America 1800-1940*; *Pleasure, Profit and Proselytism: British Culture and Sport at Home and Abroad 1700-1914*; *The Cultural Bond: Sport, Empire, Society*, *From Fair Sex to Feminism: Sport and the Socialization of Women in the Industrial and Post Industrial Eras*; *Freeing the Female Body: Inspirational Icons*; *Kicking Off A New Era: Soccer, Women and Sexual Liberation* and *Struggles for Status: Sport and Ethnicity*.

Contents

Acknowledgements/1

Straws Blowing in the Wind (Foreword) (J. A. Mangan)/1

Preface (Dong Jinxia)/1

Part One: Social Perspective

Chapter 1 Overview of the Olympic Culture/3
1. Concepts and Classification/3
  (1) Culture/3
  (2) Olympic Culture /4
2. Contents/5
3. Characteristics/6
  (1) Common Cultural Features/6
  (2) Unique Features/7
4. The Philosophic Foundation of Olympic Movement/8
  (1) Philosophy of Life/8
  (2) A Universal Social Philosophy/10

Chapter 2 The Institutional Dimension of the Olympic Culture/12
1. The Structure of the Olympic Family/12
  (1) IOC/12
  (2) International Sports Federations (IFs) — the Experts in Olympic Sports/19
  (3) National Olympic Committees (the NOCs)/20
  (4) The Organising Committee of the Olympic Games (OCOG)/22
  (5) Olympic Athletes/22
2. Relations between the Olympic Family Members/23

Chapter 3　The Olympics: Organisation/27
　1. Bids for the Games/27
　2. Organising the Games: Procedures /30
　(1) Structure of the Organising Committee/30
　(2) Obligations of the Organising Committee/30
　3. Variations in Organising the Games/31
　4. Organising the Games: Advantages and Disadvantages/33
　(1) Social Impact/33
　(2) Urban Regeneration/33
　(3) Economic Impact of the Olympics/35
　(4) Environmental Impact of the Olympics/37

Chapter 4　The Olympics: Architectural and Technological Evolution/40
　1. Architecture/40
　(1) Greek Stadiums/41
　(2) Roman Amphitheatres/42
　(3) Modern Olympic Constructions/43
　(4) Issues Relevant to Sports Architecture/50
　2. Technology/52
　(1) Equipment/52
　(2) More Accurate Measurement of Performance/53
　(3) Monitoring Judges and Referees/53
　(4) Technology and Performance/54
　(5) Technology and Greater Audience Choice /54

Chapter 5　The Olympics Mass Media/57
　1. Media Power/57
　2. Mass Media Forms/58
　(1) Press/59
　(2) Radio/59
　(3) Film/60

(4) Television/63
(5) Internet/65
3. Broadcasting /67

Chapter 6　The Olympic Games: Ceremonies/74
1. Lighting of the Flame /74
2. Torch Relay/75
3. Opening Ceremony/80
4. Victory Ceremony/82
5. Closing Ceremony/85
6. Ceremonial Ritualism: the Opening Ceremony in Detail/86

Chapter 7　The Olympics and the Arts/91
1. Brief Historical Overview /91
2. Modern Olympic Cultural Programmes/98
3. Modern Olympic Music/101

Part Two　Historical Perspective

Chapter 8　The Ancient Olympics/107
1. The Ancient Greek Civilisation /107
   (1) Religion/108
   (2) War and Olympic Culture/109
2. The Evolution of the Ancient Olympic Games/110
   (1) Festival, Games and Olympia/110
   (2) Regulations/113
   (3) Programme/114
   (4) Competition and Cheating/115
3. The Decline of the Ancient Olympic Culture/117

Chapter 9　The Olympic Games: Revival and Resurgence/122
1. The Creation of the Modern Olympics/122

  (1) Ideological Background/122
  (2) The Industrial Revolution/123
  (3) Bourgeois Education Reform/124
  (4) Internationalisation of Sport/124
  (5) Archaeological Excavation/125
  (6) Events to Revive the"Games"/125
 2. The Emergence of the IOC/127
 3. The Evolution of the Modern Olympics/129
  (1) Gradual Construction of the Organisational Model/132
  (2) Impact of Major Wars on the Olympics/133
  (3) Expansion of the Games: Examples/133
  (4) Location of the Host City and its Impact on the Games/134
  (5) Modern Transformation/135
 4. Future of the Olympic Movement/137

Chapter 10 The Modern Olympic Movement: Confrontation between Idealism and Realism/143
 1. Amateurism and Professionalism/143
 2. Philanthropy and Commercialisation/146
 3. Evading Politics and Embracing Politics/147
 4. Fair Play and Foul Play/150
  (1) Doping/151
  (2) Other Problems/156
 5. Male Dominance and Gender Equality /157

Chapter 11 Olympic Marketing: The Olympic Movement as a Business/164
 1. Olympic Marketing in Historical Perspective/165
 2. Unique Characteristics/168
 3. The Principle Sources of Olympic Marketing Revenue/168
  (1) Sponsorship/168

(2) Olympic Ticketing/172
(3) The Olympic Coin Programme/173
(4) Olympic Philately /173
4. Management of Olympic Marketing/174
(1) Structure of Management/174
(2) Distribution of Marketing Revenue/175
(3) Protection of Marketing Intellectual Properties/176
(4) Challenge of Over-Commercialisation/176

Part Three　The Olympics and China

Chapter 12　The Olympics and China: Evolution/181
1. Establishing Relations/181
2. Breaking Relations (1949-1979)/183
3. Normalising Relations (1979-1992)/184
4. Hosting the Olympics: Ambitions (1993-2001)/188

Chapter 13　Towards the Beijing 2008 Games/197
1. Infrastructural Construction /197
(1) Transport/198
(2) Stadiums and Parks/199
(3) Telecommunication Network/200
(4) Environmental Protection/200
2. Organisational Construction/201
(1) Management of Competition/202
(2) Marketing/202
(3) Sponsored Contests/203
(4) Competence Training/203
(5) Preparation for the Paralympics/204
3. A Humanistic Olympics/204
4. Athletic Performance and the Beijing Games/206
5. Opportunities and Challenges/207

(1) Opportunities/207
(2) Charllenges/208

Appendices

Appendix 1　Main Contents of Olympic Charter/217
Appendix 2　List of IOC Active Members/219
Appendix 3　Information of the Summer Games Over Time/223
Appendix 4　Information of the Winter Games Over Time/225
Appendix 5　Women's Participation in the Summer Games/227
Appendix 6　Women's Participation in the Winter Games/228
Appendix 7　Venues for the Beijing Games /229

Bibliography/231

Acknowledgement

With the approach of the 2008 Olympic Games, Beijing has become the centre of the world's attention and the Olympic Culture has been the heated topic that interests the global public. Based on the optional course "Olympic Culture" that was introduced in the University of Peking since 2002, *Olympic Culture:An Introduction(A Bilingual Textbook)* is written through years of modification, renew and improvement. Therefore, the completion of the book is to certain extent attributed to the support, aegis and funding by the Department of Teaching Administration of Peking University and the students who attended the course over the years. We are also greatly grateful to Ms Tian Wei, the editor of the book. Her intellinence, patience and assistance as well as her attention to detail encouraged and spurred on the authors to overcome various difficulties to improve the manuscript which is finally turned into the book.

Dong Jinxia   J. A. Mangan
April,2008

Straws Blowing in the Wind
(Foreword)

In 2007 I addressed a South East Asian Conference in the Republic of Korea on the need to recognise the fact that the global language of academia was English due to a set of historical coincidences and circumstances. The point was well made recently by a distinguished geneticist, Professor Steve Jones. He wrote that as a school student he was forced to study German on the grounds that it was the language of science. He commented : "It wasn t and had not been for decades for the world's scientists all talk and write in English. "Even as I spoke, however, I was aware that politically, culturally and linguistically there was happening a seismic global tectonic movement West to East. I suggested that in the future the three main global languages would be English, Chinese and Spanish—in that order. Not overnight but eventually and inevitably.

Over the last decade China has thrust itself into world prominence and this is just the beginning. The statistics of ascendancy are everywhere. Scarcely a day goes by without an addition. Merely one example: Goldman Sachs, the international investment bank, recently forecast that that by 2049 China would be the world's leading economy! A leading English business journalist, Mark Kleeman, not long ago informed his somnabulent readers that"…the level of commitment in our educational system to teaching Mandarin—which makes no mistake about it, will emerge as the new language of commerce in the 21st century—is laughable. " The state may be asleep but the far-sighted entrepreneurial middle-class is wide awake. It has noted which way the straw metaphorically is being blown to the East. The most read English quality newspaper, The Daily Telegraph, recently contained an article which under the main heading "It's as easy as yi, er, san" carried a sub-heading, "High – achieving parents are rushing to sign up Mandarin nannies". Among comments to ponder are, "Forget⋯French lessons, the latest trend for children from parents determined to give them every opportunity is a Mandarin nanny." Who specifically are these parents the commercial elite, "⋯ high-powered international business people who are making an investment for their children's future. They have realised that Mandarin will be an essential language for the next generation and they want their children to have a headstart".

For the Chinese, English is as important. Make no mistake about it. It is and will remain a leading global language (if not the leading language) of diplomacy, commerce and academia. No international diplomat, commercialist or academic can afford, or will be able to afford to be without it. The fact that the Chinese in their millions are learning it makes its enduring importance more certain than ever.

These comments above are by way of an explanation for this bilingual publication. It is a trail-blazer. It cuts a path others will follow as students in the East embrace English and students in the West embrace Chinese and both increasingly appreciate that bilingual publications assist and reinforce their linguistic development.

There is one more compelling and immediate reason for this publication the Beijing Olympics. Millions of Chinese students are now learning about the Olympic Movement. After Beijing 2008 the East led by China will come to have more and more involvement in and influence within the Movement. There is every possibility that English will be initially the language of intercommunication between East and West within the Movement but that Chinese will be heard increasingly in Lausanne and other relevant venues. In this respect also this publication is a harbinger of things to come.

J. A. Mangan

Preface

To ask the peoples of the world to love one another is merely a form of childishness. To ask them to respect one another is not in the least utopian; but in order to respect one another, it is first necessary to know one another. (Pierre de Coubertin, 1934) [1]

The Olympic Movement has become a global phenomenon. It seeks international cooperation between nations in the spirit of friendship, goodwill and fair play. It desires for individuals the harmonious development of body, mind and will. Its functions are multiple:

The Functions of the Olympic Movement
* the enhancement of national identity and prestige;
* communal integration, cooperation and consolidation;
* commercial development, job creation and economic prosperity including promotion of the economic generation of inner city areas;
* increasing personal and community involvement in and enjoyment of sport;
* promoting good skill and recreational opportunities;
* enhancing cross-cultural understanding between nations, ethnicities and races;

The highlight of the Olympic Movement is the two-week long Olympic Games which now brings together the peoples of the world through the medium of sport. The Olympic Games is the biggest and best supported sporting event of all time in terms of its number of sports, the number of participating athletes and the number of different countries united in a place at one time. Therefore, it is widely accepted that the Olympic Games offers the best means to demonstrate both the similarity and diversity of human cultures, and provides a significant opportunity to promote intercultural and international understanding and tolerance. At the same time the Games provides the inspiration to strive for personal dreams through lessons learnt from the striving, sacrifice and determination of the athletes. At its best, the Games shows how humanity can overcome political, economic, religious and racial barriers through sport. Ideally the significance of the Olympic Movement and its Games lies in the combination of competition with cooperation, mind with body, reason with passion, rules with freedom, and nationalism with internationalism.

The Olympic Movement is thus a unique cultural phenomenon. It has not only competitions, but also values which guide the Movement. Therefore, it is necessary to explore the Olympic Movement in the context of culture in order to understand fully the nature of the movement and demonstrate the similarity of the Movement to other social manifestations such as education and art.[2]

As the 2008 Olympic Games draw closer, the Olympic Movement has become widely popular in China. The International Olympic Committee (IOC) members and National Olympic Committee (NOC) members are now public figures, and the medias pay considerably more attention to the Olympics than other sports events; universities devote entirely to sport and physical education now have faculties specializing in Olympic affairs; some comprehensive universities, and even some elementary and secondary schools now have courses on the history and humanism of the Olympics; Olympic studies centres have been established in a number of universities;[3] an increasing volume of both academic and popular literature on the Olympics has emerged. As a consequence, more people than ever are now interested in the culture of the Olympics.

Olympic culture relates to the symbols, myths, ceremonies, values and artefacts that surround and permeate the Olympics. The aim of this Olympic Culture Course is to examine closely all aspects of the modern Olympic Games and Olympism in order to offer a comprehensive understanding of two key aspects of the Modern Olympic Culture:

* its historical developments and its present fundamental characteristics.
* the nature of the tensions created in the process of its evolution which

have led to recent reforms.

Approach

This book has thirteen chapters. These chapters will present diverse opinions. No particular point of view is promoted. Rather, different interpretations of modern Olympic culture are put forward, and the reader is invited to evaluate them critically.

Key Features

Each chapter is self-contained and can be studied independently. However, in order to facilitate an understanding of the complexity of Olympic culture, there are chapter cross-references.

Supplements

An Instructor's Manual with Test Bank, PowerPoint Slides, video and VCD are used as supplements to the printed manuscript.

Notes
[1] De Coubertin P (1934), " Forty Years of Olympism, 1894/1934", in Car-Diem-Institut (ed.) (1966), *The Olympic Idea: Pierre de Coubertin—Discourses and essays*, Stuttgart: Olympischedr Sportverlag, pp. 126-130.
[2] Lu xianwu (1994), "ao lin pi ke wenhua xianxiang de tezheng"[The characteristics of the cultural phenomenon of the Olympics], Beijing tiyu daxue chuban she [Beijing Sports University Press], pp. 118-120.
[3] For example, the People's Olympic Research Centre was set up in Renmin University and the Olympic Culture Research Centre was put in place in Beijing Union University in 2002.

Part One

Social Perspective

Chapter 1
Overview of the Olympic Culture

Key points of this chapter:
* The concept of Olympic Culture
* The contents of Olympic Culture
* The characteristics of Olympic Culture

1. Concepts and Classification

To understand Olympic culture, we need first to look briefly at the concept of "culture".

(1) Culture

Culture is not simply defined nor is there a consensus among scholars as to what exactly the concept should include. There are more than 100 definitions. What follows is a brief introduction to the concept. In general, culture can be defined both in a broad sense and a narrow sense.

In a broad sense, it refers to the complex cultural uniqueness of humanity when compared with other living creatures. This covers a wide range of aspects-political, economic, social and cultural and spiritual.

In a narrow sense, culture may be considered as Edward B. Tylor wrote in a famous definition in 1871: "...in its wide ethnographic sense,... that complex whole which includes knowledge, belief, art, morals, law, custom, and any other capabilities and habits acquired by man as a member of society".[1] In short, culture is both common to all humanity and specific to human groups.

Regarding the classification of culture there are different points of views. Some divide culture into two categories: material and spiritual. It is perhaps inappropriate to classify culture simplistically into material and nonmaterial categories or others as material objects are products of human ideas-secular and spiritual. Therefore, some believe that it has three components: material, institutional and spiritual. Some insist on four dimensions: material, institutional, custom, and ideas and values. Some even argue for six elements: material, social, spiritual, artistic, linguistic and custom. [2] In reality, of course, all cultural components are interwoven.

(2) Olympic Culture

What is then Olympic culture? Just as there are different definitions of culture, there are different definitions of Olympic Culture. For the purpose of this book, Olympic culture is defined as everything that has its origins in the Olympic Movement. Olympic culture is not only the Olympic Games but the ideals, ideas, activities and realities that surround it. This embraces past and present, strengths and weaknesses, successes and failures, virtues and vices.

Given that Olympic culture is the sum of material objects, institutions and spiritual products, it is classified here under three headings: material, institutional and spiritual.

Material

In terms of the Olympics, this self-evidently includes stadiums, playing fields, equipment and facilities as well as associated cultural products. [3] In essence then, it mainly comprises stadiums for the Olympic Games, the Olympic Village, the Olympic Museum, the IOC headquarters and publications, and the plethora of photographs, paintings, stamps, mascot, media projections and advertising copy.

Institutional

This concerns the regulations, laws and management structures established by Olympic Movement over time— *the Olympic Charter*, the System of Olympic Bidding, programmes and procedures of Olympic competitions, ritualistic opening and closing ceremonies, the flame-lighting ceremony, torch-relay and the medal ceremony and such like.

Spiritual

This refers to the ideals of the Olympic Movement encapsulated in its stated aims and ambitions and its espousal of cultural and art activities. [4]

The Olympic ideal, motto and tenet, are clear illustrations of this. These give the Olympic Movement its uniqueness.

2. Contents

While Olympic culture, as already stated, is much more than the Games, it is reflected in the following elements of the Games:

(i) **Opening and Closing Ceremonies** covering the whole range of Olympic symbols and values including the five rings, the flame and the doves.

(ii) **Medal Ceremonies** celebrating individual and national achievements.

(iii) **Cultural Programmes** including art, music and dance from all over the world.

(iv) **Sports Events** covering a large number of modern games and sports played throughout the world.

(v) **Equipment**—the Games is a showcase for new equipment and its contribution to enhancing performance.

(vi) **Technologies**—the Games is an ideal testing ground particularly for media innovations.

(vii) **Architecture**—the Games, constructions demonstrate some of most advanced achievements in this area—from sports facilities to complex urban designs.

(viii) **Environment**—since the early 1990s the Games has pioneered innovative solutions to acute environmental problems.

(ix) **Hobbies**—the Games represent the largest forum for sports hobbyists, including coins, philately, pins and other collections.

(x) **Educational Programmes**—typically, the host city of the Games develops educational programmes aimed primarily at young people which involve large numbers in physical and academic activities.

(xi) **Olympic Values and Norms**—ideals are written into the *Olympic Charter*.

(xii) **Tourism**—the Games give a massive boost to local, national and international tourism.

(xiii) **Gambling**—an overlooked aspect of the Olympics which involves large number of people and large amounts of money.

(xiv) **Commerce**—the Games stimulate a whole range of business activities providing a wide range of services and products-from baseball caps to burgers.

All of the above elements constitute also the image of the Olympic Games.

3. Characteristics

(1) Common Cultural Features

* Cultural values are learned by individuals as the result of belonging to a particular group.

* Culture, as corollary, constitutes that part of learned behaviour which is shared with others.

* Culture is a set of norms for adjusting both to the physical and non-physical environment.

* Culture comprises an integrated whole, which constitutes a total process. Change in one part affects all others. [5]

* Culture is dynamic and evolving as well as stable and continuing.

The Olympic Culture has all these features. [6] This fact can pose problems for Olympic harmony and for world harmony.

Case Study One: Misunderstanding between USA and Greece

The Los Angeles Olympic Committee had sold the rights to carry the Olympic flame in the United States for $3,000 per kilometre. To majority of Greeks this was sacrilegious commercial pollution of a symbol sacred to the world and to the Greek nation. To the Americans, this attitude was incomprehensible since much of the money raised was to go to youth charities. In Greece there are few private charities and the state is responsible for youth development, so the Greek authorities and journalists imagined this rationale to be a fig leaf for the naked marketing for which the Los Angeles leaders were already infamous. In frustration at these attitudes and absolutely unable to understand the true cultural sources of their intensity, the Los Angeles authorities put it about that the Greek Olympic Committee was just trying to extort exorbitant fees for putting on the ceremonies. This led to a "war" in the torch lighting between USA and Greece in 1984.... (source from *Encyclopaedia Britannica* 2002).

(2) Unique Features

The Olympic Culture, of course, has its own unique characteristics:

* **Symbolism**

Communication is based on the understanding of symbols. People send and receive messages through symbols and symbolic practices. Symbols are vehicles of meaning. Thus, they transport messages. The Olympic Games has its own symbolic messages. The Opening parade is a celebration of global goodwill, international optimism and faith in youth and its future. The parade of Olympic Champions, with which the Games conclude, also symbolises a belief in youth, its future and internationalism. It represents a visual message of the successful realisation of Olympic ideas. Olympic values and norms are also made manifest in symbolic form by means of the Olympic motto ("*Citius, Altius, Fortius*" now universally accepted to mean "Swifter, Higher, Stronger"), the Olympic flame (symbol of friendly competition and peaceful coexistence), and the Olympic Flag (symbol of global union).

* **Artistry**

The choreography and music of Opening Ceremony, Olympic medals, mascot and coins are themselves creative artefacts. In addition, the Olympic Games is the subject of, and inspiration for, various kinds of arts such as painting, sculpture, photography and stamps.

* **Ritualism**

The Olympiad includes a number of ceremonies and rituals, from the torch relay, lighting the flame, releasing doves in the opening ceremony, raising flags and playing the National Anthem of a winner at the award ceremony.

* **Combination of Nationality and Universality**

The Olympic values mentioned earlier have universal appeal. However, due to varied culture, location, history, tradition and system, different nations can employ different means to promote these values. This is clearly reflected in the design of the symbol and logo for each Olympic Games. For example, the Atlanta Games in 1996 incorporated the element of the "Star-Spangled Banner" into the Olympic emblem.

4. The Philosophic Foundation of Olympic Movement

(1) Philosophy of Life

Olympism—a state of mind arising from based on the equality of sports which are international and democratic—is the philosophical foundation of the modern Olympic movement. This philosophy was developed by the founder of the modern Olympic Movement, Baron Pierre de Coubertin (1863-1937) who gave no exact definition of this concept, but tried to explain it on several occasions from 1896 to 1935. He set out the components of Olympism in his "The Philosophical Foundations of Modern Olympism" (1935):[7]

* Religious —moral in emphasis.
* Elitist—but egalitarian and meritocratic.
* Chivalric—competion in friendly rivalry involving the suspension of exclusively national sentiments.
* Rhythmic—a reference to the ancient Olympiad as representing a "natural" cycle of time and recurrence, just like the harvest and the phases of the moon.
* Masculine—Coubertin did not approve of the participation of women in public competitions. In his Olympic Games, as in the contests of former times, their primary role should be to crown male victors.
* Aesthetic—Coubertin advocated and organised arts competitions in conjunction with the Games.
* Peaceful—Coubertin advocated mutual respect based on mutual understanding, heading to harmony, coop eration and comradeship.
* Participation—Coubertin said famously in London at the close of the 1908 Games: "Last Sunday, in the course of the ceremony organised at St Paul's in honour of the athletes, the Bishop of Pennsylvania recalled this in felicitous words: 'The important thing in these Olympiads is less to win than to take part in'...The important thing in life is not victory but struggle; the essential is not to have won but to have fought well."[8]

Olympism embraces a holistic philosophy of life—exalting the development of body, will and mind in a balanced whole; it comprises a social philosophy which emphasises the constructive role of sport in world development, international understanding, peaceful co-existence and social and moral education.

Olympism seeks to improve the individual and society, to create a way of life based on the satisfaction found in effort and the inspirational value of good example and respect for universal ethical principles developed through sport.

The Olympian should, in consequence:
* Well-rounded
* Self-improving

And should demonstrate:
* Leadership by example
* Ethical responsibility

And should treat others with:
* Dignity
* Respect

Olympism is founded on five basic human values:
- Harmony between body, mind and will
- Excellence within oneself
- Integrity in action
- Respect for others
- Joy in effort

Olympism is inclusive not exclusive; it involves not just winning but also participation; it advocates sport not just as a pleasurable activity, but also as a formative influence on the individual and society. Indeed, out of the thousands of people who enter the Olympic competitions, only a small proportion of athletes and teams reach the finals. Participation in the Games is the reality for the majority of the competitors. They have the chance of representing their country, of rubbing shoulders with an elite and the opportunity to give their best. This is the essence of the ideal Olympic Games!

Perdita Felicien, a member of the Canadian team at the Olympic Games in Sydney, caught this essence perfectly when she remarked: "... even though I was eliminated in the preliminary round of the 100m hurdles. I would do it all over again in a heartbeat. Even though the months of rigorous training and the exhausting 30 hours of flight to Sydney only meant exactly 13.21 seconds of running on the hottest track in the world... it was worth it."[9]

(2) A Universal Social Philosophy

The aim of Olympism is to place sport at the service of the development of mankind, to encourage through sport the creation of a peaceful global society concerned with the preservation of human dignity and to educate young people through sport to understand each other better. In short, the ambition of Olympism is to build a better and more peaceful world. In the words of Coubertin:

> ... *the Olympic Ideal is what qualifies sport... in general as a means for educating the whole man as a conscious citizen of the world... The Olympic Ideal is that exemplary principle which expresses the deeper essence of sport as an authentic educative process through a continuous struggle to create healthy and virtuous men[and women] in the highest possible way ("kalos k' gathos") in the image of the Olympic winner and athlete.* [10]

In summary, Coubertin, a product of late nineteenth-century liberalism and the architect of the modern Olympic Games, laid emphasis on the values of equality, fairness, dignity, rationality, harmony and excellence in the Games—the requirements of the philosophy of Olympism.

Summary

Post-Coubertin, the Olympic Games has become an impressively significant cultural phenomenon. This chapter has attempted to define the concept of Olympic culture, describe the main contents and characteristics of the culture and analyse the philosophic foundations and elements of the Olympic Movement in order to provide a basis for discussion in later chapters.

Questions
1. What do you consider the most important elements of Olympic Culture? Give your reasons.
2. What are the most admirable elements of Olympism as a philosophy? Give your reasons.

Notes

[1] Tylor, Edward B. (1871), *Primitive Culture: Researches into the Development of Mythlogy, Philosophy, Religion, Art and Custom*, Vol. 1: Origins of Culture, Gloucester, Mass: Smith,1958, 1.

[2] Zhang Dainian,Fang Keli(eds.,)(1994)*zhongguo wenhua lun*[About Chinese Culture], Beijing shifandaxue chuban she[Beijing Normal University Press],4-5.

[3] Kong Fanmin (2002), "lüe lun ao lin pi ke wenhua"[Brief Analysis of Olympic Culture], ren wen ao yun jianshe zuotan hui fayan cailiao[Speech at the Seminar of Building Humanistic Olympics].

[4] Ibid.

[5] Kendall Blanchard, et al. (1985), *The Anthropology of Sport: An Introduction*, Massachusetts: Bergin & Garvey Publishers.

[6] Ibid.

[7] Baron Pierre de Coubertin (1935), "The Philosophical Foundations of Modern Olympism",Carl-Diem-Institut(ed.), *The Olympic Ideal: Pierre de Coubertin-Discourses and Essays*, Stuttgart Olympischer Sportverlag, 1966, 130-134.

[8] Revue Olympique, July 1908, 110 (from a speech given during the London Olympic Games in 1908).

[9] Comments made on her athletics team's website, 27 November, 2000.

[10] Nissiotis, N (1987),L'Actualité de coubertin du Point de Vue Philosophique, in Müller,N. (ed.) *The Relevance of Pierre de. Coubertin Today*. CIPC,Niedernhausen,125-161.

Chapter 2
The Institutional Dimension of the Olympic Culture

Key points of this chapter:
* The Structure of the Olympic Family
* Relationships between the Members of the Olympic Family

　　The International Olympic Committee (IOC), established in 1894, is a non-profit making, non-governmental, self-elected and self-regulating international organisation with juridical status and perpetual succession. The Olympic Family consists mainly of five key members: the International Olympic Committee (IOC), the International Sports Federations (IFs), the National Olympic Committees (NOCs), the Organising Committees of the Olympic Games (OCOGs) and clubs and people belonging to the clubs, especially the athletes. Each member has its own commitments and interests, at the same time they interrelate and interact to ensure the smooth success of the Olympic Movement.

1. The Structure of the Olympic Family

(1) IOC

　　The International Olympic Committee (IOC), the supreme authority of the Olympic Movement, owns all rights concerning the Olympic Games and its main role is to promote the Olympic ideals. The IOC also makes decisions on all critical matters such as what sports should be included in the Olympic programme, which city should host the Games and how its wealth is distributed within the Olympic Family. The full details of the IOC's functions are set out in *the Olympic Charter* (see appendix 1).

The IOC has its permanent headquarters in Lausanne, Switzerland which was established in 1915. In 1981 the IOC was granted by a four Decree of the Swiss Federal Council the right to freedom of expression, freedom to meet freely and exemption from paying the national defence tax and no limitation on the number of foreign employees. Its administration has a permanent staff of about 100 people.

· **Structure**

The structure of the IOC comprises a supreme collective decision-making body—the Session (the IOC annual full meeting) and periodic Congresses and an operational body—the Executive Board (the president, vice-presidents and ten members) and Commissions (see Figure 2-1).

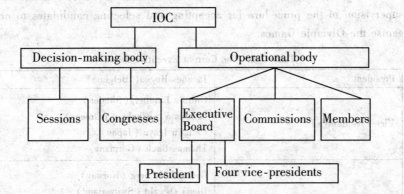

Figure 2-1 IOC Structure

* **Sessions and Congresses**

The Session is the supreme organ of the IOC. It adopts, modifies and interprets the Olympic Charter. Its decisions are final. On the recommendation of the Executive Board, it elects the members of the IOC. Once a year the IOC members meet in the Session to make important decisions. However, upon a request from over a third of IOC members, another session can be held. In 2002, two Sessions took place: the 113th, in Salt Lake City (USA) and the 114th in Mexico City (Mexico).

The Olympic Congress, held in principle every eight years, deal with strategic long-term issues. The Congress is composed of members and honorary members of the IOC, the delegates representing the IFs, the NOCs and the organisations recognised by the IOC and athletes and invited personalities.[1] The Centennial Olympic Congress celebrating the beginning of the modern Olympic Movement was held in Paris in 1994 under the slogan "Congress of Unity" and decided the fundamental role of the modern Movement in the 21st century.

* **The Executive Board**

The Executive Board (EB) consists of the President, four vice-presidents and ten additional members. All the members of the EB are elected by the Session.

The EB has many powers and duties such as determining the agenda of the Olympic Congress after consultation with the IFs and the NOCs; responsibility for the management of the IOC's finances and preparation of an annual report; recommendations regarding candidates for IOC members; supervision of the procedure for accepting and selecting candidates to organise the Olympic Games.

Table 2-1 The Current Executive Board

President	Jacques Rogge (Belgium)
Vice President(s)	Gunilla Lindberg (Sweden) Lambis V. Nikolaou (Greece) Chiharu Igaya (Japan) Thomas Bach (Germany)
Member(s)	Gerhard Heiberg (Norway) Denis Oswald (Switzerland) Mario Vázquez Raña (Mexico) Ottavio Cinquanta (Italy) Sergey Bubka (Ukraine) Zaiqing Yu (People's Republic of China) Richard L. Carrión (Puerto Rico) Ser Miang Ng (Singapore) Mario Pescante (Italy) Sam Ramsamy (South Africa)

The President of the IOC is elected by its members. He is now elected for eight years renewable once only for a further four years. However, since its establishment in 1894 the IOC has had only eight Presidents (see the following table).

Table 2-2　Presidents in the IOC History

Name	Duration	Nationality
Dimítrios Vikélas	1894-1896	Greece
Pierre, de Coubertin	1896-1925	France
Henri, de Bakker-Latour	1925-1942	Belgium
J. Sigfrid Edström	1946-1952	Sweden
Avery Brundage	1952-1972	United States
Michael Morris, Lord Killanin	1972-1980	Ireland
Juan Antonio Samaranch	1980-2001	Spain
Jacques Rogge	2001	Belgium

The President enjoys enormous power, ranging from overseeing daily operations to the right to co-opt members onto the Committee and to create or to dissolve commissions. The President is also very influential in regard to the elections of the Executive Board and its decisions though he cannot simply impose his views upon it. Therefore, the President plays a crucial part in directing the Olympic Movement. His personality, experience and values can greatly influence the evolution of the Movement. Some especially influential Presidents are described below.

IOC President Pierre de Coubertin(1863-1938)

　　Born into a French aristocrat family in Paris in 1863, Pierre de Coubertin was raised in cultivated and privileged surroundings. Interested in Ancient Greek history and education, he refused the military career planned for him by his family and renounced a promising political career. He considered education as the key to the future of society and the means to revive France which was defeated in the war with Germany in 1870, and being strongly influenced by the English Public School tradition of sport, he intended to reform French education in part in its image. Circa 1887 he wanted to revive the ancient Olympic Games. To popularize the idea, he published articles in journals, made public speeches and talked to people at home and abroad. In 1892 he openly advocated the re-establishment of the Olympic Games. Realising that sport was to become popular and universal, he accepted the proposal from a member of the Union des Sociétés Franqaisés des Sports Athletiques to organise an international congress to discuss the problem of amateurism. The Congress took place in June 1894. The revival of the Olympic Games was put forward for consideration andit received a positive response from participants. It was decide by the Congress that the first international Olympic Games was to be held in Athens in 1896 instead of Paris in 1900 as suggested by Coubertin.

　　To ensure the success of the first Games, Coubertin created a new magazine, *Revue Olympique*, in July 1894. He travelled to Athens to persuade the Greek royal family and other Greeks to support the Games and gave a stirring speech to the Parnassus Literary Society. This speech was considered a landmark in the history of the Olympic Movement. Thus it was Coubertin's vision, energy, enthusiasm and determination that created the modern Olympic Games.

IOC President Avery Brundage (1887-1975)

He had one thing in common with Coubertin. The amateur idea formed the crux of Brundage's concept of Olympism. He argued that "the Olympic Games are and must remain amateur if they are to continue. ... In order to be an Olympic amateur or eligible for the Olympic Games, a competitor always have practiced sport as a hobby, without material gain of any kind whatsoever. ... An Olympic amateur places sportsmanship above skill, nobility above fame and honour above success".

Beyond that he could not have been more different. Brundage was a highly controversial figure. He was variously described as an isolationist, an imperialist, a fascist and a communist. He considered himself a Taoist. In social background too, Coubertin and Brundage could not have been more different.

Coubertin was upper class; Brundage was working class. He was born in Detroit of working-class parents and moved to Chicago at about five years old. Shortly afterwards, his father abandoned the family. Brundage became a Chicago Tribune paperboy at twelve. While he studied in R. T. Crane Manual Training School, he combined after-school athletics with a daily schedule of 9:00 to 5:00 classes, a seven-mile trolley ride to and from school, and a two-hour pre-dawn stint of newspaper deliveries. Later he studied civil engineering at the University of Illinois. In 1912 he participated in the Stockholm Olympics and came 5th in the pentathlon. He was an amateur athlete of distinction. He was US all-around champion in 1914, 1916 and 1918. During this period he established his own company, profited from the post-war property boom and became a millionaire. Coubertin was a privileged aristocrat; Brundage was a self-made capitalist. He became the second Vice-President of American Athletic Union in 1925 and then President in 1928. He was elected as a member of the IOC in 1936 and appointed as Vice-President of the IOC in 1944. He presided over the IOC for twenty years on election to President in 1952.

Source from Otto Schantz, "The presidency of Avery Brundage (1952—1972)", in *1894—1994 The International Olympic Committee—One Hundred Years: The Idea-The Presidents-The Achievements (II)*, Lausanne: International Olympic Committee, 1995, pp. 65-90.

IOC President Juan Antonio Samaranch (1920-)

Juan Antonio Samaranch, the son of a textile manufacturer, was a middle class industrialist. His rise to the top of the Olympic Movement began by the unusual path of roller-skating: he led the Spanish team to the world title.

> Elected as an IOC member in 1966, then Chief of Protocol in 1968, his qualities as an untiring worker were soon put to use within various commissions. In 1970, he became a member of the Executive Board, and Vice-President of the IOC from 1974 to 1978. In 1977 Samaranch was appointed Spanish Ambassador to Moscow (1977-1980). He returned to the Executive Board in 1979 as Chief of Protocol and was elected to the presidency of the IOC the next year.
>
> From the time he took up office, he tried to give a new direction to the Olympic Movement which was badly shaken by the political difficulties of the XXII Olympiad, and undertook a long voyage around the world to establish numerous contacts with Heads of State and sports leaders and to defend the Olympic cause. He secured the IOC's status as an international non-governmental organisation and restructured and advanced its finances. He kept the Olympic spirit alive during the crisis years of boycotts (Moscow 1980 and Los Angeles 1984). It was through his efforts that the Olympic Museum was built in Lausanne (1993).
>
> When the IOC found itself in crisis because of abuses of trust by some of its members, he undertook major reforms to the structure of the institution.
>
> Samaranch's Presidency ended in June 2001 in Moscow, and he was elected Honorary President for Life.

Each of these Presidents came from different backgrounds; each served the Olympic Movement in different ways as a consequence of different priorities; each faced different challenges born of the times they lived in; each had their own priorities as an outcome of their own personal values and the predicaments they encountered. However all three demonstrated commitment to a concept, determination to see it prosper and skill in ensuring its success. Coubertin convinced the world of the significance of reviving the Olympic Games; Brundage resuscitated the Games in the immediate aftermath of the horrific Second World War; Samaranch secured the IOC's status as an international non-governmental organisation and reorganised its growing finances.

None was perfect: Coubertin was committed to the exclusion of women; Brundage was an opinionated authoritarian; Samaranch failed to curb corruption and drug abuse. However all ensured the forward momentum of the Olympic Movement to a unique position in modern sport. And all three, however imperfectly, kept alive the spirit of idealism that lay at the heart of its creation.

· **IOC Members**

The members meet once a year at the IOC Session. The term of office for all members is eight years, renewable every eight years. They can retire at the age of 70 (except for those who were elected before 11 December 1999; they can retire at the age of 80).

IOC members are elected and co-opted from the qualified candidates who reside in a country with an NOC recognised by the IOC. In contrast to most international organisations, the members of the IOC are its representatives in their respective countries and not delegates of their countries within the IOC. This implies that its members should be politically independent of national governments. However, this is far from the reality. Among the IOC members there are a number of diplomats, royalty and state officials. Thus, it is hard, if not impossible, for these IOC members to be independent of national governments.

The distribution of IOC membership between countries is much debated, because at present more than half of the 202 member countries are not represented at all, and most of those that have held the Games such as the UK, the USA, Switzerland or Russia, are allotted two members, with the result that there is ample room for disaffection among the unrepresented.

· **Commissions**

The IOC President sets up specialised Commissions to deal with relevant issues and make recommendations on them to the Executive Board.

∗ **The Olympic Solidarity Commission** attempts to that all athletes have the same chance to participate in the Games. This commission creates programmes to improve the sports infrastructure in various countries and offers financial assistance by awarding scholarships to athletes in preparation for the Games. The funds can be used for access to high-level sports facilities, specialised coaching or medical supervision as well as for participation in Olympic qualifying competitions.

∗ **The Medical Commission** supports research into sports sciences including sports medicine, biomechanics and sports physiology and nutrition. Its main priority is the fight against doping.

∗ **The Women and Sport Working Committee** is concerned to increase women's participation in sports at all levels and to increase the number of women in sports coaching and management.

∗ **The Commission for Culture and Olympic Education** promotes the relationship between sport and culture. To celebrate the cultural diversity of the Olympic Movement, the Commission, in collaboration with the NOCs, organises cultural and educational activities such as literature, painting and sculpture exhibitions, arts festivals and cultural programmes.

* **The Sport and Environment Commission** is concerned with ecology and the need to ensure the harmonious and sustainable development of sport and the environment.

There are other Commissions including the Olympic Games Coordination Commission, the Finance Commission, the International Relations Commission, the Ethics Commission, the IOC Juridical Commission, the Nominations Commission, the Olympic Games Study Commission, the Olympic Philately, Numismatic and Memorabilia Commission and the Olympic Programme Commission.

(2) International Sports Federations (IFs) — the Experts in Olympic Sports

An important member of the Olympic Family is the International Sports Federations (IFs). They are responsible for the development, administration and organisation of their sports. During the Olympic Games, the IFs govern the sports events of the Olympic Games programme. At present there are 35 such IFs (28 summer and 7 winter) responsible since 1921 for all the technical aspects of their sport including the rules, equipment, venues and judging. The affiliated members of each IFs all exceed 100.

Table 2-3　List of International Sports Federations

Summer Sports	Winter Sports
Int. Association of Athletics Federations (IAAF)	
Int. Cycling Union (UCI)	
Fédération Internationale de Natation (FINA)	
Int. Archery Federation	
Int. Badminton Federation	
Int. Baseball Federation	
Int. Basketball Federation (FIBA)	
Int. Boxing Association (AIBA)	
Int. Canoe Federation (ICF)	
Fédération Equestre Internationale (Horsesport, FEI)	
Fédération Internationale D'escrime (FIE)	
Fédération Internationale De Football Association (FIFA)	
Int. Gymnastics Federation (FIG)	
Int. Handball Federation (IHF)	
Int. Hockey Federation (FIHOCKEY)	
Int. Judo Federation (IJF)	

Con.

Summer Sports	Winter Sports
Union Internationale De Pentathlon Moderne (Pentathlon)	
Int. Rowing Federation (World Rowing)	
Int. Sailing Federation (Sailing)	
Int. Shooting Sport Federation (ISSF)	
Int. Softball Federation (International Softball)	
Int. Table Tennis Federation (ITTF)	
World Taekwondo Federation (WTF)	
Int. Biathlon Union (biathlon world)	
Int. Bobsleigh & Tobogganing Federation (bobsleigh)	
World Curling Federation (Worldcurling)	
Int. Ice Hockey Federation (Iihf)	
Int. Luge Federation (Fil-Luge)	
Int. Skating Union (Isu)	
Int. Ski Federation (Fis-Ski)	
Int. Tennis Federation (ITF)	
Int. Triathlon Union (Triathlon)	
Int. Volleyball Federation (FIVB)	
Int. Weightlifting Federation (IWf)	
Int. Federation Of Associated Wrestling Styles (Fila-Wrestling)	

Source: from the IOC website.

Not all the IFs enjoy equal status and have equal privileges. Some federations, such as the International Amateur Athletic Federation (IAAF) with 211 members or the Federation International de Football Association (FIFA) with 204 members, are much better positioned in the Family than others.[2] These two IFs are independently wealthy. The IAAF signed a US $ 91 million 4-year agreement of with the European Broadcasting in 1992, whereas FIFA is presiding over a global movement with revenue of approximately US $ 588.673 million in 2003.[3] Both federations' presidents sit on the EB and, individually, they have managed to negotiate some major concessions concerning representation of the IOC, the distribution of television revenues and the control of participants in the Games.

(3) National Olympic Committees (the NOCs)

Another important member of the Olympic Family is the National Olympic Committees (NOC). Each country that desires to participate in the Olympic Games must have an Olympic committee accepted by the IOC. National Olympic Committees equip, transport, and house their country's representatives at the Olympic Games. According to *the Olympic Charter*, the Committees must not be profit making organisations, must not associate themselves with affairs of a political or commercial nature, and must be completely independent and autonomous and resist all political, religious and commercial pressures. The NOCs have many functions in their respective countries, from the development of sport at all levels, to the creation of educational programmes, to the training of sports administrators. They are also responsible for sending athletes to the Games. Finally, they ensure that all the programmes carried out at a national level conform with the principles of *the Olympic Charter*.

The NOCs also recruit, supervise, and certify the athletes. Without certification from an NOC, no athlete can compete. Finally, with the advance of the IOC global marketing programme "The Olympic Programme", the NOCs around the world have been empowered to be sole proprietors of the five-ring circus on their national territories, stake-holders and partners of governments in promoting the Olympic Movement.

To be recognised as an NOC a country must have at least five national sports federations affiliated to the IFs. So far there are 202 such committees throughout the world: 53 in Africa, 42 in America, 44 in Asia, 48 in Europe and 15 in Oceania.

There are different types of NOCs: the NOCs that have full responsibility for all sports matters in their countries; the NOCs that co-operate with other national sports organisations; and the NOCs that work once every four years.

In addition, there is the Association of National Olympic Committees (ANOC) which brings the NOCs together at least once every two years in order to consolidate their role within the Olympic Movement. The ANOC is divided into five continental associations: Association of National Olympic Committees of Africa (ANOCA); Pan American Sports Organisation (PASO); Olympic Council of Asia (OCA); European Olympic Committees (EOC); Oceania National Olympic Committees (ONOC). These bodies promote their own interests and attempt to gain structural and financial privileges such as representation on the IOC, quotas for the Games or the distribution of sponsorship and TV rights money.

(4) The Organising Committee of the Olympic Games (OCOG)

Yet another important member of the Olympic Family is the Organising Committee of the Olympic Games (OCOG) which is set up after a city is awarded the Games. Each OCOG exists for about eight years: six or seven years of preparation and one or two years after the Games to tidy the books and make its final reports to the IOC and other appropriate institutions.

To date the Summer Games have been organised by only seventeen countries. Only six countries have hosted the Games more than once. The USA has hosted five and another five countries two. Seven countries have had the privilege of staging the Winter Games. Two countries, France and the USA, have each hosted four Games.

OCOG works with the IOC, the NOCs, the IFs, and local authorities and other important agencies to prepare the locale for both the competition and the visitors. Responsibilities include:

(i) to choose where and how to create the competition sites; the stadiums, training halls and the Olympic Village. In short, it is responsible for the infrastructure necessary for the running of the Games.

(ii) to provide an effective and efficient transport service.

(iii) to provide adequate medical services on site.

(iv) to offer a cultural programme-concerts, plays, ballets and exhibitions.

(v) to inform the public of all the preparations and respond to questions posed by the press.

(vi) to recruit and then train helpers from home and abroad. The OCOG benefits greatly from the assistance of thousands of volunteers who contribute to the success of the Games. The volunteers' activities cover such things as provision of transport, hospitality and administration.

(5) Olympic Athletes

The final important member of the Olympic Family are the athletes. The maximum number of athletes permitted for individual events is three per nation. The number, however, can be changed by the IOC in consultation with the international federation concerned. In team events only one team per country is allowed. In general, a National Olympic Committee may enter only its citizens.

Athletes with dual nationality may compete for the country of their choice. However, if they have already represented one country either at the Games or another major sports event, they may not compete for a different country within the three years. There is no age limit for competing in the Olympic Games, except for those that may be imposed by an individual IFs for health reasons. For example, to participate in the Games female gymnasts have to be 16 or over.

On their arrival in the host city athletes stay in the Olympic Village. At the Games their time is not devoted exclusively to competition. The Games are also an opportunity for them to meet other athletes. All of the inhabitants of the Village agree: it is not the comfort of the surroundings or the quality of the services that counts, what counts are the relationships created between athletes of the world. Anita L. DeFrantz, Olympian and IOC member, said of her experience in the Village: "For two to four weeks, the Village becomes the home for the elite athletes of the world. It was there that I realised that excellence comes in every shape, size, race and sex. It was there that I realised that an Olympian is one who can respect every individual based on the effort that takes to become an Olympian. It was there that I learned that each sport takes a special skill and determination for a person to ascend to the top."[4]

Whether or not they are winners, everyone involved in the Games takes home with them the memory of the exceptional experience of the Village.

To strengthen the link between active athletes and the International Olympic Committee (IOC), the Athletes' Commission was created in October 1981. This Commission is composed of active and retired athletes, holds at least one meeting each year and meets regularly with the IOC Executive Board, to which it offers recommendations. Furthermore, the Commission forms working groups to work in liaison with the Organising Committees of the Olympic Games to ensure that athletes' needs are met. At present the membership consists of eight athletes elected during the Games of the Olympiad, four elected during the Winter Olympic Games, and seven members appointed by the IOC to maintain a balance between the sexes, geographical regions and sports.

2. Relations between the Olympic Family Members

The IOC is the sole owner of the most expensive cultural commodity in the world—the Games. However, unlike other businesses, the IOC is not responsible for the production, marketing or the sales costs of the product, but has full control over the income distribution from its sale. Thus, the IOC has a great deal of influence without accountability. Thus, there is a constant tension between the IOC, the IFs and NOCs. Recently the claim was made that the IOC was redundant and the IFs and NOCs could adequately run the Olympic Movement without the IOC. The IOC replied that although without it the IFs might benefit in the short term, in the long run the Olympic Movement would collapse in chaos, because there would be no supreme regulatory body.[5] In an attempt to offer a collective voice to IOC a lobby group, the General Assembly of International Sports Federation (GAISF), was formed in 1967. To reduce the increasing power of the IFs, in 1983 the IOC created the Association of Summer Olympic International Federations (ASOIF) and the Association of the International Winter Sports Federations (AIWF).

However, under the pressure from the NOCs and the IFs for more say in IOC decisions, the IOC set out a new composition of its membership in the 2000 edition of The Olympic Charter: 15 presidents of the IFs and 15 representatives from the NOCs, 15 active athletes and 70 individuals. As a result, the IOC has to consult the IFs and NOCs more fully than in the past.

With the financial success of the Olympic Movement since the 1980s each member has demanded a greater share in the IOC's marketing income from sale of broadcast right and the TOP (The Olympic Programme) programme. To keep all the potentially conflicting interests in some sort of balance, in the late 1980s the IOC started to provide each member with a share of the Olympic revenue (see table 2-4).

Table 2-4 NOC, ISF and IWF Revenue from the IOC (in US $ million)

Olympic quadrenium	NOC	ISF	IWF	Total
1989—1992 (Albertville/Barcelona)	89.6	37.6	17	141.2
1993—1996 (Lillehammer/Atlanta)	137.9	86.6	20.3	244.8
1997—2000 (Nagano/Sydney)	191.9	n/a	50.3	242.2(pro)
2001—2004 (Salt Lake/Athens)	318.5		85.8	

Source: Olympic Marketing 2005 Fact File: www.olympic.org.

From 1997 the IOC reinvested 93% of the marketing revenue back into sport to be shared between NOCs, IFSs and OCOGs, and retained only 7% for its operational costs. The IOC provided the Nagano organizers with more than US $ 400 million and the Sydney organisers with more than US $ 1 billion, much more than either envisioned receiving from the IOC when they bid to host the Games.[6] The TV revenue for the period 2000-2004 was divided into 40% for the Olympic Movement and 60% for the OCOG, but changed after 2004 to 49% for OCOG and 51% to the Olympic Movement. Clearly, the NOCs and IFSs are the two principal beneficiaries from marketing and TV revenues.

In summary, the constitution, structure, funding and relations within the Olympic Movement reveal a complex balance of power, with those involved trying to pursue their own specific interests.

Summary

The International Olympic Committee was established in 1894. It is a non-profit making non-governmental, self-regulating international organisation. It has a family of five key members: IOC, IFSs, NOCs, OCOGs and athletes. The IOC's main role is to promote the Olympic ideals. It has an elected president, vice-president and members. The members meet annually in the Session. It also has specialised Commissions which report to it on specific issues. An important member of the Olympic Family is the International Sports Federations (IFs). Each Federation has responsibility for the development, administration and organisation of its sport. Another important member of the Family is the National Olympic Committees (NOCs). They are non-profit organisations responsible for approving, equipping, transporting and housing their national Olympic teams. Yet another important member is the Organising Committee of the Olympic Games (OCOG). Once a city is given the Games OCOG assists in preparation for the Games and evaluates the Games on their completion. The Olympic athletes themselves are also collectively an important family member.

Relations within the Olympic Family are not always good. In particular, there is a constant tension between the IOC, the IFs and the NOCs. The issue is invariably the distribution of power. The result is continual accommodation to achieve a complex balance of power.

Questions
1. Which of the especially significant recent Presidents described above do you consider the most significant for the Olympic Movement. Give your reasons.
2. Are there any additional Commissions that you would recommend to the IOC If so, explain why. If not, give reasons for your satisfaction with the present appointed Commissions.
3. Do you agree that the athletes (past and present) should advise the IOC? If so, give your reasons. If not, give your reasons.

Notes
[1] International Olympic Committee (2000), *Olympic Charter*, Chapter 1.
[2] Three presidents of IOC Bakker-Latour, Edstrom, and Brundage all had backgrounds in track and field, and for a country that wanted to take a place in the Olympic family, admission to membership in the IAAF had been considered a vital preliminary step. (Alfred E. Senn [-1999], *Power, Politics, and the Olympic Games—A History of the Power Brokers, Events, and Controversies that Shaped the Games*, Human Kinetics, 11.)
[3] *FIFA Financial Report 2003*(2004), Ordinary FIFA Congress, Paris.
[4] *Olympic Message*, No. 33, July 1992.
[5] Christopher R. Hill (1996), *Olympic Politics: Athens to Atlanta* 1896-1996 (Second edition), Manchester and New York: Manchester University Press, 69-70.
[6] *Final Report on the XXVIIth Olympiad*, 21.

Chapter 3
The Olympics: Organisation

Key points of this chapter:
* Bidding to Organise the Games
* Organising the Games
* Models of Past and Present Organisation
* The Organisation of the Games—Possible Advantageous and Disadvantageous Consequences

1. Bids for the Games

When Coubertin and his associates revived the Olympic Games they were fully aware of the efforts and resources needed. They decided that the site of the Games would rotate, thus enabling more nations and their peoples both to experience the Games and to share the responsibility of staging them.[1] Since 1908 the host city has been selected through a bidding process with the single exception of the post-war London Games in 1948.

Normally a city has to voice its wish to host the Games at least eight years in advance. For example, Athens submitted its application to host the 2004 Games in August 1996 and obtained them in September 1997. A similar time-scale was involved in the bid for the 2008 Beijing Games. After getting permission from the Chinese Central Party Committee and the State Council to go ahead to rebid (an earlier bid for 2004 failed) to host the Olympic Games in 2008, the Mayor of Beijing Liu Qi submitted an application to then IOC President Samaranch in April 1999 and in June 2000, the Beijing Olympic Bidding Committee handed in its *Report of Application* (see table 3-1) to the IOC, which included 22 issues concerning 6 areas. On July

13, 2001, Beijing defeated the other bidding cities to host the 2008 Games.

Table 3-1 Beijing's Report of Application for the 2008 Games

Volume 1	Volume 2	Volume 3
Preface * Letter of Support by President Jiang Zemin * Letter of Support by Premier Zhu Rongji * Letter from Liu Qi, Mayor of Beijing * Letter from Yuan Weimin, President of COC Introduction Theme 1 National, Regional and Candidate City Characteristics Theme 2 Legal Aspects Theme 3 Customs and Immigration Formalities Theme 4 Environmental Protection and Meteorology Theme 5 Finance Theme 6 Marketing	Introduction Theme 7 General Sports Concept Theme 8 Sports Athletics, Rowing, Badminton, Baseball, Boxing, Canoe/Kayak, Cycling, Equestrian, Fencing, Football, Gymnastics, Weightlifting, Handball, Hockey, Judo, Wrestling, Swimming, Modern Pentathlon, Softball, Taekwondo, Tennis, Table Tennis, Shooting, Archery, Triathlon, Sailing, Volleyball Theme 9 Paralympic Games Theme 10 Olympic Village	Introduction Theme 11 Medical/Health Services Theme 12 Security Theme 13 Accommodation Theme 14 Transport Theme 15 Technology Theme 16 Communications and Media Services Theme 17 Olympism and Culture Theme 18 Guarantees Conclusion

The honour of holding the Olympic Games is entrusted to a city and not to a country. The choice of the city lies solely with the IOC. Application to hold the Games is made by the chief authority of the city with the support of the national government. Applications must state that no political meetings or demonstrations will be held in the stadium or other sports grounds or in the Olympic Village and it must promise that every competitor shall be given free entry without any discrimination on grounds of religion, colour or political affiliation. This involves the assurance that the national government will not refuse visas to any of the competitors. At the Montreal Olympics in 1976, however, the Canadian government refused visas to the representatives of Taiwan because they were unwilling to forgo the title of the Republic of China, under which their National Olympic Committee was admitted to the IOC. Enforcement of the assurance is difficult and even the use of severe penalties by the IOC might not guarantee the elimination of infractions.

All candidate cities have to reply to a very comprehensive questionnaire, and present arguments in favour of their bid. In addition to municipal, social and commercial support, the government has to guarantee its support for the bid. A decision to bid for the Olympics therefore is made not by a single sport or public organisation but by the city's political authorities in alliance with commercial partners and the government. The cooperation between various agencies in putting forward a bid therefore does not require consulting the public.

In the case of Beijing's bid for the 2008 Games, government decisions and bureaucratic politics played the major part. The original idea behind the project was to use the event to stimulate the social and economic development of Beijing, to accelerate its recognition as one of the advanced cities of the world and to use the Games as a showcase for Chinese culture and increasing political and economic power. Accordingly, the Games' budget and proposed venues and installations reflected these goals. Some 134.9 billion yuan (about US $ 17 billion) is being spent on the construction of stadiums and relevant facilities. However, expenditure had to be reconsidered after the lOC warned Beijing of its concern over excessive expenditure. Thus, the initial budget of 4 billion yuan (about US $ 50.6 million) for the National Stadium called "Bird's Nest" was reduced to some 2 billion yuan (about US $ 25.3 million). [2]

Because of the potential benefits for the host city and country, candidate cities often adopt various measures from traditional lobbying to approaching key individuals on individual basis, and even use optimistic "psychological" propaganda such as changing the IOC members' hotel pillow cases the night before the vote with ones with the name of the city's main sponsor imprinted on them, in the hope of obtaining the IOC's votes. The Beijing Bidding Committee for the 2008 Olympic Games invited some sports and film stars such as Deng Yaping, Liu Xuan and Jackie Cheng to act as envoys to impress the IOC voters. This use of enthusiastic celebrities is now commonplace.

Although the IOC's rules and regulations for candidate cities have been steadily tightened malpractices continue to be exposed. Arguably the most dramatic was the scandal of the Salt Lake City's bid for the 2002 Olympic Winter Games which resulted eventually in the expulsion of six IOC members and three resignations for alleged corruption. The host city election procedure was reformed as late as 1999. The reform package contained a number of provisions for improving the site-selection process and clarifying the obligations of the IOC, the bid cities, and the National Olympic Committees:

* interested cities will be subjected to a bid acceptance procedure that will review their organisational capacity before acceptance as candidates.

* no city will become a candidate until it is selected by the IOC Executive Board.

* after acceptance as candidates, cities and their NOCs will sign a contract of acceptance.

* the candidate cities will be required to submit their candidature file and prepare for the visit of the IOC Evaluation Commission.

* no individual visits by the IOC members and vice versa will be allowed.

2. Organising the Games: Procedures

After being awarded the right to host the Games, the NOC, in partnership with municipal authorities, government agencies and commercial businesses, forms an Organising Committee (OCOG) responsible for running the Games. Usually, the Organising Committee comprises the key members and agencies involved in the bidding committee. However, some leading bidding figures have stepped down and been replaced by more national and internationally influential personalities.

(1) Structure of the Organising Committee

Once selected, the OCOG must develop an adequate organisational structure. For example, the Beijing Organising Committee for the Games of the XXIX Olympiad (BOCOG) was established on December 13th, 2001, five months after Beijing won the right to host the 2008 Games. The Committee is responsible for everything from venue planning to environmental management. At moment, it has 23 sections[3] and over 600 staff. BOCOG will expand its departments and recruit more staff in line with the demands of the Olympic preparations. By the year 2008, there will be more than 30 departments and 4,000 staff under the BOCOG umbrella.

(2) Obligations of the Organising Committee

The Organising Committee has to ensure all the infrastructure and services needed for the Games, thus it is required to provide:

* the physical and logistic infrastructure, equipment and training.

* accommodation and catering for the athletes, coaches and officials as well as media workers; For example, the Athens OCOG provided accommodation and services free of charge for 16,000 athletes and team officials.

* facilities (press and broadcasting centres) and services for the mass media; In the Athens Games in 2004 there were about 21,500 members of the media to cover the Games (16,000 broadcasters and 5,500 photo/written press members).

* essential information (documents, invitations, accreditations, event timetables, signs, results, reports) before, during and after the Games.

In addition, the OCOG must comply with the rules and standards established by the 35 International Federations whose sports are on the Olympic Programme, and ensure that there will be no social or political unrest during the Games. The OCOG has also to organise cultural events such as the youth camp, and art, music and dance events accompanying the celebration of the Olympiad.

3. Variations in Organising the Games

With the popularity and expansion of the Games there have appeared different models of organisation. The first Olympic Games in Athens 1896 were a small project compared to the centennial edition in Atlanta 1996 in terms of the scale of the Games, budgets and staff structures (see table 3-2).

Table 3-2 A comparison between Athens 1896 and Atlanta 1996 Games

	Games Comparison				Funding Sources					
	days	sports/ events	nations	athletes	Private donation	Sponsorship	TV	Tickets/ Coins / Medals	Licensing	Advertising/ stamps
Athens 1896	5	9/32	13	311	67%			11%		22%
Atlanta 1996	17	26/271	200	10,000		32%	34%	26%	8%	

Source: Olympic Theme: Running the Olympic Games

The Stockholm Games in 1912 provided a basis for the modern Games in terms of facilities, organisation, electronic timing and marketing. However, the Games had only a budget of US $681,000, and were run by unsalaried committees members. Nowadays organising the Games is the business of professionals. In Atlanta ACOG 4,000 employees were employed with a budget of US $1.4 billion and more for the seven years between 1991 and 1997.

An analysis of the Olympic Games over the years suggests that, generally, there have been three different models of organisation—*state financed*, *private financed* and *partnership financed*. Until 1984 the state driven organisation of the Games model, with necessary allowances, dominated until 1984, in which the governmental contribution represented some 80% of total cost, was dominant. The most striking example case was the 1980 Moscow Games. The former Soviet state took the responsibility of covering most of the construction, running and administrative costs but imposed the financial burden on taxpayers. The Games were a financial disaster. As the previous Olympics in Munich 1972 and Montreal 1976 were also financial disasters, there were not many cities willing to host the Games, and the need for a new model arose.

This came in the form of the first privately run Games in Los Angeles in 1984. The Games was organised by a non-profit corporation comprising the US Olympic Committee and a business syndicate. By introducing new sponsorship and TV rights, this organisation ended up with a profit of US $150 million. Other "new" commercial arrangements allowed the Los Angeles OCOG to obtain a further US $117 million for "service facilities". The Los Angeles model was repeated in Atlanta 1996 but not as successfully and produced a great deal of dissatisfaction amongst participants and spectators over poor transport and housing and very little in new infrastructures and improvements.

The third model represents a partnership between the public and private sector, and reflects the shift from purely government and purely private to a shared approach. Perhaps the best example was provided in Barcelona 1992. The Games were run by HOLSA, a company owned 51% by the federal government and 49% by the city and involved many commercial partners as investors and sponsors. The public authorities in Barcelona were very active, and the share of their investments was 77.6%. This approach resulted in significant investments in public projects and improvements. However, investment in sports facilities constituted a relatively small proportion of total investment (9.1%). Similar models were witnessed in Seoul in 1988 and in Sydney in 2000.

4. Organising the Games: Advantages and Disadvantages

(1) Social Impact

As Barcelona, Atlanta and Sydney have shown, among other places, there are many tangible and intangible long-term benefits to hosting the Games. Staging the Games stimulates organisers to address the issues of sport, education and equal opportunities, to introduce strategies, to raise public need for the harmonious development of body and mind and the significant part that sport can play in contributing to world peace, national identity and community unity.

The Olympics add an important element to social change because they contribute to enhancing national pride and mobilize social support for state projects which otherwise would not have materialized. Finally, through managing large scale complex projects that require integrated planning and close coordination, the training and expertise of the workforce in virtually every sector in the host country can be enhanced.

(2) Urban Regeneration

The Olympics also play a valuable role in urban regeneration by transforming the physical environment, renewing and building facilities, parks, recreational areas and transport infrastructure. This pleases the politicians who regard the Games as a means of generating urban change and as a means of enhancing a city's physical appearance. Cities compete to host major sporting events and since 1984 each subsequent Olympic Games have attracted over seven cities to bid to be the host. The benefits associated with an Olympic bid concern not only the host city but the other city contenders. The Manchester 1992 and 1996 Olympic bids illustrate the point. Among various tangible and intangible outcomes was a governmental subsidy of 50 million pounds to the city for the construction of a new indoor stadium for cycling and other sports. By also upgrading the transportation infrastructure, telecommunication system and the environment, the city's image was improved.

In one comprehensive study of the urban impact of the Olympic Games between 1896 and 1996,[4] three categories of Olympic cities were identified in terms of urban impact (table 3-3):

Table 3-3 Urban Impact of the Olympic Games 1896-2000

Impact	Olympic Games	Projects
Low	Athens 1896	Parathenean Stadium
	Paris 1900	No new facilities
	St. Louis 1904	No new facilities
	London 1948	No new facilities
	Mexico 1968	Modest investment—no new facilities
	Los Angeles 1984	Modest investment—no new facilities
Focus on sports facilities	London 1908	White City Stadium (a multi-sport facility)
	Stockholm 1912	New stadium & specialist facilities for separate sports
	Los Angeles 1932	New stadium, Olympic Village, facilities for other sports
	Berlin 1936	100,000 spectators stadium, substantial sports facilities, a sports forum, Olympic Village, House of German Sport administrative building
	Helsinki 1952	New stadium, Olympic Village
	Melbourne 1956	Olympic Park complex, Olympic Village
	Atlanta 1996	Olympic Stadium, Aquatic Centre, basketball gym, equestrian venue, hockey stadium
Stimulating environmental transformations	Rome 1960	New sporting infrastructure along a new road Olympic Way, modern municipal water supply system, airport facilities
	Tokyo 1964	A new road and 22 highways network, two underground railway lines, facilities
	Munich 1972	Derelict site redevelopment, restoration and pedestrianisation of a historic quarter, improved public transport, underground car parking, shopping centres, hotels, express ways
	Montreal 1976	Olympic Park, 20 km subway system, new airport, hotels and roads
	Moscow 1980	12 new sports facilities, new hotels, airport terminal, Olympic TV and Radio Centre, Olympic Communication Centre, Novosti Press Agency building

Con.

Impact	Olympic Games	Projects
Stimulating environmental transformations	Seoul 1988	Sports facilities and Olympic Village, depolluting Han River, 3 subway lines, 47 bus routes, Seoul Art Centre, National Classical Musical Institute, Chongju Museum, refurbishing shrines, garbage control and general hygiene improvement
	Barcelona 1992	15 new sports venues, Olympic Village, coastal ring road, new marina, restructuring sewage system, regeneration of the coastline, waterfront facilities, upgrading communications all designs and renovations based on green principles, new Olympic stadium and Village, buildings with solar power and water recycling
	Sydney 2000	Investment into the Olympic Proicts: 2.5 billion US $

Source: Essex, S., & Chalkley, B., (1998), "Olympic Games: Catalyst of Urban Change", *Leisure Studies*, vol. 17, no. 3, pp. 187-207.

Table 3-3 sums up the key findings of the study according to the scale of their building and investment projects. The first category (low impact) includes the cities that sought to keep expenditures to a minimum and did not build and made only modest investments in new sports facilities. The second category includes cities where major sports facilities were set up but where only modest changes to the city's environment and infrastructure were undertaken. The third category deals with cities where organisers used the Olympics to introduce large scale urban developments and improvements which went far beyond the basic necessity to construct new sporting facilities.

(3) Economic Impact of the Olympics

With regard to sport, economic impact has been defined as "the net economic change in a host community that results from spending attributed to a sports event or facility"[5]. The Olympics are now seen as a catalyst for such economic growth because of their potential to create job opportunities and generate tourist and other industries. However, until Los Angeles 1984, as made clear earlier, most Games ended up with massive financial losses. For example, the Montreal Games in 1976 left the city bankrupt. Local taxpayers were still paying off the Olympic bills until 2006. As noted earlier, it was the first privately organised Los Angeles Games that ended this state of affairs—at least for a time. The 1984 Games achieved commercial success with a US $ 225 million profit. For the economic effect of the previous five Olympic Games, see table 3-4 below.

Table 3-4 Economic Effect of the Olympic Games

	profit	economy	employment
Seoul 1988	US $ 300mIllion	grew by 12% in 1988	191,341 job opportunities
Barcelona 1992	US $ 5million	Added US $ 16.6 billion between 1986-1993	unemployment in fell from 18.4% to 9.6%
Atlanta 1996	US $ 10million	added $ 5.1 billion to the Georgia economy	77,026 job opportunities
Sydney 2000	US $ 1.756billion	add $ 6.5 billion to the Australian GDP	100,000 full-time jobs from 1994 - 2006.
Athens 2004	A debt of 8 billion US $ dollars and taxpayers will take 20 years to pay debt.	US $ 1.3 billion boost in public sector revenues & tourism	65,000 new permanent jobs

Data prior to 1992 from: Holger Pruess: "The Economics of the Olympic Games: Winners and Losers", in Barrie Houlihan (ed.), *Sports & Society: A - Z Student Introduction*, London: Thousand Oaks, New Delhi: Sage Publication, p. 262; Post-1992 data from "Beijing Olympiad: Profitor Loss?" *China Today*, Nov. S, 2004.

Often hosting the Olympic Games can lead to the development of tourism. Australia saw an 11% increase of total visitors in 2000. Interestingly, December was the busiest month (565,000 visitors), three months after the Olympic Games.

Due to using inappropriate multipliers of sales or employment, omitting costs and including spending by visitors who would be in the city anyway, some results of economic impact studies of the Olympic Games are questionable. One study in 1996 identified two basic methods— *cost-benefit analysis* and *Planning, Balance Sheet*, to measure the impact. These two methods have their strengths and weaknesses. [7] Another study in 1996 developed a simplified model for calculating the impact of the Olympics, based on the size of direct and created demand. Based on this model, the overall impact of the Olympic Games in Los Angeles, Seoul and Barcelona was calculated (see table 3-5).

Table 3-5 Overall Impact of the Olympic Games from 1984 to 1992

Criterion	Los Angeles 1984	Seoul 1988	Barcelona 1992
Multiplier	K = 3	K = 2.99	K = 2.66
Net direct injection	$ 792 million	$ 3.1 billion	$ 9.8 billion
Created impact	$ 1.584 billion	$ 6.2 billion	$ 16.2 billion
Total impact	$ 2.376 billion	$ 9.3 billion	$ 26 billion

Source: Dubi, (1996:89)

The economic impact is not necessarily positive. It can be negative. [8] The price of land, housing and renting in and around the city hosting the Games is often pushed up. In addition, major investment on the part of a host country is inevitably channelled to the Olympic city and the region during and after the Games, thus depriving other areas in need of improvement.

A usually overlooked aspect of the economic impact concerns the spin-off of the ever-increasing cost and scale of the Games on participating countries and the cost of excellence. By way of example, sending more and better prepared athletes to the Games is an objective of any National Olympic Committee but it comes at an ever increasing price.

(4) Environmental Impact of the Olympics

According to the 2005 *Global Forest Resources Assessment*, which was released by Food and Agriculture organisation of the United Nations, global annual deforestation is some 13 million hectares of the world's forests. [9] Thus, there is a growing concern for the natural environment and sustainable development. A challenge for the Olympics is to achieve a balance between ever-expanding scale of the Games and the conservation of resources.

The conflict between sport and nature was seriously addressed in the early 1970s. An environmental initiative of the organisers of the Munich

1972 Olympic Games invited all participating NOCs to plant a shrub from their country in the Olympic park, and they coined the slogan "certatio sana in naturea sana" (healthy competition in an intact environment). These first steps were gradually transformed by the IOC into well-defined strategies and actions aiming to arrest the harmful influence of sport on the environment.

The IOC took part in the United Nations' Conference on Environment and Development in Rio de Janeiro in 1992 and committed the Olympic Movement to the concept of sustainable development (the global plan AGENDA 21). Among other policies, the IOC developed a list of environmental requirements concerning the cities bidding to host the Games. It demands from the Organising Committees of the Olympic Games (OCOG) more responsibility and accountability and co-operation with appropriate agencies to plan and implement environmentally sound projects.

In the search for a solution to the conflict between sport and nature, the IOC and other authorities apply various strategies. A contractual strategy involves an agreement between OCOG, government, local community and private enterprises to confront and resolve problems. A second strategy is the normative control of environment "harassment". Sydney OCOG incorporated the concept of environmental sustainability to promote environmental awareness and innovative techniques of environmental protection by both adherence to an agreed set of principles and practical examples. Gradually the organisers of the Games are making efforts to protect the environment and provide better conservation conditions for sport in the future.

Summary

Every city that wishes to host the Games must submit a bid to the IOC after obtaining permission from its national government. There are procedural rules and regulations to avoid malpractice, corruption and manipulation. Putting a bid together is complicated and cooperation between city authorities, commercial parties and government agencies is essential. Once a city has been awarded the Games, the NOC in partnership with municipal authorities, government agencies and commercial interests form an OCOG responsible for delivering the Games.

As the Games have evolved, different models of organisation have emerged. There are now clear tangible and intangible long-term benefits to be obtained from hosting the Games and they can now be an agent of positive social change. It can also be a catalyst for economic growth although this is not always the case. Finally, recently an attempt has been made by the IOC to ensure that the Games are organised so as to protect the environment and provide improved conservation conditions associated with sport.

Questions
1. Why has the IOC recently tightened up the rules and regulations for bidding for the Games?
2. Provide one major reason why a city bidding for the Games must obtain government support.
3. Which organisational model has Beijing adopted in its hosting of the 2008 Games and why?
4. Which of the tangible and intangible benefits of hosting the Games do you consider the most beneficial? Given your reasons.

Notes
[1] www.olympic.org/ioc/facts/cities/candidate city intro e.html.
[2] Wang Junhua, "xie aoyun jingji tisu Beijing xiandaihua jincheng" [to speed up the modernisation of Beijing through Olympic economy], *Beijing Wanbao* [*Beijing Evening Daily*], Feb. 25, 2003.
[3] Including Secretariat, Overall Planning Department, International Liaison Department, Sports Department, Press and Propaganda Department, Engineering Department, Environment Department, Marketing Department, Technique Department, the Department of the Games' service, Law Affairs Department, Supervision and Audit Department, Personnel Department, Finance Department, Cultural Programme Department, Safety and Security Department, Medical Service Department and Information Centre.
[4] Essex, S., & Chalkley, B. (1998), "Olympic Games Atalyst of Urban Change", *Leisure Studies*, Vol. 17, 3, 187-207.
[5] Ibid.
[6] http://www.athens2004.com/athens2004/page/legacy? lang = en&cid = 1a1a4-70429149f00VgnVCMServer28130b0Arcrd.
[7] Crompton, J. (1996). "Economic impact analysis of sports facilities and events: eleven sources of misapplication", *Journal of Sport Management*, 9, 14-35.
[8] Dubi, C. (1996). "The economic impact of a major sports event", *Olympic Message*, 3, 88.
[9] World deforestation rates and forest cover statistics, 2000-2005, http://news.mongabay.com/2005/1115-forests.html.

Chapter 4
The Olympics: Architectural and Technological Evolution

Key points of this chapter:
* Sports Architecture
* Equipment and Technology

The popularization of the Olympic Movement throughout the world could not have been realized to the extent to which it has without architectural progress and technological innovation. These are major elements of the modern Olympics.

1. Architecture

"Architecture is primarily the art and science of designing spaces for serving the multifarious activities of human beings and for meeting their specific needs in a meaningful built environment. When various engineering services are rationally combined with Architecture's basic elements of Space, Structure and Form, the performance of human functions and the operation of mechanical utilities become efficient, pleasant and fulfilling."[1] This claim certainly holds true for sports architecture which covers many types of buildings among them modern gymnasium halls, open-air stadiums, swimming pools, velodromes and riding stables. Sports architecture literally provides the structural basis for the Olympic Games and serves both its utilitarian and aesthetic ends.

(1) Greek Stadiums

Ancient civilisations around the globe constructed monumental architectural sites for sport. The ancient Greeks, especially, were impressive architectural innovators. They built stadiums, gymnasiums and palaestras. These buildings testify to a strong relationship between sport and architecture in the ancient world. [2]

Olympia was a centre in which athletic and cultural structures combined uniquely with paintings and sculptures. The temple of Zeus was one of the most magnificent edifices of antiquity. One of the largest Doric temples built in Greece, the temple was designed by the architect Libon who built it according to a system of ideal proportions. The distance between the columns was harmoniously proportional to their height, and the other architectural elements were also constructed proportionately.

Figure 4-1　The Temple of Zeus

The Panathenaic Stadium, known as the Panathenaea, was built in 330 BC. The ancient sports competitions were held there. Interestingly, its track had an unusually elongated shape with such sharp turns that runners were forced to slow down considerably in order to stay in their lanes. Nearly two thousand years later, it was reconstructed in Athens in white marble for the athletic events of the first Modern Olympic Games in 1896.

Figure 4-2　Flavian Amphitheater

(2) Roman Amphitheatres

The Romans also created architectural works of art such as the Coliseum which served as sports venues. Officially known as the Flavian Amphitheater, it was constructed in the 1st century B. C. and was the scene of gladiatorial combats, animal hunts and naval battles. Nearby was the Circus Maximus, an enormous site where great, bloody and violent chariot races took place.[3] Roman coliseums, big ovals with raised seating for spectator viewing, sprouted in the lands that fell under the sway of their imperial rule. One of the most famous stadiums was the "Olympic Champions" palace. It was sponsored by Nero in A. D. 67 and could accommodate, and cater for, the tens of thousands of spectators. Roman thermae, circuses and amphitheatres are among the most renowned in the world. The design of arenas and tracks has scarcely altered from the time of the Roman Colosseum and Circus Maximus. Sport arenas, racetracks and public swimming pools of the present day mostly owe their origin to the ancient Romans (though certain precedents can be found in Crete and Greece). The Basilica of Maxentius, the site of wrestling contests 2,000 years earlier, was used in 1960 for the wrestling competition of the Modern Olympic Games. At the same time, another ancient site, the Caracalla Baths was used for gymnastics while the Arch of Constantine was used as the finish of the marathon. Greek and Roman sports architecture have had lasting influence on the world in more ways than one.

(3) Modern Olympic Constructions

* **Stadiums**

The Olympics have provided a stimulus to the development of the modern stadium. In each four-year period since the first modern Olympiad, the host country has usually erected a permanent stadium to mark the event. Three phases can be seen in the development of modern Olympic stadiums:

The first phase (from 1896 to 1968) can be characterised as one of a simple facility with a single function. The structure of the stadiums was far from sophisticated. The first stadium of the modern type was constructed for the IV Olympiad in 1908 at Shepherd's Bush in London. The stadium seated more than 50,000 people and the stands were partly roofed. It had a 536.45m cinder-track, surrounding it was the newly-built cycling track. It also had a swimming pool, fencing hall and boxing rings.

The Olympic stadiums of architectural note that were built before World War II include Stockholm (1912), Colombes outside Paris (1924), Amsterdam (1928), and Berlin (1936). The Stockholm Games in 1912 represented a fresh start in Olympic architecture. Since then, much effort has been made to make architecture worthy of the Olympic ideal and the evolving Olympic Movement. In 1932 the Los Angeles Coliseum Olympic stadium astounded the whole world. The stadium seated more than 100,000 and a new track of crushed peat was exceptionally fast, resulting in 10 new world records in the track events. To host the 1936 Olympic Games, a sports complex—the Reich Sports Field—was constructed in the west sector of Berlin. It covered 325 acres (131 hectares) and included four stadiums. The Berlin Olympic Stadium with the area of 100 × 70 m and 70-story (27 metres) stand was built in 1935. It had a capacity for over 90,000 spectators with seats for more than 60,000.[4]

Figure 4-3   Amsterdam Stadium

Figure 4-4   The Berlin Olympic Stadium

　　　The Helsinki stadium built for the XII Olympiad (1940), which was cancelled on the outbreak of World War II, became the site for the 1952 Olympics. It accommodated 70,000 spectators. The stadium was designed by the architects Yrjö Lindegren and Toivo Jäntti who won the architectural competition with their functionalist style. Since its completion the stadium has undergone a further eight stages of development in response to advances in both architecture and sport.

For the 1960 Olympics in Rome, the leading Italian architect engineer Pier Luigi Nervi created the Roman sports complex, which included the Palazzetto dello Sport with a ribbed-dome roof. The Astrodome was gigantic, with seating capacity for 62,000 people and a large field. Its dome, of transparent plastic panels supported by a steel lattice, had a span of 642 feet (196 metres) and rises 208 feet (63 metres) above the playing field. The entire interior was air-conditioned. Since the 1960 Games, the stadium has been used for athletic meetings and for football matches and regularly shared by Rome's two leading football clubs, A. S. Roma and Lazio. [5]

The year 1964 witnessed the first Olympic Games held in Asia. The Japanese government invested US $ 3 billion in the construction of a number of sports facilities in three parks for the Games. The large stadium took the form of two semi-circles, slightly displaced in relation to one another, with their unconnected ends elongated in-to points. The entrance was located in the concave sides. The roof was made up of a system of steel cables onto with soldered enamelled steel plates. It was supported on two reinforced concrete pillars which made possible the construction of daring new designs that were previously impossible to sustain structurally. The curving form of the roof served to make it more resistant to wind which can reach hurricane force in this region.

The second phase (from 1972 to 1999) was linked to the emergence of

Figure 4-5   The Olympic Stadium in Rome

television which made specialised lighting equipment, communication facilities, electronic measurement and display units as well as a computerised address system necessary elements of modern stadiums. The seating and the atmosphere of stadiums became more comfortable and performance design was more flexible to adjust for a variety of activities.

The park in Munich, built for the 1972 XXth Summer Olympics, was dominated by the 289 metre television and radio tower and famous throughout the world for its distinctive transparent canopy. It was constructed between 1969 and 1971. The Olympic Stadium within the park included a Warm-up Facility, a Swimming Facility and Main Sport Hall with a capaci-

Figure 4-6 The Olympic Park in Munich, 1972

Figure 4-7 The Olympic Stadium
Within the Park in 1972

ty of 69,256 spectators (57,456 seated and 11,800 standing).

Major problems characterised the Montreal Stadium for the 1976 Olympic Games. The problems anticipated and exceeded Athens 2004. The innovative retractable roof was unfinished when the Games took place because a 556 foot tower next to the stadium was only about a quarter of its planned height. In fact, the roof, made from 60,696 square feet of Kevlar weighing 50 tons, was not completed until 1987 and it took another two years before the roof became retractable. Problems with opening and closing the roof led to its permanent closure. In the spring of 1998, the orange Kevlar roof was removed and a $26 million opaque blue roof replaced it later in the year. The stadium's total cost to date has exceeded $1 billion.[6]

The massive Seoul Sports Complex of 1988 also anticipated Athens 2004. It was constructed along the Hangang River, which bisects the capital. The main stadium with an area of 32 acres was located in the Seoul Olympic Complex. The opening and closing ceremonies, the track and field events, football finals and steeplechase events all took place in the stadium. It had a capacity for 100,000 people. The Olympic park had 6 facilities for gymnastics, fencing, swimming, weight-lifting, tennis and cycling. The overriding ambition was immediate impact. Future practicality came second. An expensive facility for canoeing was also built at Misari, but it

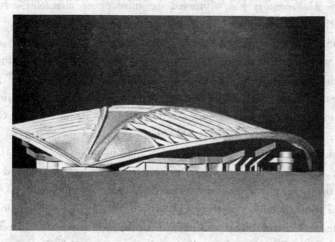

Figure 4-8 The Montreal Stadium with Roof in 1976

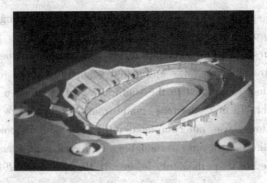

Figure 4-9 The Stadium without Roof

was unused after the Seoul Games. The velodrome, expensive to maintain, was used only for 15 days a year for several amateur contests. The cycling velodrome was even more difficult to maintain because it was made with African wood with poor resistance to Korean winters. [7]

The Barcelona Olympic Games in 1992 saw the erection of a Communications Tower beyond the large plaza in front of Palau Sant Jordi Sports Stadium, yet another technological advance.

In summary, the desire for continual improvement—to go one better than the previous Games, has stimulated the relentless search for improved materials and construction techniques.

The 21st century has witnessed the third phase characterised by the application of hi-tech, digital and environment-minded facilities and the interaction between audience and athletes through provision of computer seats. Stadium Australia in 2000, described by the IOC former President Samaranch as"the most impressive stadium I have seen in my life", is the finest example to date. The Sydney Organising Committee required the competing architects to design a beautiful and large stadium to seat Olympic crowds, but capable of being scaled down (without reconstruction) once the Games was over, in keeping with "ecologically sustainable development". It was not to adversely affect environmental resources and was to reflect the dignity and importance of the events which would take place there. The distinguished Sydney firms Bligh Voller Nied and London-Lobb won the architectural competition. The proposed Stadium Australia was oddly shaped. To some, the swooping, translucent roof looked appropriately like a boomerang. Not everyone was impressed. To the noted architect Philip Cox, however, it resembled a Pringles potato chip!

Figure 4-10　The Sydney Stadium in 2000

　　The Olympic Stadium for the 2004 Olympic Games in Athens had a seating capacity of 74,767. As a part of the Athens Olympic Sports Complex (AOSC) which also included Olympic Indoor Hall, Olympic Aquatic Centre, Olympic Tennis Centre and Olympic Velodrome, it was designed by the renowned Spanish architect Santiago Calatrava. The Stadium, which was supposed to herald a modern Athens, became the focal point of anxieties over whether the Games would even take place on time, given huge cost overruns and construction delays. The primary cause for delay was the roof, a glass and steel covering deemed necessary to protect spectators from the punishing Athens sun. By May 2004, the arches needed to support the 18,000 tonne roof hadn't even been put in place, which prompted the International Olympic Committee to suggest calling off the roof project completely. However, the bulk of the roof was finally completed by June 4 in time for the Greek track and field championships. The cost for the stadium was 170 million euros, triple the Greek government's original estimate. [8]

　　It is clear then that stadiums over time have varied markedly in design; some rectangular with curved corners, some elliptical or U-shaped. Stadiums have become more flexible, complex and gigantic and at the same time modern, technological and environmentally friendly.

* The Olympic Village

The Olympic Village of today is virtually a small city in which competitors and team officials can be housed and fed together. For example, the Olympic Village in Athens in 2004 housed 16,000 athletes and team officials during the Olympic Games and 6,000 during the Paralympic Games.[9] Athletes enjoyed many advantages in the Village. They could eat in the Village restaurant 24 hours a day, go to the hairdresser, relax in the cinema or let their hair down in bars and discotheques.

However, athletes have not always benefited from this attractive accommodation. There was no Olympic Village for the athletes until the Los Angeles Games in 1932. Athletes stayed in a variety of places: hotels, hostels or cheaper accommodation in schools or barracks. Some even slept in the boats they had taken to the Olympic city. For example, at the Amsterdam Games in 1928 the Americans, Italians and Finns stayed in the harbour.

The first Olympic Village at the 1932 Games in Los Angeles was located in Baldwin Hills, a suburb of Los Angeles. It covered 321 acres (130 hectares). The male athletes from 37 countries were housed in more than 500 bungalows and had access to a hospital, a library, a post office and 40 kitchens serving a variety of cuisines. For the first time, a hospital, a fire station and a post office were provided. However, the female athletes stayed in local hotels outside the Olympic Village. It was not until the 1956 Games in Melbourne that the Olympic Village was open to both sexes. Interestingly, a separate Olympic village was created in Otaniemi for Eastern bloc nations in the 1952 Olympic Games. This was the result of the Cold War between the two superpowers: the United States and the Soviet Union.

Now the construction of Olympic Village is taken very seriously by the organising committee during preparations for the Games. The village is located as close as possible to the main stadium and other facilities and has separate accommodation for men and women officials and performers. Only competitors and officials may live in the village.

(4) Issues Relevant to Sports Architecture

To attract maximum international exposure, a host nation and city always wants to build "showcase" facilities. The Olympic architecture, however, should be in keeping with Olympic ideals and emphasise as far as possible its dual sporting and artistic character. In addition, its silhouette must harmonise with the surrounding landscape and take advantage of it. [10] To this end, the architecture has to take the following factors into account.

* **Location**

The development of strategies for securing major government facilities and public venues requires extensive analysis of the physical site itself and the surrounding geographic areas. The analysis requires an assessment of the entire locality, including buildings, roads and access to transportation areas. Central to this analysis is an understanding of the three-dimensional spatial environment surrounding the site.

Close collaboration between man and nature is the essential feature of modern Olympic design. [11] The site chosen will necessarily influence the architectural conception. Lake Geneva, San Francisco Bay, the banks of the Thames and the Beijing plain, self-evidently, are all different. Each landscape will inspire different plans.

The location of Olympic venues should also pay attention to social criteria. It should encourage the regeneration of less developed and less affluent parts of cities, thus acting as an agent for the reduction of exclusion. [12]

* **Technology**

Technology is now able to produce facilities of great sophistication. It has become an essential component of any new sports venue. The most careful planning of its use now takes place under specific headings:

* **Scale**

Spectator numbers need to be carefully evaluated. Note that with increasing TV audiences, stadiums may be reduced in size in the future.

* **Service**

To attract the spectators, careful consideration must be given to facilities including safe and easy access, well-sited, comfortable seating, safe standing terraces and excellent catering arrangements.

* **Disabled**

Adequate access and provision for those with disabilities are now important to ensure the widest participation.

* **Viability**

Future viability needs to be taken into account. Once the Olympics are over, the costs during the remaining life of the building-for the repayment of the preliminary financing, for recurrent annual operations and maintenance and for structural rehabilitation will greatly exceed the initial capital cost. These costs must be fully anticipated, carefully evaluated and allowed for.

* **Balance**

The modern major Olympic venues represent a significant infrastructure investment. Thus, the importance of balance requires the best use of both existing and new facilities. Sustainable development (social, financial, ecological and physical) and environmental protection are crucial elements in the location, planning, design and construction of new facilities and their relationship to existing facilities.

Facilities are classified as permanent and temporary. Permanent facilities are for the long-term use and benefit of the host community. However, self-evidently no permanent facilities can support a major event without temporary facilities. These temporary facilities are needed only for the actual event and help supplement permanent facilities in order to meet obligatory guidelines for the holding of the event. For obvious reasons, decisions regarding the temporary and the permanent facilities take place at the earliest stage of planning.

2. Technology

Olympic Culture, equipment and technology have been interconnected throughout the Olympic history. The rapid development of both modern equipment and modern technology has had a strong influence on the Olympic Movement. Some examples are given below.

(1) Equipment

Prior to the First World War equipment was simply made of bamboo, metal, rubber and feather-natural ingredients. Then the process for "vulcanising" rubber altered tennis balls-and other balls and their games. Other major innovations followed. By way of example, in tennis the mid-1980s steel and aluminium innovations signalled the end of wooden rackets. Manufacturers experimented with a range of materials, including fibreglass, boron, magnesium, ceramics and graphite. These lighter materials permitted the introduction of rackets with larger heads which gave players greater power and control. In cycling, about the same time, the so called "Superbike", which depended on carbon fibre and tires inflated to a thumb-numbing 250 pounds per square inch, was introduced. Both tennis and cycling as Olympic events were transformed in terms of equipment and performance.

(2) More Accurate Measurement of Performance

Technological innovation has also led to the more accurate measurement of performance. In the 1912 Olympics electric timing devices was first introduced and the top six athletes' performances were timed to a tenth of a second. This marked a new era of performance measurement. Because of the use of electronic timing some athletic results in specific sports were recognised retroactively as official world records by some international federations. Thus, the first official Olympic records resulted. However, due to the cost of the electronic timing devices, they were not employed until the 1932 Games. These games also saw the first use of the photo-finish camera. In 1964 Seiko created quartz-timing technology, which provided the most accurate timing system to date. By the 1970s it had became an essential facility in all major international competitions. And the IAAF stipulated that the World Championships and the Olympic Games had to use the automatic timing system to measure performances to a hundredth of a second.

(3) Monitoring Judges and Referees

In North America, instant replay judging is now a common practice in hockey and football though referees initially were less than enthusiastic about the introduction of instant replay to assist or even override their decisions. The referee on the field can be over-ruled by the instant replay officials, who sit and watch the replay of the action to determine the accuracy of the on-field decision.

In addition, there are already technologies that assist umpires in sports like tennis with line calls, but it is not yet clear whether technology will evolve sufficiently to eliminate referees altogether.

In the future, simulations which could allow judges and referees to review their decisions, re-consider them from different vantage points and then evaluate their initial responses, could be developed through animation, three-dimensional modelling, and the use of actual competition footage using multiple camera angles. [13]

(4) Technology and Performance

New technologies are now used to analyze performance. For example, a rubber suit called "Datawear" has a range of sensors which span each joint on the human body, plotting their positions on computer-based graphics. Such a suit has obvious utility in monitoring the body movements of high jumpers, gymnasts and competitors in other technical events.

Nowadays computers are ubiquitously used in training athletes. Training is also becoming heavily influenced by other technology such as biofeedback, visualization and virtual reality techniques. In addition, new materials are used for boats, clothing and athletic equipment. Laser accelerometers are even used in the sprints. Boxing trainers fit punching bags with devices to measure acceleration to teach boxers to punch harder and faster. The uprights in the pole vault are now fitted with light-emitting diodes (LEDs) to measure precisely how high the athlete jumped. Finally, the battle between administrators wishing to eliminate drugs and ensure fair competition and those wanting to employ biotechnologies to improve performance is fought with competing technology.

(5) Technology and Greater Audience Choice

The emergence of new communication technology in the 1980s and 1990s instigated a process that re-shaped sports spectatorship at a global level. [14] The advent of subscription cable and satellite television, especially pay-per-view, has added a new dimension to television's relationship with sport. Pay-per-view, for example, began life in 1980 when the Ray Leonard-Robert Duran fight drew 170,000 customers, each paying $15. By the late 1990s per-per-view was the main medium for major boxing promotions.

Sky Sport adapted a piece of technology originally developed for use in the Gulf War by ORAD Hi-Tec Systems of Israel to track Saddam Hussein's Scud missiles. The technology digitally transformed sporting action to a video game-like visual format, which allowed television analysts engage the interest of spectators by reconstructing key events virtually from any angle.

In summary, technology has greatly influenced the development of sport including Olympic sport. A combination of digital and video technology provides sports performers and their coaches with the means of monitoring the biomechanical aspects of sports performance. Athletes and their coaches have welcomed these new and specialised devices that allow for ever greater achievements. Adjudicators have also taken advantage of new technologies to assist them in making decisions, and finally, media commentators, analysts and spectators have all benefited from technological advances. There will be more of these advances ahead. Technology will be an integral part of future Olympic Games.

Conclusion

Sports architecture is the structural " foundation " of the Olympic Games. This architecture and its influence, goes back centuries. Ancient Greek and Roman architecture has left its mark in modern Olympic and other sports architecture. However, over the past century, the structure, style and elements of Olympic stadiums have changed considerably with the evolution of the modern Olympic Games. Environmental protection, in particular, has increasingly played its part in promoting sophisticated changes of architectural design and structure. Equipment in the last hundred years too has become increasingly more complex due to technical innovations. Arguably, it is media technology that in recent years, has had the most significant impact of all on the Games. Very possibly, this will be the case in the future.

Questions
1. What characteristics are demanded of the modern stadium and why?
2. What is the ideal relationship between modern Olympic architecture and its environment?
3. In what ways has modern technology affected the nature of the Olympic Games and which recent technological innovations do you consider the most significant?

Notes
[1] Council of Architecture, "Practice of Architecture", http://www. coa – india. org/practice/practice. htm.
[2] Martin Wimmer (1976), *Olympic Buildings*, Edition Leipzing.

[3] David Levinson and Karen Christensen (eds.) (1996), *Encyclopaedia of World Sport: From Ancient Times to the Present*, Oxford: ABC-CLIO Ltd., 21.
[4] John Arlott (ed.) (1975), *The Oxford Companion to Sports & Games*, Oxford University Press, 735.
[5] Ibid.
[6] http://www.ballparks.com/baseball/national/olympi.htm.
[7] http://www.cyclerace.or.kr/e_cra/launching02_a.html.
[8] http://www.cbc.ca/olympics/venues/olympic_stadium.html.
[9] http://www.olympic.org/uk/games/athens/index_uk.asp.
[10] Coubertin, P. de (1976), "A Modern Olympia", in Martin Wimmer, *Olympic Buildings*, Edition Leipzig, 210.
[11] Coubertin, P. de, (1976), op. cit., 209.
[12] Architecture and International Sporting Events-Future Planning and Development, Joint Conference of International Olympic Committee and International Union of Architects, May 2002, http://multimedia.olympic.org/pdf/en_report_644.pdf.
[13] Mike Laflin, Sport and the Internet-The Impact and the Future, http://multimedia.olympic.org/pdf/en_report_60.pdf.
[14] Ellis Cashmore (2000), *Sports Culture: An A-Z Guide*, London and New York: Routledge, pp. 402-405.

Chapter 5
The Olympics Mass Media

The keys points:
* The ever closer links between the IOC and the Media.
* The ever increasing influence of television on the IOC
* The ever growing "media wealth" of the IOC

1. Media Power

This chapter discusses the relationship between the Olympic Games and the Mass Media with specific reference to the role of television in transforming the modern Olympics. Some 21,500 members of the media covered the Athens Games in 2004, among them 16,000 broadcasters and 5,500 photo/written press members.[1] Clearly, the Olympic Games meshes with the modern media. This Mass Media is an institution with multiple identities. "It is... an economic and a cultural institution,... a profit-making business,... a producer of meaning, a creator of social consciousness."[2] Therefore, the mass media can be viewed as a device for transmitting societal messages, as a wealth-pursuing, as entity responsible for the construction of reality and a source of manipulation of group awareness.

The Games are the largest sports festival watched throughout the world. It is estimated that more than 3.7 billion people in more than 220 countries and territories around the world watched the coverage of the Games in Sydney. Thus the Games is a unique advertising medium. A crucial advantage is that Games' broadcasters can insert advertising during the breaks in competition without causing viewers irritation. Furthermore, the Games contain sports with appeal to different audiences. Football and boxing mostly attract young men, rhythmic gymnastics and water ballet mostly appeal to women but the Games also includes sports with wide appeal to both sexes such as track and field events.

Advertising potential is far from being the whole story. Most people, of course, do not have the chance to attend the Games and it is the media which is a bridge between them and the Games. It transmits the values of the Olympics to the global audience, and at the same time provides details of performances, records and scores. It entertains and educates. It also controls. The power of the media is considerable. It interprets the meaning and significance of Olympic events for international and national audiences while at the same time limiting their perspectives as it chooses. It selects the events and stories to be covered. It defines Olympic reality.

The Games are the great international drama—a global theatrical performance with athletes as actors and actresses. They cover the whole spectrum of human emotions. They have public moments of tears of sadness and tears of joy; they are the venue for public success and failure; they bear witness to human greatness, courage, determination and endurance; they project physical grace, beauty and power. They are play, film, ballet and opera rolled into one for a vast audience of many millions across the globe. And the media is the means of transmission.

And more than this, it provides lasting memories of the great deeds of heroes and heroines of sport. The media stores these memories on film, tape and on pages, and reproduces them for endless later consumption. The media thus immortalises in this way, performers and performances.

2. Mass Media Forms

All forms of the mass media—press, radio and television cover the Olympics (see table 5-1 below).

Table 5-1 Accredited media representatives at the Games of the Olympiad

Games	Press	Radio and television	Total medial representatives
Rome'60	1146	296	1442
Tokyo'64	1507	2477	3984
Munich'72	3300	4700	8000

Con.

Games	Press	Radio and television	Total medial representatives
Los Angeles'84	4000	4200	8200
Barcelona'92	4880	10,360	15,740
Atlant'96	5000	12,000	17,000
Sydney'2000	5,298	10,735	16,033
Athens'2004	5,500	16,000	21,500

Source: *Olympic Marketing Fact File* : (1996—2005)

(1) Press

The printed word has been the traditional way that Olympic facts and figures have been conveyed to the international public. Sports pages and specialized sports journals began to appear in the early 19th century when men such as Pierce Egan in England began to write in the colourfully metaphoric, argot-rich prose now recognised everywhere as typical of sportswriters. Though newspapers and magazines faced first radio competition in the early 20th century and then television competition after the Second World War, for the enthusiasts' attention, thousands of specialized magazines and newspapers on a wide range of sports (and the Games) have continued to be published. Sports dailies are common in many countries. The Games now generates its own specialist books, journals and magazines. They form a genre in their own right. Newspapers devote much space to the Olympics. Despite intense competition from radio, television and the internet, the print media survives successfully and the style set by early sportswriters in many ways still persists.

(2) Radio

In the early 20th century U. S. radio pioneered the development of live sports coverage. Enthusiasts tuned in to live broadcasting of sports, including the Games. Radio stations included many hours of sports coverage. In 1920 a few thousand people owned radio receiving sets; by 1930 the figure was about 24 million and by 1940 44 million. [3] After the Second World War, radio coverage of the Olympic Games was faced with the challenge of television, but radio commentary has not been wholly replaced. In fact, many enthusiasts today turn off the television sound and listen to the radio coverage. It is often considered superior—more vivid, more detailed, more comprehensive.

(3) Film

Sports Films edited by Harvey Marc Zucker and Lawrence J. Babich in 1987 contains a list of 2,042 titles divided into 17 categories-the Olympics is one. The most famous filmmaker in this category is Leni Riefenstahl. Her film of the 1936 Berlin Olympic Games, *Olympia*, is a stunning classic. Her original use of slow motion, close-ups, and novel editing created unforgettable images of athletes in dramatic action.

Leni Riefenstahl

In 1932 Riefenstahl attended a German political rally and was impressed by the chief speaker, Adolf Hitler. She wrote to tell him so. By chance, Hitler was a fan of her recent directorial debut, *The Blue Light*. He decided she should film the 1933 Nazi rally at Nuremberg. She did-brilliantly. This won her an invitation to film the Olympics two years later. She had pits dug to film competitors in wide angle against static skies, and when the IOC balked she threw a weeping fit. Cameras were attached to balloons, which carried return labels so they could be retrieved after floating off into the Berlin suburbs. There were cameras mounted on horses' saddles to film the three-day event. Riefenstahl set out to make a beautiful film rather than a literal record, and didn't mind a bit of fakery. The pole-vault contest went on until it was too dark to film, so she got the competitors back the next day. Swimmers were filmed in close-up during training, and shots spliced into the final film. And most famously, during the virtuoso diving sequence some shots were run backwards, just because it looked good.

Numerous films have been made with the Games as a subject. Documentary films have been produced for virtually each Games. Kon Ichikawa shot the superb *Tokyo Olympiad in* 1964. It comes close to *Olympia*'s brilliance. The Munich Olympics of 1972 was the inspiration for *Visions of Eight* (1973) which brought together eight noted directors, each concentrating on a particular event or athlete. For example, Arthur Penn of *Bonnie and Clyde* covered the pole-vault; Mai Zetterling focused on weightlifting; Kon Ichikawa analysed the men's 100 metre sprint. John Schlesinger integrated the Palestinian terrorist hostage deaths into a sports story about the British marathon runner Ron Hill. [4]

Since the 1920s a number of Olympic feature films have been made (see the following list). In 1981 *Chariots of Fire*, a fictionalised account of the rivalry between Scotland's Eric Liddell and England's Harold Abrahams at the 1924 Paris Olympics, earned three Oscars—for Best Picture, Costume Design and Original Musical Score.

List of Oympic Feature Films

1925	Nine and Three-Fifths Seconds (United States). Director: Lloyd B. Carleton.
1928	Olympic Hero (United States). Director: R. William Neill.
1936	One in a Million (United States). Director: Sidney Lanfield.
1937	Charlie Chan at the Olympics (United States). Director: H. Bruce Humberstone.
1951	Jim Thorpe—All American (aka Man of Bronze) (United States). Director: Michae II Curtiz.
1954	The Bob Mathias Story (United States). Director: Francis D. Lyon.
1955	Wee Geordie (Great Britain). Director: Frank Launder.
1962	It Happened in Athens (United States). Director: Andrew Marton.
1966	Walk, Don't Run (United States). Director: Charles Walkers.
1969	Downhill Racer (United States). Director: Michael Ritchie.
1970	The Games (United States). Director: Michael Winner.
1974	My Way (aka The Winners) (South Africa). Director: Joseph Brenner.
1975	The Other Side of the Mountain (United States). Director: Larry Peerce.
1976	21 Hours at Munich (United States). Made for Forbes Television.
1977	2076 Olympiad (United States). Director: James P. Martin.
1977	Wilma (United States). Director: Bud Greenspan.
1977	The Greatest (United States/Great Britain). Director: Tom Grier.
1977	Ties to the Olympics (West Germany). Director: Stefan Lukschy.
1979	Dawn (Australia). Director: Ken Hannam.
1979	Goldengirl (United States). Director: Joseph Sargent.
1979	Ice Castles (United States). Director: Donald Wrye.

Con.

1979	Running (United States). Director: Steven Hilliard Stern.
1980	Olympiade 40 (Poland). Director: Andrzej Kotkowski.
1981	Miracle on Ice (United States). Director: Stephen Hilliard Stem.
1981	Chariots of Fire (Great Britain). Director: Hugh Hudson.
1982	Personal Best (United States). Director: Robert Towne.
1983	Running Brave (United States). Director: D. S. Everett.
1984	The First Olympics: Athens 1896 (United States). Director: Alvin Rakoff.
1984	The Jesse Owens Story (United States). Director: Richard Irving.
1985	Going for the Gold: The Bill Johnson Story (United States). Director: Don Taylor.
1986	American Anthem (United States). Director: Albert Magnoli.
1986	Sword of Gideon (United States). Director: Michael Anderson St.
1988	Blades of Courage (United States). Director: Randy Bradshaw.
1992	The Cutting Edge (United States). Director: Paul Michael Glaser.
1993	Cool Runnings (United States). Director: Jon Turteltaub.
1994	Pentathlon (United States). Director: Bruce Malmuth.
1996	Breaking the Surface (United States). Director: Steven Hilliard Stem.
1996	Blast (United States). Director: Albert Pyun.
1996	Run for the Dream (United States). Director: Neema Barnette.
1996	Rowing Through (United States). Director: Masato Harada.
1996	Prefontaine (United States). Director: Steven James.
1998	Without Limits (United States). Director: Robert Towne.
2000	The Loretta Claiborne Story (United States). Director: Lee Grant.

Source: *Encyclopedia of the Modern Olympic Movement*, p. 527.

When Olympic films are considered, one man has to be mentioned—Bud Greenspan, the current official documentary filmmaker of the Games.

> **Legendary Filmmaker Bud Greenspan**
> Born in Sept. 18, 1926, Bud Greenspan began his career as a sports broadcaster at 21 in New York City, He broadcast such programmes as Warm-Up Time and Sports Extra, the pre- and post-game coverage of the Brooklyn Dodgers and hockey, basketball, track and tennis events and others. Later, Greenspan turned to magazine writing. Since then, he has sold hundreds of fiction and non-fiction articles to major publications in the United States and abroad and is a frequent contributor to Parade Magazine. Prior to forming his own film company in 1967, Greenspan produced television commercials for the Lawrence Gumbinner Agency, Dancer-Fitzgerald-Sample, Inc. and SSC&B in New York City.
> After specialising in Olympic Games coverage, he won Emmy awards for 22-part "The Olympiad" (1976-77) and historical vignettes for ABC-TV's coverage of 1980 Winter Games; and won an 1994 Emmy award for an edited special on the Lillehammer Winter Olympics; In 1997 he was awarded a George Foster Peabody Award, the broadcast and cable industry's most prestigious honour, for his lifetime's work. Bud Greenspan has been called the foremost writer, producer and director of sports films and one of the world's leading sports historians.

Source from: http://www.goodmanspeakersbureau.com/biographies/greenspan_bud.htm.

Since 1964 he has produced dozens of films dealing with different aspects of the Olympic Movement. *Jesse Owens Returns to Berlin* (1964), *The Marathon* (1974), *The Australians* (1975), *The East Europeans* (1980), *America at the Olympics* (1984), *An Olympic Dream* (1988). The *Olympiad* series, released in 1988, included 22 parts, among them *Great Moments at the Winter Games*, *Those who Endured*, and *The Immortals*. He continued to produce Olympic films such as the *Honor of Their Country* (1991), *Measure of Greatness* (1992),[5] *100 Years of Olympic Glory* and *America's Greatest Olympians* (1996), and *The Greatest Moments at the Winter Olympics* (1997).

(4) Television

Television broadcasting is crucial to the success of the Games. It now underpins its finances. The 1936 Olympics was the first to be televised. Twenty-five large screens were set up throughout Berlin, allowing the inhabitants to see the Games for free. After the Second World War, television eventually became a mass medium. In the USA in 1949 there were about 2 percent of homes with a TV set; a year later, nearly 10 percent of homes had sets;[6] by 1965 it was 93 percent.[7] In 1964 National Broadcast Corporation (NBC) in America broadcast the Tokyo Opening Ceremony live, although it was late summer before it was certain that pictures beamed via the satellite Syncam III would be of network quality. The Mexico City Games of 1968 were first to be telecast live in colour. Live slow-motion footage was also introduced. In the decades that followed television coverage exploded. The Sydney Olympic Broadcast Organisation provided 3,500 hours of Olympic action covering more than 300 competition and ceremonial events and reached 3.7 billion viewers in a record 220 countries; while NBC televised 441 hours of the Sydney Games and then 1,210 hours of the 2004 Athens Games (70 hours per day of coverage on the seven channels).[8]

Apart from acting as a conduit to a global audience for the promotion of Olympism, television now supplies the Olympic "families" with huge amount of money through the sale of Olympic television rights (more details below). The broadcasting of Sydney 2000 accounted for 45% of all the revenue generated. This figure increased to 52% in 2004 Athens Games. For the Olympic Games staged between 1984 and 2008, the IOC negotiated television contracts worth more than $10 billion.[9] However, this situation was not achieved without struggle. Two themes pervade the history of the Olympics and television: conflict and control.

The Struggle for Television Fees

After the television rights to the Olympic Games were sold to broadcasting in 1960, Organising Committees of the Olympic Games(OCOGs), International Federations of Sports (IFs) and National Olympic Committees (NOCs) as well as the IOC, all tried to get a share of the money. The IOC was faced with one challenge after another. Therefore, in the 1960s the IOC president Brundage established a distribution formula that would bring peace to the Olympic Movement, while at the same time protect his vision of its ideals and meet the financial needs of the OCOGs. In 1966 the IOC's first formal distribution formula for television revenue was announced. From 1972, 66 percent of the television money was to be allocated to the local organisers while the remaining 33 percent would be shared by the IOC, IFs and NOCs. However, at beginning this formula was hard to implement. The Munich Olympic Organising Committee wanted to deduct a technical service fee from the sum negotiated for U.S. television rights. The IOC compromised and permitted the Munich Committee to deduct US $6 million from the US $13.5 million contract with the American Broadcasting Company (ABC). This did not happen in the following Games. The IOC banned deductions by cities wanting to host the Games. In 1977, the IOC, under its President Lord Killanin, determined that it would negotiate television contracts with the 1984 and future organising committees.

However, over the course of the next decade, this negotiation policy proved pro-

> blematic. Peter Ueberroth, president of the Los Angeles Organising Committee challenged it and claimed exclusive control of the negotiation process. Knowing that the European Broadcast Union had not been required to pay for television rights in the past, Ueberroth won the IOC's support to negotiate with the EBU. As a result, EBU paid to broadcast the Seoul Olympic Games in 1988. Direct negotiation by the city involved is now the accepted arrangement.

source: *Encyclopaedia of the Modern Olympic Games*, pp. 509-519.

Television has affected the Olympics profoundly. It has led to significant interference, for example, with the timing of events.[10] In addition, programme structure and presentational style now strongly reflect television's requirements.[11]

(5) Internet

The internet is playing an increasing part in the reporting of the Olympics. There were 186 million hits in 1996 on the official web site for the Games and 634 million hits in Nagano '98. The transformation in the use of the internet in recent years has been incredible. The internet is very much part of our daily lives. Sport is now king and attract huge audiences around the world all seeking the latest information on their favourite sport, team or player. The popular information—based sports services provide play-by-play descriptions of sporting events. SportsZone has football "Drive Charts" and basketball "Shot Charts". These graphics reveal the action diagrammatically second by second. This type of detail, impossible in newspapers due to space limitations, is being used to entice information—obsessed fans to pay monthly membership fees. News, statistics, analysis, schedules and prices, for example, can now be found online.

Selling sports "stats" is already a multi-million dollar industry.[12] Many major newspapers and broadcasting organisations have Web sites with specific sections devoted to sport, including the Olympic Games. Sport has become big business for Reuters and the internet is largely responsible. Reuters' "sports feeds" cost the average web site USD 5,000 per month. This is big business when you work out how many sports websites there are requiring content (well over 2500 sports-related web pages currently exist)[13]. Reuters have created a new department of over 80 people solely for the task of developing their sports content market and they are widely recognised as the leading source of sports information on the internet.[14] Companies like Stats, Inc. provide details like the number of running backs "stuffed" and umpire call tendencies which are available instantly for a

$30 registration fee and $0.25 per minute online charges.[15] All of the major sports services are overflowing with statistical information; ESPN's scoreline charges $0.95 a minute for scores. Motorola's sports beeper that reports on baseball games in progress costs about $50 per month. Now online services are providing customizable, real-time scrolling Java scoreboards.

The amount of sports information being distributed online is snowballing. Hundreds of sports fans have started their own information repositories as they gain access to the www. Most professional sports oversight organisations have informational web sites that they plan to use to generate revenue or solidify their fan base. Individual teams have put player information, game schedules and ticket information online. Along with other online specialty sports stores, teams are displaying and selling game merchandise.

Email, mailing lists, newsgroups and chat services are providing the sports enthusiast with a new form of communication. These services try to fulfil the basic human need for interaction and conversation with other people. Their primary drawback is that they require the user to work too hard—the discourse is often forced, uninspiring, and argumentative. Many of the most seductive aspects of sport are missing because the interactive pace and structure of email, newsgroups, and chat rooms is not conducive to intoxicating immersion.

According to Sportsbusiness. net in its January 10, 2001 newsline, www. sportsline. com, a Columbia Broadcasting Systems (CBS) website in the fourth quarter of 2000 had page views of approximately 2.8 billion, an average of 30.2 million daily page view. Sportsbusiness. net sends out a daily newsline to all its customers covering the business of sport and holds annual conferences on sports media, and sports business, including a recently held conference in Dec. 2000 in conjunction with the IOC.[16]

Online information services provide material not available elsewhere. Current systems can provide information faster than other media and in multi-media formats, but they are restricted by output devices that are less convenient and appealing than paper.

The internet has directly impacted on the Olympic Movement. As the needs for real-time information and the networking of Games services have grown, the technological challenges involved in organising the Games have skyrocketed. The IOC has developed working groups to help the OCOG and the IOC technology suppliers identify the requirements for hardware procurement, systems and application software developments and network design. The working groups also guide the implementation and operation of all technology projects. The IOC has developed its Global Technology Model to assist the interaction among all concerned. One of the more important tools for working with the OCOG and all the partners is ORIS, the Olympic Results and Information Services Manual. This sets out the technological requirements for each sport and its disciplines so everyone understands what must be delivered in each area. [17]

The internet shares with the media in general several commonalties. Its purpose is to make profits; its ambition is to provide a service; its aim is to establish a reputation as a credible source of information; its desire is to express itself in uniquely artistic form. Finally, it controls the production and transmission of messages.

3. Broadcasting

The issue of broadcasting rights is so crucial to the Olympics that it merits exploration in some detail. The role of television as a viable source of IOC revenue was identified as early as 1954 by Avery Brundage, who presided over the IOC between 1952 and 1972.

The first TV rights fees were established by the IOC for the 1960 Summer and Winter Olympic Games. CBS paid $50,000 for the rights to the Winter Olympics in Squaw Valley, California and $394,000 for the Summer Olympics in Rome. After 1960 the American television networks ABC, CBS and NBC competed fiercely for the right to cover both the Winter and Summer Games (see table 5-2).

Table 5-2 US Broadcast Rights Fees

Olympic Summer Games		Broadcast	Millions US $
1976	Montreal	ABC	25
1980	Moscow	NBC	85
1984	Los Angeles	ABC	225.6
1988	Seoul	NBC	300
1992	Barcelona	NBC	401
1996	Atlanta	NBC	456 *
2000	Sydney	NBC	705
2004	Athens	NBC	739.5 *
2008	Beijing	NBC	834.0 *

(Source: IOC 2005 Marketing Fact File, www.olympic.org)

As a result, the U.S. rights fees soared beyond the $2 million dollar mark in 1964, spiralled to $456 million from NBC for the centennial Games of 1996, reached $705 million for the 2000 Games and escalated to $739 million for the 2004 Games. It is clear from the following table that American companies dominate the broadcasting market of the Games.

Table 5-3 Olympic Broadcasters and Right Fees for the 2004 Games in Athens

Continent	Company	Right fees (US $ million)
Americas	United States National Broadcasting Company (NBC)	793.0
	Canada Canadian Broadcasting Corporation (CBC)	37.0
	Latin America Organización de la Televisión Iberoamericana (OTI)	17.0
	Puerto Rico Telemundo of Puerto Rico (WKAQ)	1.25
Asia	Caribbean Caribbean Broadcasting Union (CBU)	0.35
	Asia-Pacific Asia-Pacific Broadcasting Union (ABU)	14.5
	Japan The Athens Olympic Japan Consortium (AOJC)	155.0
	Arab States Arab States Broadcasting Union (ASBU)	5.5
	Chinese Taipei Chinese Taipei Athens Pool (CTAP)	3.65
	Korea Athens Olympic Korea Pool (AOKP)	15.5
Europe Oceania	Europe European Broadcasting Union (EBU)	394.0
	Australia Seven Network (Seven)	50.5
	New Zealand TV New Zealand (TVNZ)	3.5
Africa	Africa Union of Radio & Television Nations of Africa (URTNA) / South African Broadcasting Corporation (SABC)	9.25
	Supersport International (SSI)	3.0
Total:		1,476,911,634,

The popularity of televised sports events guarantees that the television networks will continue to offer enormous sums to cover them and commercial sponsors or governmental agencies will continue to underwrite these costs. Indeed, on June 2003 NBC extended its broadcast contract with the IOC to 2012 (see below).

NBC's a Total Package of US $ 2.201 Billion for the Games Until 2012

* US $ 2.201 billion TV rights break down as follows:

— US $ 820 million for the 2010 Olympic Winter Games (compared to US $ 614 million in Turin 2006);

— US $ 1.181 billion for the 2012 Summer Olympic Games (compared to US $ 894 million in Beijing 2008) * sponsorship of the Games by NBC's parent company General Electric in the TOP 6 and TOP 7 IOC Marketing programmes amounting to a minimum of US $ 160 million up to maximum of US $ 200 million;

* rights fees for the US Olympic trials to the sum of US $ 12 million; development of a digital TV library and archiving system for an estimated value of US $ 10 million;

* in addition, NBC has made a further multi-hundred million dollar commitment to promote the Olympic name leading up to, and surrounding the Olympic Games.

Source from: "Official IOC Press Release", 06 June 2003.

The above NBC's package represents an overall increase of 32.6% (34% for the Winter Games and 32% for the Summer Games), and a compounded annual increase of 7.5% for the Winter Games and of 7.2% for the Summer Games.[18]

Hand in hand with the increased rights fees go the increasing hours of broadcast. In 1996, NBC aired 171 hours of the Olympic Games. In 2000 it aired 441 hours. In 2004 the figure jumped to 806 hours (nearly double that of Sydney four years earlier).[19]

The return on the investment by the major television networks is impressive. It is estimated that NBC made a $ 82 million profit on its coverage of the 1988 Seoul Olympics,[20] and it generated $ 1 billion in advertising revenue from the 2004 summer Games—up from $ 900 million in revenue from Sydney four years earlier.[21] Grand moments and grand venues come at a price. NBC charged an average of $ 730,000 for a 30-second commercial spot during the Games. Hardly surprisingly, therefore, it is estimated that the company could eventually make a profit from advertising, of perhaps $ 50 million.

The sale of Olympic television rights has become the main source of the IOC's income. Table 5-4 shows the TV revenue from 1980 to 2008. The IOC generated more than US $ 1.332 billion from the sale of Sydney fees. This represents an increase of nearly 50 percent over the US $ 898 million generated by the sale of Atlanta fees. [22] In the last quadrennial the IOC generated US $ 2.4 billion from the marketing of Olympic broadcast rights and world-wide sponsorships alone, nearly US $ 900 million more than that generated in the quadrennial 1993-96. [23]

Table 5-4 Global TV revenue over time

Olympic Summer Games		Millions US $	Olympic Winter Games		Millions US $
1960	Rome	1.178	1960	Squaw Valley	0.05
1964	Tokyo	1.578	1964	Innsbruck	0.937
1968	Mexico City	9.750	1968	Grenoble	2.613
1972	Munich	17.792	1972	Sapporo	8,475
1976	Montreal	34.862	1976	Innsbruck	11.627
1980	Moscow	87.984	1980	Lake Placid	20.726
1984	Los Angeles	286.914	1984	Sarajeyo	102.682
1988	Seoul	402.595	1988	Calgary	324.897
1992	Barcelona	636.06	1992	Albertville	291.928
1996	Atlanta	898.267	1994	Lilehammer	352.911
2000	Sydney	1,331.550	1998	Nagano	513.485
2004	Athens	1,494.028	2002	Salt Lake City	736.135
2008	Beijing	1697 *	2006	Torino	833

* Rights Fees negotiated to date (Source: IOC 2005 Marketing Fact File, www.olympic.org)

Most of the revenue is distributed throughout the Olympic Movement. The IOC is now able to provide more support than ever to the OCOGs, the IFs, the NOCs, and other institutions or organisations, such as the World Anti-Doping Agency and the International Paralympics Committee. [24] Although corporate sponsorship money raised through the Olympic Partners Programme, which began in the 1980s, has diversified its revenue base—television revenue still provides 50% of the Olympic Movement's financial resources.

Linking with the media has meant the Games losing a degree of control over its own activities and destiny. Along with the benefits have come some possible costs to the Games. The Media's increasing involvement in, and control over, the Games has put it in a powerful position to dictate aspects of events. Rules for some Olympic sports have been changed and playing conditions revised so as to enhance media coverage. Gymnastics is a good example. In the past, four or six gymnasts competed on different apparatuses at the same time. To ensure virtually all competitors are camera-covered, now one or two gymnasts perform at a time. As a result, one session of competition can last hours, much longer than before. Specific timetabling changes in the Seoul Games (some competitions took place in the early morning) were made to fit in with the North American viewer's requirements. Unquestionably, the mass media is re-shaping the Olympic Games.

However, there is one thing in favour of the IOC. To promote Olympism and minimize the negative impact of commercialism on the Olympics, the IOC has decided that rights to the Olympic Games are sold only to broadcasters who can guarantee the greatest access to Games coverage throughout their countries or territories free of charge. The IOC has declined higher offers for Olympic Games broadcast rights because a broadcasters' coverage was only accessible to a limited section of the population. The Olympic Games are one of the last remaining major events in the world to maintain such a relatively free-access policy.

Conclusion

The Olympic Games and the media are now tightly bound together in a complex relationship. Newspaper, magazines, radio, television and internet promote and influence the Olympic Games. Today television is dominant, but the internet will gradually play a more and more important role. In summary, the media has demonstrated an increasing capacity to influence the character and development of the Olympic Movement, and there appeared to be little resistance to this from the governing bodies of the Olympics.

Questions
1. What is the essence of the relationship between the Olympic Games and the mass media?
2. Do you believe that television companies should dictate the times and structures of events?
3. Do you see the internet or television as the future dominant influence on the IOC?
4. Is it right that American television audiences have such an influence

over the presentation of Olympic events?

Note

[1] http://www.olympic.org/uk/games/athens/index_uk.asp.
[2] Hallin, D. C., "The American Media: A Critical Theory Perspective", in H. Forester (ed.) (1985), *Critical Theory and Political Life*, Cambridge, MA: MIT., p. 141.
[3] Ellis Cashmore (2000), *Sports Culture: An A-Z Guide*, London and New York: Routledge, 138.
[4] Ibid.
[5] John E. Findling and Kimberly D. Pelle (2004), *Encyclopedia of the Modern Olympic Movement*, London: Greenwood Press, 563.
[6] Ellis Cashmore (2000), ibid., 405-406.
[7] David Levinson and Karen Chritensen (eds.) (1996), *Encyclopaedia of World Sport*, Oxford: ABC-CLIO, 244.
[8] IOC Awards US TV Rights For 2010 And 2012 Olympic Games To NBC, 06 June, 2003, Official IOC Press Release.
[9] "IOC 2005 Marketing File", www.olympic.org.
[10] In Seoul Games, for example, the 100-metre sprint was scheduled late in the morning, Seoul time, instead of the usual time of afternoon or evening for this race.
[11] Take gymnastics as example. Gymnasts have to perform virtually one by one instead of several at a time on different apparatuses, and meanwhile warm-up time was cancelled.
[12] P. H. Lewis, "In Cyberspace, a High-Tech League of Their Own", *The New York Times*, April 5, 1994.
[13] Yahoo Sports, http://www.yahoo.com/Recreation/Sports/.
[14] Mike Laflin, "Sport and the Internet-The Impact and the Future", http://multimedia.olympic.org/pdf/en_report_60.pdf.
[15] D. Katz, "Welcome to the Electronic Arena", 1995, from Sports Illustrated Online-no longer available. Can find at http://www-white.media.mit.edu/~intille/st/electronic-arena.html.
[16] Mike Laflin, "Sport and the Internet—The Impact and the Future", http://multimedia.olympic.org/pdf/en_report_60.pdf.
[17] Electric lines and modem.
[18] Final Report on the XXVIIth Olympiad, 17.
[19] IOC Awards US TV Rights For 2010 And 2012 Olympic Games To NBC, June 6, 2003; Official IOC Press Release.
[20] Associated Press, "TV will nearly double Sydney's coverage", http://espn.go.com/oly/news/2003/0205/1504525.html.
[21] George H. Sage (1990), *Power and Ideology in American Sport*, Human Kinetics Europe Ltd, 124.

[22] George Raine, "2004 Athens Games: Advertising sporting a profit: NBC sells expansive Olympic coverage", *Chronicle Research*, August 12, 2004.
[23] Final Report on the XXVIIth Olympiad, 21.
[24] Ibid, 5.
[25] Ibid.

Chapter 6
The Olympic Games: Ceremonies

Key points of this chapter:
* The Olympic ceremonies
* IOC Ceremonial Ritualism in detail: Aspects of the Opening Ceremony

Introduction

Since the Olympic Games in Athens in 1896, Olympic ceremonies have been part of the Olympic Games. Over time these ceremonies have steadily increased in number. Today the main ceremonies comprise the Torch Relay, the Lighting of the Olympic Flame, the Opening Ceremony, the Presentation Ceremony and the Closing Ceremony. These ceremonies distinguish the Games from other sports competitions. They reflect both the culture of the Olympic Movement and the culture of host countries and now mostly involve set rituals.

1. Lighting of the Flame

The Flame symbolizes the quest for perfection, the striving for victory, the pursuit of peace and the cultivation of friendship. Perhaps the most striking of the ceremonies of the Games is the Lighting of Olympic Flame. Originally ignited during the Opening Ceremony, it burned day and night at the Olympic Stadium and other scenes of competition during the Games. Only when the Olympic Flag was lowered at the end of the Closing Ceremony was the Flame extinguished.

The first Lighting of the Olympic Flame in the modern era was in 1928 in Amsterdam in Holland. It burned at the entrance of the main stadium throughout the duration of the Summer Games. The concept of lighting a flame for the duration of the Games comes from the ancient Greeks, who used a flame lit by the sun's rays at Olympia—the site, of course, of the original Olympic Games. In 1932 the Flame was lit in Los Angeles stadium and burned atop the Coliseum throughout the Games. This was the last time that an Olympic Flame was lit at the Games site.

In 1934 the IOC ratified a Torch Relay from Olympia to the host city. Thus, Olympia became the place where the Flame was lit.

> **Flame Lighting in Olympia**
> The flame is ignited from the rays of the sun using a parabolic mirror in front of the Temple of Hera. A special ceremonial torch is used for the actual lighting. The flame is then transferred to an urn and carried into the ancient stadium by the "high priestess". After a brief ceremony the official torch is lit and carried away by the first Torch Bearer.

2. Torch Relay

The tradition of carrying the torch in relays from Olympia was established at the Berlin Games in 1936. Since then, the Torch Relay has become a major Olympic Ceremony symbolizing an embrace of the world, celebrating all humanity and illustrating the universality of the values of Olympism. To this end the Torch Bearers represent all manner of people—among them, politicians, artists, businessmen, athletes, the handicapped, the young and the elderly. To be selected as a Torch Bearer is a great honour. Therefore, it is unsurprising that the IOC vice-Chairman Kevan Gosper's 11-year-old daughter replaced a 15-year-old Australian-Greek student to be the first Australian to carry the torch caused attacks on IOC nepotism. [1]

The last torch relay runner now ignites the cauldron in the Olympic Stadium with the torch. The runner circles the track, mounts the steps, and lights the Olympic cauldron that burns night and day during the Games. In a moving variation in 1992, the Spanish Olympic archer Antonio Rebollo, a Paralympic athlete, for the first time at the Games, ignited the cauldron atop the Stadium with a flaming arrow. To great acclaim the flame soared to a height of three metres.

Figure 6-1 Igniting the Flame from the Rays of the Sun

Figure 6-2 Carrying the Flame by the Priestess

Each Relay, for obvious reasons, varies in route and scale (see table 6-1).

Table 6-1 Information on the Torch Relay of the Olympic Games in modern era

	Numbers of runners	Lasting days	Distance total	Name of last runner
2004		141	Over 78,000 km	Nikolaos Kaklamanakis
2000	11,000	126	27,000 km	Cathy Freeman
1996	Over 800 in Greece, 12,467 in USA	84	2,141 km(Greece), 26,875 km (USA)	Muhammad Ali
1992	9,849 and 599 cyclists	51	about 6,300 km	Juan Antonio San Epifanio
1988	1,467	26	about 4,700 km	Sohn Kee Chung
1984	3,636	82	15,000 km	Rafer Johnson
1980	about 5,000	30	4,915 km	Sergej Belov

Con.

	Numbers of runners	Lasting days	Distance total	Name of last runner
1976	about 1,200	4	775 km	Stéphane Préfontaine and Sandra Henderson
1972	6,000	30	5,532 km	Günther Zahn
1968	2,778	50	13,620 km	Enriqueta Basileo
1964	870 (Outside Japan), 4,374 (Japan)	50	15,508 km (outside Japan air-relayed), relayed overland 732 km,	Yoshinori Sakai
1960	1,529	13	1,863 km	Giancarlo Peris
1956	3,118 (2,830 in Australia)	20	4,912 km	Ronald William Clarke
1952	3,372	25	4,725 km	Paavo Nurmi
1948	1,416	12	3,160 km	John Marks
1936	3,331	12	3,187 km	

In 1952 the Olympic Flame was flown from Greece to Denmark and carried in a Torch Relay, Fritz Schilgenthrough Sweden to the Finnish border. A local Torch was provided by an additional Flame lit from the rays of the midnight sun on top of the Pallastunturi fell in Lapland. The two Flames were united and relayed to Helsinki. A quarter of the Finnish population came to see the Torch relayed along its route. The Torch was brought into the Stadium by the former famous Finnish athlete 55-year-old Paavo Nurmi. By 1956 the Relay had become so well established, celebrated and structured that torch bearers numbered 3,500.

Each host country strives for originality in the relaying of the Torch. For the Mexico Games of 1968, for example, the Torch Relay was planned to follow the course of Columbus's first voyage to the New World, thus symbolizing the union of the classic cultures of the Old and New Worlds. The principal intermediate points along the route of the Torch were Genoa in Italy, the birthplace of Christopher Columbus, Palos in Spain, the port from which he embarked on his first voyage of discovery; and the island of San Salvador, the first place he reached in the New World. In another act of originality, a twenty-year-old hurdler, Norma Enriqueta Basilio became the first woman in Olympic history to bring the Olympic Torch into Mexico City stadium and to ignite the cauldron.

In 1976 there occurred a technological innovation that symbolised the willingness of the Olympic Movement to embrace change. The Flame was brought from a Greek to a Canadian flame altar and then transferred with a torch to a sensor, which captured the ionised particles of the Flame and transmitted electrical impulses in sequence. Via the communication satellite "Intelsat", these impulses were transmitted to Parliament Hill in Ottawa, where they were changed back into a Flame by means of a laser beam and a parabolic mirror. The Canadian Prime Minister Pierre Elliot Trudeau then received the Flame from the hands of Lise Litz, an athlete from Ottawa. He handed it on to twelve Torch Bearers, who symbolised the ten provinces of Canada, the Yukon and the Northwest Territories. On the Opening Day 16 Torch Bearers ran in relay to the Olympic Stadium. Stéphane Préfontaine and Sandra Henderson ran the final metres and ignited the cauldron. This was the first time that a man and a woman lit the cauldron together. This event, and another, linked them together. They married and became the "dream couple" of Torch Relay history.

In 1984 another element of modernism appeared—commercialism. The Los Angeles Olympic Committee in 1984 sold the rights to carry the Olympic Flame in America for $ 3,000 a kilometer. This entrepreneurship angered the Greeks. In their view the Flame was not for sale. Some 30,000 Greek demonstrators tried to deny the Americans the Sacred Flame from Olympia, and 15,000 Greek troops sealed off access to the sanctuary at ancient Olympia. Tensions ran high and Greek President Konstantinos Karamanlis was prepared to place himself between the soldiers and the demonstrators to keep the peace. In the event, this was not needed. The American Olympic officials helicoptered directly into the cordoned-off site, took the Flame as soon as it was lit (by a "chief priestess" who received scores of deaths threats for doing so), omitted the usual rituals at Coubertin's memorial, and to the chanted curses of the crowd lifted off to a waiting U.S. government plane at a military airport near Athens.[2]

In 2000, after the Torch was lit in Olympia and conveyed to Athens,

Figure 6-3　Paavo Nurmi Ignited the Cauldron in 1952

there were brief stopovers in twelve countries of Oceania before the Torch Relay travelled around Australia for 100 days. Originality was again the order of the day. The Relay was carefully organised to maximize community involvement: half the 11,000 Torch Bearers were chosen by community committees, and the Torch made frequent lunch-time and evening stops where community cauldrons were lit. The final Torch Bearers were all women in celebration of 100 years of women's participation in the Olympic Games.

　　The Torch Relay for the Athens Games in 2004 saw a more imaginative innovation involved a twenty-first-century-style "tourist" tour. It visited each past Olympic Summer Games host city, as well as the 2008 host city Beijing and a select list of additional cities that includes New Delhi, Cairo,

Figure 6-4   Torch Relay

Cape Town, Rio de Janeiro, New York, Brussels, Geneva, Lausanne, Kiev, Istanbul, Sofia and Nicosia. In total, the Relay passed through 34 cities in 27 countries. The worldwide route embraced Australia, Asia, Africa, South America, North America and, finally, Europe. This was the largest Olympic Torch Relay in history and it passed through Africa and Latin America for the first time.

The Torch Relay has self-evidently expanded substantially over time in terms of duration and distance travelled and numbers involved. It has become global.

3. Opening Ceremony

Each Games has an Opening Ceremony with the sports stadium filled with music, singing, dancing and fire-works. The Opening Ceremony is the most viewed sports event in the world. In Britain, the ceremony in Athens in 2004 was watched by more than 8.5 million viewers (2.5 times more than the Opening Ceremony in Sydney). In France, 7.3 million viewers watched the Ceremony on France 2 Channel. In Germany, more than 12.95 million people saw the Ceremony on ZTF(3.5 times more than the Ceremony in Sydney). In the United States, more than 56 million viewers watched the Ceremony on NBC. [3]

The Ceremony, as already mentioned, has evolved over time. The London Games in 1908 was the first Olympics to have a Ceremony. The participating athletes paraded behind their respective national flags on their entry into the White City Stadium. However, the parade was marred by political controversy. The Finnish team protested publicly against Russian rule in Finland, many Irish athletes refused to compete as subjects of the British crown and were absent from the parade and the Games, and a running feud between the Americans and the British began when the American shot-putter Ralph Rose would not dip the U. S. flag in salute to King Edward VII. This refusal later became standard practice for U. S. athletes in the opening parade.

The Ceremony of the Los Angeles Games in 1932 set both patterns and precedents for pageantry and showmanship. Hundreds of flags flew above the Coliseum. National banners and the five-ringed Olympic flag graced the peristyle at the east end. The peristyle itself bore Coubertin's classic statement: "The important thing in the Olympic Games is not winning, but taking part. The essential thing is not conquering, but fighting well." A 250-piece band and a choir of 1,200 voices delivered impassioned music. With the delegation from Greece at its head, the parade of athletes marched crisply from the Coliseum's main tunnel, drew up in neat columns across the field, and stood smartly to attention. [4]

In 1936 the German organisers, for ideological reasons, transformed the ceremony. The association of sport with the National Socialist Cult of the Warrior was made clear in the festival performance of "Olympische Jugend", which Karl Diem had written for the Opening Ceremony. The exuberant Games of Youth were followed with a fourth scene with the theme "Heldenkampf und Totenldage" (Fight of the Heroes and Death Moans). Then in the "Schwertertanz der Jinglinge" (Dance of the Swords of the Young Men), a heroic battle between young soldiers occurred, which ended in the sacrifice of their life, and women in mourning—danced by Mary Wigman[5] and the avant-garde of German dance. With the sacrifice of the lives of the heroes, a huge dome of spot lights arched over the stadium, created by special effects, and 15,000 singers sang Schiller's and Beethoven's "Ode an die Freude." [6]

The 1996 Atlanta Games had a five-hour Opening Ceremony celebrating American culture. In 2002, the Sydney Opening Ceremony involved the depiction of the nation's culture was arguably, more evocative and moving: the presentation of the land and its traditional inhabitants, the importance of fire and water to the island continent, the coming of immigrants, and the creation of a vibrant and technologically advanced nation. The initial segment was especially poignant: "Deep Sea Dreaming" introduced the Aboriginal notion of the dreamtime and the importance of the ocean to the island inhabitants of Australia.

The Opening Ceremony of the Athens Games in 2004 went one better and won worldwide acclaim for its stunning tableau of 3,000 years of Greek history and culture. Four hundred drummers imitated a human heart-beat before a flame raced across the stadium's 80-metre-high roof to light the logo of the modern Olympics on a man-made lake in the arena, symbolizing the Aegean Sea. A boat carrying a boy glided across the lake to be greeted by President Stefanopoulos, the IOC President Jacques Rogge and the Athens 2004 Chief Executive, Gianna Angelopoulos Daskalaki. Then came the centrepiece of the ceremony with human figures that looked as though they were brought to life from Greek frescoes, mosaics, sculptures and paintings. The performance provided a chronological procession of images ranging from prehistoric to modern times. It was intended to be entertaining and educational giving the audience a graphic history lesson on both Greece and the Olympics. The Ceremony combined ancient history with modern technology. The flooded arena that contained two million litres of water was drained in just 3 minutes in preparation for the next stage. Throughout—perfectly timed fireworks lit the sky around the arena as the performance unfolded.

4. Victory Ceremony

The Presentation Ceremony is an old Olympic custom. The winners are presented with medals, a diploma and an olive or laurel branch. In the ancient Games, the simple crown of wild olive was sufficient to immortalize the victor, his family and his city. The crown made of olive leaves came from a wild olive tree in the Altis, which was called the olive of the Beautiful Crown. Olive trees, which supplied the Greeks with olive oil-bathing oil and a base for perfumes, were an important resource in the dry and rocky Greek environment. A Greek legend credited the hero Herakles (Hercules) with introducing the olive tree to Greece.

Figure 6-5　Old Award Ceremony

Design of the Medals

The design of the medals varies with each Olympic Games and they are the responsibility of the host city's organising committee. Solid gold medals were first awarded in 1912. Since 1928 the medals have been standardised. Olympic medals must be at least 60 millimetres in diameter and at least three millimetres thick. Gold and silver medals must be made of 92.5 percent pure silver; the gold medal must be gilded with at least six grams of gold. The obverse medals show a figure of Victory holding a wreath in one hand and a palm frond in the other. The reverse side has to show a victorious athlete on the shoulders of the crowd. Since 1972, however, only the obverse of the medal has remained the same. The reverse is now modified for each Olympiad.

However, the Winter Games medals are not subject to the same constraints. There are no rules stipulating a particular shape or design. Other materials may even be introduced along with the basic gold, silver and bronze. The medals of the Albertville Games (France) included a crystal disc. The Lillehammer (Norway) medals had a granite elementand. The medals of the Nagano Games (Japan) were partially worked in lacquer. In fact, every Olympic Winter Games has seen a different medal design.

Figure 6-6   Medals of the Beijing 2008 Olympic Games

At the first modern Games in Athens in 1896 winners were rewarded with an olive wreath and a silver medal, while the runners-up received a bronze medal and a laurel wreath. Gold, silver and bronze medals were not awarded until 1904. The 1932 Olympic Games saw the appearance of the national anthems and the raising of flags in honour of the victors during the medal ceremonies. These ceremonies would take place henceforward at the competition site immediately after the end of the event how instead of all together on the closing day. Since the Olympic Winter Games in Lake Placid in 1932 (USA), the medals have been awarded to winners standing on a podium.

The first eight in each event receive a diploma and their names are read out. In Athens in 2004, 301 presentation ceremonies took place over a period of 16 days.

The moment of Olympic glory occurs when the athlete steps onto the podium to receive his or her medal which is usually presented soon after the conclusion of each event. The gold medallist stands in the centre on the highest step, the silver medallist on the right and the bronze medallist on the left. The medals, attached to a chain or ribbon, are hung around the necks of the athletes by a member of the IOC, and the flags of the nations concerned are raised to the top of the flagpoles while an abbreviated form of the national anthem of the winner is played. The spectators and the three successful athletes stand and face the flags.

5. Closing Ceremony

The Closing Ceremony takes place on the last day of the Games after the final event, which is usually the equestrian Prix des Nations. At the Closing Ceremony of the 1932 Games, a parade of nations' flags replaced the parade of athletes. Trumpets and artillery salutes marked the lowering of the five-ringed Olympic flag, which the mayor of Los Angeles accepted for safekeeping until it would rise in Berlin in 1936. The huge crowd joined massed bands and a thousand-voiced chorus in an emotion-filled moment, singing "Aloha" as the sun dropped below the horizon. Throughout the subsequent Games, athletes were identified by nation.

However, the closing ceremony in Melbourne was different. Based on the idea of an adolescent Chinese-Australian student, "... during the march there will only be 1 NATION..., no team is to keep together and there should be no more than two team mates together, they must be spread out evenly...", the Closing Ceremony created "a prophetic image of a new future for mankind—the athletes of the world not now sharply divided, but..., marching as one in a hotchpotch of sheer humanity, a fiesta, {of} friendship...". [7] Since then, the Closing Ceremony of the Olympic Games has been a less formal affair.

The Closing Ceremony of the Games is also frequently full of music, song and dance. In the Closing Ceremony of the Athens Games, for example, 3,691 volunteer performers from 15 countries and 2,200 volunteer in support from 32 countries, were involved. "Let the dances last" was the first song and many others followed sung by some of the best Greek singers including Charis Alexiou, and Dimitra Galani. Then the Medal Ceremony for the Men's Marathon followed, for the first time in the Olympic Closing Ceremony. After short speeches by the Presidents of the Athens Organising Committee and the IOC, the national anthems of Greece and China were played and the Olympic flag was handed over to Wang Qishan, the mayor of Beijing, the host city of the next Olympic Games. Then the IOC President Jacques Rogge declared the Athens 2004 Olympic Games closed, and some 170 Chinese artists then presented an eight-minute performance directed by the famous film director Zhang Yimou.

In summary, the Closing Ceremony now includes:

* A parade of athletes, six from each nation, march mixed together signifying the friendly bonding of the Olympic performers.

　　* The handing over of the Olympic flag to the next Olympic host city. Then the President of the IOC calls the youth of the world to assemble in four years to celebrate the Games of the next Olympiad.

　　* The mingling of all the athletes in the stadium symbolising global friendship.

　　* The extinguishing of the Flame. A fanfare is sounded. The Flame is then extinguished.

　　* The declaration of the end of the Games by the IOC President. To the strains of the Olympic anthem, the Olympic flag is lowered and the Games are over.

6. Ceremonial Ritualism: the Opening Ceremony in Detail

　　Certain elements of the Opening Ceremony are laid down by the IOC in great detail—from the moment when the head of state of the host country is received by the president of the IOC and the organising committee at the entrance to the stadium to the end of the proceedings when the last team files out. These are:

　　(1) *the entry of the athletes into the stadium with their delegations* (in alphabetical order except for Greece which goes first and the host country which brings up the rear). Each contingent, dressed in its official uniform, is preceded by a shield with the name of its country, while an athlete carries its national flag.

　　After the 1924 Games in Paris, it was common for the athletes to hold their arms to the right when they marched into the stadium. In Berlin the German athletes entered the stadium with the German greeting, arm held in front of the body, while passing the Fuhrerloge, as did the Austrians. When the French team marched in with the Olympic greeting, the 100,000 spectators rejoiced, because they thought the French were using the German greeting. This scene can be seen in Riefenstahl's Olympic film. At the 1980 games, some of the countries protesting against the Soviet Union's involvement in Afghanistan carried the Olympic flag in place of their national flag.

The Olympic Flag

In the stadium and its immediate surroundings, the Olympic flag is flown together with the flags of the nations taking part. The Olympic flag, presented by Coubertin in 1914, has a white background, and in the centre there are five interlaced rings—blue, yellow, black, green, and red. The blue ring is farthest left, nearest the pole. The five rings represent the international nature of the Games. Designed in 1913 by Pierre de Coubertin, the flag was first displayed in Paris during the celebration of the twentieth anniversary of the reorganisation of the Olympic Games in June 1914, but it never appeared at an Olympic gathering until 1920. According to Coubertin, the five entwined multicoloured circles, on a white background, symbolize the five parts of the world united by Olympism and, at the same time, reproduce the colours of every nation.[8]

The Olympic Rings are seen as the most potent of all global marketing symbols. In a survey conducted by Sponsorship Research International in 1996, 78% of the world's population recognised the Olympic Rings and their significance to the Olympic Movement. This percentage topped the listing ahead of the symbols of Shell, McDonalds, Mercedes and the Red Cross.

The Olympic flag became the official symbol of the Games in 1920 and the Olympic flag flew above and inside all sports facilities throughout the Games.

Figure 6-7　The Olympic Flag

(2) *the declaration of the opening of the Games by the Head of State of the host country* (Before the head of State proclaims the Games open, the president of the organising committee delivers a brief speech of welcome, followed by another brief speech from the president of the IOC).

(3) *the entry of the Olympic flag into the stadium* (A fanfare of trumpets is sounded as the Olympic flag is slowly raised).

(4) *the Olympic Anthem*

The Olympic Anthem expresses the spirit of the Olympics. An Olympic Anthem composed by Spyros Samaras (music) and by Kostis Palamas (lyrics) was first played at the Games of the First Olympiad in Athens. Thereafter, a variety of musical offerings provided the backgrounds to the Opening Ceremonies until 1960 when the Samaras/Palamas composition became the official Olympic Anthem. [9]

Olympic Anthem

Immortal spirit of antiquity,
Father of the true, beautiful and good,
Descend, appear, shed over us thy light
Upon this ground and under this sky
Which has first witnessed the unperishable Flame.

Give life and animation to those noble games!
Throw wreaths of fadeless flowers to the victors
In the race and in the strife!
Create in our breasts, hearts of steel!

In thy light, plains, mountains and seas
Shine in a roseate hue and form a vast temple
To which all nations throng to adore thee,
Oh immortal spirit of antiquity!

---

(5) *the release of doves (a symbol of peace)*

At the Antwerp Games in 1920 doves of peace were for the first time released at the Opening Ceremony. They are still part of it.

(6) *the oath sworn by an athlete and an official from the host country.*

In the ancient times, the athletes with fathers, brothers and other male relations met the judges and before the statue of Zeus swore that they had the correct qualifications, citizenship and had never committed a crime. The Belgian fencer and water polo player Victor Boin was the first to take the modern Olympic Oath in 1920. Since then the Olympic Oath has been a part of the Olympic ceremonial. According to established custom, one athlete, representing all athletes, promises to adhere to the rules during the Games. The first Officials' Oath was sworn at the 1972 Olympic Games in Munich.

Figure 6-8 Release of Doves

The 2000 Sydney Games Oath

Athlete's Oath: "In the name of all competitors, I promise that we shall take part in these Olympic Games, respecting and abiding by the rules that govern them, in the true spirit of sportsmanship, for the glory of sport and the honour of our teams, committing ourselves to a sport without doping and without drugs."

Official's Oath: "In the name of all the judges and officials, I promise that we shall officiate in these Olympic Games with complete impartiality, respecting and abiding by the rules which govern them in the true spirit of sportsmanship."

Conclusion

The Lighting of the Flame, Torch Relay, Opening Ceremony, Presentation Ceremony and Closing Ceremony are now established Olympic rituals and highlights of the Olympiads. Over time they have evolved, expanded and changed. They have been transformed from mainly local events into global events. Music, song and dance are integrated into these Ceremonies to create a friendly, festival atmosphere. Of global impact and significance, the Ceremonies are regulated by the IOC, but at the same time host cities are encouraged to create unusual and innovative settings or performances to impress themselves on the world. Politics, technology and education and entertainment are now ingredients of the Ceremonies. And advanced technology is the means of their promotion.

Questions
1. Would you make any changes to the Opening Ceremony of the Beijing Games? If so, why?
2. Do you applaud the changes to the Closing Ceremony that now involve the participants marching together as a cosmopolitan crowd?
3. How should the Beijing Games integrate traditional Chinese elements by means of modern advanced technology in the Opening and Closing Ceremonies to do justice to Chinese culture? What would you suggest?
4. Are there any changes you would make to any of the now established Ceremonies? If so, why and what?

Notes
[1] John Pye, "Olympic Ceremony Sparks Uproar Gosper under Fire for Giving Daughter Torch", *The Associated Press Sydney, Australia* (AP), Thursday, May 11, 2000.
[2] Encyclopaedia Britannica, 2002.
[3] "Athens Olympic Opening Ceremony New TV Viewing Record: IOC", http://english.people.com.cn/200408/23/eng20040823_154349.html.
[4] John E. Findling and Kimberly D. Pelle (eds.) (2004), *Encyclopaedia of the Modern Olympic Movement*, London: Greenwood Press.
[5] Mary Wigman, born on Nov. 13, 1886 and died on Sept. 18, 1973, was a major pioneer of the German modern dance. Her impact on dance throughout the West was immense. Her students included Hanya Holm, who exerted a major influence on the development of American modern dance, and thousands of other original choreographers.
[6] John E. Findling and Kimberly D. Pelle (eds.) (2004), op. cit.
[7] Ibid., 152.
[8] Roland Renson, "Antwerp 1920", in John E. Findling and Kimberly D. Pelle (2004), *op. cit.*, 74.
[9] Charles Beck (ed.) (1896) *Oi Olympiakoi Agones, 776 P. X. -1896* (*The Olympic Games, 776 BC-1896*), Athens 1896.

Chapter 7
The Olympics and the Arts

Key points:
* The Arts and the Ancient Olympics
* The Olympics, Arts Competition, Cultural Festivals and Cultural Olympiads
* Music and the Modern Olympics

1. Brief Historic Overview

Sport should be seen as a producer of art and as an art opportunity. It produces beauty since it creates the athlete who is a living sculpture. It is an art opportunity through the buildings dedicated to it, the spectacle, the celebrations it generates (Coubertin, 1919).[1]

One of the elements of modern Olympism as conceived by Coubertin was the aesthetic pleasure to be derived from the arts. For Coubertin the arts were an integral part of the modern Olympiad.

The ancient civilisations of Egypt, Sumer, Greece and Rome left numerous examples of sport in art. In ancient Greece, art and sport were seen as perfect partners in achieving harmony of body and mind. The earliest work of art connected with athletics was *the Ramping Horseman* [2], the creation of a great Athenian artist just before the middle of the 6th century B.C. Greek ceramic vases with elaborate paintings of wrestling, boxing, running, jumping and other sports fill whole rooms in dozens of museums from Athens to New York. Attic vase-painting alone include 1,571 representations of sportingscenes.[3] Furthermore, "the ancient history of Hellenism with its countless artistic forms and its intellectual life is to be found

Figure 7-1   the Ramping Horseman (550BC)

Figure 7-2   Painting on a Vase

concentrated at Olympia."[4] Consequently, there was intense competition between artists for the honour of the inclusion of their work at Olympia.

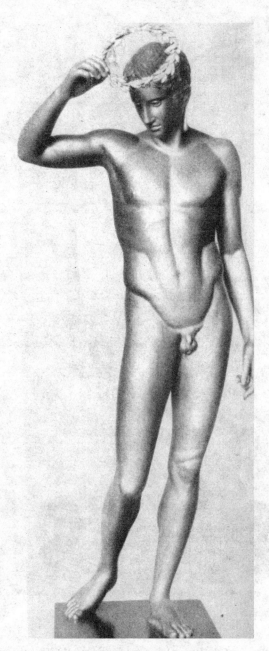

Figure 7-3 Olympic Champion (5th B.C.)

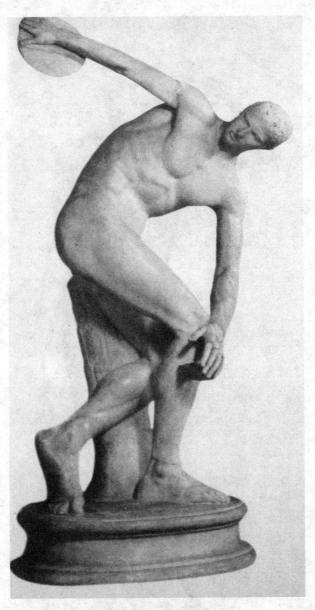

Figure 7-4   Discus Thrower

The existence of these works of art is due to the fact that the figures of the victors were commemorative votive offerings to the gods. The presence of the Gods themselves was also invoked by their ritual effigies. The most famous statues of Zeus by Phidias are still visible at the site of Ancient Olympia.

The Romans copied Greeks bronze statues in bronze or marble. However, they were more inhibited and when making replicas of Greek art, they covered the genitals with fig leaves (one way to tell an original Greek work from a Roman copy). In contrast to the Greeks, however, and as a reflection of their brutal sports, the Romans favoured art illustrating the bloody combats of armed men in mortal combat, men fighting against wild animals and great naval combats in flooded arenas.

Figure 7-5   Heracles

At the time of the revival of the Olympics and the early growth of mod-

Figure 7-6 Zimmerman et sa Machine (Lautrec, 1895)

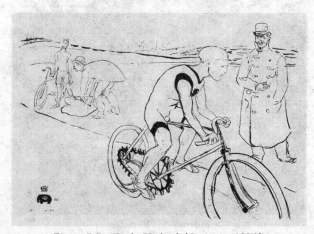

Figure 7-7 Cycle Michael (Lautrec, 1896)

Fiugre 7-8　Indian Ball Game (George Catlin)

ern sport, athletic contests of all kinds attracted artists. Tennis, foot-races and bicycle races were especially favoured. Henri de Toulouse-Lautrec (1864-1901), one of the great post-impressionists, drew not only the cycle races, but also portraits of a number of champions such as Zimmerman, Warburton, Michael and Fournier. Eventually, sport as a painters' subject became so popular that an exhibition entitled "Sport in Art" was mounted at the Georges Petit Gallery in 1885. Well aware of these trends in art, Coubertin advocated the integration of art into the Olympics in 1906 proposing an "Advisory Conference on Art, Science and Sport" in Paris.[5] He suggested that the Olympic Games include competitions for unpublished works in architecture, sculpture, painting, music and literature directly inspired by sport. He expected that these competitions would attract the participation of the great artists of his time.

The Stockholm Games in 1912 was the start of the lasting marriage between sport and art through the introduction of art competitions.[6] Artistic contests called the "Pentathlon of the Muses", were organised in parallel with the sports competitions until 1948. Arrangements changed considerably over time. For example, the Paris Games in 1924 included an international artistic and literary competition. Medals were offered in five categories: architecture, literature, music, painting and sculpture. At the Paris Games of 1924 French intellectuals embraced the Olympics. Novelists, poets and essayists filled newspapers and magazines with odes to athletic endeavour. The Nobel prize winners Selma Lagerl and Maurice Maeterlinck served on the literary jury set up to determine the most outstanding literary contributions.

The Olympic Fine Arts Competition in Los Angeles in 1932 contained over 1,100 works from 32 nations, including painting, sculpture, architecture, graphic arts, literature and music. Prize-winning paintings, watercolours, prints, and drawings had titles such as "Struggle", "Jackknife" and "Stadium". An honourable-mention went to "Indian Ball Game" by the Native American artist Blue Eagle. The first prize for sculpture was awarded to Mahonri Young of the United States for "The Knockdown". The venerated Canadian sculptor R. Tait McKenzie's "Shield of the Athletes" was placed third. Architectural design awards included second prize for Yale's Payne Whitney Gymnasium in New Haven, Connecticut and an honourable mention for the Stanford Stadium in Palo Alto, California. Awards in the fine arts competition as those for athletic events were announced in the Stadium. Two giants of American Letters, William Lyon Phelps and Thornton Wilder, judged the literary entries. Avery Brundage's essay "The Significance of Amateur Sport" was given an honourable mention.

In contrast to other previous host cities where the arts had played a relatively minor role despite Coubertin's hopes, the so-called "Nazi Games" of Berlin in 1936 staged a cultural festival of unprecedented size and nature. There were few non-western medal winners because of judging controversies and predilections associated with restricted publicity, the difficulty in transporting objects, and perhaps most significantly, a general lack of interest in or even knowledge of the events. [7]

Arts Competitions during the Olympic Games were discontinued after 1948 and replaced by Arts Olympiads or Cultural Olympiads which were completely separate from the sports competition. The result has been a feast of artistic and cultural programmes of various kinds.

2. Modern Olympic Cultural Programmes

In the 1952 Helsinki Games the artistic competitions were formally replaced by exhibitions, festivals and performances. In the 1956 Melbourne Games, for the first time the arts festival included three sections—Visual

Arts, Literature and Music and Drama. The Visual Arts section included exhibitions of architecture and sculpture, painting and drawing and the graphic arts. The Literature section included early Australian works of historical interest, contemporary books by Australian authors and exceptional examples of Australian printed books. The Music and Drama section was divided into three sub-sections: theatre, orchestral music and chamber music.[8]

Since Melbourne there has been a tendency to stage exhibitions that demonstrate the art of the host country. However, the Mexico and Munich programmes were international in approach. Since Melbourne also, successive cities have had very different approaches to the cultural component of the Games. In Munich, theatrical companies, music groups, artists, dancers and other performers from many nations performed on the Spielstrasse and exhibitions, including one devoted to the Art of Ancient Olympia at the Deutsches Museum, were arranged. Sport in art was portrayed in an outdoor display of reproductions and a special art book was published for the occasion. The posters for various events were particularly attractive but special mention should be made of those especially commissioned for the Games by artists of international fame such as Kokoschka, Vaserely, Hartung, Poliakoff, Hockney, Jones and Wonderlich.

In 1960 Rome's organising committee mounted an enormous exhibition of "Sport in History and Art" which lasted for six months and included 2,300 works. In 1968, Mexico hosted a year long programme that included an international film festival and events covering among other things folk art, sculpture and poetry. Various exhibitions on Olympic philately, the history and art of the Olympic Games and sports research were organised. These were held in museums and auditoriums, along busy thoroughfares, and in the city's green and spacious Chapultepec Park. One element of this cultural fiesta, still visible in the city, was the group of nineteen abstract, monumental concrete sculptures crafted by an international team and erected along a seventeen-kilometre stretch of the southern Periferico (the circumferential highway around the capital) named the "Route of Friendship"; these sculptures straddled both sides of the Olympic Village. The impressed IOC President Avery Brundage expressed the hope that Mexican's imaginative cultural programme would mark a return to "the purity, beauty and simplicity" of the Olympic tradition.

The themes of Olympic cultural programmes have varied from strongly rooted national festivals to international festivals, from a focus on popular events to a focus on elitist activities—here are some illustrations.

The already mentioned cultural festival of Munich (1972) was completely integrated within the Olympic sporting events. It also presented the arts component in spontaneous way. This was evident in the so-called "Avenue of Entertainment" which was composed of street theatre shows, mimes, clowns and acrobats. Thus, to an extent it set a standard for subsequent arts festivals in terms of structure and approach. Montreal (1976) mounted a small scale but highly popular spontaneous festival with a marked national character. Los Angeles (1984), in contrast, was a large festival which focused on elite national and international events. There were few open-air popular events. Seoul (1988) combined both international elitist and popular events.

It is worth noting that in the 1960s and 1970s some art forms attempted to fuse fine art with popular culture. Like the art of Ancient Greece that exalted beautiful athletes on everyday domestic pottery, "pop" art celebrated the sports heroes and heroines of the time.

The Barcelona Games (1992) saw the establishment of the concept of the Cultural Olympiad, a programme of cultural celebrations that lasts the four years between the Olympic Games, with a "Cultural gateway" in 1988, the "year of Culture and Sport" in 1989, the "Year of the Arts" in 1990, the "Year of the Future" in 1991 and the "Olympic Art Festival" in 1992. Atlanta also organised four year programme of festivals, with two main themes: "Southern Connections" and "International Connections". Sydney offered illustrations of the many and diverse Australian cultural communities with its indigenous festival in 1997, a festival dedicated to multicultural groups and migration waves in 1998 and then provided international festivals in 1999 and 2000. [9] In 2000 the "Olympic Art and Sport Contest 2000" took place in Sydney. This competition addressed two categories of artist: students of art and athletes. All works had to be related to the theme of sport. Between June 1998 and November 1999 the jury composed of celebrated personalities from the world of art and presided over jointly by the IOC President and the President of the IOC Culture and Education Commission, deliberated. The event received 68 sculptures and 113 graphic art works from fifty-four National Olympic Committees. In March, 2000, the prize winners were announced (see table 7-1). [10]

Individual appropriate artistic works, incidentally, have won the attention and support of the IOC. By way of example in 2001, the Mexican artist Nieto painted three animals—a hare, coyote and bear—to represent the Olympic motto: swifter, higher and stronger. This painting was called "Olympic Power". He also created a painting for the 2002 Salt Lake City Olympic Winter Games, entitled "Peace and Loyalty".[11]

Table 7-1   List of Winners of the Olympic Art & Sport Contest 2000

	Sculpture			Graphic Works		
	Title	Artist Name	Nation	Title	Artist Name	Nation
First Prize	Speed	Konstantin Kostuchenko	Belarus	Clinging	Chen Chi-Ran	Chinese Taipei
Second	Sphere	Deborah C. V. West	Australia	Free from Power	Chung Tai-fu	Hong-Kong China
Third	Competitors	Grzegorz Witek	Poland	The Fire of Olympus	Darya Moroz	Belarus
				Olympic Sport	Zakria Mohamed Soliman	Egypt

3. Modern Olympic Music

Fashions have undergone many changes over two thousand years, but music has remained the factor which best conveys the emotion within a crowd, and which best accompanies the amplitude of a great spectacle. (Coubertin, 1919)

Coubertin considered that music was of special significance to the Olympics. He ensured that it had a place in the modern Games. And it retains this place to this day.

In ancient Greece at the Games musical contests were held alongside athletic competitions. In early twentieth century Greece, music was part of the first modern Games. Its presence has continued. It is part of the twenty-first century Games. Music, thus, has always been integral to the Games. In 1896, the Philharmonic Band of Corfu led a parade which included singers singing "The Sailor Lad" followed by the band playing selections from Wagner's Lohengrin. In 1896 also, the first official Olympic Hymn was sung—the music was composed by the Greek composer Spiros Samaras and Kostis Palamas wrote the words. The Samaras version remained the official Olympic Hymn until 1912. Thereafter, at various times various new hymns were used. Samaras' hymn was reintroduced for the Games of 1960 and continues to be used today at the Opening and Closing Ceremonies.

Music has not only been a feature of ceremonial but also of publicity and entertainment. For Los Angeles (1932), for example, a chorus of 1,200 members rehearsed for several months before the Games and performed over the radio on several occasions prior to the Games to help promote them. The chorus also performed with the 1000-member Olympic Band at the Opening and Closing Ceremonies as well as at the demonstration football game. In addition to the band and chorus, groups of trumpeters performed fanfares at the Marathon and Opening and Closing Ceremonies, in the Olympic Village and on other occasions during the Games. Massed bands of the Brigade of Guards (200 members) played at the Opening Ceremony at London (1948). The massed bands also performed the national anthem. A fanfare was also played during the ceremonial release of the doves symbolizing peace. 1,200 singers made up the choir. At Helsinski (1952) a new Olympic Hymn and a cantata (A Finnish Prayer) by Taneli Kuusisto were performed by a 526 member mixed chorus. At the opening Olympic Banquet for the Games, a double quartet of men's voices performed. Later a men's choir of 2,500 gave a concert. Trumpeters dressed in medieval costumes played a fanfare after the King's opening speech. The choir of the Swedish Choral Association sang a national air following a cheer for the King. The athletes left the grounds to the Olympic Games Triumphal March composed by Dr. H. Alexandersson. This piece was awarded first prize (Gold Medal) in a competition held by the Swedish Olympic Committee. Other musical events included Lynyrd Skynyrd, The Giants of Jazz, Travis Tritt, Yoel Levi, and William Fred Scott. Also featured was the Australian Youth Orchestra, the Atlanta Youth Orchestra and the Atlanta Symphony Orchestra and Chorus in a joint programme which included a performance of Mahler's Symphony No. 2, The Resurrection. Many of these performers were also included in the Opening and Closing Ceremonies. [12]

The theme music of the Olympics—1984, and 1988 ("Hand in Hand") and 1996 ("Summon the Heroes") was written by John Williams, one of America's most famous composers. Williams is probably best known for the many great film scores he has composed for such popular movies as the Star Wars trilogy, E. T., Jurassic Park, the Raiders of the Lost Ark, Jaws, Superman, Home Alone and Hook.

What is clear from this brief outline is the major role of music in the history of the Olympic Games. There are good reasons for this-the common features of the music. Virtually all the music at the Olympics is intended to promote the ideas of friendship, peace and justice and at the same time to portray the national cultural traditions of the host countries. Prior to the Second World War Western classical music, opera and religious music were the main sources of Olympic music. After the Second World War, especially after the 1970s, with the successful hosting of the Olympic Games in Asia and America, folk music and pop music became popular. Whatever its nature, music, first endorsed by Coubertin, has shared with the other cultural activities of the Games the purpose of uniting the people of the world at this famous gathering of the nations of the world.

Summary

The Olympic Movement has been closely linked with cultural programmes which have evolved over time in terms of scale, organisation and content. In Olympic history—both ancient and modern—the arts have been used to express the drama of sport and the emotions of athletes. The main forms of artistic expression associated with the Olympics are paintings, sculpture, and, above all, music.

Coubertin advocated the integration of the arts into the Olympics through competitions in architecture, sculpture, painting, music and literature. Competitions existed between 1912 and 1948 and were later replaced by Arts Olympiads or Cultural Olympiads, but the arts, once part of the ancient Games, have remained an essential part of the modern Games.

Questions
1. Do you think it is good idea to reinstate Arts Competitions in the Olympic Games? If so, why and if not, why?
2. What cultural activities should the Beijing Cultural Olympiad include?

Should these activities be national or international?
3. Do you favour Arts Competitions or Festivals or Exhibitions or all these? Give your reasons for your preference.

Notes
[1] J. Durry, (1998), "The Cultural Events at the Olympic Games and Pierre de Coubertin's Thinking", *Proceedings of the 38th Session of the International Olympic Academy*, p. & J.
[2] The Rampin Horseman is a masterpiece of Archaic art, which blends Attic seriousness with the rich decorative tradition of eastern Greece. This male head, which was found on the Acropolis in 1877, was sculpted around 550 BC. (Greek, Etruscan, and Roman Antiquities: Archaic Greek Art (7th-6th Centuries BC), http://www. louvre. fr/llv/oeuvres/detail_notice. jsp?
[3] D. W. Masterton, "The Contribution of the Fine Arts to the Olympic Games", http://www. ioa. leeds. ac. uk/1970s/73200. htm.
[4] N. Yalouris, (1971), "The Art in the Sanctuary of Olympia", *Report of the Eleventh Session of the International Olympic Academy*, Athens, 90.
[5] Coubertin, P. de (1967), "The Olympic Idea: Discourse and Essays", Cologne, 16.
[6] Martin Wimmer (1976), *Olympic Buildings*, Edition Leipzig, 27.
[7] Beatriz Garcia Garcia, *The Concept of Olympic Cultural Programmes: Origins, Evolution and Projection*, Centre d'Estudis Olympics I de 'Estport (UAB), International Chair in Olympism.
[8] John E. Findling and Kimberly D. Pelle (eds.) (2004), *Encyclopaedia of the Modern Olympic Movement*, London: Greenwood Press.
[9] Beatriz Garcia Garcia, op. cit.
[10] Art & Sport 2000 Olympic contest, http://www. olympic. org/uk/passion/museum/temporary/exhibition_uk. asp? id = 17&type = 0.
[11] This painting depicts a wolf at the feet of an American Indian chief who is wearing a war bonnet and holding an eagle feather. Nieto claimed that the eagle feather is a universal symbol of strong values; the wolf represents the relationship between humans and canines, and the loyalty associated with kinship.
[12] William K. Guegold(1996), 100 *Years of Olympic Music: Music and Musicians of the Modern Olympic Games* 1896-1996, Golden Clef Publisher.

Part Two
Historical Perspectives

Chapter 8
The Ancient Olympics

Key points:
* Greek civilisation and the Ancient Olympic Games
* Evolution, Regulations and Programme of the Ancient Olympic Games
* Decline of the Ancient Olympic Games

The Ancient Olympic Games were held in Greece as early as 776 BC. Why did the Olympic Games emerge in Greece and not in other civilised nations such as China and Egypt? To answer this question it is necessary to consider these Games within the framework of ancient Greek civilisation.

1. The Ancient Greek Civilisation

Greece is a Mediterranean nation state at the top of the Balkan Peninsula in south-eastern Europe. It is a mountainous, rocky country with a highly indented and crenulated coast. In ancient times these physical characteristics produced independent small city-states.

The ancient Greeks valued education. For them it had a particular meaning. The term "education" implied "the cultivation of the whole man and could not be divided into physical and mental education because the mind cannot exist without the body and the body has no meaning without the mind"[1]. Therefore, body and mind were of equal and inseparable importance and only through their mutual development was man's potential realised.

Ancient Greece, the birthplace of the Olympic Games, is known as the "Cradle of Democracy and Western civilisation". Its famous philosophers Socrates, Plato and Aristotle were essential to the evolution of its democratic and educational principles and practices. Socrates (470-399 BC) once claimed: "no citizen has right to be an amateur in the matter of physical training; it is a disgrace for a man to grow old without ever having seen the beauty and strength of which his body is capable... ."[2] Plato (427-347 BC) was a splendid athlete. His original name Aristocles was changed by his wrestling coach to Plato (broad shouldered). He advocated physical activity for boys and girls. Aristotle (384-327 BC) criticised unbalanced development, saying: "Right from the start the legislator must see to it that the bodies of young men become excellent".[3] These thinkers had their influence so did the need to be prepared for war. Consequently, physical exercise was widespread. It is claimed that as many as 173 athletic contests of a formal type were organised all over Greece each year.[4]

Beautiful bodies were the representative icons of the society. The ancient Greeks even depicted their many gods as ideal humans, as shown, for example, in the sculptures of the demi-God Hercules at Olympia. The statues and paintings of the gods reflected the image of the naked perfect male body: lean, muscular, athletic. Sport and nudity were inseparable concepts in ancient Greece. Gymnasium and gymnastics both derive from the same root *yuuvos* meaning naked. In the gymnasium, athletes trained naked, and outside, the statues honouring the greatest of them, were correspondingly nude.

(1) Religion

As in the daytime there is no star in the sky warmer and brighter than the sun, likewise there is no competition greater than the Olympic Games. (Pindar, Greek lyric poet, 518-438 B. C.)

The various athletic festivals of ancient Greece evolved over time and included religious ceremonies at which the Greeks honoured their Gods to whom sacrifices were made and of whom favours were asked. Thus, Games in Greece were closely connected with religious ceremonies that formed part of the worship of the gods. There was no famous religious festival and no great sanctuary in Greece that did not link worship of the Gods with the holding of Games. Indeed, at the Games the first competitive locations were the forecourts and surrounding areas of the temples with gods as the main spectators.

Greek Gods left their places on mountain tops, mingled with the populace and enjoyed the events. To the Greeks their Gods (and Goddesses) were participants made in the image of the most beautiful men (and women).

The Games, therefore, brought humankind into contact with these Gods and this explains why the Games were always held under their tutelage in the most sacred sanctuaries of Olympia, Delphi, Nemea and Isthmus. The Olympic Game were held in honour of Zeus, the king of the Greek gods, at Olympia in the city-state of Elis. A sacrifice of 100 oxen was made to Zeus on the middle day of the festival. [5]

Over time, the Games flourished, and Olympia became the main site for the worship of Zeus. Individuals and communities donated buildings, statues, altars and other dedications to him. The most spectacular sight at Olympia was the gold and ivory cult statue of Zeus enthroned, which was made by the sculptor Pheidias and placed inside the temple. The statue was one of the Seven Wonders of the Ancient World and stood over 42 feet high.

While the Games retained their early function within religious custom for several centuries, they later underwent a gradual transformation and became essentially sporting occasions.

(2) War and Olympic Culture

In the centuries before Christ, as already noted, Greece was composed of many small independent states and cities often isolated by natural barriers. These communities were fiercely defensive of their freedom. Due to continual wars, every Greek citizen had to be constantly prepared for combat. Thus, participation in preparatory physical activity was regarded as a way of life for Greeks. Local conflicts interrupted Festivals and Games. Then in 884 BC the local rulers, King Iphitus of Elis, Lycurgus of Sparta and Archon Cleosthenes of Pisa, instituted a truce at Olympia. [6] An inscription describing the truce written on a bronze discus was displayed there. During the truce covering the Olympic Festivals, wars were suspended, armies were prohibited from entering Elis and legal disputes and the implementation of death penalties were forbidden. Thus, visitors could travel safely to and from Olympia. Violation of this truce was punishable by death. The political and military neutrality of the Olympic site was one of

Figure 8-1　Temple of Zeus

the reasons for the continuity of the ancient Olympics. The sacred truce lasted three months each year to allow all who wished to attend the Games in safety.

2. The Evolution of the Ancient Olympic Games

(1) Festival, Games and Olympia

In ancient Greece, it was automatic that birth, marriage, death, good harvests, winning contests, completion of a boat, triumph in battle, were all celebrated with a festival. The associated Games, such as the Olympics, originated from informal contests of and funeral games. The connection of athletic games with funeral customs was due to the belief that life and death stood in a dialectical relationship to each other—the dead earth gives birth to the new shoot and the youths involved in the competitions draw strength from the dead heroes in whose honour they were competing.

Figure 8-2 Olympia

Figure 8-3 Stadium in Olympia

By the end of the 6th century BC at least four of the Greek sporting festivals: the Olympic Games held at Olympia, the Pythian Games at Delphi, the Nemean Games at Nemea and the Isthmian Games at Corinth had achieved major importance. The Olympic Games, however, were considered the most significant throughout the Greek world.

> **Olympia**
>
> In the territory of Elis, Olympia is located in the extreme west of the Peloponnese between the rugged mountains of Arkadia and the inhospitable coast of the Ionian sea. In contrast to most Greek sites, Olympia set amidst groves of trees, is green and lush.
>
> There was a prehistoric Iron Age settlement at Olympia in the twelfth century BC after the Doric invasion from the north and ruins suggest that Olympia played a significant political and military role in the troubled history of antiquity and extended its authority throughout the Greek world. Thousands of votive offerings found there dating from at least the tenth century BC illustrate this. The sanctuary of Olympia preserved as its main mission the cultivation of the spirit of competition.[7] For over a thousand years, in peace and war, the Greeks assembled here to celebrate this great festival. "In Olympia the great Themistocles was acclaimed, Herodotus read a part of his history, Plato spoke and Demosthenes, Hippias, Prodicus, Anaximenes, Pindar, Simonides, Thucydides, Polus, Gorgias, Anaxagoras, Diogenes, and Lucian came as spectators."[8]

The ancient Olympic Games were certainly held continuously for at least 1168 years (776 BC-AD 393). However, it is generally accepted that the Games had been probably at least 500 years old by 776 BC. There are records of the champions at Olympia from 776 BC to AD 217. The first recorded Olympic champion was Coroebus of Elis.

Held every four years between August 6 and September 19 in late summer and early autumn, a period of rest from agricultural work, the Games occupied such an important place in Greek life that time was measured by the interval between them—an Olympiad. Olympia's fame was extraordinary. Large crowds used to come every four years to worship at the sanctuaries, admire the great works of art, listen to historians, poets and rhapsodists and watch the statuesque men, well-built boys and fleet-footed horses competing in fascinating contests. Olympia became the meeting-place for the whole Greek world. As already made clear, all the Panhellenic festivals were much more than athletic meetings. At an early date various states, many of them from overseas colonies, sought to secure themselves a permanent standing at the sanctuary by dedicating temples or treasuries. Thus, the site became immensely richer than could have been possible from local resources alone.

The Games flourished far from the great centres of Greece. Nevertheless, as stated above, the Games were so famous that they brought together not just the best athletes, but also the finest sculptors, poets, writers, speakers and politicians.

(2) Regulations

The Games were very different from the Games today. Here are a few examples. The Games were originally restricted to freeborn Greeks. The competitors travelled hundreds of miles from all over the mainland and the colonies of the Greek city-states, which were as far away as modern-day Spain, Italy, Libya, Egypt, the Ukraine and Turkey (see the following map).[9]

Athletes were 'amateur' in the sense that the only prize was a wreath or garland, but were often rewarded by their city-states if they did well. The athletes underwent a most rigorous period of supervised training. Even-

Figure 8-4 Map of the Colonies of the Greek City-States

tually they were de facto professionals. Not only were there substantial prizes for winning but the Olympic champion also received adulation and generous benefits from his city. With the result that athletes eventually became full-time specialists, a trend that in the modern Games caused a long and bitter controversy over amateurism.

(3) Programme

The Games included preliminary contests to select the best athletes for the final competition. On the first day of the Games the athletes and the judges swore that they would respectively compete and judge honestly. On the second, third and fourth days different contests were held. The main event at Olympia was the stadion or single-course race, and the winner of that race gave his name to the whole Olympiad. On the fifth day, at the conclusion of the Games, each victor was awarded a crown of wild olive leaves.

> **The Olive Crown**
> The olive crown was the greatest honour for the contestant, his family and his city. It was an honour that could never be outranked either by money or official position. The victors were linked to the immortals, celebrated by poets and sculptors, and often lived for the rest of their lives at public expense.

There was apparently only one event, the stadion in 776 BC but other events were added over the ensuing decades, for example, the diaulos in 724 BC and the dolichos (a long-distance race possibly to be compared to the modern 1,500 or even 5,000-metre event) in 720 BC. Runners sprinted for 1 stade (192 m.) or the length of the stadium. The other races were a 2-stade race (384 m.) and a long-distance run which ranged from 7 to 24 stades (1,344 m. to 4,608 m). Therefore, there were different types of races at Olympia.

Wrestling and the pentathlon that consisted of the long jump, javelin throw, discus throw, foot race and wrestling appeared in 708 BC. Like the modern sport, a wrestler needed to throw his opponent on the ground, on a hip, shoulder or back for a fair fall. 3 Throws were necessary to win a match. Biting was not allowed, and genital holds were also illegal. Breaking your opponent's fingers, however, was permitted.

Boxing was introduced in 688 BC. Boxers fought without rounds until one man was knocked out or admitted he had been beaten. Unlike the modern sport, there was no rule against hitting an opponent when he was down. There were no weight classes within the men's and boys' divisions; opponents for a match were chosen randomly. Instead of gloves, ancient boxers wrapped leather thongs around their hands and wrists which left their fingers free.

A chariot race was included in 680 BC. There were both 2-horse chariot and 4-horse chariot races. Another race was between carts drawn by a team of 2 mules. The course was 12 laps around the stadium track (9 miles).

In 648 BC the pankration—a gruelling combination of boxing and wrestling—was added in the programme. In this event punches were allowed, although the fighters did not wrap their hands with the boxing leather thongs. Rules outlawed only biting and gouging an opponent's eyes, nose, or mouth with fingernails. Kicking an opponent in the belly, which is against the rules in modern sport, was perfectly legal. Like boxing and wrestling, this event had separate divisions for men and boys.

There were, of course, no stopwatches to record the time of a race. Neither was the length of a jump or of a javelin or discus throw precisely measured. Team games were unknown. No water sports were included in the programme. Women could not compete.

(4) Competition and Cheating

Until the 77th Olympiad (472 BC) all the contests took place on one day; later they were spread, with perhaps some fluctuation, over four days, with a fifth devoted to the closing-ceremony presentation of prizes and a banquet for the champions. Women, except for the priestess of Demeter, were not allowed as spectators.

Ancient athletes, as stated above, competed as individuals and not as part of a team as in the modern Games. The emphasis on individual athletic achievement through public competition was related to the Greek ideal of individual excellence. Men who attained this ideal, through their outstanding words or deeds, won permanent glory. Those who failed to measure up to this ideal realistically feared public shame and disgrace.

Such pressure could lead to intense competition in which some took dishonest measures to win. Those who were discovered cheating were fined

Figure 8-5 Wreseling

Figure 8-6 Ancient Boxing

116　The Olympic Culture: An Introduction

and the money was used to make bronze statues of Zeus, which were erected on the road to the stadium. The statues were inscribed with messages describing the offence, warning others not to cheat, reminding athletes that victory was won by competence and emphasizing the Olympic spirit of fair competition and respect for the Gods.

The earliest recorded cheat was Eupolus of Thessaly, who bribed boxers in the 98th Olympiad. Callippus of Athens bought off his competitors in the pentathlon during the 112th festival. Two Egyptian boxers, Didas and Sarapammon, were fined for fixing the outcome of their match at the 226th Olympics. All these men were recorded as cheats for posterity in the writer Pausanias' 2nd century AD guidebook to Greece, in which he describes the statues at Olympia and recounts the men's misdeeds.

3. The Decline of the Ancient Olympic Culture

Greece lost its independence to Rome in the middle of the 2nd century BC and the support for the competitions at Olympia and other places fell off considerably in the next century. The Romans found the Greek sports pointless and preferred the Etruscan sport of gladiatorial fighting. Whereas the Greeks educated their youths to seek perfection, the Romans educated theirs to conquest.[10] Most Romans looked on athletics with contempt—in their view, to contend naked in public was degrading. Some Romans appreciated the value of the Greek festivals, however, and Emperor Augustus (63 BC-AD 14), who had a genuine love for athletics, staged athletic games in a temporary wooden stadium erected near the Circus Maximus. Emperor Nero (AD 37-68) was also a keen patron of the festivals in Greece.

The Romans enjoyed their Games as much if not more than the Greeks enjoyed theirs. By the 4th century AD, Rome, with its population of more than 1,000,000, had well over 150 holidays for Games. There was chariot racing in the Hippodrome and horse racing in the Circus Maximus. In the Coliseum humans and animals were maimed and slaughtered in the name of sport. Public Games were held in abundance but for the Romans athletic events occupied a secondary position. The only ones that really interested them were the fighting events—wrestling, boxing and the pancratium. A major difference between the Greek and Roman attitudes was that the

Greeks organised their games for the competitors and the Romans for the public. One was primarily competition; the other entertainment. The Greek festivals were described as agones (contests); the Roman as ludi (games).

The period following the subjection of Greece by the Romans in 146 BC was crucial for Olympia. To the ruins left by earthquakes and continuous warfare between the Greeks, were added the fearful sackings and devastation of the Roman civil wars fought on Greek soil. During this period there was a general economic, social and moral collapse. Most of the local Games ceased to be held and the Pan-Hellenic Games barely survived.

Two factors, however, made an important contribution to keeping alive the Panhellenic Games during this time of great difficulty. The first was the great prestige for the Greeks of these Games. The second was the importance for the Greeks of the gymnasium as an institution. The gymnasium occupied an important position in the life of the Hellenistic cities. After the Roman conquest, the conquered Greeks used their limited autonomy to meet in the gymnasium. It became the centre for the expression of their national identity and they continued within it to engage in permitted sporting, intellectual and social activities. Therefore, for sound and sensible political reasons the Romans despite their indifference to athletics and their distaste for Greek athletic customs, did not suppress either the Games or the Gymnasiums. To do so could have antagonised the Greeks. Although the Romans left the gymnasium untouched as an institution, they frequently intervened in its administration to ensure they maintained control in Greece.

The existence of the Panhellenic Games in general, and of Olympia in particular, was subjected to a severe threat by Sulla[1]'s plundering of Olympia during the Mithridatic wars of the first century BC. Eventually, the ancient Olympic Games were banned by the Emperor Theodosius I (the first Christian emperor) in AD 394. He was opposed to the Greek concept of Gods for religious reasons. The last Games, the 293rd, therefore, were in AD 393.

In summary, the ancient Olympic Games experienced three developmental phases:

* **Initial phase (800 BC-600 BC)**

At this time slavery was new (freeborn athletes required the slavery system to free them to train for the Olympics), economic production was low, the transport system was undeveloped and thus, communication be-

Figure 8-7 Exterior of the Coliseum

tween different city-states was difficult. Therefore, the Olympic Games were festivals only for the city-states of Peloponnesus. Only later did they involve other city-states of Greece.

* **Peak phase (600 BC-400 BC)**

In this period Athens experienced its Golden Age: the maturing of the democratic system of government under the Athenian statesman Pericles, the building of the Parthenon on the Acropolis the creation of the tragedies of Sophocles, Aeschylus and Euripides and the founding of the philosophical schools of Socrates and Plato. Against this background the Games evolved and established their own cultural traditions.

* **Expiry phase (400 BC-394 AD)**

This was a lengthy period of great tension and change. There were slave uprising and continued fighting between various city-states. Then the Peloponnesian War between Athens and Sparta (431-404 BC) broke out and lasted 29 disastrous years. And then the Greeks lost their independence to the Romans and then the Roman Empire experienced internal conflict, and finally Christianity took a hold of Rome. These events collectively had a huge negative impact on the Olympic Games which, as already stated, were finally suppressed in 394 AD by the Christian Emperor Theodosius.[11]

Conclusion

The ancient Olympic Games were inseparable from the philosophical, political, economic and social environment of ancient Greece. Greek educational ideals stressed the education of mind and body The continuous confrontations between the city-states of Greece made physical activities as a training for war an integral part of daily life. The frequent conflicts between city-states required physically fit warriors. Sports competitions were thus emphasised. Therefore, to ensure the continuity of the Olympic Games a truce was signed between those city-states at war at the time. The ancient Olympic Games, of course, were also a religious festival of great importance in honour of the God Zeus.

Conquest of the Greeks by the Romans led to the decline of the Olympic Games. The Romans in general despised Greek athletics and mostly did not support the Games. Then wars, earthquakes and Christianity led eventually to the complete demise of the Games in 394 AD.

The ancient Olympic Games lasted over twelve centuries and were very different from the modern Games. There were fewer events and only free men who spoke Greek could compete. The Games were always held at Olympia never at other sites. Games have left the world an impressive cultural heritage and have had a far-reaching influence on modern world sport. In particular, the ancient Olympic ideal with its emphasis on peace, friendship, fair play and excellence has had a powerful impact on the modern Games.

Questions
1. Why was physical activity so important to the citizens of the Greek City-States?
2. Why were many ancient Olympic events para-military events involving weapons and extreme physical aggression?
3. What were the specific reasons for the decline and demise of the ancient Olympic Games?
4. Were the ancient Olympic Games amateur?

Notes

[1] Iris, Douskou, *The Olympic Games In Ancient Greece*. Athens: Ekdotike Athenon, 1982.
[2] John T. Powell (1994), *Orignins and Aspects of Olympism*, Champaign, Illinois: Stipes Publishing Company, 37.
[3] Aristoles (1878), *The Rhetoric of Aristotle*, London: G. Bell, Translated by J. S. Walson Book III, 13; 6.
[4] John T. Powell (1984), "Ancient Greek Athletic Festivals", *Olympic Review*, 63.
[5] Gray Poole (1963), *The Ancient Olympic Games*, London: Vision Press, 17.
[6] C. Palaeologos, (1964), "The Ancient Olympics". Paper presented at the Proceedings of the International Olympic Academy, University of Leeds. (www. greekembassy. org/press/pressreleases/truce/TRUCE. html)
[7] Nicolaos Yalouris, (ed.) (1979), *The Eternal Olympics: The Art and History of Sport*, New Rochelle, New York: Caratzas Brothers, Publishers, 77.
[8] Paleologos, 1964.
[9] http://www. perseus. tufts. edu/Olympics/site. html.
[10] David Levinson and Karen Christensen (eds.), *Encyclopedia of World Sport: From Ancient Times to the Present*, Oxford: ABC-CLIO Ltd. , 1996,21.
[11] Diane L. Dupuis, Marie J. MacNee, Christan Brelin, and Martin Connors (1993), *The Olympics Factbook*. Detroit: Visible Ink Press.

Chapter 9
The Olympic Games: Revival and Resurgence

Key points:
* Revival of the Games
* Resurgence of the Games
* Challenges to the Games

For over thirteen centuries the ancient Olympic Games were forgotten due to natural disasters that had destroyed and buried the site. It was not until 1896 that the modern version of the Olympic Games came into being. Why were the Olympic Games revived? And what has been the nature of the resurgence?

1. The Creation of the Modern Olympics

The revival of the Olympic Games was the consequence of long term political, economic, cultural and social change in post-medieval Europe.

(1) Ideological Background

The period from 15th to 18th centuries saw three great European Movements—the Renaissance, the Reformation and the Enlightenment. They gave rise to fundamental changes. These Movements paved the way for the development of capitalism, democracy, science and technology.

> **Concepts: The Renaissance, Reformation and Enlightenment**
>
> The 15th century *Renaissance* witnessed the growth of modern individualism in opposition to the collectivism of the Middle Ages, the revival of classical literature and the rediscovery of classical sculpture, painting and architecture lost for a thousand years in Europe.
>
> The 16th century *Reformation* was the religious movement which, while ostensibly aiming at an internal renewal of the dominant Roman Catholic Church, led to a great revolt against it, and the weakening of its power.
>
> The 18th century *Enlightenment* was a significant intellectual movement. Influential thinkers and writers believed that human reason could be used to combat ignorance, superstition and tyranny and build a better world. Their principal targets were religious superstition and hereditary authority.

Gradually individualism and liberalism replaced collectivism and despotism and became essential European values. Religion survived, but weakened and often transformed almost beyond recognition. The separation of state from church proved favourable to the development of intellectual freedom of thought. Simultaneously the hereditary monarchy and aristocracy was reduced in significance. Of particular and specific importance for the later recreated Olympic Games was the fact that Renaissance "humanists" argued that the proper worship of God involved admiration of his creation—humanity. They tried to recapture the pride, spirit and creativity of the ancient Greeks and Romans, to replicate their successes and to go beyond them. The Renaissance painters, architects, musicians and scholars all exercised their powers in a new atmosphere of freedom in which Ancient Greece was admired for its "humanist" values.

(2) The Industrial Revolution

The Industrial Revolution that began in Britain in the late 18th century had a dramatic impact on society and sport. The invention of the steam engine[1] greatly facilitated industrialization and brought great wealth to Britain.

The dramatic changes that characterised the Industrial Revolution also transformed the sport of first Britain, then Europe and then North America, and then much of the rest of the globe. Initially, in Britain, the new wealth, "new" (expanded) middle classes, "new" (expanded) educational agencies, new leisure and new technologies brought in their wake a new attitude to sport and new sports to enjoy.[2] Then the great invention of the engine in the form of the steam train and the steam ship spread these sports widely and shortened distances between regions and nations. Thus, first national and then international competition became increasingly possible to nations throughout the world.

(3) Bourgeois Education Reform

During the late Industrial Revolution, educational transformation occurred in Britain and other European countries.

The European middle classes progressively embraced the educational values of the Classical world. Mind and Body became an educational concern. However, the source of much modern sport was England for rather different reasons. In the second half of the nineteenth century it had a hugely prosperous middle class as a consequence of industrial growth and imperial expansion. Schools for the middle class expanded greatly in number in consequence. They were mostly boarding schools for boys. They were known as "public schools"! Prior to 1850 those few in existence were brutal places with no organised games and considerable pupil freedom. The result was extensive pupil indiscipline.

Modern games were systematically developed in these schools to exhaust, control and keep the boys within the school boundaries. Academic standards were low; games-playing standards were high; games-playing was prized above scholarship. It created strong, fit and assertive schoolboys for imperial leadership:[3] "Sports seemed to have developed not only the boys' enviable physical prowess but also their character. They projected a sturdy self-confidence that their teachers attributed to their hours at cricket, soccer, and rugby."[4] This self-confidence attracted the attention of Coubertin concerned at the military humiliation of France at the hands of Prussia in 1870 and impressed by the successful imperialism of Britain. In his view, English middle class sport had much to commend it. England, therefore, directly laid the foundation for the popularity of modern sport and indirectly for the revival of the Olympic Games.

(4) Internationalisation of Sport

As a consequence of the middle class espousal of sport, initially in Europe and the USA, sports clubs and associations came into being. By the late 19th century, sports such as golf, football, tennis and gymnastics were popular in the industrialized world. Sport began to transcend national boundaries and international sports competitions and exchanges were organised. In these circumstances, international sports organisations for different sports came into being one after another. The first international sports organisation—the Federation of International Gymnastics—was created in 1881. In 1892 another two organisations: the International Rowing Federation and the International Skating Federation came into being. The establishment of these organisations turned sports competitions from local events into international evens. Towards the end of the nineteenth century the internationalisation of sport became an irreversible trend. With the increase of international sports organisations for individual sports and competitions, large-scale comprehensive Games that would include most sports were called for. Therefore, the internationalisation of sport in the late 19th century paved the way for the emergence of the modern Olympic Games.

(5) Archaeological Excavation

Prior to 1766 archaeologists from Britain, France and Germany had been prevented by the Turks from exploring the site of ancient Olympia. It was now part of their Ottoman Empire. In 1766, however, the Englishman Richard Chandler was permitted to go to Greece to undertake exploratory excavations. He found the ruins of Ancient Olympia. This aroused the interest of many archaeologists. In the following years English, French and Germans all worked there, but it was more than 100 years later, between 1875-1881, that the German archaeologist Ernst Curtius and others progressively exposed the mud-covered remains. By 1876 archaeologists had discovered 50 structures and 130 statues in the ruins of Olympia. This aroused considerable interest in the Ancient Games in European educated circles. By 1881 the main parts of the site of the ancient Olympia had been uncovered. In 1887 discoveries from ancient Olympia were displayed in Berlin which further stimulated curiosity in the Ancient Olympic Games.

(6) Events to Revive the "Games"

Between the 17th and 19th Centuries there were various attempts to "recreate" the Olympic Games in different parts of the world (see the following table 9-1).

Table 9-1   List of attempts at re-establishing the Olympic Games before 1896

1604	revival of the "Olympic Games" by Robert Dover in the Cotswold Hills, England; lasted intermittently until 1857; re-established in 1952
1819	Highland Games of Celtic origin revived in St. Fillans, Scotland and spread by Scottish emigration to Australia, Canada, New Zealand, South Africa and the USA
1839	An "Olympic Games" in Sweden
1844	"Travelling Olympic Games" organised in Germany also visited the western section of Poland then occupied by Prussia
1849	Olympic Games organised by William Penny Brookes in Wenlock, Shropshire, England
1853	Franconi' Hippodrome in New York, USA featured 'many of the most attractive games of ancient Greece and Rome
1859	Evangelios Zappas attempted to revive the Olympic Games in Athens
1862	First Olympic Festival in Liverpool, England organised by the Athletics Club of Liverpool
1863	Second Olympic Festival in Liverpool
1864	Third Olympic Festival in Liverpool
1866	First Olympic Festival organised by the Athletic Society of Great Britain in Llandudno, Wales
1867	Second Olympic Festival organised by the Athletic Society of Great Britain in Liverpool, England
1870	Second attempt to revive the Olympic Games in Greece (Athens)
1873	Local, "Olympic Games" organised in the Polish town of Grodzisk Wielkopolski (then under German occupation)
1875	Third Olympic Games at Athens
1888	Fourth Olympic Games at Athens
1892	An "Anglo-Saxon Olympiad" proposed by J. Astley Cooper; unsuccessful but initiated the idea of the British Empire Games later called the Commonwealth Games

Though most of these attempts were unsuccessful, they helped build a bridge between the ancient and the modern Olympics. Among the above attempts, the most impressive occurred in Athens between 1859 and 1889—due to the generosity of the Greek philanthropist Evangelis Zappas, the

Games were held there four times. However, as the Games were only open to Greek participants they attracted little foreign attention. It was the Wenlock Games that had a direct influence on Coubertin—the founder of the modern Olympic Games. The Wenlock Games were initiated in 1850 by a Shropshire doctor, William Penny Brookes. These Games were held annually at Linden Fields, Much Wenlock and consisted of traditional English sports. Coubertin was invited by Brookes to attend these Games in 1890.

2. The Emergence of the IOC

The modern reincarnation of the Olympic Games was the brainchild of the French nobleman Baron Pierre de Coubertin—inspired in turn by the games-cult of the English public schools. He sought to invigorate the young men of France through athletic exercise and competition which were absent in their school curriculum.

> **Pierre, Baron de Coubertin**
> The architect of the modern Olympics was Pierre de Coubertin. He was born in Paris on Jan. 1, 1863. His father was an artist and his mother was a musician. He was raised in cultivated aristocratic surroundings. He sought the means to make France confident once more after its humiliating defeat in the Franco-Prussia War of 1870. Inspired by the educational system of the English middle class, he saw sport in this role. An active sportsman keen on boxing, fencing, horse-riding and rowing, he was convinced that sport was a prime source of national energy. Like most Frenchmen, the young Coubertin burned with a desire to avenge the defeat and to recover the lost provinces (two eastern provinces of Alsace and Lorraine). As he grew older, he became less chauvinistic and was drawn more to a humanistic version of a peaceful world but remainedconvinced of the value of sport in international relations. As an aristocrat his social position barred him from bourgeois occupations. Family tradition pointed to an army career or politics, but Coubertin decided that his future lay in education which he considered the key to the future of society. By the age of 24 he decided he should help reinvigorate the youth of France by reforming its old-fashioned and unimaginative education system along English middle class lines. He was also concerned to promote goodwill through sport between the young of the world. Inspired then by the example of the role of sport in the English Public School, and motivated by his friendships with Penny Brookes and with Greek revivalists such as Vikelas, Coubertin sought to reinvent the Olympic Games as an international multi-sport festival. In 1892 he announced at a meeting of the Union of French Societies of Athletic Sports (USFSA) of which he was Secretary General that he wanted to revive the Olympic Games. Though his statement was greeted with little

enthusiasm, he did not give up. After two years of tireless effort he gathered enough public support to organise the International Athletic Congress of 1894 in Paris. At this Congress in June 1894 in which 79 delegates of 49 organisations from nine countries participated, Coubertin raised again the possibility of the revival of the Olympic Games but in a new guise. Though only a few were really interested in reviving the Games, the proposal was accepted by unanimous vote at the end of the Congress which was later considered the First Olympic Congress. At the Congress the International Olympic Committee with 15 members was established and it was agreed that an Olympics is going to be held in Athens in April of 1896. It was. And the modern Olympic Games was born. Coubertin served the Olympic Movement until 1925 when he retired from it to devote himself to his pedagogical work, which he termed his "unfinished symphony".

In 1931 at the age of 69 Coubertin published his "Olympic Memoirs" in which he emphasized the philosophical nature of his enterprise and his wish to "place the role of the IOC, right from the start, very much above that of a simple sports association". Pierre Coubertin suddenly died of a heart attack on 2 September, 1937 and his "symphony" remained unfinished. The city of Lausanne had decided to award him the honorary citizenship of the city, but he died just prior to the ceremony. In accordance with Coubertin's last wishes, he was buried in Lausanne and his heart was placed inside a stele erected to his memory at Olympia.

Figure 9-1　The first IOC Members.
From left to right: Willibald Gebhardt, Pierre de Coubertin, Jiri Guth, Dimitrios Vikelas, Ferrenc Kemeny, Aleksei Butovsky, Viktor Balck.

By selecting the Ancient Olympic Games as an inspiration for modern sport, Coubertin found a novel way of perpetuating the principles of Greek Idealism which had been inherited by Europe and had influenced European culture since the Renaissance. The Games exalted sport but at the same time subordinated it to idealism.

3. The Evolution of the Modern Olympics

It should be made clear that the "...modern Olympic Games were not intended to be a historically genuine revival of the Olympic Games of classical antiquity when they were inaugurated in 1896"[5], they were intended to be a means by which to create broadly in their image, a modern global "festival" of sports. In the course of a century or more, the Games have expanded both in magnitude and in popularity to meet this end (see table 9-2).

Table 9-2 Information on the Summer Olympic Games over time

	Date	City	Country	No. of nations	Athletes		Number	
					Total	Female	events	sports
1	4.6-15 1896	Athens	Greece	14	241	0	43	9
2	5.20-10.28 1900	Paris	France	19	997	19	166	24
3	7.1-11.23 1904	St. Louis	USA	12	651	6	104	6
4	4.27-10.31 1908	London	UK	22	2008	36	110	21
5	5.5-7.22 1912	Stockholm	Sweden	28	2407	57	102	13
7	4.20-9.12 1920	Antwerp	Belgium	29	2626	77	154	21
8	5.4-7.27 1924	Paris	France	44	3089	136	126	17
9	5.17-8.12 1928	Amsterdam	Neitherland	46	2883	290	109	14
10	7.30-8.14 1932	Los Angeles	USA	37	1332	127	117	14
11	8.1-8.16 1936	Berlin	Germany	49	3963	328	129	19

Con.

	Date	City	Country	No. of nations	Athletes Total	Female	Number events	sports
14	7.29-8.14 1948	London	UK	59	4104	385	136	17
15	7.19-8.3 1952	Helsinki	Finland	69	4955	518	149	17
16	11.22-12.8 1956	Melbourne	Australia	72	3314	371	151	17
17	8.25-9.11 1960	Rome	Italy	83	5383	610	150	17
18	10.10-24 1964	Tokyo	Japan	93	5151	683	163	19
19	10.12-27 1968	Mexico City	Mexico	112	5516	781	172	18
20	8.26-9.11 1972	Munich	Germany	121	7134	1058	195	21
21	7.17-8.1 1976	Montreal	Canada	92	6084	1247	198	21
22	7.19-8.3 1980	Moscow	USSR	80	5179	1124	204	21
23	7.28-8.12 1984	Los Angeles	USA	140	6829	1567	221	21
24	9.17-10.2 1988	Seoul	Korea	159	8391	2186	237	23
25	7.15-8.9 1992	Barcelona	Spain	169	9364	2707	257	24
26	7.19-8.4 1996	Atlanta	USA	197	10,318	3516	271	26
27	9.15-10.1 2000	Sydney	Australia	199	10735	4069	300	28
28	8.13-29 2004	Athens	Greece	201	10625	4,412	301	28

Source from DK, *The Olympic Games: Athens 1896- Athens 2004*, London: Dorling Kindersley Limited, 2004, pp. 253-367.

Table 9-3　Information on the Winter Olympic Games

	Date	City	No. of nations	Athletes Total	Female	Number Sports	Events
1	1924.1.24-2.5	Chamonix France	16	258	13	5	14
2	1928.2.11-2.19	St. Moritz Switzerland	25	464	26	6	14
3	1932.2.4-2.13	Lake Placid (USA)	17	252	21	5	14
4	1936.2.6-2.16	Garmisch-Partenkirchen (Germany)	28	646	80	6	17
5	1948.1.30-2.8	St. Moritz Switzerland	28	669	77	7	22
6	1952.2.14-2.25	Oslo Norway	30	694	109	6	22
7	1956.1.26-2.5	Cortina d'Amperzzo	32	821	132	6	24
8	1960.2.18-2.28	Squaw Valley USA	30	665	143	6	27
9	1964.1.29-2.9	Innsbruck Austria	36	1091	200	8	34
10	1968.2.6-2.18	Grenoble France	37	1158	211	8	35
11	1972.2.3-2.13	Sapporo Japan	35	1006	206	8	35
12	1976.2.4-2.15	Innsbruck Austria	37	1123	231	8	37
13	1980.2.13-2.24	Lake Placid (USA)	37	1072	233	8	38
14	1984.2.8-2.19	Sarajevo Yugoslavia	49	1272	274	8	39
15	1988.2.13-2.28	Calgary Canada	57	1823	313	8	46
16	1992.2.8-2.23	Albertville France	64	1801	488	10	37

Con.

	Date	City	No. of nations	Athletes		Number	
				Total	Female	Sports	Events
17	1994. 2. 12-2. 27	Lillehammer Norway	67	1737	520	10	61
18	1998. 1. 7-1. 22	Nagano Japan	72	2176	787	14	68
19	2002. 2. 8-2. 24	Salt Lake City USA	77	2399	886	7	78
20	2006. 2. 10-2. 26	Dulin Italy	80	2508	960	7	84

Source from DK, The Olympic Games: Athens 1896- Athens 2004, London: Dorling Kindersley Limited, 2004, pp. 267-367

From the above tables a number of implications are clear.

(1) Gradual Construction of the Organisational Model

The tables reveal that the modern Olympic Games developed gradually and purposefully over time. Initially, the IOC had little authority. Instead, the host nations had the autonomy to decide the number and type of sports to be included and, indeed, many other things. As a consequence, a great deal of flexibility characterised the organisation and operation of the early Games. At the first modern Games, for example, any one who wished could participate. As a result, several entrants were tourists who had unexpectedly stumbled upon the Games. The Paris Games in 1900 lasted over a period of five months and most competitions took place in inadequate venues. This Games and the one in St. Louis that followed were merely appendages to the World Exhibition in Paris and the Purchase Exhibition in Louisiana[6] respectively. Due to poor organisation, ineffective marketing and low profiling, officials and athletes were hardly aware that they were participating in the Olympics. In short, the first three Olympic Games were often poorly organised, regulations were far from perfect and equipment and facilities were underdeveloped.

The 1908 London Games were organised more systematically and for the first time by official sports bodies. Then the Stockholm Games in 1912 adopted an even more systematic approach with greater public commitment and very careful planning. By 1924 International Federations had gained more influence over their respective sports and standardized their rules and regulations for competitions. In the meanwhile national Olympic organisations in most countries had started to conduct trials to ensure that the best athletes were sent to compete. Thus performance levels improved significantly.

The structure of the Games was gradually established. In 1920 the Olympic Flag was introduced at the Antwerp Games of 1920 and the Olympic Flame at the Amsterdam Games of 1928. The Winter Games was created in parallel to the Summer Games in 1924. The Olympic Village was established in 1932 and at the same time the duration of the Games became fixed at about two weeks. In 1936 a runner carried the Olympic Torch to light the Olympic Cauldron. Twenty years later the less formal parade of athletes at the Closing Ceremony was initiated in the Melbourne Games of 1956. With the increasing incidents of drug-taking and controversy over gender identity, drug testing and female gender verification were conducted for the first time in the Mexico City Games of 1968. With the development of modern technology, media coverage, TV in particular, became popular and crucial from the 1960s. Broadcasting rights became the most important source of IOC revenue.

(2) Impact of Major Wars on the Olympics

Due to the First and Second World Wars the Games of 1916, 1940 and 1944 were cancelled. The post-First-War Games were awarded to Antwerp in hopes of bringing a spirit of renewal to war-torn Belgium. Due to the very short time available to clean up the rubble left by the war and to construct new facilities for the Games, the athletics stadium was unfinished when the Games began and athletes were housed in crowded rooms furnished with folding cots. The defeated nations of the War—Germany, Austria, Hungary, Bulgaria, and Turkey—were not invited to the Games.

After the Second World War, with barely two years' notice, London shouldered the responsibility for hosting the 1948 Games which were to provide an release from the strains of the war. Again, Germany and Japan, the major defeated nations, were not invited to participate.

(3) Expansion of the Games: Examples

Since the Olympic Games in Athens in 1896 the modern Olympic

Movement has experienced continual, extensive expansion for over a century. Three examples: first, the number of competitors increased significantly at the Games of 1960, 1972 and 1996 (see figure 9-2).

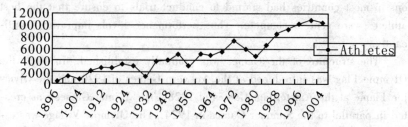

Figure 9-2　Number of Participants in the Olympics

Second, the number of member NOCs has been rising. By 1968 it exceeded 100 and by 2000 it had reached over 200 (see figure 9-3).

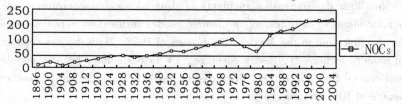

Figure 9-3　Number of NOCs within the IOC

Third, the Olympic Games are held by different nations of the world. The majority of host cities prior to World War II were European and the Olympians were mostly Westerners. This began to change after 1945. For example, the 1956 Games were awarded to Australia—the first nation in the Southern Hemisphere to host the Games. In 1964 The Games were held at Tokyo. Africa is now the only continent that has not hosted the Olympic Games.

(4) Location of the Host City and its Impact on the Games

It is clear from table 9-1 that the three games, including the St. Louis Games in 1904, the Los Angeles Games in 1932 and the Melbourne Games in 1956, had fewer participants than the previous Games. This could be related to the location of the host cities. Europe was the major force in the Olympic Movement in the early 20th century. To go to Los Angeles, the European athletes had to travel to New York first by boat and then cross the

American continent by train, which took three weeks. Besides, some competitors had to save up their holiday entitlement for three years in order to have the ten weeks' leave they needed for the Olympic adventure. In addition, America was considered by some Europeans as a remote and uncivilised place. They had no wish to participate in the Games there. Thus, in 1904 about 76% participants were Americans. Both the USA Games of 1904 and 1932 saw a decline in participants. So did the 1956 Games in Australia. As Australia is far from Europe and America, and there were two international crises[7] and equestrian events were moved to Stockholm due to Australian quarantine restrictions, the number of athletes at the 1956 Games was less than the immediately previous Games.

The 1968 Games were held in Mexico City. Its high altitude was both a benefit and a hindrance to track-and-field competitors. The sprinters and field athletes thrived in the thin air. The Americans Bob Beamon (long jump) and Lee Evans (400-metres), for example, set new world records that shattered previous records. African middle distance runners, who trained at high altitudes, had an advantage; Kip Keino of Kenya did particularly well earning gold and silver medals.

(5) Modern Transformation

Modern Olympism has already undergone several major reforms:

First, with use of modern technology, such as electric timing devices and a public address system in 1912, televised events in 1936, a computer system to record results in the 1960s and the advent of subscription cable and satellite television in the 1990s, the Olympic Games have steadily become unrecognisable from the Games of 1896.[8]

Second, the IOC has changed from being a regional to being a global organisation. When the IOC was created in 1896 most of the IOC members were Europeans. Now the 116 member of the IOC are from 79 nations/ regions.

Third, principles such as male only participation and amateurism have been abandoned. In 1896 there were no women competitors. In 1900 women began to participate in the Olympics, but only in tennis and golf. A century later, 4069 women participated in 25 sports and 132 events at the Sydney Games. In the Athens Games women participated in 26 sports and 135 events.

However, these transformations have not been without difficulties. Women's entry into the Olympics was not easy. It took women 28 years to

Figure 9-4 The Century Jump of Bob Beamon

get track-and-field and gymnastics added to the women's events and 72 years for the number of female Olympians to reach four figures.

In the new millennium, the Olympic Movement has undergone, and will undergo further, massive transformations. The bribery scandals with respect to Salt Lake City's bid to host the Winter Olympic Games in 2002 were a recent catalyst for change. There had been criticism on IOC's corruption before 1998 but the revelation of the Salt Lake City Bidding Scandal by a TV reporter in November 1998 shocked the world. It was alleged that a number of IOC members accepted bribes—in the form of cash, gifts, entertainment, business favours, travel expenses, medical expenses and even college tuition for members' children in exchange of their votes for the Salt Lake City as the site for the 2002 Winter Games.[9] Accusations of impropriety were also alleged in the conduct of several previous bid committees. The Sydney bidding committee was one of them.

Allegations of widespread corruption among IOC members forced the IOC to react quickly. First, for the first time six members were expelled from the organisation after the IOC conducted its own investigation—four resigned and one had died before the decision. Ten other members received warnings. In addition, the IOC decided to reform its policy, structure and the process of selecting future Olympic host cities. For example, site visits to Olympic bid cities of the IOC members are not now allowed. In addition, athletes now play a more important part in decision making voicing their opinions on important IOC issues. These changes will have, it is hoped, a far reaching influence on the Olympic Movement. In addition, the fundamental ethical values underpinning the Olympic ethos are to be stressed more than ever, and responsibility, inclusiveness, transparency, accountability and democracy will be emphasised to ensure a "pure" Olympic Movement.

4. Future of the Olympic Movement

The Olympic Movement faces a number of challenges in the twenty-first century.

* **First, with increasing involvement of government and corporations the IOC's autonomy is under increasing threat.**

The IOC has always opposed any use of the Olympic Games as a tool for political purposes, but this has never been completely realised. The recurring boycotts in the past and public statements of state heads during the recent voting contest of the host cities illustrate this. In addition, the IOC is in a dilemma—encouraging commercialisation of the Games while at the same time trying to minimize the interference of commerce in the Games. Compromises have often to be made as reflected in changes of competition venue and time. [10] There is even a claim of excessive compromise, namely that the IOC sold the 1996 Games to Atlanta-based multinational corporations such as Coca-Cola and the Cable News Network (CNN). [11]

Second, the corruption of Olympic officials has led to public loss of confidence in the Movement.

The recurring scandals regarding the selection of host cities of the Olympic Games led to questions about the behaviour of the IOC members and the IOC's credibility was at stake. Sponsors became wary of continuing their financial support of the Olympic Movement. How to fully restore public faith in the IOC will be a crucial task facing the organisation in the immediate future.

Third, drug-taking athletes threaten the future of the Movement.

The Olympics is linked overtly and specifically to the idea of fair play and illegal doping remains the "number one threat to the credibility of sport" (Jacques Rogge, 2001) and the decent image of the Olympics. To eliminate illegal drug-taking, the IOC has imposed increasingly harsh punishments and introduced ever advanced and more frequent testing. However, "the fight against doping is a highly complicated affair involving science, law and ethnics". [12] Drug tests cost huge amounts of money and often cause controversy and lawsuit cases as reflected in the following Reynolds Case. [13]

Reynolds Case

In 1992 a US federal judge in Ohio awarded Harry "Butch" Reynolds, then world 400 meters record holder, $26 million after determining that the IAAF had acted in error to ban him from competition for two years for testing positive for drugs. The IAAF did not accept the relevance of the jurisdiction of the Ohio court and opted not to defend the case on the assumption that no order could be enforced.

Reynold's lawyer pursued their award, obtaining orders in several US states in which the IAAF held assets. The IAAF was forced to respond and appealed against the oringinal decision. Eventually, the case reached the Supreme Court. In 1993 a US Court of Appeal overturned the Reynolds award ruling that the Ohio judge had no jurisdiction over the IAAF, which was then based in London.

The case prompted the IAAF to establish legal defences against any recurrence. Prior to the Atlanta Summer Olympic Games of 1996 all competitors were made to sign a declaration that in the event of a dispute over drug testing, they would not seek legal redress outside the Court of Arbitration for Sport. [14]

The above episode involving Reynold vividly reflects the intrusion of biotechnological commercial companies into the Games. The commercialisation of sport makes illegal drug elimination difficult, if not impossible. While the IOC wishes to eliminate illegal drugs and maintain "fair" competition not a few people, including some national and local politicians, coaches, scientists and athletes, want to employ biotechnologies to improve performance. The battle against illegal doping is, therefore, hard to win.

Fourth, gigantism makes the Games difficult to manage.

As the Olympic Games have expanded over time, Gigantism has become a problem. Nowadays the operating cost of hosting the Olympics is about $2 billion for the Summer Games and $1.5 billion for the Winter Games. To manage the Games becomes more demanding and difficult especially for small and developing countries. This will challenge the Games' principle of universality. How to reduce the size and complexity of the Olympic Games has been concern of the IOC under the leadership of Jacques Rogge. However, this is not an easy process as more sports want to become part of the Olympic programme, and those that are already included don't want to be removed. The repeated call to scale-down the Games by Rogge since 2001 has not seen any concrete result. The difficulties of reducing sports are considerable. This battle is still going on.

Fifth, security has become the central issue of all parties—bidding and organising committees of the Games, sponsors, participants and spectators.

Security began to attract more attention from the IOC and the Organising Committee of the Games after the massacre of Israeli athletes by Pakistan terrorists in the 1972 Games. Security has been a specific item of the Games' budget and has been rising over time. Greater resources and more sophisticated technology have been continuously utilised. In 1988, for example, about 100,000 security personnel were recruited given Seoul's proximity (30 miles) to North Korea and the possibility of student demonstrations for reunification. Though extra security precautions were taken in the Atlanta Games in 1996, a pipe bomb exploded in Centennial Olympic Park and led to two deaths. The terrorist attacks on the World Trade Centre in New York and on the Pentagon in Washington on September 11, 2001 made anxiety about security more acute. The security costs for Salt Lake City that hosted the 2002 Winter Games reached over $310m. [15] The security costs in Athens in 2004 were estimated $1.2 billion far more than the estimated $750m. security budget. Some 71,000 trained security personnel, the seven-nation Olympic Advisory Group, and the NATO allies were mobilised. [16] Partly because of the huge cost in security, Athens was left with a huge debt after the 2004 Games. [17] The rising expenses and complexity of security have raised important questions: Will small countries be able to afford these security measures and be capable of undertaking them? Does the spiralling cost place the Games even further out of the reach of "developing" countries? Will major cities now want to take the risk of staging the Games? Will athletes, officials and spectators be prepared to travel to the Games? And if not, what effect will this have on subsequent media and commercial interest? Will the future Olympic Games look like a sporting spectacle or a military exercise? Undoubtedly, the issue of security will have a major direct and indirect impact on the Olympic future.

Summary

Many factors over time-political, economic, cultural and social-have contributed to the birth of the modern version of the Olympic Games at the end of the 19th century. In particular, the Renaissance, Reformation, Enlightenment, the Industrial Revolution, European bourgeois educational reform with its emphasis on mind and body, the archaeological discovery of Ancient Olympia, English middle class educational precepts and practices, the internationalisation of sport and particularly, the tireless efforts of Coubertin, all played their part in ensuring the creation of the modern Olympic Games.

The nature of the modern Games, therefore, has been gradually established over time. And there have been major transformations. The modern Games have developed impressively in some one hundred years from a regional centred into a global centred sports competition. Transformation is not over. In the twenty-first century, the IOC has been under pressure to reform its policies, structures and practices to curb the epidemic of corruption among its members. The result has been a package of reforms. However, how to confront political interference, the commercialisation of the

Games, doping, corruption, gigantism and security, remain present and future challenges. More transformations lie ahead.

Questions
1. What major early historical events in Europe contributed to the eventual revival of the Olympic Games and which do you think was most influential?
2. Why did Pierre de Coubertin want to revive the Ancient Olympic Games?
3. Which of the transformations of the Olympic Games over the last hundred years do you consider most important? Give your reasons for your choice.
4. Which of the challenges facing the future Olympics is most serious? Give your reasons for your choice?

Notes
[1] The first modern steam engine was built by the engineer Thomas Newcomen in 1705 to improve the pumping equipment used to eliminate seepage in tin and copper mines. In 1763 James Watt, an instrument-maker for Glasgow University, began to make improvements on Newcomen's engine. He made it a reciprocating engine, thus changing it from an atmospheric to a true "steam engine".
[2] David Levinson and Karen Christensen (eds.) (1996), *Encyclopaedia of World Sport: From Ancient Times to the Present*, Oxford: ABC-CLIO Ltd., 391.
[3] For a full and updated discussion of the role of the games in the public schools, J. A. Mangan (1981), *Athleticism in the Victorian and Edwardian Public School*, Cambridge University Press.
[4] Allen Guttmann (1992), *The Olympics: A History of the Modern Games*, Chicago: University of Illinois Press, 9.
[5] Joachim K. Ruhl (2004), "Olympic Games before Coubertin", John E. Findling and Kimberly D. P Pelle, *Encyclopaedia of the Modern Olympic Movement*, London: Greenwood Press, 3.
[6] The Games originally were scheduled for Chicago, but the location was changed to St. Louis when Olympic Committee officials decided to combine the Olympics with the Louisiana Purchase Exhibition, a large fair celebrating the 100th anniversary of the U.S. acquisition of the Louisiana Territory.
[7] Egypt, Lebanon, and Iraq boycotted in protest of the Israeli invasion of the Sinai Peninsula in October. A few weeks before the opening of the Games, the Soviet army entered Budapest, Hungary, and suppressed a popular uprising against the government; The Netherlands, Spain and Switzerland boycotted the Games in protest of the Soviet invasion.
[8] Ellis Cashmore (2002), *Sports Culture: An A-Z Guide*, Routledge, pp. 402-405.
[9] Details can be found in Lex Hemphill, "Salt Lake City 2002" in John E. Find-

ling and Kimberly D. Pelle (eds.) (2004), op. cit., pp. 424-427.
[10] To meet the requirement of American TV broadcasters, whose audience were mainly American residents, the time of competitions for a number of sports at the Seoul Games had to move from afternoon or evening to early morning—a rare experience for athletes.
[11] Alfred E. Senn (1999), *Power, Politics, and the Olympic Games: A History of the Power Brokers, Events, and Controversies that Shaped the Games*, Human Kinetics, p. 249.
[12] Jacques Rogge, 2001.
[13] Michael Janofsky, "Track And Field: Reynolds Case Spotlights Battle of the Regulators", *The New York Times*, October 11, 1991.
[14] Ellis Cashmore (2002), op. cit., pp. 356-357.
[15] Di shi jiu jie dongji ao yun hui longzhong kaimu [Grand Opening of the 19th Winter Olympic Games], http://61.135.180.163/xwzx/tpxw/5945.shtm
[16] Gianna Angelopoulos Daskalaki, "We Are Ready to Compete on the World Stage Again", *The Daily Telegraph*, August 12, 2004.
[17] "Yadian aoyun ji xiang caiwu shuju daigei Beijing de qishi" [Revelations that some financial figures of the Athens Games bring to Beijing], *tiyu chanye xinxi* [Informaiton of Sports Industry], 10, 2004.

Chapter 10
The Modern Olympic Movement:
Confrontation between Idealism and Realism

Key points of this chapter:
* Amateurism and Professionalism
* Philanthropy and Commercialisation
* Evading Politics and Embracing Politics
* Fair Play and Foul Play
* Male Dominance and Gender Equality

The modern Olympic Movement has now existed for more than one hundred years and none of the explicit or implicit values of Olympism has yet been perfectly fulfilled. Tensions have characterised these years—between amateurism and professionalism, between philanthropy and commercialism, between political amity and political hostility, between foul play and fair play in various forms, between male dominance and gender equality. Nevertheless, it has been through the management of these tensions that the Olympic Movement has evolved to become the world's largest sporting manifestation. Therefore, it is necessary to understand the attempts to resolve these tensions in order to grasp the nature of the success of the Movement.

1. Amateurism and Professionalism

Amateurism and professionalism have long been issues in the modern Olympic Games. They were issues in the Ancient Games. From the 5th century BC onwards, the financial rewards for winning athletes became increasingly larger. Though ostensibly the prize at the Panhellenic Games was simply a crown of olive leaves, as already mentioned, a number of cities began to honour their victors by offering them goods or money or privileges that could be measured in terms of money. During the Hellenistic period (323-331 BC), some athletes competed solely for money, some even accepted money from an opponent in exchange for conceding victory.[1]

In modern sport amateurism and professionalism have existed in ideological opposition to each other since its emergence. An amateur participates in sport without material reward and participates essentially for pleasure. A professional performs essentially for reward.

Amateurism was emphasized when modern sport developed in late nineteenth century England. Much of modern sport began there in the schools of the privileged. Many pupils from the schools on leaving formed sports clubs. These clubs were amateur. The members played for pleasure not material reward. Briefly, this is the origin of modern amateurism. The rise of professionalism in modern sport went broadly hand in hand with the rise of amateurism. Professional players played for money, and professionalism gradually increased in conjunction with rising commercialism, the growth of "spectatorism" and the improvement of performances.

Before the 1970s the Olympic Games were officially restricted to amateurs as this rule made clear:

A person who has ever competed in sports as a professional, who has ever coached sports competitors for payment, or who is engaged in or connected with sport for personal profit is not eligible to serve on a national committee. The rules provide that exceptions to these categories may be made by the Executive Board of the I.O.C. on the recommendation of the National Olympic Committee concerned. National Olympic Committees that do not conform to IOC rules and regulations forfeit their recognition and their right to send participants to the Olympic Games. [2]

> **Jim Thorpe's Medals**
>
> Jim Thorpe, a Native American, won the pentathlon and decathlon by huge margins, setting world records in both events in the 1912 Olympics. At the Awards Ceremony, the King of Sweden told Thorpe, "Sir, you are the greatest athlete in the world." But the following year Thorpe's name was struck from the roll of Olympic champions and his medals were taken back by the IOC after it was revealed that he had earlier been paid for playing minor league baseball. The amount involved was miniscule (US $15 per week). It was not until 1982 that the IOC reversed its decision and after an interval of 70 years the medals were returned to the family of their rightful owner.

As a consequence of this ruling, some sports and athletes were thrown out of the Olympics. For example, after the 1924 Games, tennis was dropped from the Olympics because of the many non-amateur participants in the sport. Tennis did not return to the Olympics until 1988.

Since the 1970s the rules regarding athlete's eligibility have been gradually relaxed. In 1971 the IOC decided to eliminate the term amateur from the Olympic Charter. Subsequently, the eligibility rules were amended to permit "broken-time" payments to compensate athletes for time spent away from work during training and competition. The IOC also legitimized the sponsorship of athletes by National Olympic Committees, sports organisations and private businesses. In some sports, including track and field, figure skating and skiing, athletes had to place income from commercial endorsements and sponsorships in a restricted trust fund controlled by their national federation.

The Olympic rule requiring participants to be amateurs was finally replaced in 1986 and decisions on professional participation were left to the governing bodies of particular sports. Professionals in ice hockey, tennis, soccer and equestrian sports were permitted to compete in the 1988 Olympics, although their eligibility was subject to some restrictions, and professionals from sports other than track and field became eligible for Olympic track-and-field events.

The change of ruling was closely associated with public demand for entertainment. In 1992, for example, the U.S. men's basketball team, the "Dream Team", crushed each of its opponents to win the gold medal easily. The team had 11 professional basketball stars including Michael Jordan, Scottie Pippen, Earvin ("Magic") Johnson and Larry Bird; all crowd-pullers! In the early part of the 20th century 98 percent of the

Games' competitors made no money from their participation; in the early part of the twenty-first century Games competitors for the most part, are far from amateur. [3]

2. Philanthropy and Commercialisation

Initially the funding of the IOC was exclusively private. In the first modern Olympic Games of 1896, 60% of funding was donated by one man, the wealthy Greek benefactor George Averoff. However, this situation led to future difficulties. Prior to 1981 the IOC could hardly manage to cover its operating costs or to pay its members' expenses.

Thus, since the early 1980s the Olympics has embraced commercialism. Commercialism is perhaps best explained by the term "commodification"—objects and people become commodities in a market. "Commodification" is a consequence of the emergence of a consumer-based economy within capitalism. It nurtures a mercantile culture keen to trade and profit whenever the opportunity presents itself. In the 1984 Games, for example, a place in the Torch Relay team sold for $3,000 per kilometre. [4]

As a consequence of "commodification" corporate sponsorship has become the important source of IOC revenue. The IOC budget has increased significantly as a result from US $14.1 million between 1972-76 to US $1.7 billion between 1992-96. Private enterprises from soft drink producers to automobile companies now compete to be an official sponsor of the Games. Coca-cola, for example, paid $22 million for the guarantee that no competitor's soft drinks be allowed to display the Olympic symbol at the Seoul Games. [5]

While the need for support from the commercial sector is widely recognised, there is growing concern about the extent of the support. Criticism has been voiced regarding the over-commercialisation of the Olympics. It has even been claimed, as noted earlier, that the IOC sold the 1996 Games to Atlanta-based multinational corporations such as Coca-Cola and the Cable News Network (CNN). [6]

To curtail uncontrolled commercialisation, the IOC is committed to the following key policies:

* **No venue advertising is permitted**. The Olympic Games are the only major sporting event in the world where there is no advertising in the stadium or on the athletes.

* **Control over the number of major corporate sponsorships and greater support from fewer partnerships** ! For example, the Salt Lake Organising Committee and the IOC generated greater marketing support and more revenue for Salt Lake 2002 with significantly fewer commercial partnerships than for the substantially larger Centennial Games in Atlanta 1996. This fact illustrates the enhanced value of Olympic marketing partnerships and demonstrates the IOC's effort to control the commercialism that underpins the staging of the Games.

3. Evading Politics and Embracing Politics

The Olympic Charter states that "the International Olympic Committee is to oppose any political abuse of sport and athletes". The IOC President A. Brundage (1952-1972) claimed: "Sport has nothing to do with politics". However, the Olympic Games have often been influenced by political events and been occasionally used as a powerful political tool. For more than a century, the Olympic Movement has experienced various political interventions by governments and political movements. Three Olympic Games were cancelled due to World Wars. In 1920 Austria, Bulgaria, Germany, Hungary and Turkey were not permitted to participate because of their role in the First World War. One of the most politically influenced Games was the Berlin Games of 1936. When the Games were awarded to Berlin in 1931, no one suspected that Adolf Hitler and Nazi Germany would have control of the Games. Though Hitler used the Games as a display of political strength, he failed to "prove" his theory of racial superiority as Jesse Owens, an American black athlete, won four gold medals in the 100m, 200m, long jump and the 4 × 100m relay.

After the Second World War, the London Games of 1948 saw the communist countries compete for the first time, but Germany and Japan were refused entry due to their roles in the war. Then due to the Israeli-led takeover of the Suez Canal, Egypt, Iraq and Lebanon did not take part in the 1956 Melbourne Games. Spain and Switzerland boycotted the Games as well, in protest to the Soviet invasion of Hungary. In 1960, South Africa was banned from the Olympic Games due to its policy of Apartheid. The IOC restored recognition of the South African Olympic Committee in 1991.

South Africa competed in the 1992 Barcelona Games.

The 1968 Olympic Games in Mexico City were the most politically charged Olympics since the 1936 Games in Berlin. Ten days before the Games were to open, students protested about the Mexican government's use of funds for the Olympics rather than for social programmes. The students were surrounded in the Plaza of Three Cultures by the army and fired upon. More than 250 protesters were killed and over a thousand injured. Then at the victory ceremony for the men's 200-metre run, Americans Tommie Smith and John Carlos (gold and bronze medalists, respectively) stood barefoot with heads bowed and with a single black-gloved fist raised during the national anthem. The athletes described the gesture as a tribute to their African American heritage and as a protest over the living conditions of minorities in the United States. Officials from the IOC and the U.S. Olympic Committee judged the display to be counter to the ideals of the Games; both athletes were banned from the Olympic Village and sent home.

One of the most horrifying political events linked with an Olympic Games happened at the 1972 Games in Munich. On 5 September, eight Arab terrorists broke into the Israeli team headquarters. The terrorists killed 2 people immediately and another 9 were murdered after a rescue attempt by the German police failed at the airport. The world was stunned. A memorial service took place the next morning in a packed Olympic stadium. Competition resumed later that day with the consent of the Israeli team who returned home immediately. In the following days and months there was considerable controversy over the IOC President Avery Brundage's decision to continue the Games after the attack.

Boycotts—the voluntary severing of relations with a person, country or other group in order to exert pressure—at the Olympic Games occur officially when a government refuses to allow its athletes to attend. The Soviet Union's invasion of Afghanistan in December of 1979, for example, disrupted the 1980 and 1984 Games. A number of non-communist nations decided to boycott the 1980 Moscow Games. Tit-for-tat politics came into play at the 1984 Games in Los Angeles with a last minute boycott by the Soviet Union and other communist countries. The standard of competition was affected at both Games by the boycotts. Boycotts continued. In 1988 at the Seoul Games, North Korea, Cuba, Ethiopia and Nicaragua did not participate for political reasons.

Figure 10-1　Black gloved fist

With their international Visibility, the Olympic Games have considerable potential as a political tool. While the reverse is true, the Olympics can be used to improve relations between countries and communities. De facto, the Olympics represents a political project, in the sense that, to aspire for equal global opportunities and world participation in sport, to achieve international understanding and peace, require political decisions and actions involving constructive compromise. After Juan Samaranch became President of the IOC in 1980, the IOC adopted a pragmatic position: "the Olympic Movement is an integral part of society and therefore has a duty to come to terms with the public authorities". Nevertheless, if the Games are used for negative political ends, Olympic idealism is threatened.

Figure 10-2   The Olympic Flag Lowed Half in 1972

4. Fair Play and Foul Play

The Olympic tradition emphasises fair play. Fair play is a set of aspirations including rule-adherence, respect for others, modesty in success, dignity in defeat and generosity in victory with purpose of creating lasting

150   The Olympic Culture: An Introduction

positive human relationships in sport.

However, in the Olympic Movement foul play is often seen. Doping is an example.

(1) Doping

Doping is cheating. Doping is akin to death. Death physiologically, by profoundly altering, sometimes, irreversibly, normal processes through unjustified manipulations. Death physically, as certain tragic cases in recent years have shown. But also death spiritually and intellectually, by agreeing to cheat and conceal one's capabilities, by recognising one's incapacity or unwillingness to accept oneself, or to transcend one's limits. And finally death morally, by excluding oneself de facto from the rules of conduct required by all human society.

H. E. Juan Antonio Samaranch, President of the IOC (1980-2001)

∗ Doping in the world

The issue of drug-abuse in sport—the deliberate or inadvertent use by athletes of substances or methods that may enhance performance has a long history.[7] However, it was in the mid-1950s when cyclists were tested drug positive that the issue of drug abuse attracted international attention.[8] Alarmed by the increasing numbers of athletes using drugs to enhance performance, the IOC passed a resolution against doping in 1962. In 1967, the IOC established a Medical Commission to provide medical control service for the 1968 Olympic and Olympic Winter Games. Since 1972 full-scale testing has been carried out.

The government inquiry in Canada that followed the positive test on Ben Johnson at the Seoul Games (1988) was a crucial event, perhaps the crucial event, in the worldwide crusade against drug-abuse in sport. More than 13 years after Johnson report was published, a major breakthrough in the war against drugs was to end the conspiracy of silence, which involved competitors, coaches, trainers, physicians and administrators.

Ben Johnson Case

At the Seoul Olympics in 1988 Ben Johnson ran the 100 metres in 9.79 seconds making him the fastest human ever. It was a proud dream in Canadian athletic history that quickly turned into a nightmare. Only 62 hours later Olympic officials entered Johnson's room and walked out with his gold medal. Ben Johnson had tested positive for steroid use and lost millions in endorsements and sponsorship fees. He was suspended from competition for two years.

Prior to Ben's meteoric rise to the pinnacle of the track and field world, Charlie Francis, his Canadian Olympic track coach told him that a sprinter couldn't hope to go world class without steroids. Johnson, like many of his competitors, began using steroids six years before his stunning victory. The fateful dose was administered by Dr. Jamie Astaphan, his team doctor, during a rest session in St. Kitts just prior to Seoul Games. The doctor allegedly warned Johnson and his coach that Johnson could test positive at the Games as a result and asked for $1 million to keep quiet. Johnson's coach did nothing and allowed him to compete. Although Johnson knew that he used steroids, he trusted his coaches and medical advisor, which proved to be a fatal mistake.

In the early 1990s Johnson attempted to climb to the top once again. Unfortunately, in 1993, he tested positive again after a Montreal track event and was banned by the International Amateur Athletics Federation (IAAF) for life. This time, Ben insisted that he was clean. Records showed that he had been tested three times Jan 15, Jan 17 & Jan 21. Only the Jan 17 sample tested positive. Johnson maintained that it was impossible to be clean two days prior and four days later but didn't have the money to dispute the results in court. His brilliant athletic career was finally over.

He continued to train and in 1999 a Canadian arbitrator ruled that Johnson had not received due process in 1993 and would be allowed to compete in Canada. The IAAF, however, upheld the lifetime ban. This meant that although Johnson could now technically run in Canada he couldn't compete. His competitors would be considered "tainted" and also barred from international competition. In October 1999 he raced against a thoroughbred, a pacer, and a stock car at a charity event. Johnson came third after the stock car became bogged down in the mud.

Johnson was in the headlines again last summer after he accepted a three month job to train Libyian dictator Muammer Gaddafi's son, a soccer player.

Ben Johnson still lives in Toronto, He's never held down a job and lives on an income of a few hundred dollars a week. He trains at York University with his first coach Percy Duncan for races that may never come. Ben Johnson is adamant that he is history's supreme sprinter, despite having used drugs to fuel his victories. He said: "Most people loved the entertainment and they know the game. The sport will never be clean".

source from "Dying to Win: The Ben Jonson Story", www.tv.cbc.ca/witness/doping/dopmain.htm, Feb. 21, 2001.

Some athletes and officials claim: "testing in competitions only catches the careless and the ill-advised". This is because competitors, their coaches and medical advisers usually ensure that all traces of hormone drugs have left their athletes' bodies before they have to give a urine sample. It remains a moot point whether Johnson was careless or ill-advised. For a country whose people often feel themselves in the shadow of the United States, Johnson's victory over Carl Lewis, the great American athlete, was an opportunity to stand in the Olympic limelight. In part, this was the motivation for a stupid action.

The failure of many sports bodies to treat the drug-abuse problem seriously and to take more effective means to detect the illegal use of drugs has also contributed to the extensive use of enhancing drugs by athletes. A further problem has been that when an athlete was detected using performance-enhancing drugs only the athlete was disciplined. No responsibility was attached to coaches, physicians or to the relevant athletic organisation.

Drugs samples taken at the outdoor US National Championships during the summer of 2003, as well as out-of-competition tests, indicated widespread use of a new drug tetrahydrogestrinone (THG), a designer steroid. THG has been sold in the guise of a dietary supplement. While little is known about THG's specific effects because it is new, its close chemical similarity to other well-known steroids means it could well pose the same risks as anabolic steroids that have been shown to have dangerous side effects, including liver damage, heart disease, anxiety and rage..

After criticism of its handling of drugs cases prior to the 2000 Sydney Olympics, the USA Track & Field (USATF) agreed to delegate such matters to the USA Anti-drug Agency (USADA). This action, however, came too late to prevent the past returning to haunt the USATF at the World Championships in Paris in August 2003. It was revealed that Jerome Young, a member of the victorious US 4 ×400 metres squad, had been allowed by the USATF to run despite testing positive for nandrolone in 1999. The image of the USATF was also damaged in the same year by the case of Kelli White, the double sprint champion in Paris, who failed a drugs test. Other American athletes also failed drug tests. [9]

In fact, the IOC has known for years that testing at competition time was an inadequate method of detection and deterrence and has said so, yet the idealistic image of clean and fair competition has been too often maintained while those directly involved in sport knew the reality.

The World Anti-Doping Agency (WADA) has been set up with code of conduct, and is supported by most countries and international federations. This body has been struggling to secure agreed funding from several governments.[10]

* **Doping in China**

In 1989 the spread of drugs prompted China to announce a three-pronged anti-drug- abuse policy of "strict prohibition, strict examination and strict punishment" (*yanli jinzhi, yange jiancha, yanli chufa*). Subsequently, drug tests were introduced in major domestic competitions.[11] In 1990 some 165 athletes were screened and 3 tested positive (1.82 per cent).[12] However, those drug violators were neither punished nor named publicly. Instead, the excuse "misusing Chinese medicine" (*wufu zhongyao*) was offered to explain away these positive tests.

In January, 1998 Chinese swimmers became the target of accusations over drug abuse. Growth hormone was found in a flask in the Chinese swimmer Yuan Yuan's luggage at Sydney airport on January 8, 1998.[13] One week later four other swimmers failed the pre-competition drug tests[14] during the World Swimming Championships in Perth. These events reinforced the long-existing suspicion that the Chinese were involved in a systematic national drug programme. The Chinese sports authorities reacted quickly.

The Xinhua New Agency quoted Yuan Weimin, vice-president of the Chinese Olympic Committee, as saying: "We will not only make unremitting efforts to fight doping, but also reject biased attacks by a few sports officials with double standards". Despite this spirited and prompt response, however, many athletes and officials from other nations remained uneasy and called for the expulsion of the entire Chinese swimming team from the world championships and for a boycott of a World Cup event in China the following month.

Hugely embarrassed, Chinese sports officials promised a tightening of doping control. Drastic action was taken in the run-up to the Sydney Olympics. Some forty athletes and officials including fourteen track and field athletes, four swimmers, two canoers, and seven rowers who failed last-minute blood tests, were dropped from its delegation to Sydney.[15] As a result, no Chinese athlete tested positive during Sydney and Athens Games.

* **IOC's anti-doping policies**

Competitors who participate in the Olympic Games are governed by the

Eligibility Code. This Code states that competitors must abide by the IOC Medical Code. The Code prohibits doping, publishes a list of permissible products, establishes lists of the classes of prohibited substances and procedures, obligates competitors to submit themselves to medical controls and examinations and makes provision for sanctions to be applied in the event of a violation of the Code. The IOC provides a complete updated list to all International Federations, National Olympic Committees, athletes, coaches and team doctors before the Olympic Games.

Table 10-1   The IOC List of Categories of Banned Substances (Feb., 1994)

Doping Classes	Functions
Stimulants	These act directly on the athletes' nervous system to speed up parts of their brain and body. This can speed up reaction time and slow fatigue.
Narcotic Analgesics	These are pain killers or depressants. Athletes take them to enable them to train and compete despite pain and injury.
Anabolic Agents	These are substances such as the hormone testosterone which develop athletes' muscles.
Beta-Blockers	These stop an athlete from trembling, reduce their blood pressure, slow their heart rate and have a calming effect.
Diuretics	These increase the amount of urine that athletes pass from their bodies. Therefore, they could be used by athletes in sports with weight divisions, who have difficulty keeping their weight down to qualify.
Peptide Hormones & Analogues	These help the body to grow muscle and determine height. Growth hormones encourage muscle growth and promote speed and strength.

Blood doping pharmacological, chemical and physical manipulation drugs are subject to restriction. The following substances are allowable up to certain limits: Alcohol, Local Anaesthetics and Corticosteroids.

Any competitor refusing to submit to a medical control (drug test/ urine sample) or who is found guilty of drug abuse is excluded by the IOC from the current and future Olympic Games. If a competitor is a member of a team, the competition, event or match during which the infringement took place may be considered as forfeited by that team. If an infringement of the Medical Code occurs, a medal may be withdrawn.

The IOC Medical Commission is responsible for the collection, sealing and numbering and delivery of urine samples to the laboratory accredited for the Olympic Games. The IOC has 24 accredited laboratories to carry out the testing for illegal substances.

From 1968 to 1992, urine samples were taken and analysed in accordance with the Medical Code. However, at the 1994 Olympic Winter Games in Lillehammer, blood tests were performed in the Nordic Skiing events under the exclusive control of the International Ski Federation.

During the Olympic Winter Games in Nagano, the IOC-NAOC medical team conducted 700 doping control tests. There were no positive cases. During the Olympic Games in Sydney, the IOC-SOCOG team performed 2,076 in-competition tests, 404 out-of-competition tests, and 307 EPO tests. The IOC found eleven athletes guilty of doping offences. [16]

The IOC, through the Medical Code, is pressurising the International Federations to adopt the IOC Medical Code for all of their international competitions. In December 2003 the IOC Executive Board took the important decision to re-test the samples collected during the XIX Olympic Winter Games in Salt Lake City for the new designer drug THG based on advice from experts who confirmed that it is legally and scientifically possible to do so. The IOC Executive Board decided in February, 2004 that Muehlegg and Danilova from the Salt Lake City Games were to be disqualified and their medals were to be withdrawn. The Executive Board also agreed to consider the period from the Opening of the Olympic Village to the Closing Ceremony of the Olympic Games as an in-competition testing period. [17]

In conclusion, by entering the Olympic Games athletes are making a commitment to respect the Olympic values and agree to undergo doping tests. Throughout the Games, tests are carried out under the authority of the IOC and its Medical Commission. Tests may also be conducted during the pre-Games period. After each event, the first four athletes are tested along with two other athletes chosen at random.

(2) Other Problems

Other types of "foul play", such as bribery, also exist in the Olympic family. A recent blatant example, already noted, in November 1998, involved unethical behaviour of Salt Lake City bid officials and IOC officials, Some IOC members as stated as earlier, were accused of having accepted bribes-in the form of cash, gifts, entertainment, business favours, travel expenses, medical expenses, and even college tuition for members' children—from members of the Salt Lake City Bid Committee for the 2002

Winter Games. On December 11, 1998, the IOC Executive Board appointed an ad hoc commission to investigate all available tangible substantiated evidence. Later both the Salt Lake Organising Committee (SLOC) and the United States Olympic Committee (USOC) launched investigations. As a result of the IOC investigation, the IOC membership voted to expel six members. Four others under investigation resigned and one other had died prior to the decision. Ten other members received warnings.

This event led to a crisis of belief in the Olympic Movement. To recover its untainted image, the IOC had to take measures to prevent corruption from spreading in the organisation. Immediately, an IOC 2000 reform commission was set up. In December 1999 a 50-point reform package covering the selection and conduct of the IOC members, the bid process, the transparency of financial dealings, the size and conduct of the Games and drug regulations was endorsed. An independent IOC Ethics Commission was established.

5. Male Dominance and Gender Equality

In the Ancient Olympic Games, as stated earlier, women were forbidden to take part. Married women were forbidden to even enter the competition areas as spectators. If they were caught, they were thrown off Typeum, local high precipitous cliffs. Callipateira, disguised as a trainer, brought her son to compete at Olympia. Her son, her brothers and her father were all Olympic champions. She was caught watching, but she was not punished because of their performances. However, as a result, a law was passed that all trainers must strip before entering the arena.

Therefore, women created their own Games dedicated to the goddess Hera. Hera was the sister-wife of Zeus. It is said that Hippodamia, in gratitude to Hera for her happy marriage to Pelops selected 16 women and with them inaugurated these Games and dedicated them to the Goddess. The choice of the 16 women arose from the time when Damaphon, tyrant of Pisa was particularly cruel to Eleans. After he died, the people of Pisa and Elis wished for friendship amongst themselves. So one woman from each of the 16 Elean cities was chosen. These 16 were entrusted with the management of the Games.

When the Olympic Games were revived in 1896 the founder Baron Pierre de Coubertin did not agree with women's participation in the Games.

Figure 10-3   Women's Tennis in the Early Years

"...the true Olympic hero, in my view, is the individual adult male."[18] Thus, the Olympic Games in Athens in 1896 were an exclusively male preserve. When women made their Olympic debut four years later at the Paris Games in 1900, only two sports were open to them—tennis and golf. In early 20th century society, women athletes had to cope with a great deal of prejudice. There were fears that they would lose their femininity, grow unattractively muscular or become sterile. Such prejudices faced the first Olympic female athletes.

In London at the 1908 Games there were 36 women competitors in the figure skating and tennis events. After these Games there was a recommendation from the British Olympic Association that women swimmers, divers and gymnasts be allowed to compete in future Games. As a consequence, the Swedish Organising Committee included two swimming events and one diving event for women at the 1912 Stockholm Games in which the Australian Fanny Durack won the 100m freestyle to become the first female champion; impressively, her time was the same as the men's winner.

In reaction to the limited events available to women in the Olympics, in 1919 the first Women's Games were created in Paris and in one day alone, 20,000 spectators saw world records broken in track and field. In

1921 Jeux Feminins, the first all-women "Olympics" was held in Monaco. Three hundred women from five countries competed in many sports not permitted to them in the Olympic Games such as track and field and basketball. The "Olympics" were so successful that they were held again in 1922 and 1923. In 1924 the IOC decided to allow a larger participation of women in the Games. The first "women's Olympic Games" were one-day track meet in Paris in 1922. The second Game were held in Gothenburg, Sweden in 1926 with entries from 10 nations. And they lasted until 1934. Future Women's Games were cancelled in exchange for a nine-event Olympic programme for women in the 1936 Olympic Games.

However, the road to equal participation was not without difficulties and confrontations. In 1928, several women collapsed at the end of the 800m and the event was declared dangerous to women and banned until 1960. Incidentally, the British women stayed away from the 1928 Games to protest at the lack of women's Olympic events. This is the only feminist boycott in Olympic history.

Gradually, women earned their place at the Games-sport by sport and event by event. Nevertheless, there were only 5 women's sports in the London Games of 1948. After the Games there was a marked increase in the participation of women in sport throughout the world. During the 1970s the increase of women participating in the Games became more extensive reflecting the increased awareness of the positive contribution that sport can make to the well-being of women. After the 1976 Games, the number of sports offered to women began to increase significantly. In 1991, the IOC decided that any new sport seeking to be included in the Olympic programme had to include women's events. Thus, more sports are now available to women in the Olympic programme. At the 1996 Atlanta Games there were 26 sports and 97 events open to women; there were 163 events open to men. At the Sydney Games in 2000, women competed in 25 sports (out of 28) and 132 events. These figures improved in 2004—135 events. In Athens, women competed in all sports with the exception of baseball (softball for women) and boxing. Several new events were added for women in wrestling, fencing and sailing.[19] Finally, the percentage of women athletes at the Olympic Games has been steadily increasing. It was 34.2% in Atlanta (1996), 38.2% in Sydney (2000) and 40.6% in Athens (2004).

Women have participated in the Olympics not only as athletes but also as coaches, referees and officials. In 1981 the first two women were coop-

Figure 10-4 Women's Tennis in the 21st Century

ted as IOC members. Women began to play a part in the IOC's leadership. In 1994, *The Olympic Charter* was amended to include an explicit reference to the need for promoting women's participation in leadership: "The IOC strongly encourages, by appropriate means, the promotion of women in sport at all levels and in all structures, particularly in the executive bodies of national and international sports organisations with a view to the strict application of the principle of equality of men and women."[20] A "Women and Sport" working group was established in 1995. It was composed of athletes and representatives of the IFs, NOCs and specialists, to advise the IOC Executive Board on measures to be taken to promote the advancement of women in executive positions within sport. The working group also works with Olympic Solidarity to hold training seminars and symposiums. A world conference is also held every four years to evaluate progress made in the Olympic Movement, share experiences and identify priorities for the future. In 2004 the group was renamed as the Women and Sport Commission.

In 1995, the IOC decided to set as an objective for NOCs and IFs: at least 10% of all decision-making positions be held by women by 31 December 2000. This percentage was to reach at least 20% by the end of 2005.

Through persistent and concerted effort, progress has been made in promoting women's representation. In 1996 American woman Anita DeFrantz was elected as the IOC's first woman Vice-President between 1997 and 2001. By 2001, about 66% of NOCs and 43% of IFs had met the objective of 10 percent of women in decision-making positions. By December 1, 2003 thirty-two Olympic IFs (91%) had at least one woman on their executive body. Gunilla Lindberg from Sweden was elected as the IOC Vice-President in 2004. In the same year Nawal El Moutawakel became the first woman to lead the IOC's Review Committee. However, the road to women's equality is still not smooth. By December 1st 2003, only 20 (57%) out of the 35 Olympic IFs had achieved the objective of 10%, and only eight Olympic IFs (23%) had more than 20% of women on their executive body.[21]

Summary

Idealism is a laudable component of modern Olympism but it has always had to coexist with realism. Tensions in the more than one hundred years of the Olympic Movement involving amateurism and professionalism, philanthropy and commercialism, political harmony and disharmony, fair play and foul play and male dominance and gender equality have characterised its history. Nevertheless, idealism remains extant and the efforts of the Olympic Movement to reduce associated tensions and ensure global idealism in sport remain energetic and are to be applauded.

Questions

1. Has professionalism had any significant deleterious effects on the Olympics?
2. What impact will future commercialisation have on the Olympics?
3. Will international politics continue to adversely interfere with Olympic idealism?
4. Do you think that doping can be eliminated?

5. What do you think of the future prospects for women in the Olympics?

Notes:

[1] "Professionalism in Athletics", www.athens2004.com.
[2] IOC, The Olympic Charter, 1964.
[3] David Levinson and Karen Christensen (eds.) (1996), *Encyclopaedia of World Sport: From Ancient Times to the Present*, Oxford: ABC-CLIO Ltd., 81.
[4] *Encyclopaedia Britannica*, 2002.
[5] David Levinson and Karen Christensen (eds.) (1996), op. cit., 81.
[6] Encyclopaedia Britannica, http://www.britannica.com/eb/article? eu = 137628.
[7] Doping was first reported in modern sport in 1865. After 1879 cyclists favoured ether and caffeine to delay the onset of sensations. In the 1930s some cyclists used strychnine and other stimulants, which were later adopted by body-builders, footballers and track athletes. For the details, see Ellis Cashmore (1996), *Making Sense of Sports* (Second Edition), London and New York: Routledge, 150.
[8] The Sports Council, "History of doping in modern sport", Craig Donnellan (ed.) (1995), *Drugs and Violence in Sport: Issues for the Nineties*, No. 26, Cambridge: Independence Educational Publishers, 27.
[9] David Powell, "Americans Stand Accused of Doping Conspiracy", *Times Onlne-Sport*, October 17, 2003.
[10] John Goodbody, "Inquiry into Drug Use Created Long-term Positive Effects", *Times Online-Sport*, September 24, 2003.
[11] In 1989 the National Sports Commission issued the "Provisional Regulations on Testing for Banned Drugs in National Sports Competitions" (*quangguo xing tiyu jingsai jiancha jinyong yaowu de zanxin guiding*).
[12] Guojia tiyu zongju zhongguo aoweihui [The National Sports Bureau and the Chinese Olympic Committee], "Zhongguo fan xinfenji shinian" [The Decade of Fight against Drug Abuse in China], http://www.sports.gov.cn.
[13] According to medical sources, there was enough of the drug Somatotropin to serve the entire Chinese team of 23 in Perth for the duration of their stay. Yuan Yuan was banned for four years and her coach for 15 years (Crag Lord, "Caught Red-Handed—Amid Global Cries Of 'I Told You So,' China Awaits Its Fate In The Great Doping Scandal", *Sunday Times*, 11 January 1998).
[14] The urine samples of female swimmers Wang Luna, Wang Wei and Cai Huiyu and a male swimmer Zhang Yi contained traces of Triamterene, a diuretic, which can be used as a masking agent to cover any traces of banned substances. Its use is interpreted as trying to manipulate a test and is therefore read as a positive result.
[15] http://www.guardian.co.uk/print/0,3858,4060177 – 105268,00.html. Accessed 21 May 2005.
[16] Final Report on the XXVIIth Olympiad, 37.
[17] IOC Executive Board Concludes Last Meeting Of The Year, International Olympic Committee Press Release, Friday 5 December 2003.

[18] *Le Sport Suisse*, 31st year, 7 August 1935, 1.
[19] "New record participation of women at the Olympic Games", http://www.olympic.org/uk/organisation/commissions/women/full_story_uk.asp?id=1017, August 19, 2004.
[20] Rule 2, paragraph 5, Olympic Charter.
[22] Women in the Olympic Movement (Updated July 2004), http://multimedia.olympic.org/pdf/en_report_846.pdf.

Chapter 11
Olympic Marketing:
The Olympic Movement as a Business

Key points:
* History, Character and Sources of Olympic Marketing
* Management of Olympic Marketing
* Distribution of Marketing Revenues
* Protection of Marketing(Intellectual) Properties
* Marketing and Over-Commercialism

Sport without money is impossible today... The Olympics is of course a business, but it has not become a product one can consume.

(Samaranch, the former IOC President, 1986).

The goal of the Olympic Movement, as has been made clear over and over again in previous pages, is to achieve a better world by encouraging excellence, equality of opportunity, international goodwill and fair play in sport. To realise this goal huge resources are needed. Olympic marketing, therefore, is crucial. As a phenomenon that attracts the attention of the media and the interest of the entire world, the Olympic Games provide one of the most effective international corporate marketing opportunities in the world. According to a survey by the Chinese company Lingdian Diaocha (Zero Survey) in 2004, some 79.9% of respondents looked more favourably on companies that had sponsored the Olympic Games than others; some 75.1% would buy or use the products that had the Olympic five rings. These two figures reached 87.7% and 80.1% respectively for the age group between 18 to 25. [1] This is also true in other countries (see table 11-1). Sponsoring the Olympic Games can hugely enhance the brand image of corporate products, enhance the corporation's attraction for clients and increase its profits.

Table 11-1 Olympic Sponsor Brand Survey Data

	Total (N = 3,200)	US (n = 1,274)	China (n = 724)	CIS (n = 199)	India (n = 338)	UK (n = 193)	Germany (n = 277)	France (n = 195)
Increase Premium Image	79	78	91	91	94	70	39	64
More positive Image	78	78	92	88	96	68	34	60
More attention & awareness	77	77	89	81	97	67	36	53
Buying opportunities by promotion	75	77	90	83	83	69	36	55
Want to buy Sponsor product	66	65	74	80	95	46	28	44

Source from the Samsung Company in China.

Without doubt the Olympic Rings are the most recognised symbols in the world. As the sole owner of the five interlocked rings, the IOC possesses a marketing logo of immense lucrative potential. Consequently, Olympic marketing is a global programme for the promotion of the Olympic Games and for the securing of the financial stability of the Olympic Movement. This marketing directly relates to the marketing of sport and is indirectly linked to the marketing of the consumer goods of multinational and other companies.

1. Olympic Marketing in Historical Perspective

Olympic marketing can be traced back to the first modern Olympic

Games in 1896 when companies provided revenue through advertising in the souvenir programme. One of the advertisers was Kodak which continues its support as a partner in The Olympic Partner (TOP) programme today (more detail later). In 1912 approximately ten Swedish companies purchased "Sole-rights", primarily to take photographs and sell memorabilia of the Olympic Games in Stockholm. One company purchased the rights to place weighing machines in the grounds for spectators. The official programme of 1920 Antwerp Games was replete with advertising. Olympic Games venue advertising was permitted in 1924—the first and only time in Olympic history. Four years later, the IOC made a stipulation that the stadium, grounds and buildings should not be disfigured with posters, but advertising was allowed in the programmes. The Coca-Cola Company, a current TOP Partner, began its long-standing association with the Olympic Games in this year. The OCOG in 1932 approached business organisations and retail stores to provide free merchandising and advertising tie-ins. In 1952 an IOC sales department sold various rights to do on-site business at the Olympic Games. For the first time an international marketing programme was attempted with companies from eleven countries donating value-in-kind products ranging from food for the athletes to flowers for medal winners. By 1964 the number of corporations associated with the Games had grown to 250. A new cigarette brand called "Olympia" generated over US $ 1 million in revenue for the Tokyo OCOG (The tobacco category was later banned). In the Munich Games of 1972 a private advertising company was licensed to use the official logo of the Games. The Games' Rights to use the official emblem were sold and several types of licensing and advertising agreements were available. There was also the first official mascot, "Waldi", whose image was licensed to private firms. [2]

Although there were sponsors and suppliers participating in the official sponsor programme which was further broken down into official sponsors, official supporters and official promoters, only US $ 7 million was generated for the Montreal OCOG in 1976. When Samaranch was elected as IOC President, he understood that unless the Olympic Movement could develop an independent financial base and revenue source, it would not survive. The 1984 Los Angeles Olympic Games, which marked the beginning of the most successful era of corporate sponsorship, further strengthened his belief. For the first time, the Organising Committee of Los Angeles Olympic Games separated sponsors into three categories; "Official Sponsor", "Official Supplier" and "Official Licensee". The profit from the Games was US

$215 million. Arguably the Games in Los Angeles were the watershed in Olympic marketing though the marketing programme was limited to the host country and U.S. companies. Prior to 1984 no real international Olympic marketing existed and less than ten NOCs generated any revenue from marketing programmes. After the Games Olympic marketing became a co-ordinated activity on a global scale with the establishment of the IOC's TOP programme in 1985. In 1996 long-term broadcast and sponsor agreements were agreed until 2008.[3] This helped to secure the financial future of the Olympic Movement. Through ticket sales, licensing and the sale of broadcasting rights in addition to sponsorship, revenue generated from the marketing has soared since 1980 (see table 11-2).

Table 11-2 Olympic Marketing Revenue Evolution by Quadrennium 1980-2004

	Moscow / Lake Placid	Angeles / Sarajevo	Seoul / Calgary	BarcelonaAlbertville	Lillehammer/ Atlanta	Nagano / Sydney	Salt Lake City/ Athens
Revenue (million US $)	350	790	1,150	1,870	2,630	3,770	4,264

Source from "Olympic Marketing 1980-2001: Two Decades of Unprecedented Support for Sport".

Table 11-3 Olympic Marketing Revenue Generation:
The Past Three Olympic Quadrenniums (million US $)

Source	1993-1996	1997-2000	2001-2004
Broadcast	1,251	1,845	2,236
TOP Programme	279	579	603
Domestic sponsorship	534	655	736
Ticketing	451	625	608
Licensing	115	66	81
Total	2,630	3,770	4,264

Source from "The Olympic Marketing Fact File, 2005", p.17, www.olympic.org.

2. Unique Characteristics

The Olympic Games is the most expensive global cultural commodity. For example, the 2004 Athens Games cost about 11.6 billion US dollars billion to stage. [4] As a non-profit organisation, the IOC is involved with two major markets: its contributors (or partners in Olympic terms) who provide cash or services to the organisation, and its clients, the members of the Olympic Family including National Olympic Committees, International Federations and the Organising Committee of the Olympic Games and athletes. The IOC marketing programmes have to cater equally for the Olympic Movement contributors and for its clients. The IOC deals with business or commercial enterprises to the mutual benefit of both parties. IOC clients are the recipients of its money and services and at the same time, the producers and consumers of the product—the Games. This unique feature makes Olympic marketing challenging, as reflected in the frequent disputes within the Olympic Family over the distribution of its wealth, and the constitution of the IOC. [5]

Unlike a typical business, the IOC has little or no responsibility for the production, sales and marketing costs of the Games. The preparation of athletes is a prime responsibility of their clubs, national associations and governments. The staging of the Games is largely the duty of the host city and country—though a substantial part of their budget is covered by the TV rights and sponsorship money mediated by the IOC.

3. The Principle Sources of Olympic Marketing Revenue

In general, Olympic revenue comes from TV rights, sponsorship, tickets, licensing, coins and philately. The chart below shows the contribution of different financial sources to the IOC marketing revenue during the period from 2001 to 2004. With the extension into new sources of financing in the past two decades, the contribution of the TV rights revenue was reduced to around 50%.

(1) Sponsorship

Sponsorship has become the second source of Olympic financing.

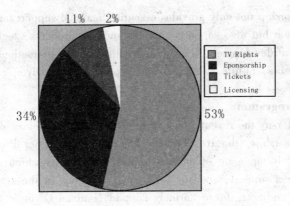

Figure 11-1 Sources of the 2001-2004 Olympic Revenue

Sponsorship accounts for 30%-40% of Olympic marketing revenue. The aim of sponsorship is to ensure an independent financial stability, continual support for, and an equitable revenue distribution throughout the Olympic Family. All sponsorship programmes are co-ordinated by the IOC and operate on three levels: international, with a worldwide programme known as TOP (The Olympic Partners); host country, with the local programmes of the OCOG; national, with the NOC programmes.

Table 11-4 Number of Enterprises Advertising with the Olympic Games from 1976 to 2000

	1976 Montreal	1980 Moscow	1984 Los Angeles	1988 Seoul	1992 Barcelona	1996 Atlanta	2000 Sydney
No. of enterprises	742	325	98	80	107	119	109

Source from *Olympic Marketing Fact File* (1976—2001).

Table 11-5 OCOG Revenues from Sponsoring Olympic Games (without licensees) (million US $)

	1976 Montreal	1980 Moscow	1984 Los Angeles	1988 Seoul	1992 Barcelona	1996 Atlanta	2000 Sydney
revenues	40	88	219	215	550	588	588

Source from *Olympic Marketing Fact File* (1976—2001).

Sponsorship not only provides essential financial support for the Olympic Movement but also supports services such as products, technical support and staff development. Furthermore, through the promotional activities of the sponsors, public awareness and support for the Olympic Movement can be increased.

* **TOP Programme**

To diversify the revenue base of the Olympic Movement and gain additional sponsorship, the IOC created The Olympic Partner Programme in 1985. TOP is made up of multi-national organisations which are able to provide direct support, sponsor services or expertise in the staging of the Games. In addition, these Partners support National Olympic Committees and the Olympic teams that participate in them by providing cash and value-in-kind contributions. TOP partners in return for their financial commitment are guaranteed exclusive and worldwide marketing opportunities within an agreed category such as soft drinks, television and audio, office equipment and so on. This means that their competitors may not align themselves with an Olympic team or the Olympic Games anywhere in the world. In addition to their exclusivity, the TOP Partners have the opportunity to use all of the Olympic symbols on their products, to obtain and use Olympic footage, to take advantage of hospitality opportunities at the Games, to secure preferential access to broadcast advertising, on-site concessions/ franchises and product sale/showcase opportunities at the Games. Therefore, to be part of TOP programme can greatly advance a brand image. The Korean company Samsung is a good example. In the early 1980s, Samsung was an ordinary regional enterprise. It joined the TOP Programme in 1988 when the Summer Games took place in Seoul. This move turned Samsung into a global brand. In 2001 the value of the Samsung brand reached $6.4 billion, ranking 43rd globally and climbed to 34th a year later with value of 8.3US $. Because of the obvious benefits that sponsoring the Olympic Games can bring, companies compete vigorously to become the TOP partners.

TOP programmes have been assigned numbers such as TOP I (1985-1988), TOP II (1989-1992) and so on. Twelve premier international corporations including Coca Cola, Atos Origin, GE, Kodak, Manulife, Macdona, Omega, Panasonic, Sumssung, Visa, Lenovo Johnson-Johnson participated in TOPVI programme. Lenovo[6] was the first Chinese company to join the TOP Programme. Since its introduction in 1985, the number of TOP Partners has stayed around 10, but the entrance fees have increased steadily over time. As a consequence, TOP has made great contribution to the IOC's financial stability (see Table 11-6).

Table 11-6　Number and Contribution of TOP Partners over Time

	TOP I (1985-88)	TOP II (1989-92)	TOP III (1993-96)	TOP VI (1997-00)	TOP V (2001-04)	TOP IV (2005-08)
No. of TOP Partners	9	12	10	11	10	11
Contribution in total (million US $)	96	172	279	579	663	866

Source from: The Olympic Marketing Fact File, 2005.

Olympic sponsorship also operates on national level. National programmes are managed by the OCOG and the National Olympic Committees in each country but sponsors for national programmes cannot be in the same product category as the international sponsors.

Table 11-7　Domestic Sponsorship Revenue (million US $)

	Atlanta 1996	Nagano 1998	Sydney 2000	Salt Lake 2002	Athens 2004
No.	111	26	93	53	38
Sponsorship	426	163	492	494	242

* **The Olympic Suppliers programme**

The Olympic Suppliers programme is further category of commercial relationship. It offers less than the TOP programme in marketing rights and opportunities. Marketing rights are more restricted for Suppliers and generally do not include any direct support for the staging of the Games. The Suppliers arrangement is geared towards furhter assisting the IOC in its government of the Olympic Movement and support of the athletes.

* **The IOC Licensing programme**

The IOC Licensing programme is an agreement between the IOC, NOC or the OCOG and commercial companies for the right to use the Games emblem and mascots on their merchandise, which usually includes commemorative items such as T-shirts, pins and baseball caps. In return, these companies pay a royalty fee of between ten and fifteen percent. Licensing programmes are brand driven, designed to promote the Olympic image and convey the culture of the host region within a controlled commercial environment. The table below presents facts and figures on the success of recent licensing programmes and the revenue generated to support the Olympic Games and Olympic Winter Games.

Table 11-8 Olympic Games Licensing (million US $)

Olympic Games	1988	1992	1996	2000	2004
	Seoul	Barcelona	Atlanta	Sydney	Athens
Licensees	62	61	125	100	23
Revenue to OCOG	18.8	17.2	91	52	56

Source from the *Olympic Marketing Fact* File from 1988 to 2005.

Olympic licensing programmes act as creative and pro-active custodians of the Olympic brand and serving as a visual window to the Games that inspire consumers, whilst maintaining high merchandising standards to enhance the Olympic image and to ensure quality goods for the public.

These Licensing Programmes cover officially licensed products from the Organising Committees for the Olympic Games (OCOGs), the National Olympic Committees (NOCs) and the International Olympic Committee (IOC). These products carry the emblems and mascots of the Olympic Games or Olympic teams and are designed to commemorate the Olympic Games and Olympic teams. There are three tiers of licensing within the Olympic Movement.

(2) Olympic Ticketing

Olympic ticketing is probably the most complex ticketing exercise of any international sports event. The IOC expects the OCOG to provide an accessible, transparent and equitable distribution of tickets among its member nations. At the same time, the OCOG must also generate its targeted revenue from ticketing. From the following two tables it is clear that OCOG's ticketing and its distribution has varied.

Table 11-9 Comparison of Tickets Sold for the Olympic Games from Munich 1976 to 2008 (million)

		1976	1980	1984	1988	1992	1996	2000	2004	2008*
Ticket	Total	5	6.1	6.9	4.4	3.9	11	7.6	5.3	9
	sold	3.2	5.3	5.7	3.3	3.021	8.318	6.7	3.8	7
	%	74	90	80.6	75	80	82.3	88	72	77
revenues (million US $)		56.56	6.1	156	36	79	425	551	228	166.4

* Estimated by Bidding Committee Beijing (2000)

Sources: PREUSS (2002); "2005 Marketing Fact File"; Bidding Committee Beijing (2000)

The above table shows the financial potential of ticketing. The high revenues at the Los Angeles 1984, Atlanta 1996 and Sydney 2000 Olympics were reached due to the large number of tickets sold at relatively high prices. [7] Because the average Athens 2004 ticket price was 34% less expensive than the average Sydney 2000 ticket price, the revenue from ticketing in 2004 was less than that in the 2000 Games.

(3) The Olympic Coin Programme

Huot has written: "today the value of a coin is determined by its face value which, for the most part, has little to do with its intrinsic value. This difference between intrinsic and face value, referred to as seignorage, is a very important source of revenue for governments of all nations". [8] It is also an important source of revenue for the IOC.

The first government to use an Olympic coin (500-Markaa silver coin) to commemorate the modern Olympic Games was the Finnish government in 1951. It is reckoned that the 605,000 coins issued over two years generated a profit of $1 million for the Finnish mint, part of which was used to cover the cost of staging the Games.

Since the success of this innovation in 1951, more than 350 million Olympic coins have been sold globally raising more than $1.1 billion for the authorities and the Olympic Family. The peak of this source of revenue was reached in Munich 1972, when the coins financed the major part of the Games. In 1984 Los Angeles Games' revenue from Olympic coins was only surpassed by those from the TV and brought the OCOG and the USOC $73.5 million. In 1992 the IOC introduces an Olympic coin programme to celebrate the Centennial of the founding of the IOC and the first modern Olympic Games in 1896. This international coin programme, managed by the IOC and using the combined resources of mints from five nations, closed in December 1996. Worldwide sales of US $48 million from 90,000 gold and 500,000 silver coins made this the most successful Olympic coin programme to date. [9]

(4) Olympic Philately

The revenues from Olympic philately are substantial. In 1896 a Greek philatelist proposed the issue of commemorative Olympic stamps to finance the building of Olympic venues. In 1928 the OCOG of Amsterdam covered 1.5% of expenditures with philatelic programme revenue. Portugal issued stamps to finance its Olympic team's participation in the Amsterdam Games. Purchase of the stamp was obligatory in Portugal for three days. In 1992 some 137 countries issued 1,230,000 stamp series bearing the Olympic rings. In 1994 four albums of stamps commemorated the Olympic Movement centennial. In 1996 more than 150 countries issued a total of 15 million Olympic stamps. In 1998 three albums of Olympic stamps commemorated the Games of Nagano. In 2000 five albums of Olympic stamps commemorated the Olympic Games. More than 48 million stamps and first day covers were produced. More than 10 million Olympic stamps were sold during the course of the Games. For the first time, the host country issued stamps honouring each Australian gold medallist the day after competition.[10]

4. Management of Olympic Marketing

For nearly 20 years Olympic marketing has managed to secure the sound financial stability of the Olympic Games. The management structure underpinning this success is set described below.

(1) Structure of Management

The overall direction of the Olympic marketing policy and the management of various programmes is the responsibility the IOC, its Executive Board and its specialised Marketing Department founded in 1989. Their work is assisted by the following specialist agencies:

* Meridian Management S. A. (co-ordinates the management of the TOP programme, and acts as NOCs marketing liaison).

* Olympic Television Archive Bureau (OTAB co-ordinates the management of, and holds exclusive rights to Olympic footage and historical image archive of the Olympic Movement. TWI manages special programming and is the world's largest sports television producer.

* Olympic Photo Archive Bureau (OPAB manages the historical archive of the Olympic Movement and develops special Olympic photographic projects. OPAB is managed by Allsport, the world's sports photographic library).

* Sponsor Research International (SRI executes IOC global market-

ing research).

* Sports Marketing Surveys (SMS executes the IOC broadcasting data analysis).

To ensure the support of commercial and media partners in the pursuit for "fair play", in 1997 the Olympic Marketing Code was established and the sports industries leaders such as Nike, Adidas, Reebok, Mizuno and Asics all signed an agreement that their advertising would be in line with Olympic ideals. In addition, every broadcaster who signs up with the IOC, is contractually obliged not only to transmit the Games but to promote the Olympic Movement.

(2) Distribution of Marketing Revenue

The IOC distributes approximately 92% of Olympic marketing revenue to organisations throughout the Olympic Movement to support the staging of the Olympic Games and to promote the worldwide development of sport. The IOC retains approximately 8% of Olympic marketing revenue for the operational and administrative costs of governing the Olympic Movement.

Table 11-10 Olympic Marketing Revenue Contributions to NOCs (million US $)

Olympic Quadrennium	Broadcast Revenue	TOP Programme Revenue *	Total Revenue to NOCs
Albertville / Barcelona 1989/1992	51.6	35	86.6
Lillehammer / Atlanta 1993/1996	80.9	57	137.9
Nagano / Sydney 1997/2000	118.7	93	211.7
Salt Lake / Athens 2001/2004	209.5	109	318.5

* The figures presented above do not include the contributions to the USOC and the host country NOCs.

Table 11-11 Olympic Marketing Revenue Contributions to IFs (million US $)

	Summer Games				Winter Games			
	1992	1996	2000	2004	1992	1994	1998	2002
Revenue to IFs	37.6	86.6	190		17	20.3	49.4	85.8

Table 11-12 Olympic Marketing Revenue Contributions to OCOGs (million US $)

	Summer/Winter Games	
TOP Programme	50%	
Broadcast	prior to 2004 60%	After 2004 49%

(3) Protection of Marketing Intellectual Properties

As already made very clear, the Olympic symbol of five interlocking rings and other Olympic icons are valuable marketing intellectual properties. They are the cornerstones, in fact, of all Olympic marketing programmes and invaluable to the generation of revenue. Over the past four years, the IOC has set out to enhance and protect the value of these Olympic properties using legal strategies and practices consistent with those used to promote commercial brands. For example, in Australia, there are the *Olympic Insignia Protection Act* (1987), and the *Sydney Games (Indicia and Images) Protection Act* (1996). In Britain there is the *Olympic Symbols (Protection) Act* (1995). The Olympic brand is, in the words of John Moore (Marketing Director Sydney OCOG 2000), "a rich and complex living synthesis of endeavour, sport and multi-culturalism". It still has possibilities for development which will allow its phenomenal success to continue. Its potential is far from exhausted.

(4) Challenge of Over-Commercialisation

With the increased role of sponsors, the IOC faces the substantial challenge of protecting the Games from over-commercialisation despite the fact that the Games are the only major sporting occasion where there is no advertising within the stadiums or on the competitors. As already noted, there is a concern that marketing is stressed too much as a financing source and that in consequence, there is a real danger of "over-commercialising" the Games. A survey during the Sydney Games in 2000 (n = 1973) revealed that 53.4% questioned saw commercialisation as a threat for the Olympic Games in the coming 20 years. In a smaller survey 66% of German tourists (n = 212) and 72.3% of P. E. students (n = 628) were also conscious of this threat.[11] To protect the image of the Olympic Movement, as pointed out already, the IOC insists on the practice of no venue advertising and "clean" telecasting by the Olympic Games broadcasters, and carefully controls the number of major corporate sponsorships. Will this be sufficient in the future?

Summary

Olympic marketing is crucial for ensuring the successful future global development of the Olympic Movement. Olympic marketing is not new, but international Olympic marketing did not exist until 1984. After the TOP programme was endorsed in 1985 Olympic marketing became a co-ordinated activity on a global scale. In general, Olympic revenue comes from TV rights, sponsorship, tickets, licensing and philately. For the past two decades the sound financial stability of the Olympic Games has been secured through various Olympic marketing approaches. To promote the interests of the members of Olympic Family—the OGOC, IFs, NOCs—the IOC has established and adjusted over time, its policy of distributing its revenues. The recent past has seen immense marketing success. How to protect the Games and the Movement from over-commercialisation, however, will be a challenge to future Olympic marketing.

Questions
1. What unique characteristics does Olympic marketing have?
2. Do you think it is necessary to restrict the number of TOP companies? If so, give your reasons fully.
3. Should the Beijing Games in addition to the TOP programme, attract yet more commercial sponsorship?

Notes
[1] "Tiyu yingxiao shi tisheng qiye de pinpai zhiming du yu pinpai xingxiang de" [Sports marketing helps enterprises promote the brand popularity and image], *zhonghua gongshang shibao* [China's Industry and Commerce Newspaper], Dec. 10, 2004.
[2] The Olympic Marketing Fact File, 2004. www.olympic.org.
[3] "Olympic Marketing 1980-2001: Two Decades of Unprecedented Support for Sport", *Marketing Matters* (The Olympic Marketing Newsletter), 19, July, 2001.
[4] Athens Games most expensive Olympics in history, http://english.people.com.cn; Nov. 14, 2004.
[5] Girginov Vassil(2005), *The Olympic Games Explained*, London: Routledge.
[6] Lenovo Group is the largest computing technology equipment manufacturer in Chi-

na. The Group's own brand PCs have been the best seller in China since 1997 and in the Asia Pacific region (excluding Japan). Lenovo Group has been actively involved in supporting sports activities including sponsoring China's National Women's Soccer Team in 1999 and Beijing's successful bid to host the 2008 Olympic Games.

[7] Holger Preuss (2002), "Economic Dimension Of The Olympic Games", Centre d'Estudis Olímpics i de l'Esport (UAB), *International Chair in Olympism*.
[8] Huot, R., *Letter*, June 20, 1997.
[9] IOC, "2005 Olympic Marketing Fact File", www.olympic,org.
[10] Yi ming, "2000 nian xini aoyunhui jinian youpiao"[Memorable stamps of Sydney Olympics], Coll. org. cn, Dec. 6,2006.
[11] Preuss, H. (2001), "The Economic and Social Impact of the Sydney Olympic Games", in IOC, *Proceedings of the 41st Session of the International Olympic Academy*, Lausanne, 94-109.

Part Three
The Olympics and China

Chapter 12
The Olympics and China: Evolution

Key points:
* Chinese Olympic Involvement in the 20th and 21st Centuries
* Chinese Olympic Ambitions, Strategies and Successes

China is playing an indispensable part in promoting the Olympics throughout the world. This is reflected in its remarkable athletic achievements—for example second in the gold medal table in the 2004 Games, the increasing number of Chinese on various committees of the IOC, and more importantly, the successful Beijing bid to host the 2008 Olympic Games. All this is a result of sustained effort for over eighty years on the part of Chinese to pursue recognition by the international community. This has been characterized by struggle, challenge and even confrontation. Therefore, it is necessary to devote a chapter to the evolution of the Olympic Movement in China in order to demonstrate the complex relationship between international and national politics, sports policies and national and international identity.

1. Establishing Relations

When the modern Olympic Games was inaugurated in 1896, China was in the throes of Western invasion and partial colonisation—a consequence of the Opium Wars that turned China from a feudal dynasty and a politically centralised, but economically decentralised agrarian society into a semi-feudal and semi-colonial society. As a result, the imperial Chinese government had no time or energy to give consideration to the Olympic

Games even though the IOC sent China an invitation. Sport was secondary to national survival. Then in 1922 the high ranking Chinese diplomat and sports official Wang Zhengting[1] became a member of the IOC and the formal relationship between Olympic Movement and China was established.

Humiliated by the earlier Western invasion, the Chinese were determined to modernise their ancient nation. A Westernization Movement (1860-1890) and a National Reform Movement (1896) were launched. One of the measures adopted was educational reform. Western-type schools were established one after another and modern sports, including gymnastics, fencing, boxing, football, track and field, swimming and gymnastics became part of the school curriculums. [2] By the 1920s physical education was a subject in most schools and universities and specialised sports schools and colleges had been created. Regional and national modern sports competitions had also appeared by the early twentieth century. From 1872 onwards students were sent to England, France, Germany, United States and Japan to study and became familiar with modern sport. All these developments paved the way for the Chinese to get involved in the Olympic Games.

In 1924 three Chinese played in the tennis demonstration match in the Paris Games. In 1928 Song Ruhai[3], an official from the Ministry of Education, was sent to Amsterdam to observe the Games. Three years later the Chinese Society for Sport Promotion, established in 1924, was regarded by the IOC as the national Olympic body. A Chinese athlete Liu Changchun, the only athlete of the five-person Chinese delegation, competed at the Olympic Games in Los Angeles in 1932. His participation in the Games was essentially a political attempt to block the Manchuguo, the puppet state installed by Japanese invaders in the North East of China, from sending a sport delegation to the Olympics Games.

With the rapid development of modern sport in schools and universities, it became increasingly possible for China to send more athletes to the Olympic Games. In 1936, just before the outbreak of the Japanese invasion of China, a delegation of 69 athletes including women and 34 officials participated in the Olympic Games in Berlin. The Chinese competed in football, basketball, boxing, weightlifting, track and field, swimming, cycling and demonstrated Wushu (traditional Chinese martial arts). However, except for the latter their performances were far below those of the Western nations.

The chaos of civil wars (1927-1937 and 1945-1949) and the Anti-

Japanese War (1937-1945) made it hard, if not impossible, for the Chinese to participate in the Olympic Games. [4] While the Civil War was underway, thirty-three basketball, football, track and field, swimming and cycling athletes participated in the London Olympic Games in 1948. Unsurprisingly, their performances were far from satisfactory, but disgracefully, the Chinese Nationalist government did not finance the delegation's return home. It had to find its own resources. After experiencing months of hardship, it finally reached home.

2. Breaking Relations (1949-1979)

The establishment of the People's Republic of China (PRC) in 1949 marked a new era in Chinese history. To win international recognition and respect and to maintain its sovereignty and territorial integrity were the important and immediate tasks of the new regime. Thus, the 1952 Helsinki Olympic Games were considered an opportunity for the New China to enter the world through sport. Although Taiwan, ruled by the Nationalist Party, was invited to the Games (but withdrew from the Games at the last minute), New China sent a forty-one strong delegation including twenty-four male basketball and football players and two female swimmers. However, due to the late arrival of most Chinese participants in Finland—a result of the delayed invitation from the IOC which was thrown into confusion by the "two Chinas Policy", [5] only one swimmer Wu Chuan-yu took part in the competition. He was to remain the only Olympic athlete of the People's Republic of China for the next 28 years. [6]

To prepare for the 1956 Melbourne Olympic Games, in which the Chinese keenly wanted to demonstrate the superiority of socialism over capitalism, China held preliminary competitions for seven sports in October, in which about 1400 athletes from twenty-seven provinces, municipalities and autonomous regions took part. Ninety-two athletes were chosen to prepare for the Games. However, as the IOC under the presidency of Avery Brundage recognised both the NOCs in Beijing and Taiwan, which violated the principle of one NOC per country as stipulated by the Olympic Charter, China protested and boycotted the Games. [7] Later in 1958, China formally withdrew from the IOC and eight other international sports organisations. [8] This action demonstrates the extent to which Chinese competitive sport has been strongly dependent on state politics and has served the purpose of politics.

In spite of isolation from the IOC for over 20 years, Chinese ambitions to win Olympic victories did not vanish. Elite sport developed steadily across the country. The National Games was initiated in 1959 to motivate the coaches and athletes, and more importantly, to demonstrate to the world the progress of China's sport.

3. Normalising Relations (1979-1992)

The year 1979 marked a significant turning point in the IOC and in the history of Olympism in China. The IOC, led by Lord Killanin, who became president in 1972, finally recognised the legitimacy of a Chinese place on the Olympic Committee in November,1979. [9] While the Olympic Committee of the PRC would be recognised as the "China Olympics Committee" and its national flag and anthem would be used in all ceremonies, the name of the Olympic Committee in Taiwan would be the "Chinese Taipei Olympic Committee" with a new flag, anthem and emblem. This unique "Olympic compromise" made it possible for athletes from both Chinese Taipei and China to compete at the same Olympics.

China began to prepare to take part in both the 1980 Winter and Summer Games. China for the first time sent athletes and coaches to Germany, America and the former Soviet Union to train for several months. Twenty-six Chinese men and women made their debut at the 13th Olympic Winter Games at Lake Placid in 1980. However, politics and sport remained closely intertwined. China joined America and other Western nations in boycotting the Moscow Summer Games in response to the Soviet invasion of Afghanistan. Regrettably, this boycott brutally deprived a number of Chinese athletes of the possibly once in a lifetime chance to participate in the Olympics, and also delayed the Chinese impact on this significant international sports event for another four years.

The 1984 Olympic Games formed a great divide in Chinese Olympic history. China, for the first time, sent a large delegation of 225 athletes to the Games. The Chinese not only broke their "nil" record in the Olympic medal chart, but also won 15 gold medals. This astonishing achievement greatly changed the Chinese image in the world and inspired Chinese from all walks of life to work hard to strengthen and modernise the Chinese nation. As a consequence, an intense nationalism was aroused in all Chinese at home and abroad. [10] After the 1984 Games Chinese became steadily involved continually and comprehensively in Olympic Movement.

Figure 12-1　Chinese Women's Volleyball Team

In 1985 China created an Olympic Strategy that later became the blueprint for all Chinese elite sports programmes. In line with the Strategy, emphasis was shifted to Olympic sports and all available resources in China were concentrated on a few key sports in which athletes had the best chance of winning medals in the Olympic Games. However, the road to world supremacy was full of twists and turns. Inspired by the achievements in the 1984 Olympic Games, the Chinese were very optimistic about the Seoul Games of 1988. The conservative goals set by the National Sports Commission were to win eight to ten gold medals and become one of the top six nations at the Games. [11] But popular expectation was that China would come fourth and win fifteen to twenty gold medals. [12] To this end, a large delegation of 445 members, including 298 athletes (46 percent were women) were sent to South Korea. Unfortunately, the results were disappointing: Chinese athletes won only five gold medals and China was placed eleventh behind even South Korea. [13] For most Chinese this was a total fiasco—a "defeat of the troops in Seoul" (bingbai hancheng). [14] However, this defeat did not put an end to the Olympics-focused policy. Instead, the Olympic strategy was stressed even more than ever.

Figure 12-2　Li Ning Won 6 Medals in 1984

After Beijing successfully staged the Asian Games in 1990, at which Chinese athletes harvested a crop of medals and swept away the memory of the poor showing in 1988, China immediately directed its attention to the coming Barcelona Olympic Games. In 1991 the National Sports Commission (NSC) gave the status of "key Olympic sport" to sixteen sports including athletics, swimming and gymnastics. These sports enjoyed favourable treatment in virtually every aspect from budgets to training arrangements.[15] Olympic performance was the unblinking focus of state sports officials. To secure Olympic success, therefore, early in the 1990s the National Sports Commission (NSC) adjusted its policies on the National Games. First of all, the timing of the National Games was changed from the year before the

Fgure 12-3   Gold Medallist Zhang Shan
(who defeated male shooters in 1992 Barcelona Games)

Olympics to the year after. Thus, the Seventh National Games were postponed from 1991 to 1993. To further stimulate local enthusiasm for the Olympics, the NSC announced in 1991 that Olympic results in 1992 would be incorporated into the scoring system of the National Games in 1993. [46] These changes saw immediate results at the Barcelona Games in 1992. China won 16 gold medals and came 4th in the medal count.

In addition to athletic participation in the Olympics, in the eighties and nineties Chinese were also involved in the management of the Olympic Movement through membership on various IOC committees and its affiliated organisations. For example, in 1981 He Zhenliang[17] became a member of the IOC, then the member of the executive board in 1985 and the vice-president of the IOC in 1989. Lü Shengrong[18] became the president of international Badminton Federation and then member of the IOC in 1992. More and more Chinese faces were seen in various international sports organisations.

4. Hosting the Olympics: Ambitions (1993-2001)

The ability to host big international sports events has been a symbol of Chinese political stabilisation and economic prosperity. Through sport China has made a powerful political statement. The considerable success of the 11th Asian Games in Beijing in 1990 increased Chinese confidence in their ability to host large-scale international sports event. At the closing ceremony of the Asian Games, there appeared in the stands a huge banner which read: "With the success of the Asiad, we look forward to hosting the Olympic Games." On March, 1991 the Beijing 2000 Olympic Games Bid Committee was announced. On December 4, Beijing formally handed in its application to the IOC President J. A. Samaranch in Lausanne.

The intention of China to make an Olympic bid dates back to 1908 when the *Tianjin Youth* magazine asked: "When can China send an athlete to participate in the Olympic Games? When can China send a team to participate in the Olympic Games? When can China host an Olympic Games?" As the first two questions had been already answered, the last question was now to be answered. In fact, as early as 1945, China intended to bid to host the 15th Olympic Games of 1952.[19] Chinese success at the 1992 Barcelona Olympic Games (16 gold medals and fourth position in total medal number) boosted Beijing's enthusiasm to the Olympic bid. To promote public interest in the 2000 bid further, various sport-related activities were organised from 1991 to 1993. Under the theme of "Bid to host the 2000 Olympics", June 1992 was named "Sports Month" in Beijing. Over 30,000 participants were attracted to 123 activities. In the same month, the bid slogan: "Opened Up China Wants the Olympics" appeared prominently in the *People's Daily*. In addition, in anticipation of a successful bid, Beijing's infrastructure was greatly improved. Beijing had already established 76 percent of the stadiums that were needed for hosting the Olympic

Games. The successful performance by Chinese athletes at the 1992 Games (16 gold medals and 4th place in terms of the medals in total) further stimulated Chinese enthusiasm for the Olympic bid. In early 1993, Beijing submitted to the IOC a candidature file. On June 20, 1993 Chinese President Jiang Zemin wrote a letter to all IOC members reaffirming Chinese government support for the Beijing's bid for the 2000 Olympics. This first bid won overwhelming support (98.7%) of Beijing residents. Beijing's bid greatly aroused people's interest in the Olympic Movement and helped to promote the Olympics throughout the country. In the early 1990s Olympic studies became a subject in physical educational institutions and Olympic research centres were established in universities. In addition, there appeared various related publications including an *Olympic Encyclopaedia*, *Olympic Mass Readings*, *Olympic Stories for the Elementary Students*, *Olympic Knowledge for Secondary Students* and *The Olympic Movement for University Students*.[20]

Despite all this effort and all the investment involved, unfortunately, Beijing lost the bid by two votes to Sydney.[21] The whole nation was plunged into depression when the news was reported by the media. However, the defeat did not end the Chinese Olympic dream. It strengthened China's determination to become an Olympic force through outstanding athletic performance. To synchronise national and local practice in a drive for athletic excellence, the National Sports Commission issued a directive in 1993 to the effect that only Olympic sports and the traditional Chinese Martial Arts would be incorporated into the 1997 National Games. This action demonstrated explicitly the national determination to achieve major Olympic successes in the future.

This national Olympic-oriented policy also led to the re-organisation of provincial and municipal sports teams throughout the country. Non-Olympic sports teams were substantially reduced. By 1995, non-Olympic sports athletes comprised only 7.34 percent of all athletes. In addition, team sports that demanded more investment than individual sports and that had no medal potential were terminated in most provinces and municipalities.

To secure victory at the 1996 Atlanta Games a special fund for Olympic-related sports facilities, nutrition and sports research reached 65 million yuan (US $7.8179 million). Over 200 researchers were involved in 56 Olympic-related projects.[22] Moreover, between 1994 and 1996 China assembled 960 athletes across the country, more than twice that of the actual participants, to prepare for the universal sports event.[23] This was undoubtedly an expensive approach. Although the details of expenditure for the 1996 Olympic Games are not available, it has been claimed that the expense was that double of the Games four years earlier. The various actions bore fruit at the 1996 Olympic Games—China retained its fourth place in both the gold and total medal counts. In the last decade of the twentieth century China had consolidated its fourth position in the Olympic rankings.

After the market economy was encouraged in 1992 internal economic and general reform accelerated together with contact with the external world. Economic, social, political and cultural changes were now underway in a fast-forward transition to a market economy. By the mid-1990s China had already fulfilled its original target of quadrupling the 1980 GNP by the year 2000. People's living standards had improved dramatically. Beijing as the capital had also shown great potential for economic growth with its gross domestic product surging to 201.6 billion yuan (US$24 billion) in 1999, registering a per capita GDP of more than 16,800 yuan (US$2,000). Beijing's GDP was just 46.98 billion yuan (US$5.4 billion) in 1990.[24]

With increased national performance, prosperity and confidence, in November 1998 Beijing re-launched its bid to host the Olympic Games. The motto "New Beijing, Great Olympics" indicated that Beijing had undergone great changes since 1992 due to far-reaching social and economic reforms. Appropriately and pointedly, the emblem of Beijing's bid, a traditional handicraft known as the "Chinese Knot" resembling a person doing taiji shadow boxing, had the same colours of the Olympic rings. The graceful, harmonious and dynamic design of the emblem deliberately symbolized friendship, cooperation and interaction between the peoples of the world.

To ensure a successful bid, a number of carefully-planned activities were organised from 1998 to 2001. Celebrities, including the Sydney Games' champion Liu Xuan and the film stars Gong Li and Jackie Cheng, were officially appointed as promoters of the Beijing Games to sway IOC voters; some 1,100 non-governmental Groups from various fields including hi-technology, commerce, construction, sports, education, sanitation and environment, wrote a letter to the IOC president Juan Samaranch in support of Beijing's bid.[25] A public poll conducted by Gallup organisation in Beijing in November 2000 showed that 94.9% percent of the residents in Beijing strongly supported the city's bid to host the 2008 Olympics and 62.

4% were fairly confident that Beijing would win.[26] Finally in 1999 Beijing invested 5.97 billion yuan (US $746.25 million) in environmental projects.

In 2001 the bid campaign was intensified. In February, a 1260-metre-long colourful Olympic bid billboard appeared towering over a highway; the first Olympic bid bus began to run on the Chang'an Avenue; the Australian Olympic painter Charles Billich presented the Beijing Olympic Bid Committee with a painting entitled "Beijing Millennium Cityscape", to indicate his personal support; a special magazine "Beijing-2008" was made available on aircraft from Beijing to San Francisco; exhibitions of Centennial Olympic Philately and China's Sports were organised in the Century Altar of China; Olympic Reading Books for the Masses and the Chinese version of Olympic Charter were published. About 10,000 people from 92 sports associations affiliated to Beijing General Sports Society bicycled in the Tian'an'men Square to express their support to the bid.[27] People from all walks of life were involved in the bid campaign. The following chart shows the major events in the bid process.

Table 12-1 Major dates and events of Beijing's bid for the 2008 Games

Date	Events
25 Nov., 1998	Announcement of Beijing's bid for the 2008 Games
9 Jun. 1999	Beijing 2008 Olympic Games Bid Committee (BOBICO) is established in Beijing. Liu Qi, Mayor of Beijing acted as the President and COC President Yuan Weimin as the Executive President.
2 Jan. 2000	Logo, motto ("New Beijing, Great Olympics") and website of BOBICO are officially launched.
28-29 Aug., 2000	Lausanne—Beijing, Istanbul, Osaka, Paris and Toronto were accepted by the IOC Executive Board as the candidate cities (Cairo, Seville, Kuala Lumpur, Bangkok and Havana were eliminated).
9 Sept., 2000	Chinese President Jiang Zemin writes to IOC President Juan Antonio Samaranch to express the Chinese Government's support to Beijing's bid.
13 Dec., 2000,	Lausanne—Ten-minute presentation by each of the Candidate Cities to the IOC Executive Board.
17 Jan., 2001	Submission of Candidature File to the IOC

Con.

Date	Events
20-25 Feb., 2001	IOC Evaluation Commission visits Beijing to inspect the city's capacities to host an Olympic Games.
15 May, 2001	Report of IOC Evaluation Commission to the Executive Board. Beijing's bid is appraised as "excellent". The report says that Beijing would stage an "excellent Olympic Games". Designation by the IOC Executive Board of Candidate Cities to be submitted to the IOC Session for election.
13 Jul. 2001	The 112th IOC Session in Moscow Selection for the host city for the 29th Olympic Games.

Figure 12-4　Celebrating the Victory of Olympic Bid

When the former IOC President Juan Samaranch declared on 13 July 2001 that Beijing had beat on Osaka, Paris, Toronto and Istanbul[28] and won the right to host the Games of the 29th Olympiad in 2008, Beijing and China as a whole exploded with joy. Thousands of Beijingers poured into the city centre to join celebrations of national pride. Chinese President Jiang Zemin made an unannounced appearance and gave the exuberant crowd his "warmest congratulations".

The Chinese successful bid for the 2008 Games coincided with China's accession to the World Trade Organisation. The two events would leave their marks on the course of Chinese modernisation. This will be considered in the next chapter.

Summary

When the modern Olympic Games were revived at the end of the nineteenth century, China was in the throes of Western invasion and partial colonisation. Understandably, the imperial Chinese government had no time or energy to take the Games into account although it received an early IOC invitation. The chaos of Civil War and the Anti-Japanese War in the following decades made it hard, indeed almost impossible, for Chinese athletes to participate in the Games. The establishment of the People's Republic of China in 1949 fundamentally changed the situation. Sport was to be promoted as a political statement. However, the new regime was faced with political complexities which threatened China's standing in world sport. In protest to the IOC's acceptance of "two Chinas", China withdrew from the IOC in 1958. This delayed the Chinese impact on the international sports community for over two decades. It was not until 1979 when its membership of the IOC was renewed. Since then the Chinese have become steadily, enthusiastically and successfully involved in Olympic Movement. Both success and defeat in the Olympics since 1984 greatly stimulated China to become an Olympic power. This led to the introduction of an Olympic Strategy and remarkable and effective changes in sports policy, the competition system and investment structures. With the result that the position of China in the Olympic Medal Table moved from 4th in 1992 and 1996 to third in 2000 and second (in terms of gold medals) in 2004—and China finally won its bid to host the Olympic Games in 2008. The "Olympics" now became the most popular word in the country.

Questions

1. Why did China not participate in the Olympic Games before 1932?
2. What were the factors which caused China's withdrawal from the IOC in 1958?
3. What are the motives to become an Olympic Power?
4. Why did the Chinese achieve great advances in the Olympics over the past two decades?

Notes

[1] He got his PH. D. from Yale University in 1910. He was the Foreign Minister and Ambassador during the rule of the Nationalist Party government. From 1921

Wang Zhengting became the principal of the China University in Beijing. A year later, he was elected as member of the IOC, the first one of China and the second one from the Far-east region. In 1924 Wang was appointed as the honourable chairman of the newly found "National Sports Promotional Association of China" and he became the board chairman of the organisation. He led the Chinese Sports Delegations to the Olympic Games twice (in 1936 and 1948). After 1952 he lived in Hong Kong and passed away in 1961.

[2] *Tiyu shiliao* [*Sports History Information*], no. 1-4, 1980; Jonathan Kolatach, *Sport, Politics and Ideology in China*, New York: Jonathon David, 1972, pp. 8-11.

[3] Song Ruhai was the honourable secretary of the National Sports Promotion Society in China at the time. As he was in the USA as a visiting scholar in 1928, he was sent to Holland from there to observe the Olympic Games. This is the fist time that China sent a representative officially to the Olympic Games.

[4] In the Chinese delegation to the 11th Olympic Games in 1936, Li Sen was the only woman of the 22 athletes.

[5] Both Taiwan and the Mainland demanded sole recognition of their own NOC and total exclusion of the other. The Taiwan Chinese based their case on legalistic arguments, the Mainland Chinese on the claim that they were now the actual representatives of 600 million people. Tired of the political invective hurled from both sides the IOC looked for a compromise solution. For further details, see Jonathan Kolatch (1972), ibid., pp. 171-174.

[6] See Jonathan Kolatch(1972), ibid., pp. 171-174.

[7] According to the Olympic Charter only one NOC per country could be recognised. the People's Republic of China and Taiwan fought in the IOC. Under the presidency of Avery Brundage there was a heating debate within the IOC on which NOC should be accepted and the final decision was that both sides got invitations to the Olympic Games. For further details, see Jonathan Kolatch(1972), ibid., pp. 171-174.

[8] Including international federations of swimming, athletics, basketball, weight-lifting, shooting, wrestling and cycling as well as the Asian Table Tennis Association.

[9] On October 25 1979 the Executive Committee of the IOC drafted a resolution that the Chinese Olympic Committee was China's legal representative in the organisation. The Taiwan Olympic Committee was regarded as one of its local institutions and remained in the IOC. This resolution was passed by the IOC with 62 votes to 17 votes one month later.

[10] Susan Brownell (1995), *Training the Body for China: Sports in the Moral Order of the People's Republic*, Chicago and London: University of Chicago Press.

[11] "Tiyu jie de yici duihua"[A Dialogue in the Sports Community], *Tiyu luntian* [Sports Forum], no. 1, 1988, 9.

[12] According to a poll "how many gold medals the Chinese would win", co-sponsored by *China's Sports Daily* and American Kouda Company, there were only

1,536 out of 200,000 respondents predicting 5 or below gold medals going into the Chinese pocket (Zhao Yu, "Qiangguo meng – dangdai zhongguo tiyu de wuqu"[The Dream of Being a Superpower – the Trap of Contemporary Chinese Sport], *Dangdai* [Contemporary], no. 2, 1988, 9).

[13] Guojia tiwei [The NSC] (1986), "Qi wu qijian tiyu bixu jianchi gaige, kuochong daolu, zhixing fenlei zhidao yi qude gengda de chengjiu—quanguo tiwei zhuren gongzuo huiyi baogao"[During the "Seventh Five – year" Period Sport Must Insist in Reform, Further Development and Conduct Management Considering the Characteristics of Sports in order to Make Greater Progress-Reports of the National Meeting of Sports Commissions Directors], *Tiyu gongzuo qingkuang fanying* [Reflections on the Situation of Sports Affairs], no. 9 (April), p. 3.

[14] It is a name of a literary work written by writer Zhao Yu, *Tiyu Wenti baogao wenxue ji* [The Report of Zhao Yu Tiyu Wenti], Zhongguo shehui kexue chuban she [China Social Science Press], 1988.

[15] Chen Jinhua, "1993 nian quanguo jingji shehui fazhan jihua wancheng qingkuang de baogao ji 1994 nian quanguo jingji shehui fazhan jihua de caoan" [A Report on the Implementation of the 1993 National Economic and Social Developmental Plan (NESDP) and a Draft of the 1994 NESDP], *Renmin ribao* [People's Daily], March 25, 1994.

[16] Guojia tiwei [NSC] (ed.) (1993), *Zhongguo tiyu nianjian*, 49-91 *jinghua ben (xia ce)* [China's Sports Yearbooks, 49-91 Hard Cover (second volume)], Beijing: Renmin tiyu chuban she [people's Sports Press], p. 202.

[17] He Zhenliang, IOC member and Chairman of Cultural and Olympic Education Communion, International Olympic Committee(IOC). Graduate from Fudan University in Shanghai in 1950, he attended the 15th Olympic Games held in Finland in 1952 as an interpreter. After he moved to the State to the National Sports Commission (NSC) in 1955, he has been working in the sports community. While he was appointed the vice-director of the Dept. of the International Liaison under the NSC, he was elected the member of the IOC. In 1985 he was promoted to be the vice-minister of the NSC and at the same year he was elected the member of the executive board of the IOC. Between 1989 and 1993 he was the vice-president of the IOC. He was elected twice again as the member of the executive board of the IOC in 1994 and 1999 respectively. He made great contribution to the resumption of Chinese seat in the IOC and the successful bid of Beijing to the 2008 Olympic Games.

[18] After Lü Shengrong graduated from the Foreign Language University of Beijing in 1964, she worked in the International Affair Dept. of the Chinese Women's Association until 1972. Then she came to the International Liaison Dept. of the National Sports Commission. After 1980 she became involved in the management of badminton community at national and international levels. She was elected as the president of the International Badminton Federation in 1993. Three years later she became the first Chinese woman to be elected as an IOC mem-

ber.
[19] A programme was drafted and put forward to the representatives of a national sports meeting in 1945. Details see "Olympic Bids: Bid for 2000", Chinese Olympic Committee Website, 2003.
[20] Ren Hai, "China and the Olympic Movement", 2002 Centre d'Estudis Olímpics de 'Esport (UAB).
[21] Beijing was ahead of Sydney in the first three rounds but at the last round of voting, Beijing lost to Sydney by two votes. After it was revealed in 1999 that Australia bribed two members of the IOC before the final vote, the Chinese were furious and questioned the reliability of the bid.
[22] Zhang Tianbai (1996), "Di 26 Jie aoyunhui ji zhongguo tiyu daibiaotuan cansai qingkuang" [The Situation of the Chinese Delegation at the 26th Olympic Games], *Tiyu gongzuo qingkuang* [Situation of Sports Work], no. 16-17 (vol. 624-625), 14.
[23] Yuan Hongheng, "Zengqiang jinzhen, cujin gaige – Wu Shouzhang zai aoyun xuanba sai shang de jianghua" [Increase Competition, Promote Reform-Wu Shouzhang's Remarks on the Trials for the Olympic Games], *Beijing wanbao* [Beijing Evening Daily], June 2, 1996, 8.
[24] Yi Ming (2004), *Olympic bid ABC*, http://wjhsqxx.wjedu.net/web_ztwz/2008_beijing/2008/Article_Class2.asp? ClassID = 28
[25] *People's Daily*, Feb. 20, 2001.
[26] Lai Hailong, "cong zijingcheng wumen zouxiang2008" [Moving towards 2000 from the Midday Gate of the Forbidden City], http://www.chinanews.com.cn/zhonghuawenzhai/2001-08-01/txt3/12.htm.
[27] The Important Issues on Feb., 2001, www.beijing-2008.org.
[28] Votes of the two rounds are: Beijing 44/56; Istanbul 17/9; Osaka 6; Paris 15/18; Toronto 20/22 (http://olympic.sportsol.com.cn, July 7, 2002)

Chapter 13
Towards the Beijing 2008 Games

Key points:
* Overall preparation for the Beijing Games
* Beijing 2008: Opportunities and Challenges

Needless to say, the 2008 Beijing Games are hugely significant for the Chinese. They are expected to power the national modernisation drive; to provide a broad bridge to the West; to pave the way to a greater role for China in world affairs; to allow China to showcase its recent impressive advance as a modern nation; to signal the end of a century of humiliation and subordination to the West and Japan.[1] For all these reasons, the Chinese are making a massive effort to ensure that the Games are the best in Olympic history. Money is no object. Chinese Central and Beijing Municipal governments have promised to provide funding if or when any shortfall occurs.[2]

1. Infrastructural Construction

To organise the Games is a complex and complicated organisational undertaking, which requires numerous facilities and venues, a modern communication network, a trouble free traffic system, ample modern hotels and guaranteed food hygiene. After Beijing won the bid to host the 2008 Games in 2001, Beijing embarked immediately on a vast investment and construction programme and an investment in preparation for the Games on which China plans to spend more than 280 billion yuan (US $35 billion).[3]

(1) Transport

Traffic jams are a major problem in Beijing. To reduce them for the Games, Beijing plans to invest 90 billion yuan (about US $ 11.25 billion) to construct subways, light railways, express ways and airports. By the year 2008, the urban railway system is expected to carry between 1.8 and 2.2 billion passengers per year. To ease traffic pressure, Beijing is to boost its bus system by spending billions of yuan. the capacity of Beijing's buses and trolley buses will reach 4.5 billion passengers per year and the number

Figure 13-1   The City of Beijing

of buses will reach 18000. Eight new subway lines will be built in the urban area and the number of public transit lines will increase to over 650. To ensure easy access to the venues, there will be 62 roads and 4 bridges constructed around the venues in Olympic area.[4] A special "Olympic Express Way" will be linked to the 3rd and 4th ring roads and 38 special Olympic lines will be linked to the 16 venues. They will operate 14 days prior to the Games and close three days after the Paralympics Games.[5] During the Games, travelling from residential places to competition venues will take no more than 30 minutes. It is expected that by adopting 3S-based core technology a highly effective intelligent traffic network system will be built and the capacity and efficiency of Beijing's passenger and freight transport will catch up with the rest of the world. In addition, the environment around the venues and approach roads will also be improved.[6]

(2) Stadiums and Parks

To stage the best ever Games in history, Beijing plans to build the most advanced venues and facilities ever. Of the required 37 stadiums, 31 will be located in Beijing including 11 new stadiums, 9 temporary stadiums and 11 old stadiums which will be modernised and expanded (see appendix 5). In addition, forty-one training venues and five facilities which are directly related to the Games will be needed. Thus, direct investment in the construction of Olympic venues and facilities will amount to 13 billion yuan

Figure 13-2   The "Bird's Nest" Stadium

(US $1.8 billion) in the lead-up to the Games. [7] All the stadiums are ready by late April, 2008.

The National Stadium, known as "Bird's Nest" [8] for its giant latticework structure of irregularly angled metal girders, costs about 3.5 billion yuan (US $486 million), much less than the originally planned 4 billion yuan (US $506 million). In keeping with the requirements of the IOC the retractable roof was not constructed. [9]

The Olympic Village, which is expected to accommodate 16,000 athletes and officials and will cover a total area of 66 hectares, is at the north end of Beijing's central axis and has the Olympic Forest Park to its north and the major Olympic venues to its south. The residential area of the village will consist of 22 six-floor buildings and 20 nine-floor buildings, as well as a clinic, restaurants, a library, a recreation centre, gyms, swimming pools, tennis courts, basketball courts and jogging tracks. Once the Games are over, the village will be transformed into a luxury residential estate. [10]

(3) Telecommunication Network

In the information era a communication network, of course, is crucial for the success of the Games. The information system of Beijing 2008 will have five parts: the timing and scoring system, the results management system, the Intranet/Internet Information Query System, the management system and the communication and network system. Thus, Beijing will spend 30 billion yuan (US $3.797 billion) on the construction of information technology including a digital communication system, a software and intelligent management system for competition and a fibre-optic network for journalists or officials to get video pictures of what is happening at any site.

(4) Environmental Protection

One of the reasons for the failure of 1993 Olympic bid was the unsatisfactory environment of China. Since then Chinese environmental problems have received attention. To some extent the increasing public enthusiasm for environmental protection helped Beijing win the Games. In keeping with a "Green Olympics"—one of the three goals put forward in the bid report, Beijing will invest 57 billion yuan (US $7.92 billion)[11] "to turn the skies bluer, the water cleaner and earth greener" (*rang tian geng lan, rang shui geng qing, rang di geng lü*). As a result, there will be more green belts and parks in the future. Environmental protection methods will be used in several renovation projects. Thus, forty factories causing heavy pollution moved out of the city in 2002 and further 150 factories were moved out of the capital city by 2005. [12]

Figure 13-3 The Environmental Symbol of Beijing Olympics

To enhance the harmony between people and the environment through hosting the Games is one of Beijing's objectives. To this end, Beijing plans to apply modern digital, network-broadband, environmental and energy—and water-saving technologies such as Regenerated Energy, solar energy, earth heat and wind energy to the construction of venues and the installation of telecommunications and transportation facilities. Electric motor automobiles will be used in the Olympic village and competition venues to decrease air pollution.

2. Organisational Construction

The Beijing Organising Committee for the Games of the 29th Olympiad (BOCOG) was established on December 13, 2001 five months after Beijing won the right to host the Games. On March 2004 the Committee consisted of 18 departments with 90 commissioners and 240 staff. By March 2006, five more departments[13] with 389 had been added. [14] In all probability, BOCOG will gradually expand further in terms of the number of its departments and staff. By the year 2008 it is anticipated that there will be more than 30 departments and 4,000 staff. At the moment its executive board has 17 members including three women with Liu Qi, the Party General Secretary of Beijing, as its head.

In addition, other Games-related committees have been put in place one after another. For example, in June 2002 the Science and Technology Committee for the Games of the 29th Olympiad was founded. With the result that the Beijing Olympic Media Centre was unveiled on November 1, 2004. This marked the official opening of a window to promote "New Beijing, Great Olympics" in the run up to the Games, while the Beijing Olympic Broadcasting Co. Ltd (BOB) was established in 2005.

To ensure high calibre staff BOCOG advertised world wide for applicants in 2002. Within two weeks responses reached 3,515 including 301 overseas Chinese. [15] In 2004 a second recruitment drive took place. BOCOG, it is believed, now has some 10,000 specialists covering 27 specialisms preparing for the Games.

(1) Management of Competition

As is commonplace, not all the Games' events will be in the capital. Football events, for example, will be staged in Tianjin, Shanghai, Shenyang and Qinhuangdao, while the equestrian events will be in Hong Kong. The Coordination Working Group for Competitions and the Events Committee both of BOCOG, have responsibility for the smooth organisation of these disparate occasions.

(2) Marketing

In 2002 BOCOG began sponsorship negotiations with major domestic and international enterprises in such industries as telecommunication, banking, insurance, automobiles, petrifaction, electronic appliances and aviation. In April 2004 a promotion conference was convened in Beijing at which 370 projects involving infrastructure, environmental protection, hi-tech, manufacturing industries and tourism, worth about 100 billion Yuan, were on offer. [16] So far, BOCOG has signed deals with eleven companies[17] making them official partners at the Games. One is Adidas, the German sportswear and sporting goods giant, who is also outfitting the Chinese Summer and Winter Olympic teams and providing staff uniforms for the Summer Olympics—a contract worth US $50 million. [18] In addition, BOCOG has appointed 10 sponsors and 15 suppliers. [19] In total, BOCOG has also approved more than 300 licensed products.

(3) Sponsored Contests

BOCOG has initiated various contests including for the design of sports venues, for sculpture, for the motto, for the mascots, for the theme songs and for the choreography of the Opening and Closing Ceremonies. The contest for the design of the Mascots for both the Summer Games and Paralympics Games took place from August 1 to December 1, 2004. Of the entries some 614 (92.75%) were from mainland China, 11 from Hong Kong and Macao and 37 from foreign countries. The contests for the Olympic Motto was organised in January 2005. Altogether 210,000 slogans were submitted. The slogan "One World One Dream" was chosen. Calligraphic presentation of the slogan and posters featuring the slogan have been solicited from all over the world. [20] BOCOG has also invited proposals for the Opening and Closing Ceremonies. Winners have been invited to join the design team for the ceremonies. [21] A "Contest of Sculpture Designs for Beijing 2008 Olympics" was organised in August 2005. In addition, from 2003 onwards BOCOG requested suggestions for the themes songs. Ten songs are selected each year. A final selection was made from the accumulated songs in 2008.

(4) Competence Training

Initially there was a shortage of competence in a number of areas including management and marketing. Competence training was an early priority. [22] A Coordination Committee for Competence was set up in 2005. It provided programmes at four levels for:

1) general officials and staff, sports managers, coaches and referees;
2) volunteers, ceremony officials and the like;
3) media, security, service and related industries;
4) general Beijing residents. [23]

To ensure the success of the programmes consultants were hired from both home and abroad. [24] In addition to the above, personnel in technology, appropriate sciences and administration were selected by BOCOG for study abroad. Competition administrators, for example, were attached to the Athens Organising Committee for six months. BOCOG also has been providing training courses for an additional 2000,000 staff in 11 industries since 2006.

BOCOG has also encouraged courses on the Olympics and Olympism in educational institutions. Courses for students have been established at many universities and schools. Olympic research centres have been created in a number of higher education establishments and "Olympic Education Model Schools" have been set up across the country to ensure that many young will be especially familiar with Olympic issues prior to the Games. It is not only BOCOG that has taken responsibility for competence training, incidentally, individual national sports management centres have organised courses for their personnel in Olympic Studies and English.

Finally, an exchange programme "True Love Knot" involving 200 schools nation-wide has been organised to establish links involving Olympics topics with schools around the world. [25]

(5) Preparation for the Paralympics

In addition to the Summer Olympics, incidentally, Beijing will also be responsible for the Paralympic Games in 2008. A Planning Office was set up under the control of BOCOG in 2004. The emblem for the Beijing Paralympics announced on July 13, 2004.

3. A Humanistic Olympics

A humanistic Olympics (or People's Olympics) is one of the three aims of Beijing's bid slogan. The whole nation will contribute to the Games that will reflect by definition the Olympic ideals of fair play, friendship and harmony between men and nature. The Games have been promoted across the nation and beyond. CCTV has started a new programme "Beijing 2008" on its sports channel and other local TV Stations have also transmitted Olympic theme programmes such as "My 2008" on Hunan Satellite TV. Newspaper columns are being devoted to Olympic topics, for example, in the *Beijing Evening Daily* and *Competition Daily*. The Olympic promotion video "New Beijing, Great Olympics" directed by internationally-acclaimed Zhang Yimou, with its strong humanistic emphasis, won three top awards at the Milan international festival in 2003. [26]

Proud of its historical heritage, China wants to present its traditional culture through the chosen emblem, "Chinese Seal—Dancing Beijing". It features a single Chinese character on a traditional red Chinese seal with the words "Beijing 2008" written in an eastern-style brush stroke. The IOC president Mr. Rogge commented: "In this emblem, I saw the promise and potential of a New Beijing and a Great Olympics".[27]

Fuwa, the official mascots of Beijing 2008 Olympic Games, consists of five little children embodying the natural characteristics of the Fish, the Panda, the Tibetan Antelope and the Swallow together with the Olympic Flame. Jointly they carry a message of friendship, peace and blessings from China to children all over the world.[28]

The Opening and Closing Ceremonies will reflect the unique aspects of the Chinese culture. The opening ceremony of the Athens Games won worldwide acclaim for its evocative tableau of 3,000 years of Greek history and culture. This put the Chinese under pressure to create better, or at the very least as good, ceremonies as Athens.

BOCOG announced in May 2007 the plan of torch relay which will begin from 24 March, 2008 and end on August 8, 2008, the day of the Opening Ceremony of the Beijing Games. The torch will pass through 28 foreign and 70 Chinese cities throughout the five continents. There will be about 15,000 torch bearers. It is worth mentioning that the torch, for the first time, will be carried over the world's highest mountain: Mount Everest (Zhu Mu Lang Ma).[29]

The Chinese are intense patriots. This patriotism is fired by the Games. As one athléte has put it: "Having the Olympics here will let foreigners see what a great and powerful country this is".[30] For this reason, the Beijing Games have received considerable support from the public. A survey showed that about 95% of residents in Beijing wish to volunteer their services for the Games.[31] On June 5, 2005 Beijing officially launched its "Volunteers Project" and simultaneously issued its "Volunteers Action Plan" together with a volunteer logo. On the same day an International Forum on "Volunteers and the Humanistic Olympics" was held in the Beijing Hotel. Some 100,000 volunteers will have specific responsibilities such as assisting visitors, ensuring safety and translating.

Increasingly in recent years China has become part of the global community, especially on admittance to the World Trade Organisation in 2001. The Olympic Slogan: "One World, One Dream", clearly demonstrates future aspirations. At the same time, it fully reflects China's interpretation of the essence of the Olympic ideals: unity, friendship, harmony.[32] Beijing, too, has become increasingly more open to the outside world.[33] The

Games have advanced this development. As already stated, BOCOG invited proposals, among other things, for a slogan, theme songs and ideas for the opening and closing ceremonies from all parts of the world; foreign financial institutions have been encouraged to invest with domestic banks in BOCOG projects; and an Australian, Bob Elphinston,[34] is an international consultant to BOCOG. [35]

Without doubt, the Games have accelerated international interaction and will continue to do so with implications for change at many levels of the Chinese nation.

4. Athletic Performance and the Beijing Games

Chinese performances will be an important indication of the success of the Games. They will provide a golden (literally) opportunity for the Chinese to realise their longstanding dream of becoming a foremost, if not the foremost, Olympic power. As host country, China will have the self-evident host advantage in terms of support. To ensure Chinese success, the "Plan to Win Glory in the 2008 Olympics" was drafted in 2002. According to the plan, Chinese athletes will participate in all 28 sports competitions and intend to obtain more medals in more events than in past Games aiming to be at least one of the top three nations. Specifically, the Chinese wish to win 180 medals from the 298 events. Women, once again, will play a major part in achieving this goal. Over eighty percent of medals could be won by women. [36] Furthermore, to realise the "Glory Plan", each sports management centre has put forward its own "Project to Implement the Plan to Win Glory in the 2008 Olympics".

To ensure medals in 2008 scientific research is crucial. The National State Administration has allocated a special budget for Olympic-related research projects. The budget in 2002 was 14 million yuan, of which 4.7 million yuan went to "the superior and potentially superior" sports, and over 6 million yuan were spent on the projects focusing on athletics, swimming and water sports that could produce 119 Olympic gold medals. [37]

In addition, to stimulate provincial performances the central government plans to use 3 million yuan from its sports budget to award the provincial-level sports sections that produce the top eight Chinese athletes at the Games. In consequence, 26 provinces hope to produce these eight top athletes. In addition, 22 provinces aim to win gold medals and 28 provinces aim to win medals.[38]

5. Opportunities and Challenges

(1) Opportunities

In 2007 China reached $2.137 trillion in trade[39] and surpassed Japan as the world's third-largest market. Coupled with WTO accession, preparations for the Games have led to, and will further lead to, an inflow of investment from overseas. The unprecedented global attention on China and associated investment will provide a major economic boost to China's economy. Billions of dollars spent on building and related activities are expected to boost China's annual GDP by 0.3 percent. One study indicates that Beijing will fulfil the goal of 6,000 US $ per capital GDP two years earlier than planned.[40] It is estimated that about 1.94 million new jobs will be created between 2002 and 2007[41] (for specific job opportunities, see the following chart).

Table 13-1 Business Opportunities for Various Industries

* Environmental Technologies, products and services (wastewater treatment, pollution control and reduction devices, remediation, recycling, alternative power sources, etc.);
* Energy, Energy Conservation and Renewable Energy Resources (building technologies, light emitting diodes, renewable energy, fuel cell technology, etc.);
* Construction Services, Construction Equipment, Construction Materials;
* Information Technology and Telecommunications;
* Multimedia;
* Security, Surveillance, X-ray and security scanning equipment;
* Transportation and Transportation management equipment;
* Architectural and Project design;
* Project Management;
* Medical Devices, Instrumentation and Health Care Infrastructure;

Con.

* Tourism and Hospitality, Hotel and Restaurant Supplies and Management;
* Food, Beverage and Wine Exports;
* Computer, Software, Hardware and related products;
* Professional Services including Banking, Law and Accounting;
* Television Broadcasting and Syndication;
* Licensing, Branding, Sponsorship Rights;
* Industrial Machinery, Electronic and Electrical Equipment.

The Games will result in over 141.7 billion yuan in direct investment which will lead to Beijing's economic growth of 8.783 billion yuan or 2.07 percent annually between 2002 and 2007. [42] In addition, the Games will inject tremendous vitality into Beijing's real-estate market which will grow in value due to improved infrastructure and environmental conditions. The market will heat up, attracting people both at home and abroad. In a word, staging the 2008 Olympic Games will provide Beijing with a chance to showcase to the world a confident, sophisticated, modern metropolis with consequent fiscal advantages.

(2) Challenges

As the capital city of a heavily populated and developing nation, Beijing faces many problems such as air pollution, a shortage of water resources, traffic congestion and dilapidated housing, but the more acute problem in the immediate context of the Games is the shortage of high quality sports managers, sports marketing agents, journalists and lawyers who understand international rules and practices. [43]

Another problem will be language, especially English. As a non-English speaking country, language will be a big challenge to Chinese. Though most Beijingers have said, including taxi drivers[44], they are learning English, the language barrier is not easy to overcome. Misunderstandings could easily occur between different language speakers.

Security is also a challenge that will lead to increases in the Games' budget. It will be more expensive than originally estimated. [45] Terrorism is increasingly expensive to thwart and the cost rises every year for all major sports occasions.

Furthermore, given the high patriotic expectations, "if the Olympics were not satisfactory or if Chinese athletes did not perform well, negative consequences, for example, violence against rivals and criticism against the government could result"[46]. Athletes, coaches and officials will be under intense pressure.

Summary

The unprecedented global attention on China due to the Games and the associated investment will provide a major economic boost to China's economy. But China wants more. Due to the contemporary global significance of the Olympic Games, to become an Olympic power has been a persistent Chinese ambition. The Games will provide a golden opportunity to achieve this ambition. In addition, by delivering a "Green Olympics", a "Hi-Tech Olympics" and a "People's Olympics", Beijing aims to be acknowledged as a twenty-first century international city. However challenges exist with opportunities: there is concern over language proficiency in English; there is anxiety over terrorism and the cost of its prevention; there is the matter of the crushing pressure to perform on national performers.

Nevertheless, Beijing (and China) confidently prepare together for the greatest Games in the history of the Games.

Questions

1. What impact do you think the Beijing Olympic Games will bring to Beijing and China as a whole?
2. To what should Beijing pay most attention in preparation to the 2008 Games?
3. What results do you think the Chinese athletes will achieve in the 2008 Olympics? Please give your reasons.

Notes

[1]   John W. Garver (1993), *Foreign Policy of the People's Republic of China*, Englewood Cliffs, NJ: Prentice Hall, 20.
[2]   Daniel Covell (eds.) (2003), *Managing Sports Organisations: Responsibility for Performance*, Thomson: South-western, 296.
[3]   Wang Junhua, "xie aoyun jingji tisu Beijing xiandai hua jincheng" [To speed up

the modernisation of Beijing through the Olympic economy], *Beijing wanbao* [Beijing evening daily], Feb. 25, 2003.

[4] "Olympic Venue Construction Making Remarkable Headway", http://en.beijing-2008.org/19/82/article211668219.shtml, Sept. 20, 2005.

[5] Xie yongli, "2008 aoyun jinxing qu shunchang" [The preparation of the Beijing Olympic Games is smooth], www.bjd.com.cn, Aug. 6, 2006.

[6] Olympic Projects Progress on Course, beijing2008.com, Dec. 8, 2006, http://www.china.org.cn/english/sports/191730.htm.

[7] Wang Junhua, ibid.

[8] "Bird's Nest" was designed by Swiss architects Jacques Herzog and Pierre de Meuron and the China Architecture Design and Research Group. It stood out of the 13 entries for the international design competition for the stadium from home and abroad in Mar., 2003.

[9] Zhao Liping, "niaochao shoushen yuanyu jingji wenti, yao jinkuai fugong jiandi sunshi" [The scale down of the 'Bird's Nest' resulted from the economic problem. It is necessary to go back to work as fast as possible in order to lessen the damage", *Jinghua shibao* [Jinghua Daily], Aug. 27, 2004.

[10] BOCOG, "Beijing 2008: Construction Starts On Beijing Olympic Village", June 29, 2005, Official website of Beijing 2008.

[11] Beijing aoyun touru 300 yi yuan yongyu xinxi hua jianshe [The Beijing Games invest 30 billion yuan to the construction of information system], *diyi caijing ribao* [The First Financial Times], Jan. 25, 2007.

[12] Zhu Ying, "wei 'lvse aoyun' ranglu, Beijing 40 jia gongchang qianchu sihuan" [40 factories in Beijing moved out of the 4th ring road for the requirement of the Green Olympics], www.zhongxinnet.com, Oct. 30, 2002.

[13] The twenty-three departments are: General Office, Project Management Department, International Relations Department, Sports Department, Media and Communications Department, Construction & Environment Department, Marketing Department, Technology Department, Legal Affairs Department, Games Services Department, Audit and Supervision Department, Human Resources Department, Finance Department, Cultural Activities Department, Security Department, Media Operations Department, Venue Management Department, Olympic Logistics Center, Paralympic Games Department, Transport Department, Olympic Torch Relay Centre, Accreditation Department, Opening & Closing Ceremonies Department.

[14] Gao Peng, Wang Yong, "Beijing aozuwei jinnian gongzuo renyuan shuliang jiang zengjia yibei" [the staff of the BOCOG will double this year], www.XINHUANET.com, March 16, 2006.

[15] Wang Yong, "Beijing aozuwei queding shoupi gongkai zhaopin renyuan bishi mingdan" [BOCOG announced the namelist of the first group of openly recruited staff for the written test], www.xinhuanet.com, Nov. 22, 2002.

[16] Beijing seeks investment for 2008 Olympics, CCTV. com, March 24, 2004.
[17] They are: Bank of China, CNC, Sinopec, CNPC, China Mobile, Volkswagen, Adidas, Johnson – Johnson, Air China, PICC, State Grid.
[18] "Adidas races in for staff uniforms at Beijing Olympics", http://www.tdctrade.com/imn/05020301/clothing162.htm, Feb 3, 2005.
[19] The 10 sponsors: UPS, Haier, Sohu.com, Yili, Tsingtao Beer, Yan Jing Beer, BHPBhilliton, Heng Yuan Xiang, Tongyi Fast Noodles; The 15 exclusive suppliers: Great Wall, Kerri Oil & grains, Gehua Ticketmaster Ticketing, Mengna, Vantage, Yadu, Snickers, Qingxihe, Synear, Beifa, Technogym, Royal, Staples, Aggreko, Schenker.
[20] "BOCOG Calls for Olympic Art, 10? August? 2005", http://www.olympic.org/uk/games/beijing/full_story_uk.asp?id=1449
[21] "Beijing Seeks Olympic Ceremony Proposals", crienglish.com, March 1, 2005.
[22] "Beijing aoyun rencai 'jiao ke', daibiao jianyi quanmian qidong peixun gongcheng" [The Beijing Olympics is short of talents. Delegations propose to start an overall training project], http://news.xinhuanet.com/newscenter/2005 – 03/06/content_2659524.htm.
[23] *Renmin ribao* [People's Daily], July 5, 2002.
[24] Liu Hao, "Beijing jin 20 wan chuangkou hangye congye renyuan canjia aoyun peixun huodong" [Nearly 200,000 people from the service industry attend Olympic training activities] http://www.beijing2008.com/44/19/article212031944.shtml, July 30, 2006.
[25] Up to the opening of the Olympic Games, the students who join the "True Love Knot" will learn the language, culture, history, geography, customs and protocol of the paired foreign country or region and exchanged events will be organised. By the time of the Olympics representative teachers and students of the schools will have attended the welcome ceremony at the Olympic Village, watch excises to cheer for the involved countries or regions and during the Olympics invite athletes to their schools, etc.
[26] http://english.people.com.cn/200311/13/eng20031113_128200.shtml.
[27] "Luoge: 2008 aoyun huihui tixian 'xin Beijing xin aoyun' chengnuo" [Rogge: the emblem of the Beijing Olympics reflects the promise of New Beijing and Great Olympics], http://www.china.com.cn/chinese/zhuanti/zgy/378582.htm, Aug. 4, 2003.
[28] The Official Mascots of the Beijing 2008 Olympic Games, http://en.beijing2008.com/80/05/article211990580.shtml.
[29] Gao Peng, "2008 nian aoyunhui huoju chuandi bianji wu da zhou" [the Torch relay of the 2008 Olympics will reach the five continents], http://news.xinhuanet.com/olympics/2006 – 04/18/content_4444401.htm, April 18, 2006.
[30] Daniel Covell (ed.) (2003), ibid., 296.
[31] "Liu Qi tan Beijing aoyun 'qiantu' zhengqian tongshi yao rang minzhong dedao

shihui" [Liu Qi mentioned that the Beijing Games should benefit the citizens while marketing to earn money], http://www.tongxin.org/j-sys-news/page/2005/1116/17331_106.shtml, Nov. 16, 2005.

[32] Getty/Guang Niu, BEIJING 2008: One World, One Dream, http://www.olympic.org/uk/games/beijing/full_story_uk.asp?id=1370,June 28, 2005.

[33] Ibid.

[34] He successively assumed the posts of Physical Education Officer of Sydney 2000 Olympic Games, Secretary-General of Australian Olympic Committee, Sports Consultant of International Olympic Committee (IOC) and Vice President of International Basketball Federation (FIBA). He also took part in four Summer Olympic Games, i.e., Los Angeles (1984), Barcelona (1992), Atlanta (1996) and Sydney (2000), and three Winter Olympic Games, i.e., Lillehammer (1994), Nagano (1998) and Salt Lake City (2002).

[35] Zhang Yu, "Bob Elphinston Becomes the Sports Consultant of BOCOG", http://en.beijing-2008.org/92/71/article211667192.shtml.

[36] Guojia tiyu zongju jingji tiyu si [the Cometpitive Sport Dept. of the State Sports Administration], "ge sheng zizhiqu zhixia shi beizhan 2004 nian 2008 nian aoyunhui diaoyan qingkuang baogao" [report on the survey of preparing for the 2004 and 2008 Olympic Games of each province and municipal city across the country], *quanguo jingji tiyu gongzuo huiyi cankao ziliao zhiyi* [reference material of the national conference of competitive sport affairs], 2003.

[37] Lin Wen, "beizhan aoyun, 144 ge keyan gongguan keti zhaobiao" [to prepare for the Olympic Games, 144 research projects invite public bid], *shichang bao* [Market Newspaper] Feb. 26, 2003.

[38] Guojia tiyu zongju jingji tiyu si [the Competitive Sport Dept. of the State Sports Administration], 2003, op. cit.

[39] China's total trade volume may exceed $2.1 till this year, www.chinaview.cn, Oct. 28, 2007.

[40] Liu yan, "aoyun dacan shui yu zhenggeng" [Who will compete for the Olympic Market], *Beijingxiandai shangbao* [Beijing Modern Commerce Post], April 4, 2003.

[41] Wang Junhua, op. cit.

[42] "1417 yi yuan aoyun touzi tisu Beijing jingji" [141.7 billion investment speeds up Beijing economy], www.jingbaonet.com, March 24, 2005.

[43] Yang runsheng, "aoyun cuisheng duozhong xin zhiye" [the Olympics creates many new occupations], *Jingbao* [Competition Post] Aug. 29, 2005.

[44] Taxi drivers are expected to be able to speak the most frequently used 100 English sentences for taxi services. Thus, they have to pass English tests before they get their driving licences.

[45] http://www.china.com.cn/chinese/2003/Aug/378176.htm.

[46] Dong Jinxia, "Women, Nationalism and the Beijing Olympics: Preparing for Glory", speech at the International Conference of "Sport, Society and Identity", Athens, 2004.

Appendices

Appendices

Appendix 1
Main Contents of Olympic Charter

1. Fundamental Principles and Significance

The Olympic Charter (OC) is the codification of the Fundamental Principles of Olympism, Rules and Bye-Laws adopted by the International Olympic Committee (IOC). It governs the organisation, action and operation of the Olympic Movement and sets forth the conditions for the celebration of the Olympic Games. Anyone or organisation belonging to the Olympic Movement has to subject to the regulations described by the Olympic Charter.

2. Evolution of Olympic Charter Over Time

The first version of the Olympic Charter was drafted by Coubertin and passed by the IOC in June 1894. In the course of the following one century and more, the Olympic Charter has been revised and renewed for a number of times. The last updated version was passed by the IOC on September 1, 2004.

3. Major Articles

Olympic Charter consists of the five chapters: Fundamental principles, The Olympic Movement, The International Olympic Committee

(IOC), The International Olympic Committee (IOC), The International Olympic Committee (IOC).

Chapter 1 comprises Supreme Authority, Role of the IOC, Belonging to the Olympic Movement, Recognition by the IOC, Patronage by the IOC, Periodic Consultation with the IFs and with the NOCs, Olympic Congress, Olympic Solidarity, Olympic Games, Olympiad, Rights over the Olympic Games, Olympic Symbol, Olympic Flag, Olympic Motto, Olympic Emblem, Olympic Anthem, Rights to the Olympic Symbol, Flag, Motto and Anthem, Olympic Flame, Olympic Torch.

Chapter 2 comprises Legal Status, Members, Composition of the IOC – Recruitment, election, admittance and status of IOC members; Obligations, Cessation of membership, Honorary President for life, Honorary Members, List of members in force as from 4 July 2003, organisation, Sessions, Executive Board, Composition, Election, Terms of office and Renewals, Vacancies, Powers and Duties, The President, IOC Ethics Commission Measures and Sanctions, Procedures, Ordinary Procedure, Procedure in case of urgency, Languages, IOC Resources.

Chapter 3 comprises Recognition of the IFs, Role of the IFs.

Chapter 4 comprises Mission and Role of the NOCs, Composition of the NOCs, The National Federations, Country and Name of a NOC, Flag, Emblem and Anthem.

Chapter 5 comprises organisation and administration of the Olympic Games, Celebration of the Olympic Games, Election of the host city, Site of the Olympic Games. Programme of the Olympic Games, Pre-Olympic Events Organised by the OCOG, Protocol: Invitations, Olympic Identity and Accreditation Card, Opening and Closing Ceremonies, Victory, Medals and Diplomas Ceremony etc.

Appendix 2
List of IOC Active Members

Last name, First name	NOC	Year of election	Games participation
Havelange, João	BRA	1963	1936/52
Hodler, Marc	SUI	1963	
Mzali, Mohamed	TUN	1965	
Smirnov, Vitaly	RUS	1971	
Tallberg, Peter	FIN	1976	1960/64/68/72/80
Gosper AO, Richard Kevan	AUS	1977	1956/60 * *
Magvan, Shagdarjav	MGL	1977	
Pound, Richard W.	CAN	1978	1960
Filaretos, Nikos	GRE	1981	
He Zhenliang	CHN	1981	
Carraro, Franco	ITA	1982	
Coles, Phillip Walter	AUS	1982	1960/64/68
Dibos, Iván	PER	1982	
Igaya, Chiharu *	JPN	1982	1952/56/60 * *
Matthia, Anani	TOG	1983	
Muñoz Peña, Roque Napoleón	DOM	1983	
Schmitt, Pál	HUN	1983	1968/72/76 * *
Liechtenstein, la Princesse Nora de	LIE	1984	
Adefope, Henry Edmund Olufemi	NGR	1985	
Elizalde, Francisco J.	PHI	1985	
Monaco, le Prince Albert II de	MON	1985	1988/92/94/98/02
Nikolaou, Lambis V. *	GRE	1986	
Defrantz, Anita L.	USA	1986	1976 * *
Geesink, Anton J.	NED	1987	1964 * *
Princess Royal, The	GBR	1988	1976

Con.

Last name, First name	NOC	Year of election	Games participation
Mendoza Carrasquilla, Fidel	COL	1988	
Wilson, Tay	NZL	1988	
Wu Ching-Kuo	TPE	1988	
Ruhee, Ram	MRI	1988	
Kaltschmitt Luján, Willi	GUA	1988	
Nyangweso, Francis W.	UGA	1988	1960
Stankovic, Borislav	SCG	1988	
Bello, Fernando F. Lima	POR	1989	1968/72
Tröger, Walther	GER	1989	
Okano, Shun-ichiro	JPN	1990	1968 * *
Carrión, Richard L. *	PUR	1990	
Indrapana, Nat	THA	1990	
Rodríguez, Antonio	ARG	1990	
Oswald, Denis *	SUI	1991	1968/72/76 * *
Rogge, Jacques *	BEL	1991	1968/72/76
Vázquez Raña, Mario *	MEX	1991	
Bach, Thomas	GER	1991	1976 * *
Al-Sabah, Ahmad Al-Fahad	KUW	1992	
Easton, James L. *	USA	1994	
Reedie, Craig	GBR	1994	
Pescante, Mario	ITA	1994	
Heiberg, Gerhard *	NOR	1994	
Ljungqvist, Arne	SWE	1994	1952
Sealy, Austin L.	BAR	1994	
Mitchell, Robin E.	FIJ	1994	
Diallo, Alpha Ibrahim *	GUI	1994	
Gilady, Alex	ISR	1994	
Tarpischev, Shamil	RUS	1994	
Borzov, Valeriy	UKR	1994	1972/76 * *
Fasel, René	SUI	1995	
Killy, Jean-Claude	FRA	1995	1964/1968 * *
Ramsamy, Sam	RSA	1995	
González López, Reynaldo	CUB	1995	
Vázquez Raña, Olegario	MEX	1995	1964/68/72/76
Vrdoljak, Antun	CRO	1995	

Con.

Last name, First name	NOC	Year of election	Games participation
Hickey, Patrick Joseph	IRL	1995	
Khoury, Toni *	LIB	1995	
Larfaoui, Mustapha	ALG	1995	
Ali, Shahid	PAK	1996	
Chang Ung	PRK	1996	
Lindberg, Gunilla *	SWE	1996	
Maglione, Julio César	URU	1996	
Lee Kun Hee	KOR	1996	
Verbruggen, Hein	NED	1996	
Cinquanta, Ottavio *	ITA	1996	
Borbón, l'Infante Doña Pilar de	ESP	1996	
Drut, Guy	FRA	1996	1972/76 * *
Szewinska, Irena	POL	1998	1964/68/72/76/80 * *
Luxembourg, le Grand-Duc de	LUX	1998	
Sabet, Mounir	EGY	1998	
Moutawakel, Nawal El	MAR	1998	1984 * *
Sanchez Rivas, Melitón	PAN	1998	
Wallner, Leo	AUT	1998	
Orange, le Prince d'	NED	1998	
Ng, Ser Miang	SIN	1998	
Moudallal, Samih	SYR	1998	
Blatter, Joseph S.	SUI	1999	
Diack, Lamine	SEN	1999	
Bubka, Sergey *	UKR	1999	1988/92/96/00 * *
Ctvrtlik, Robert	USA	1999	1988/92/96 * *
Di Centa, Manuela	ITA	1999	1984/88/92/94/98 * *
Popov, Alexander	RUS	1999	1992/96/00/04 * *
Aján, Tamás	HUN	2000	
Kasper, Gian Franco	SUI	2000	
Keino, Kipjoge	KEN	2000	1964/68/72 * *
Nuzman, Carlos Arthur	BRA	2000	1964
Palenfo, Lassana	CIV	2000	
Sérandour, Henri	FRA	2000	
Yu Zaiqing *	CHN	2000	
Fok, Timothy Tsun-Ting	HKG	2001	

Con.

Last name, First name	NOC	Year of election	Games participation
Singh, Randhir	IND	2001	
Coates, John D	AUS	2001	
Hayatou, Issa	CMR	2001	
Samaranch Jr, Juan Antonio	ESP	2001	
Breda Vriesman, Els van	NED	2001	
Abdulaziz, Nawaf Faisal Fahd	KSA	2002	
Lazarides, Kikis N.	CYP	2002	
Park Yong Sung	KOR	2002	
Chamunda, Patrick S.	ZAM	2002	
Al-Thani, Tamim bin Hamad	QAT	2002	
Holm, Kai	DEN	2002	
Ndiaye, Youssoupha	SEN	2002	
Wiberg, Pernilla	SWE	2002	1992/94/98/02 * *
Kurri, Jari	FIN	2002	1980/98 * *
Sondral, Adne	NOR	2002	1992/94/98/02 * *
Craven, MBE, Sir Philip	GBR	2003	
Zelezny, Jan	CZE	2004	1988/92/96/00/04 * *
Guerrouj, Hicham El	MAR	2004	1996/00/04 * *
Fredericks, Frank	NAM	2004	1992/96/04 * *
Elwani, Rania	EGY	2004	1992/96/00
Kendall, Barbara	NZL	2005	1992/96/00/04 * *

* Executive Board member
* * Olympic medalist

★ It is clear from the above names that IOC members are from 79 countries. SUI occupies 5 seats; ITA and NED have 4 members each; RUS, USA, AUS, GBR, FRA have 3 IOC members each; BRA, CHN, HUN, SWE, UKR, KOR, ESP, NZL, MEX, EGY, GER, JAN have 2 members each.

Appendix 3
Information of the Summer Games Over Time

order	date	cities	no. of nations	no. of athletes
1	1896. 4. 6 – 4. 15	Athens	14	241
2	1900. 5. 14 – 10. 28	Paris	24	997
3	1904. 7. 1 – 11. 23	Saint Louis	12	651
4	1908. 4. 27 – 10. 31	London	22	2008
5	1912. 5. 5 – 7. 22	Stockholm	28	2407
7	1920. 4. 20 – 9. 12	Antwerp	29	2626
8	1924. 5. 4 – 7. 27	Paris	44	3089
9	1928. 5. 17 – 8. 12	Amsterdam	46	2883
10	1932. 7. 30 – 8. 14	Los Angeles	37	1332
11	1936. 8. 1 – 8. 16	Berlin	49	3963
14	1948. 7. 29 – 8. 14	London	59	4104
15	1952. 7. 19 – 8. 3	Helsinki	69	4955
16	1956. 11. 22 – 12. 8	Melbourne	72	3314
17	1960. 8. 25 – 9. 11	Rome	83	5338
18	1964. 10. 10 – 10. 24	Tokyo	93	5151
19	1968. 10. 12 – 10. 27	Mexico City	112	5516
20	1972. 8. 26 – 9. 11	Munich	121	7134
21	1976. 7. 17 – 8. 1	Montreal	92	6084

Con.

order	date	cities	no. of nations	no. of athletes
22	1980.7.19 – 8.3	Moscow	80	5179
23	1984.7.28 – 8.12	Los Angeles	140	6829
24	1988.9.17 – 10.2	Seoul	159	8391
25	1992.7.15 – 8.9	Barcelona	169	9364
26	1996.7.19 – 8.4	Atlanta	197	10,318
27	2000.9.15 – 10.1	Sydney	199	10,735
28	2004.8.11 – 8.29	Athens	201	10,625

Appendix 4
Information of the Winter Games Over Time

order	date	cities	no. of nations	no. of athletes
1	1924.1.25 – 2.5	Chamonix (France)	16	258
2	1928.2.11 – 2.19	St. Moritz (Swiss)	25	464
3	1932.2.4 – 2.13	Lake Placid (U.S.A)	17	252
4	1936.2.6 – 2.16	Garmisch – Partenkirchen (Germany)	28	646
5	1948.1.30 – 2.8	St. Moritz (Swiss)	28	669
6	1952.2.14 – 2.25	Oslo (Norway)	30	694
7	1956.1.26 – 2.5	Cortina D'ampezzo (Italy)	32	821
8	1960.2.18 – 2.28	Squaw Valley (U.S.A)	30	665
9	1964.1.29 – 2.9	Innsbruck (Austria)	36	1091
10	1968.2.6 – 2.18	Grenoble (France)	37	1158
11	1972.2.3 – 2.13	Sapporo (Japan)	35	1006
12	1976.2.4 – 2.15	Innsbruck (Austria)	37	1123
13	1980.2.13 – 2.24	Lake Placid (U.S.A)	37	1072
14	1984.2.8 – 2.19	Sarajevo (Bosnia)	49	1272
15	1988.2.13 – 2.28	Calgary (Canada)	57	1423
16	1992.2.8 – 2.23	Albertville (France)	64	1801

Con.

order	date	cities	no. of nations	no. of athletes
17	1994.2.12 – 2.27	Lillehammer (Norway)	67	1737
18	1998.2.7 – 2.22	Nagano (Japan)	72	2176
19	2002.2.8 – 2.24	Salt Lake City (U.S.A)	77	2399C
20	2006.2.10 – 26	Turin (Italy)	80	2508

Appendix 5
Women's Participation in the Summer Games

Year	Sport	Event	Nation	Parti-cipant	%	Year	Sport	Event	Nation	Parti-cipant	%
1896	–	–	–	–		1956	6	26	39	384	16.1
1900	2	3	5	22	1.6	1960	6	29	45	610	11.4
1904	1	2	1	6	0.9	1964	7	33	53	683	13.3
1908	2	3	4	37	1.8	1968	7	39	54	781	14.2
1912	2	6	11	48	2.2	1972	8	43	65	1058	14.8
1920	2	6	13	77	2.9	1976	11	49	66	1247	20.7
1924	3	11	20	136	4.4	1980	12	50	54	1125	21.5
1928	4	14	25	290	9.6	1984	14	62	94	1567	23
1932	3	14	18	127	9	1988	17	86	117	2186	25.8
1936	4	15	26	328	8.1	1992	19	98	136	2708	28.8
1948	5	19	33	385	9.4	1996	21	108	169	3626	34.2
1952	6	25	41	518	10.5	2000	25	132	199	4069	38.2
						2004	26	135	201	4329	40.7

Appendix 6
Women's Participation in the Winter Games

Year	Sport	Event	Nation	Parti-cipant	%	Year	Sport	Event	Nation	Parti-cipant	%
1924	1	2	7	13	5	1972	3	13	27	206	20.5
1928	1	2	10	26	5.6	1976	3	14	30	231	20.6
1932	1	2	7	21	8.3	1980	3	14	31	233	21.7
1936	2	3	15	80	12	1984	3	15	35	274	21.5
1948	2	5	12	77	11.5	1988	3	18	39	313	22
1952	2	6	17	109	15.7	1992	4	25	44	488	27.1
1956	2	7	18	132	17	1994	4	27	44	532	30
1960	2	11	22	143	21.5	1998	6	31	54	788	30
1964	3	13	28	200	18.3	2002	7	37	55	886	36.8
1968	3	13	29	211	18	2006	7	40	60	960	38.3

Appendix 7
Venues for the Beijing Games

1. Beijing

(1) 12 Newly Built Venues

National Stadium
National Aquatics Centre
Beijing Shooting Range Hall
Laoshan Velodrome
Wukesong Indoor Stadium
National Indoor Stadium
Triathlon Venue
Tennis Courts at the Olympic Park
China Agriculture University Gymnasium
Beijing University of Technology Gymnasium
Peking University Gymnasium
Beijing Science and Technology Gymnasium

(2) 11 Renovated Venues

Fengtai Softball Field
Workers' Stadium
Workers' gymnasium
Beihang University Gymnasium
Olympic Sports Center Stadium
Olympic Sports Center Gymnasium

Ying Tung Natatorium
Laoshan Mountain Bike Course
Beijing Shooting Range CTF
Capital Indoor Stadium
Beijing Institute of Technology Gymnasium

(3) 8 Temporary Facilities

Fencing Hall at the National Conference Centre
Wukesong Baseball Field
Hockey Field at the Olympic Park
Beach Volleyball Ground
Archery field at the Olympic Park
Shunyi Olympic Rowing – Cannoeing Park
Urban Cycling Road Course
BMX Field

2. Stadiums outside Beijing

(1) Newly Built Facilities

International Sailing Centre in Qingdao
Tianjin Stadium
Qinhuangdao Stadium

(2) Refurbished Facilities

Shenyang Wulihe Stadium)
Shanghai Stadium
Hong Kong Shatin Race Course

Bibliography

English

1. Books

Alfred E. Senn, *Power, Politics, and the Olympic Games—A History of The Power Brokers, Events, and Controversies That Shaped the Games*, Human Kinetics, 1999.

Aristoles, *The Rhetoric of Aristotle*, London: G. Bell, 1878, Translated by J. S. Walson Book III, 13.

Allen Guttmann, *The Olympics: A History of the Modern Games*, Urbana and Chicago: University of Illinois Press,1992.

Carl-Diem-Institut(ed.), *The Olympic Ideal: Pierre de Coubertin - Discourses and Essays*, Stuttgart Olympischer Sportverlag, 1966.

Charles Beck (ed.) *Oi Olympiakoi Agones, 776 p. X.-1896 (The Olympic Games, 776 BC-1896)*, Athens 1896.

Christopher R. Hill, *Olympic Politics: Athens to Atlanta 1896 - 1996 (Second edition)*, Manchester and New York: Manchester University Press, 1996.

Craig Donnellan (ed.), *Drugs and Violence in Sport: Issues for the Nineties*, No. 26, Cambridge: Independence Educational Publishers, 1995.

Daniel Covell, eds., *Managing Sports Organisations: Responsibility for Performance*, Thomson: South-western, 2003.

David Levinson and Karen Christensen (eds.), *Encyclopedia of World Sport: From Ancient Times to The Present*, Oxford: ABC—CLIO Ltd., 1996.

Diane L. Dupuis, Marie J. MacNee, Christan Brelin, and Martin Connor, *The Olympics Factbook*. Detroit: Visible Ink Press, 1993.

Douskou, Iris, *The Olympic Games In Ancient Greece*. Athens: Ekdotike Athenon, 1982.

Dong Jinxia, "Women, Nationalism and the Beijing Olympics: Preparing for Glory", in Boria Majumdar and Fan Hong (eds.), *Modern Sport: The Global Obsession—Politics, Religion, Class, Gender; Essays in Honour of J. A. Mangan*, Lodon and New York: Routledge Taylor & Francis Group, 2007.

Ellis Cashmore, *Making Sense of Sports* (Second Edition), London and New York: Routledge, 1996.
Ellis Cashmore, *Sports Culture: An A—Z Guide*, Routledge, 2002.

FIFA Financial Report 2003, Ordinary FIFA Congress, Paris, 20 and 21 May 2004.
Olympic Message, No. 33, July 1992.

Girginov Vassil, The Olympic Games Explained, London: Routledge 2005.
Gray Poole, *The Ancient Olympic Games*, London: Vision Press, 1963.

H. Forester (ed.), *Critical Theory and Political Life*, Cambridge, MA: MIT., 1985.
Hai Ren, "China and the Olympic Movement", 2002 Centre d'Estudis Olímpics de' Esport (UAB). Holger Preuss, Economic Dimension Of The Olympic Games, Centre d'Estudis Olímpics i de l'Esport (UAB), International Chair in Olympism, 2002.

International Olympic Committee, *Olympic Charter*, 1964.
International Olympic Committee, *Olympic Charter*, Sept. 11, 2000.

John Arlott (ed.), *The Oxford Companion to Sports & Games*, Oxford University Press, 1975.
John E. Findling and Kimberly D. Pelle, *Encyclopedia of the Modern Olympic Movement*, London: Greenwood Press, 2004.
John T. Powell, *Orignins and Aspects of Olympism*, Champaign, Illinois: Stipes Publishing Company, 1994.
Jonathan Kolatach, *Sport, Politics and Ideology in China*, New York: Jonathon David, 1972.
John W. Garver, *Foreign Policy of the People's Republic of China*, Englewood Cliffs, NJ: Prentice Hall, 1993.

Kendall Blanchard (et al), The Anthropology of Sport: An Introduction. Massachusetts: Bergin & Garvey Publishers, 1985.

Martin Wimmer, *Olympic Buildings*, Edition Leipzing, 1976.

Nicolaos Yalouris ed., *The Eternal Olympics: The Art and History of Sport*, New Rochelle, New York: Caratzas Brothers, Publishers 1979.

Susan Brownell, *Training the Body for China: Sports in the Moral Order of the People's Republic*, Chicago and London: The University of Chicago Press, 1995.

Tylor, Edward B., *Primitive Culture: Researches into the Development of Mythology, Philosophy, Religion, Art and Custom*, vol. 1: Origins of Culture, Gloucester, Mass: Smith, (1871) 1958.

Yalouris, N. *The Art in The Sanctuary of Olympia*. Report of the Eleventh Session of the International Olympic Academy. 90. Athens 1971.

2. Magazine

Essex, S., & Chalkley, B., (1998), "Olympic Games Atalyst of Urban Change", *Leisure Studies*, Vol. 17, no. 3, 187-207.

J. Crompton, "Economic impact analysis of sports facilities and events: eleven sources of misapplication", Journal of Sport Management, 9, 1996, 14-35.

C. Dubi, "The Economic Impact of a Major Sports Event", Olympic Message, 1996, 3.

Coubertin, P. de: "A Modern Olympia", in Martin Wimmer, *Olympic Buildings*, Edition Leipzig, 1976.

George Raine, "2004 Athens Games: Advertising Sporting a Profit: NBC Sells Expansive Olympic Coverage", *Chronicle research*, August 12, 2004.

John T. Powell, "Ancient Greek Athletic Festivals", *Olympic Review*, 1984.

3. Newspaper

P. H. Lewis, "In Cyberspace, a High-Tech League of Their Own", The New York Times, Tue Apr. 5, 1994.

Michael Janofsky, "Track and Field; Reynolds Case Spotlights Battle of the Regulators", *The New York Times*, October 11, 1991.

Gianna Angelopoulos Daskalaki, "We Are Ready to Compete on The World Stage Again", *The Daily Telegraph*, August 12, 2004.

John Pye, "Olympic Ceremony Sparks uproar Gosper under Fire for Giving Daughter Torch", The Associated Press, Sydney, Australia (AP), Thursday, May 11, 2000.

"Olympic Marketing 1980-2001: Two Decades of Unprecedented Support for Sport", *Marketing Matters* (The Olympic Marketing Newsletter), No. 19, July, 2001.

David Powell, "Americans Stand Accused of Doping Conspiracy", Times Online-Sport, October 17, 2003.

John Goodbody, "Inquiry into Drug Use Created Long-term Positive Effects", Times Online-Sport, September 24, 2003.

Crag Lord, "Caught Red-Handed—Amid Global Cries Of 'I Told You So,' China Awaits Its Fate In The Great Doping Scandal", *Sunday Times*, 11 January 1998.

C. Palaeologos, "The Ancient Olympics", Paper presented at the Proceedings of the International Olympic Academy, University of Leeds, 1964.

William K. Guegold, "Volunteerism and Olympic Music Venues", papers of the Symposium held in Lausanne, 24-26 Nov., 1999.

Chinese

1. Books

Guojia tiwei [NSC] (ed.), *Zhongguo tiyu nianjian*, 49 - 91 *jinghua ben* (*xia ce*) [China's Sports Yearbooks, 49-91 Hard Cover (second volume)], Beijing: Renmin tiyu chuban she, 1993

Xie yalong (ed.), *ao lin pi key yanjiu* [Olympic Studies], Beijing: Beijing tiyu daxue chuban she, 1994.

Zhang Dainian, Fang Keli (eds.,), *zhongguo wenhua lun* [About Chinese Culture], Beijing shifandaxue chuban she [Beijing Normal University Press],1994.

Zhao yu, zhaoyu tiyu wenti baogao wenxue ji [Collection of Zhao Yu's Repertoire Literatures], Beijing: zhongguo shehui kexue chuban she [China Social Science Press], 1988.

Kong Fanmin, "lve lun ao lin pi ke wenhua"[Brief Analysis of Olympic Culture], ren wen ao yun jianshe zuotan hui fayan cailiao [Speech at the Seminar of building Humanistic Olympics],2002.

Guojia tiyu zongju jingji tiyu si [the Comeptitive Sport Dept. of the State Sports Administration], "ge sheng zhizhiqu zhixia shi beizhan 2004 nian 2008 nian aoyunhui diaoyan qingkuang baogao" [report on the survey of preparing for the 2004 and 2008 Olympic Games of each province and municipal city across the country], *quangguo jingji tiyu gongzuo huiyi cankao ziliao zhiyi* [reference material of the national conference of competitive sport affairs], 2003.

2. Magazine

Tiyu chanye xinxi [Sports Industry Information], 10, 2004
Tiyu shiliao [Sports History Information], 1-4, 1980
Tiyu luntan [Sports Forum], 1, 1988
Dandai [Contemporary],2, 1988.
Tiyu gongzuo qingkuang fanying [Reflection of Sports Work Situation], 9, 1986
Tiyu gongzuo qingkuang [Situation of Sports Work], 16-17, 1996

3. Newspapers

Zhonghua gongshang shibao [China's Industry and Commerce Newspaper], Dec. 10, 2004
Beijing wanbao [Beijing Evening Daily],June 2, 1996; Feb. 25, 2003
Shichang bao [Market Newspaper],Feb. 26, 2003.
Renmin ribao [People's daily],March 25, 1994;Jan. 2, 2002;July 5, 2002

Jinghua shibao [Jinghua Daily], Aug. 27, 2004
Beijing ribao [Beijing Daily], June 2, 1996..
Beijing xiandai shangbao [Beijing Modern Commerce Post] April 4, 2003
Jing bao [Competition Post] Aug. 29, 2005

Websites

www. olympic. org
http://www. athens2004. com
http://news. mongabay. com/
http://www. coa – india. org
http://www. ballparks. com/baseball/national/olympi. htm
http://www. cyclerace. or. kr/e_cra/launching02_a. html
http://www. cbc. ca/olympics/venues/olympic_stadium. html
http://www. olympic. org/uk/games/athens/index_uk. asp
http://multimedia. olympic. org/pdf/en_report_644. pdf
http://multimedia. olympic. org/pdf/en_report_60. pdf
http://www. olympic. org/ 2005 Marketing File/
http://www. yahoo. com/Recreation/Sports/
http://multimedia. olympic. org/pdf/en_report_60. pdf.
http://www – white. media. mit. edu/ ~ intille/st/electronic – arena. html
http://espn. go. com/oly
http://english. people. com. cn
http://www. olympic. org/uk
http://www. louvre. fr
http://www. ioa. leeds. ac. uk/
http://www. perseus. tufts. edu/Olympics/site. html
http://61. 135. 180. 163/xwzx/tpxw/5945. shtm
www. athens2004. com
http://www. britannica. com/eb/article? eu = 137628
http://www. sports. gov. cn.
http://www. guardian. co. uk/
http://www. chinanews. com. cn/zhonghuawenzhai/2001 – 08 – 01/txt3/12. htm
www. beijing – 2008. org
http://olympic. sportsol. com. cn
www. bjd. com. cn
http://www. china. org. cn/english/sports/191730. htm
www. xinhuanet. com
http://www. china. com. cn/chinese/2003/Aug/378176. htm
CCTV. com (2004-03-24)
http://www. tdctrade. com/imn/05020301/clothing162. htm
http://www. forbes. com/columnists/free_forbes/2004/0524/043. html